PROFESSIONS AT BAY

The first Stirling Professions and Management Conference was held in August 1993. Over 100 participants were drawn from the UK, Europe, Australasia and the USA and 75 papers were presented.

The main theme of the conference was the character of late twentieth century UK management, with a strong emphasis on the changing situations of professionals who have long been the bulk of the UK's managers. Over 30 of the conference papers have now been published in three co-edited books as part of Ashgate's Stirling School of Management Series. *The Professional-Managerial Class* (edited by Ian Glover and Michael Hughes) deals with the more general aspects of the main theme. *Professions at Bay* (same editors) focuses on the situations of eleven professions as they face the onslaught of managerialism, commercialism and consumerism. Most of these professions, and UK professions in general, are seen to be adapting to external changes and processes quite effectively, some showing surprising resilience and cunning and others facing unexpected long term problems. *Beyond Reason: the National Health Service and the Limits of Management* (edited by John Leopold, Ian Glover and Michael Hughes) is effectively a sector case study of the main themes. It asks whether 'science plus will' in the form of managerialism allied to commercialism is consumerism are likely to make the National Health Service more effective, or debilitate it. Professions at Bay, appearing later than the other two volumes, contains three new papers not given at the conference, and extended introductory and concluding chapters, and takes the arguments about the general theme beyond those of *The Professional-Managerial Class* and *Beyond Reason.*

Professions at Bay

Control and encouragement of ingenuity in British Management

Edited by
IAN GLOVER
MICHAEL HUGHES
Department of Management and Organization
Faculty of Management
University of Stirling

Routledge
Taylor & Francis Group
LONDON AND NEW YORK

First published 2000 by Ashgate Publishing

Reissued 2019 by Routledge
2 Park Square, Milton Park, Abingdon, Oxon, OXl 4 4RN
52 Vanderbilt Avenue, New York, NY 10017

Routledge is an imprint of the Taylor & Francis Group, an informa business

A Library of Congress record exists under LC control number:

ISBN 13: 978-1-138-73871-3 (hbk)
ISBN 13: 978-1-138-73870-6 (pbk)
ISBN 13: 978-1-315-18459-3 (ebk)

Contents

Figures and tables

List of contributors

Stephen Ackroyd is Professor of Organizational Analysis in the Department of Behaviour in Organizations. The Management School, University of Lancaster and an organizational consultant. He has researched widely in private and public sector organizations, and his books include *Data Collection in Context*, with John Hughes (second edition, 1992) and *Organizational Misbehaviour* with Paul Thompson (1998).

Don Bathie is Director of the Management Centre at the University of Teeside. His main research interests are business failure prevention, supply chain networks, and relationship marketing.

Charles Booth is a Senior Lecturer in Strategic Management at British Business School of the University of the West of England. His research interests are in strategic networks, public sector management and in the area of critical management studies. He set up and runs the critical management and management history email networks. He is an associate editor of the *Electronic Journal of Radical Organization Theory*, and in the past worked in local government for ten years.

Colin Bryson is a Senior Lecturer in the Department of Human Resource Management at Nottingham Trent University. His main research interest is in flexible employment and his main publications have been on the management of information technology and in human resource management and industrial relations.

Stephen Bull is a PhD Student in the Department of Management & Organization at the University of Stirling. He is studying organizational and technological change in the ship repair industry. Formerly he was in the Royal Navy and he has also worked in engineering and for the Ministry of Defence.

Timothy Clark is Reader in Management at King's College of the University of London. His main research interests are the nature of knowledge intensive workers, especially management consultants and gurus and transnational management studies. Since he began his doctoral research into the executive search and selection industry in 1968 he has conducted studies into different aspects of management consultancy. More recently his research has focused on their impact and success. He is Associate Editor of *Human Relations* and the author of numerous papers and co-editor of six books which include *Managing Consultants* (Open University Press, 1995), *European Human Resource Management* (Blackwell, 1996), *Advancement in Organizational Behaviour* (Ashgate, 1997), and *Experiencing Human Resource Management* (with C. Mabey and D. Skinner, Sage, 1998).

Wendy Currie is Professor of Strategic Information Systems at Brunel University. Her main research interests are in IT outsourcing, internet commerce, and the theory and practice of managing information systems. Her latest book is *Rethinking Management Information Systems* (OUP, 1998), co-edited with Robert Galliers.

Stuart Davies is a Lecturer in Strategic Management at the University of Leeds. His research interests are in management issues within UK and European cultural and heritage industries. His books include *By Popular Demand* (1994), an assessment of the market for UK museums.

John Flood is Professor of Law and Sociology and Director of the Centre for Graduate Studies at the University of Westminster. He has held posts at the American Bar Foundation, Indiana University and the European University Institute. Recent publications include *Insolvency Practitioners and Big Corporate Insolvencies* (1995), *The Professional Restructuring of Corporate Rescue: Company Voluntary Arrangements and the London Approach* (1995), *Reconfiguring the Advocacy Services Market A Case Study of London and Four Fields of Practice* (1996).

Ian Glover is the Director of the Doctoral Programme in the Department of Management and Organization at the University of Stirling. He has been a consultant for the Department of Industry regarding management quality in the UK and abroad, and in 1994 and 1995 he was a member of an ESRC-funded panel of experts on Professions in Late Modernity. His main research interests are managerial work and occupations in the UK and abroad, and age, employment and management.

Jane Goodsir is a Consultant working in the area of regeneration and social action. Educated at University College London and the University of Bristol, she was Director of the charity Release for six years, and has also worked in the commercial and university sectors.

Mark Hughes is a Senior Lecturer in Organizational Behaviour in the Department of Finance and Accountancy at the University of Brighton Business School. His research focuses on Management and organizational behaviour in financial services. He is co-author of *Bank Lending Beyond the Theory* (1993).

Michael Hughes is Professor of Management in the Department of Management and Organization at the University of Stirling. His main research interests are in the area of comparative management and international business. He is currently studying the management of the transition process in Central and Eastern Europe.

Michael Kelly is Professor and Head of the School of Social Science at the University of Greenwich. His main research interests are medical sociology, health promotion and disease prevention. His books include *Colitis* (1992) and *Healthy Cities* (1993).

Tony Millman is Professor of International Business and Marketing at the University of Buckingham. He was formerly a member of the Marketing Group at Cranfield School of Management. As a Chartered engineer and Fellow of the Institution of Mechanical Engineers, he has closely followed the development of his profession and took an active part in the 'unification' debate in the mid-1990s.

Barbara Paterson is a self-employed human resource consultant. She has worked in senior human resource management posts in manufacturing, finance and local government. Her doctoral thesis is on the work and knowledge used by personal specialists.

Robin Roslender teaches accountancy at the University of Stirling. In addition to the accountancy profession and the conditions of accounting labour, Dr. Roslender has research interests in strategic positioning accounting, accounting for the worth of employees, and the application of interdisciplinary and critical perspectives in management studies. He is currently researching developments at the interface of management accounting and marketing.

Graeme Salaman is Professor of Organizational Studies in the Faculty of Social Science, the Open University. He is currently carrying out, with Paul du Gay, an ESRC funded study of management consultants and discourse of enterprise; and with Timothy Clark, a study of managers' use of management consultants. He has published extensively over many years on the sociology of work and organizations, and human resource strategies.

Acknowledgements

This book arose out of the first Stirling conference on Professions and Management in 1993. We are grateful to all of the participants in that conference who helped shape the debate and to the contributors, other colleagues and anonymous professional interviewees who subsequently helped us develop it including the participants of the 1994 and 1995 ESRC Seminar Series on Professions in Late Modernity and the content of all three of the books that resulted from the conference.

Anne Keirby at Ashgate was a very understanding and flexible administrator who always managed to solve our technical problems.

We are greatly indebted to Pauline McBeath and Terry Middleton for their considerable accuracy and skill, and for the remarkable speed of their work, and for their calmness, humour and patience when coordinating the contributors' and editors' contributions.

List of abbreviations

AAT	Association of Accounting Technicians
AI	Artificial Intelligence
ASC	Accounting Standards Committee
APRA	American Planning Association
ASPA	American Society for Public Administration
AMC	Area Museums Councils
APC	Auditing Practices Committee
BASW	British Association of Social Workers
BBC	British Broadcasting Corporation
BCS	British Computer Society
BCCI	Bank of Credit and Control International
B.Eng.	Bachelor of Engineering
CA	Chartered Accountant
CA.	California
CACA	Chartered Association of Certified Accountants
CCAB	Consultative Council of Accounting Bodies
C/DMS	Certificate/Diploma in Management Studies
CEF	Capital Extensive Firm
CEng	Chartered Engineer
CEI	Council of Engineering Institutions
CIB	Chartered Institute of Bankers
CIMA	Chartered Institute of Management Accountants
CIP	Canadian Institute of Planners
CIM	Chartered Institute of Marketing
CIPFA	Chartered Institute of Public Finance and Accountancy
CJA	Criminal Justice Act
CCT	Compulsory Competitive Tendering
CPD	Continuing Professional Development
CUH	Computer Users' Handbook
CUP	Cambridge University Press
CT.	Connecticut

DC.	District of Columbia
DCF	Discounted Cash Flow
DipEM	Diploma in Engineering Management
DTI	Department of Trade and Industry
EFTPOS	Electronic Funds Transfer from the Point of Sale
EngTech	Engineeering Technician
EU	European Union
FEANI	Federation Europeenne d'Associations Nationales d'Ingenieurs
GCE	General Certificate of Education
HMSO	Her Majesty's Stationery Office
HRM	Human Resource Management
IBRM	Institute of Baths and Recreation Management
ICAEW	Institute of Chartered Accountants of England and Wales
ICAI	Institute of Chartered Accountants of Ireland
ICAS	Institute of Chartered Accountants of Scotland
ICE	Institution of Civil Engineers
ICEF	Information Extensive Firm
ICI	Imperial Chemicals Industries
ICSA	Institute of Company Secretaries and Administrators
IEng	Incorporated Engineer
IEE	Institution of Electrical Engineers
IEEIE	Institution of Electronics and Electrical Incorporated Engineers
IEHO	Institute of Environmental Health Officers
ILAM	Institute of Leisure and Amenity Management
IMarE	Institute of Marine Engineers
IMechE	Institution of Mechanical Engineers
IMfgE	Institution of Manufacturing Engineers
IOH	Institute of Housing
IPD	Institute of Personnel and Development
IProdE	Institution of Production Engineers
IPM	Institute of Personnel Management
IS	Information Systems
IStructE	Institution of Structural Engineers
ISSC	Information Systems Steering Committee
IT	Information Technology
ITEC	Information Technology Executive Committee
ITSA	Institute of Trading Standards Administration
JMS	Journal of Management Studies
KIF	Knowledge Intensive Firm
KIFOWs	Knowledge Intensive Firms, Organizations and Workers
KPMG	Klynweld Peat Marwick Group
LA	Library Association
MA	Museums Association
M&A	Mergers and Acquisitions

MBA	Master of Business Administration
MCI	Management Charter Initiative
MDP	Multidisciplinary Practice
MEng	Master of Engineering
MGC	Museums and Galleries Commission
MIT	Massachussetts Institute of Technology
MSc	Master of Science
M-TCEF	Global Manufacturing and Trading Conglomerate
NAPM	National Academy of Public Administration
NHS	National Health Service
NPM	New Public Management
PACE	Police and Criminal Evidence Act
PEST	Political Economic Sociological and Technological
R&D	Research and Development
RAeS	Royal Aeronautical Society
RINA	Royal Institution of Naval Architects
RIPA	Royal Institute for Public Administration
RPL	Revenue Per Lawyer
RTPI	Royal Town Planning Institute
SHEFC	Scottish Higher Education Funding Council
SICC	Standard Industry Classification Code
SME	Small and Medium Sized Emterprises
SRHE	Society for Research into Higher Education
STH	Science leads to Technology leads to Hardware
SWOT	Strengths Weaknesses Opportunities and Threats
TOPP	Training Outside Public Practice
TPIC	Town Planning Institute of Canada
TQM	Total Quality Management
TUC	Trades Union Congress
UK	United Kingdom
USA	United States of America
USSR	Union of Soviet Socialist Republics

For our colleagues, our teachers, Dumyat Hill and J G Drake

With the drawing of the Love and the voice of this Calling
...And all shall be well and
All manner of thing shall be well
When the tongues of flame are in-folded
Into the crowned knot of the fire
And the fire and the rose are one

T.S. Eliot, Little Gidding, 1942

Watching the morning come in on the land
See the moon roll over Skeabost
See the young men late in the glen
All with camans in hand
Sea winds out on the wilds
Sea waves crash onto Uig
See the black homes strung out on a line
Across the island of Skye

Should have been home before daylight
Buts it's not easy when you're down and hungry
One from the late run rolled up in a coat
I make my way across the moor
For a late summer in '84
But now there's a new day dawning
I've heard the Braes men talk in Portree
The news from Glendale

Still the morning comes in on the land
See the new sun red and rising
See the corn turn ripe in the fields
See the growth of the glen
And Macpherson's in Kilmuir tonight
What a night for a people rising
On God not before time
There's justice in our lives

And I can't believe
That it's taken all this time
I can't believe
My life and my destiny
After the clans, after the clearings
Here I am
Recovering

Recovery, by Calum and Rory Macdonald, of Runrig, from Recovery, Ridge Records, 1981.

Part I

Introduction

1 The challenge to professions

Ian Glover and Michael Hughes

Introduction

Our aim in this book is to discuss and consider the recent, contemporary and future situation of professions in the UK. More specifically, we are interested in the sources of conflict and change which affect professional occupations, with the responses of such occupations to such forces, and with the possible or likely outcomes for the character of British management.

In this introductory chapter we first describe and discuss the general context of professional occupations in the UK. Then we describe and consider the various challenges which they have recently faced, are facing and are likely to face in the future. These include commercialism, managerialism and developments in higher education. Then we briefly consider the appropriateness and the possible future of professional producer-consumer relationships in different kinds of sectoral and organizational context. We go on to discuss the relevance of professional resources in the twenty-first century before offering brief outlines of each of the subsequent sections and chapters of the book. The next three sections of the book consist of thirteen chapters on independent, public sector and organizational professions. The final discussion and conclusion section consists of one chapter on the relevance of the book's contents to the future of management in the UK.

The general context

In some sectors of the UK's economy professionals virtually *are* the management, and in others they supply significant proportions, but by no means all, of those who run things. Examples of the former case have included health care, the construction industry, much of local government, and higher education, and most of the major religious denominations. Examples of the latter include most sectors of manufacturing and retailing, management consultancy, banking and central government.

The UK's education system was not designed and developed, as it expanded during the nineteenth century and for much of the twentieth, to ensure that UK-based commerce and manufacturing attracted and were managed by their fair shares of the most able or socially advantaged members of each generation. Until long after the end of the Second World War many of the most able school leavers were encouraged to set their sights on central government, the armed forces and the independent and learned professions like the law, medicine, the clergy and university research and teaching. Only very slowly and following the demise of the Empire and of its relatively easy markets after 1945, and mainly during the 1960s and 1970s and in the face of growing foreign industrial and commercial competition, did national priorities begin to change. Throughout the nineteenth century and until long into the twentieth there was much of what Western Europeans and North Americans would have regarded as a vacuum in higher education regarding the production of relevantly educated graduates for industry and commerce. It was filled, incompletely but to some useful effect, by the efforts of employers, professional associations and lecturers and teachers employed by local commercial and technical colleges. Accountants, engineers of many kinds and surveyors were amongst their main products. Such people formed the majority of senior and middle managers across many sectors. However the highest and some less elevated managerial positions tended, also, to be reserved for graduates in liberal arts and pure science subjects from the traditional universities.

In the civil service and the armed forces, and in larger commercial and industrial employing organizations with staffing policies which followed theirs, senior jobs tended to be dominated by such people, with professionally qualified specialists 'on tap but not on top', supporting them from below. At the top of the civil service the gentlemanly, amateur, philosopher-king liberal arts or pure science graduates were the 'custodians' (Glover, 1977) the 'generalists' who formed its top Administrative Class. Beneath them were the 'specialists', often members of the more lowly Executive Class, the 'outstretched arm' of their Administrative betters, there to inform and to implement the decision-making of the latter. This approach to the staffing and organization of management has been called the 'metropolitan' one because of its association with major national employing organizations very often based in London and the Home Counties, run by graduates of Oxford, Cambridge and London and other traditional universities (Glover and Kelly, 1987).

However in medium-sized and more provincially-based companies and in local government, the National Health Service (NHS) and in most of the public corporations and industries nationalized by Labour governments between 1945 and 1951, there was a different and in most respects opposed, 'provincial' (Glover and Kelly, 1987) way of staffing and organizing management-level work (also see Burrage, 1973). Here the professional specialists generally *were* 'the management' and they tended, in the public sector, to be directly responsible only to elected politicians, who tended to be unfamiliar with the details of their work.

The generally accepted strengths of the custodians were the objectivity and impartiality which resulted from their having quite rigorously trained minds, usually in non-relevant subjects, often uncluttered by much detailed knowledge of specialist tasks. Their generally accepted weaknesses were the lack of such knowledge, and an arms'-length stance towards messy practical necessity and reality. The strengths and weaknesses of the professionals tended to be the opposite of these. So professionals, while relatively narrow in outlook, training, abilities and sympathies, were competent within their ambit, and much more practical and 'hands-on' in general than the custodians. Of course many custodians were willing to dirty their hands and many professionals broadened themselves through self-education and experience, but they tended to be thought of as exceptions even if they were not.

The main remedies advocated in the twentieth century, especially in its last third, as cures for the weaknesses implied by this account, have been US-influenced management training and business education and a more general shift in emphasis in higher education from the academic to the vocational. Post-experience management courses have helped to teach the custodian something useful, such as accountancy, marketing and personnel management. The narrow accountant has learnt about marketing and operations management, the marketing specialist about the latter and finance and personnel, the engineer about finance, markets, people, and so on. Business and management studies have been amongst the fastest growing subjects in higher education since the 1940s and most courses leading to professional and other higher-level specialist practical qualifications are nowadays taught in universities to full-time students, rather than in commercial and technical colleges to part-time ones. Further, specialist professional degree courses tend to be much broader than their counterparts of a generation or two ago. Architects, doctors and engineers learn about money and markets and accountants learn about markets, personnel and operations management, and so on. As we write there is public debate about how top police officers should be equipped with financial and other 'managerial' skills and about whether business expertise should be bought into police forces/services, with some top job holders being employed without any experience of police work.

However equivalent degree or similar courses on the continent of Europe aimed at senior posts in industry, commerce and government, have long been equally or more technocratic. Higher education institutions responsible for engineering, business economics and administrative education in France, Germany, Scandinavia and the Low Countries and elsewhere on the Continent, have long produced broadly educated and commercially and financially and/or technically knowledgeable expert people who are both specialists and generalists. In the case of engineers these people are 'true' technocrats and in the case of graduates in business economics and administration they are broadly-defined ones. What we mean by this is that all such people are powerful because of their mastery of technique, and technocrats in a general sense, and that those amongst them whose main expertise is technical, especially engineers, are the most completely and truly technocratic of all. Such people have tended to be both educated and trained before their university or equivalent studies are complete. Engineers, for example, have generally taken courses lasting for about six years following a much broader secondary education than their UK counterparts have received. The first half of their engineering studies is mainly theoretical, for example in physics, thermodynamics, economics and mathematics, and the second half consists mainly of practical project work under the tutelage of professors with significant to very substantial records of industrial experience and/or achievement (Chisholm, 1975; Hutton and Lawrence, 1981; Lawrence, 1992).

In Japan and elsewhere in the Far East a similarly technocratic philosophy tends to prevail but while the relevant forms of expert labour are also recruited from higher education, where 'theory' is also inculcated, it is trained and developed beyond its theoretical base by employers. These broad and general differences are summarised within the following schema:

> *Professional-Managerial:*
> Expert labour is developed partly in full-time education and partly through on-the-job experience and post-experience education and training. Expert labour of this type is often subordinated to general management. Examples include the Anglo-Saxon countries, such as the UK, the USA, Canada, Australia, New Zealand and India.
>
> *University-formed Technocratic:*
> All or most expert labour is produced in full-time higher education (often with employer help) and management is part of technical expertise and not vice-versa. Examples include France, Germany, Sweden, the other Scandinavian and the Benelux countries.
>
> *Company-centred Technocratic:*
> Expert labour is recruited from higher education but is trained and developed beyond its theoretical base by employers. Management tends to be subordinated to or to be part of technical expertise. Examples include Japan and other Far Eastern countries.

Source: Glover and Tracey (1997)

In *The Professional-Managerial Class* (Glover and Hughes, 1996b, p. 5) the above differences were also partly summarised by outlining two master, contrasting, depictions of ways of constructing and organizing 'management-level and expert "professional" occupations, tasks, qualifications, expertise and divisions of labour' (p. 4). These were 'what Albert (1993) called the Rhine and the Neo-American versions of capitalism, and what Fores, Glover and Rey (1976) call *Technik* and (later, Business) Management. The former tends to emphasize the value of production, process, the long term, management *in* specialist activities, and the more positive side of the state's role in economic life. The latter, the neo-American or the (Business) Management model, stresses consumption, outcome, the short-term, management *of* specialist activities, and the more negative side of the state's role' (Glover and Hughes, 1996b, p. 5).

All of the above points were made at greater length in *The Professional-Managerial Class* (chapter 1). However they have since been added to and qualified in articles by Glover and Tracey (1997) and Glover, Tracey and Currie (1998). In the latter of these two articles a number of points about the long-term resilience, also hinted at in *The Professional-Managerial Class*, of the Business Management approach and of the societies responsible for it, especially the UK and the USA, are spelt out more fully. In the first article Glover and Tracey (1997, pp.773, 774) added the category of manager to those of technocrat, custodian and professional, discovered above. Since writing this article it occurred to Glover and Tracey that the category of manager would have benefited from putting the word business in front of it. This is apparent in the following quotation from the paper, which depicts characteristics and typical examples of all four categories:

> Regarding our typology of top job holders, we would now add the category of manager to those of technocrat, custodian and professional, so as to cover the whole range of alternative backgrounds (apart from that of the unqualified "practical man" [Barnett, 1972, pp. 95-96; Locke, 1984, 1989])'. A typical "manager" would have a business studies or business degree or an MBA; a typical "technocrat" a Continental engineering Diploma (Dipl.Ing.), or a UK M.Eng., or B.Eng. degree plus a relevant Masters degree, such as an MSc in Technology Management or an MBA; a typical "custodian" an arts or natural or social science degree or degrees. A typical "professional" would be a chartered accountant, architect, chartered engineer, high-level marketing researcher, personnel specialist, surveyor, or of course lawyer or doctor (Glover and Tracey, 1997, pp. 773, 774).

The article goes on to note how many individuals combine elements of two or more of the above in their backgrounds, and to say that 'Management-level people in the UK tend to be professional-managerial but are evolving into a mixture of products of all three ways of producing people - they are becoming more technocratic - with elements of the custodian still around' (op cit. p. 774).

Why, after discussing the UK's professions and professionals in terms which are neither especially unfriendly nor especially pessimistic, are we doing so in a book whose main title, *Professions at Bay*, suggests that they are under threat? The answer is that while the attributes and characteristics of professionals have been and are in general being underpinned, developed and added to in the UK setting, since the 1960s they have been subjected to a great deal of public criticism and externally induced change, much of which has been openly hostile. Markets which independent fee-taking professionals operate in have been deregulated, subjecting them to often considerably heightened competition. The jobs of some public sector professionals have been lost, and others contracted out or otherwise made less secure during cost-cutting exercises, with public-sector professional work increasingly subjected to tough and even oppressive managerial(ist) control. In the private sector, other organizational professionals have also been operating since the 1960s in more demanding competitive environments, with job losses, job insecurity and tough management control very common.

The sources of public and private criticism of professions have by no means all been part and parcel of the Thatcherite project of deregulation. It is true that the public sector professionals, in the NHS, education, the civil service and local government and so on, were for most of the twentieth century, and certainly since 1945, major beneficiaries of big government, the welfare state and of relatively high levels of public expenditure. It is also true that many independent (or partly so) fee-taking professional occupations, like accountancy, architecture, civil engineering, law, surveying, private medicine, veterinary surgery, and so on, have been both lucrative and open to varying degrees to accusations about rigging markets. Thus cosy public sector employment and monopolistic practices in the private sector have led many right-wing and other critics of professions to focus in a sometimes crude and general way on their presumed economic inefficiency.

However a number of other criticisms, mainly of the 1970s, were equally fundamental but rather different in emphasis. They drew on international comparisons of management and organization and they were also historically informed (Glover, 1978a, 1980, 1985; Child et al, 1983; Locke, 1984, 1989; also see Dingley, 1996). They did not offer blanket criticisms of professions; and they approved strongly of the ethical, social and vocational dedication of many professionals and their occupations, and they believed, too, that notions of professional jurisdiction and expert 'practice' did often function to serve the individual and public or general good. What these writers did do was to make a number of specific points about the origins, nature and role of professional activities in different contexts. As this book does, they distinguished between the independent (traditional, original, fee-taking) professions, and the public sector and organizational ones. The traditionally independent professions such as the law and medicine did, it was felt, still deserve to enjoy most of their original monopoly powers and to be subjects of relatively high expectations regarding their ethics, insofar as their services were often of great and sometimes overriding value to their clients. They continued to be archetypical professionals, with 'origins...those of a small-town big shot from the eighteenth century, pre-industrial life...an adviser, or a consultant...[whose output was rated by clients and peers]...as much by elements of rectitude, such as rightness or truth against a scale, as by market criteria such as ability, price and date of delivery' (Glover, 1978b). In the public sector and in commercial sectors in which producers also wield potentially great power over individual clients or consumers because of the nature of their outputs, as in education, health care and construction, the relevance of professional standards of responsibility to the general public and to individual clients was also quite clear (Child et al, 1986).

However in largely or purely commercial settings the professional approach had much less relevance. Market criteria prevailed there: a person buying a dress, a car, a shirt or a compact disc player did not need to pay a fee for some expert advice before deciding which one to buy. The organizational professional, the accountant, engineer or the IT, market research or personnel expert, working as a salaried employee of a business firm, was only a professional by virtue of their qualifications and expertise and general sense of responsibility for their actions. Overt exercise of a sense of communal or public responsibility is the exception rather than the rule with such people. Many of the criticisms made of professions in the years preceding the deregulation of professions and the growth of New Public Management in the 1980s were directed at organizational professions' and professionals' attempts to profit from their association with the status, ethos and relative independence of the liberal and the public sector professions. They had proliferated around such core line management activities as operations and production or sales in the private sector, often at their expense, as when accounting, technical or personnel management considerations prevailed over commercial ones in manufacturing (Child et al, 1983).

Their ethos tended to be rational, ordered, concerned with giving advice, reflective and static, and knowledge-specific, whereas management-level work, at least in the private sector, including its expert specialist professional components, tended to have very different characteristics. Thus it tended to be ingenious, relatively chaotic, concerned with output rather than advice, intuitive and active, and skill-specific. The obvious solutions to the tendency of professional 'staff' expertise to weaken the authority and the power of the 'line' in management are for the latter to reassert its authority and to require staff specialists to take on line responsibility and authority, making them work in teams with other kinds of professional and to learn some of their outlook and skills (see, for example, Leveson, 1996).

The challenges: professions outflanked, undermined, subordinated?

Organizational professionals like engineers, accountants, research and development scientists, specialists in personnel and human resource management, and marketing and IT experts have long competed for power, status and financial reward (Child, 1982; Armstrong, 1984). They have done so, too, with many other manifestations of expert and managerial labour, including many highly qualified former specialists who have first and often long embraced administrative or managerial roles and identities, and many who have non-relevant qualifications or none at all. When levels of qualification have been high, as with many engineers and scientists, and when the most senior posts in relevant sectors and organizations have not been dominated by holders of such qualifications, there has been clear evidence of dissatisfaction on the part of the relevant professionals with their careers, work situations or status. Further, many organizational professionals do not belong to professional associations, either because they are unqualified, because their qualifications are unsuitable, or because, although qualified, they see no benefits in joining 'talking shops' which exert little or no influence over employers.

In the UK, the USA and the other former British Empire countries recognition as a "profession" was important to occupations not only because it was associated with traditional gentry status, but also because its traditional connotations of disinterested dedication and learning legitimated the effort to gain protection from competition in the labour market. Given the prevalence of the *laissez-faire* philosophy, 'only quite special excuses could justify the state-sanctioned creation of a market shelter' (Freidson, 1983, pp. 24, 25). However in Europe the more active part played by the state in organizing education, training and employment meant that both the traditional professions of law and medicine and the new senior, middle-class occupations of the nineteenth century, such as those of civil servants and engineers, came to depend far more on the generally very high status of their elite educational backgrounds and of their careers, rather than on their occupational specialism and professional affiliations (Jarausch, 1990; Overy, 1992; McLelland, 1991). For Freidson, following Maurice (1972), Fores and Glover (1978) and Glover (1978b), professions, as institutions, belong to a particular period and 'with only a limited number of nations' in it (Freidson, 1983: 26). The study of a wide range of sources concerned with the establishment of professional associations in the UK and the USA would suggest that the high point of profession-formation in the UK was probably around start of the twentieth century, with the corresponding date for the USA being about thirty or forty years later. The USA was far 'ahead' of the UK, of course, in the development of business and management education, and these differences in timing are mostly, at least ultimately, attributable to the UK being the much older and in some relevant respects the more conservative nation.

Since the 1960s and the expansion of higher education and of the vocational emphasis within it, UK organizational 'professionals' have become more and more diverse, as well as much more numerous. The extent to which the products of UK higher vocational education manifest professional characteristics has reduced, as the numbers of business and management, social science and other expert kinds of non-professional specialist graduate have risen. Smith (1991) implied that only about a third, at most, of the UK's graduate or equivalently-qualified and eligible engineers join the relevant professional engineering associations. We think that if IT specialists are defined as engineers the figure would only be about a quarter. Roslender (1992) thought that only about a half of the UK's practising accountants belonged to professional accountancy associations: most of those suitably qualified did belong, but many had been trained by employers, or were partly or wholly self-taught. Similar kinds of estimate have been applied to scientists and personnel specialists, and the proportion of marketing and sales experts or 'professionals' who belong to the Chartered Institute of Marketing is particularly low, as we might expect given the totally commercial character of the tasks of the vast majority of the relevant practitioners (Bathie, 2000).

However the most important single fact about the out-flanking of professions and professionals in the UK concerns the overall number of graduates currently being produced compared with the overall numbers of members of professional qualifying associations. According to data discussed by the Engineering Council (1994) the total number of the latter in the early 1990s could not have been much more than one million. A proportion approaching nearly two fifths of all school-leavers will soon to be attending universities, many of them taking specialist vocational courses which overlap with or are substitutes for those taken by professionals, and the influence of organizational professionals who are fully paid up members of professional associations in the private sector looks likely to be diminished further. However the situation in the public sector, most obviously in health and education perhaps, looks much different, with professionals still occupying most of the line management positions in spite of influxes of business 'managers', and often keen to regain ground lost to the latter.

The undermining of professions by commercialism, by the commercialisation of management practices, is perhaps the most direct form of assault on them. Part of the onslaught on professions associated with the 1980s has been one on functional specialist management. As suggested earlier, to make commercial organizations act in more proactively and aggressively commercial ways, it was important for line and staff functions to work more closely together at least, and ideally for them to unify (cf. Child et al, 1983; Lawrence, 1980). Staff specialists like those in R and D, personnel, management services and even some of those in accountancy and finance and market research, needed to refrain from pursuing their own occupational (professional) interests, and to pull together in the causes of organizational unity, of commercial and technical as opposed to political and departmental empire-building innovation, and of sales and the bottom line. When professionals have been employed widely as staff specialists, attacks on fragmented and divisive forms of functional specialist management will have had a base in reality. However when professionals have themselves made up much or most of 'the line', as they do in many public services, changes which go beyond encouraging or training them to be more effective need some other justification. This justification appears to have come partly from the pages of America and other intellectually and morally lightweight 'pop management' and 'management guru' books, which habitually demonize vaguely specified 'bureaucracy', while romanticizing the supposedly greater and more 'democratic' effectiveness of flexible, organic, management and organization.

This most obvious reason for commercialising the work of professionals is the improvement of their productivity which, it has often been argued, is often less than it might be because they have a tendency to 'place application of their expertise ahead of any objectives... articulated by their employers' (Chaston and Badger, 1993). These authors undertook a survey of managers in local government and the NHS in order to explore the effectiveness of their attempts to create customer-responsive organizations in the public sector. They found, apparently, that 'the dominant influence of professionals in the culture, structure and strategies of these organizations' was a major retardant of the development of interdepartmental cooperation, internal customer chains, external customer satisfaction, the use of 'concepts such as Customer Care and Total Quality Management' and the establishment of customer-driven cultures in general. The results suggested strongly that departments were managed in rather autocratic and small-minded ways which encouraged insularity of outlook amongst staff, and 'senior managers in different departments' appeared to be very reluctant to trust each other 'to put the needs of internal customers ahead of intra-departmental objectives' (p. 6). Although departments had been merged, management layers reduced, information systems developed to enhance decision-making, service units made smaller and more autonomous, training in customer care given, and strategic planning introduced, managers persisted in using traditional methods of allocating resources. Doctors in the NHS and department heads with professional qualifications and responsibilities in local government constituted the majority of those who became senior managers. There was also a 'lack of common managerial language among different professionals' (p. 8). The authors advocate more post-experience management training for professionals as part of their solution. It should, they felt, use a common language and emphasize responsiveness to customers. The other part of their solution consisted of 'Artificial Intelligence [AI] Engines', as substitutes for professional labour. This seems to be rather naïve regarding both the long-term effects of management exhortation and training courses, and the practical potential of AI compared with that of combined human experience and unpredictable ingenuity (cf. Fores, Glover and Lawrence, 1991).

Ackroyd (1994, p. 10) noted how effectively the UK's public sector professions had been in achieving a degree of market closure, partly by differentiating themselves 'sharply... from political and executive power on the one side, and routine administration on the other'. They had thus preserved their professional beliefs over long periods by *persistently* distinguishing themselves from management. Their ability to do this was undoubtedly long underwritten by the general character of UK local government and of UK society in general. The qualifications of the custodians who dominated the upper, metropolitan, reaches of public administration in Whitehall for over a century generally consisted of degrees from prestigious universities. Their counterparts in local government were generally people without degrees and very often without professional qualifications, or more recently, graduates from provincial universities (old and new). Similarly, local politicians have generally also had less prestigious educational and occupational backgrounds than those of their national counterparts. Until quite recently professionals have been clearly the most highly and relevantly qualified people available to fill local government posts. More permanent than local politicians, more heavyweight than local administrators, and far more able to justify their actions by using professional expertise and mystique than most local government managers, professionals in local government long enjoyed relatively secure bases of power. Ackroyd noted how such professionals had usually enjoyed at least some control over the education and licensing of practitioners, how they have focused closely on their own specialisms, and how the division of function between public service managers and professionals has been protected and preserved by both groups (also see Clarke and Newman, 1992). Thus although many public sector managers were recruited from professional groups, and maintained 'a protective... attitude towards the services they manage (Ackroyd et al, 1989), [they] see themselves as managers not practitioners, and tend to be regarded as such by practitioners'. Clearly such a distinction is self-reinforcing insofar as rising practitioners can develop either within or outwith their professional departments and insofar as those who remain in the middle ranks of their professions generally enjoy higher rewards and prestige than their counterparts in management. Managers at all levels have relied, of course, on the existence of professional services for their employment, irrespective of their own qualifications and occupational backgrounds. Such points help to explain why the respondents whose views were discussed by Chaston and Badger, junior and middle managers in local authorities and the NHS in South West England, provided such firm evidence of resistance to the customer service and total quality cultures in their organizations.

Professionals and managers of all kinds are encouraged by their education, training and occupational socialization to develop their own specialist norms and practices, and both career structures and formal divisions of labour continually reinforce each other and the process in general. Long-term and fundamental changes in attitudes and behaviour are hardly likely to result from training courses or managerial attempts to manipulate 'culture' in such circumstances. An external threat to a whole organization or profession is the only kind of force which is likely to be strong enough. Such forces are experienced more often in the private sector than the public one. Thus while professionals have always been more vulnerable to threats to their values, control over their work, and their power, income and status in the private sector than in the public one, the character and operation of such process as developments in IT, the internationalization of economic life and changes in the boundaries between the private and the public may all only have a background and relatively slight influence on these things (Green and Whitney, 1996; Greenwood and Lachman, 1996; Scott, 1997).

Even in the private sector there are important differences in terms of vulnerability to commercialisation of professional work, between sectors of employment whose purposes are completely commercial and those in which an element of a professional fiduciary relationship exists between buyers and sellers. In the former, as in the case, for example, of a chain of shops selling clothes, managerial pressures on professional specialists like accountants and personnel staff which encourage them to be governed almost entirely by commercial criteria (when they are not already) are unlikely to meet with much resistance. Paterson (1991, 2000) found, in interviews with personnel specialists, mainly in the private sector, in the early-mid 1980s, that they were fully aware of how they and their professional association had long deployed the habits and rhetoric of professionalism in order to establish themselves within management teams. Their main short-term target was 'credibility' in the eyes of line managers, and they regarded political astuteness as a major weapon for obtaining it. In the threatening, and worse, economic and employment climate of the early-mid 1980s, they had thus been very prepared to drop much of the traditional rhetoric of personnel professionalism, of being umpires of the conflict between the 'two sides' of industry and commerce, in favour of that of the bottom line and 'tough' human resource management practices.

In the case of commercial sectors in which professional fiduciary relationships continue to prevail to a large degree, such as construction and law, the nature of the product and the market generally serve as powerful breakwaters against the tides of commercialism (see Flood, 2000, on lawyers). The professional archetype of the relatively disinterested and learned service-provider is clearly far more relevant to the purchaser of a house, office block, or the services of solicitor or barrister, than it is to the same person buying a motor car, clothing, or a ticket for a rugby match. This is not merely a matter of differences in cost.

The more *public* as well as the longer-term ramifications of the relevant purchase are also crucial to the difference. However, and as Barrett (1993a, 1993b) noted, the forces driving UK professional practices towards a greater business orientation were considerable, and included the increased availability of computing power, improvements in management education in the professions, the abolition of scale fees and more demanding clients. Further, various restraining forces had been reduced, such as when professional associations had relaxed their bye-laws governing advertising and internal divisions of labour in professional practices. These pressures were forcing construction professionals to be more efficient but entirely along traditional lines. In other words commercial forces were making them more effective as providers of services which were no different from the ones which they had always provided, and they were thus probably *strengthening*, not weakening, the power bases of such services as architecture and surveying.

In the NHS, advances in medical techniques and the growth of chronic illness relative to acute illness, as a result, partly, of the Service's achievements, had led successive governments since the 1960s to seek savings in public spending on health care and ways of restraining the power and the apparently related profligacy of doctors (Dopson, 1996). The application of the concept of the internal market in health care had eventually followed numerous largely failed attempts to subvert the power of doctors, and a little less unsuccessfully, to involve them directly in management. Eventually, doctors, who had traditionally been very highly qualified super health technicians rather than true medical technocrats capable of managing all aspects of health care provision, had begun to fight back against the threats of commercialism and managerialism by taking a much more active interest in the non-medical aspects of health care management, and by taking various new and relevant masters level and other health care management qualifications (Fitzgerald, 1996). Both the centrality of their knowledge and tasks to health care, and possibly their intellectual superiority over most of their non-medical management colleagues, would appear to augur well for the continuation of medical dominance in the NHS.

For McNulty, Whittington and Whipp (1996) the concept of a 'practice' (MacIntyre, 1990; Keat, 1991) was highly relevant for understanding professional responses to market-driven changes. Their study of four NHS hospitals and four R and D laboratories explored ways in which such changes of emphasis, from control by hierarchies to control by markets, has involved the creation of internal markets in both cases and contracting out in the latter. A practice was defined as a complex cooperative set of activities which produces, not only external goods for relevant segments of the wider community, but also internal ones which partly define the activities of practitioners. These internal goods are produced as practitioners develop their skills, and help to extend professional powers and capabilities. To belong to a practice was to submit to its standards of excellence and to obey its rules. Practices clearly include most crafts and professions. For Keat (1991) consumer power threatened that of producers, involving reduction in the deference accorded to producers by consumers, with the latter increasingly determining the 'form, nature and quality of goods and services'.

However, McNulty, Whittington and Whipp found that relationships between practitioners, organizations and markets were more varied and complex than Keat had suggested. They found that consumers varied in terms of the degrees of deference that they gave to producers' expertise and knowledge. Doctors received more deference than R and D professionals. Different organizational managers interpreted and responded to market forces in different ways; and they rigged, or did not rig, their internal markets differently too. McNulty and his colleagues felt that emphasis on market-driven change was not such a threat to professional 'practices' as many had feared. With Barrett (1993a) above, they implied that greater efficiency *and* viability are likely to result. For McNulty, Whittington and Whipp, poor management of client relationships and inadequate involvement of practitioners in contracting and marketing, meaning reduced control over work, were the biggest threats to professional practices. In itself commercial management of practices was a neutral force. Dopson (1996) made a similar point about bureaucracy: it could both underpin and stifle creative work.

The evidence that UK professionals are being outflanked by well-qualified competitors from non-professional educational and occupational backgrounds appears, so far, to be more conclusive than that which suggests that they are being undermined by rampant market forces. However the relationships between the two aforementioned forces need to be explored further, and the roles of other possibly relevant ones considered too. One of the latter is managerialism. To what extent are those, including directors and employers, who are employed above professionals in the upper reaches of organizational hierarchies, deliberately curbing their power, and why?

There is a fair amount of evidence from the UK private sector of 'delayering', 'downsizing' and simplification of managerial hierarchies. However the degrees to which these changes have frustrated or supported specific professional groupings within specific employment sectors are largely unknown. Sensibly, Ackroyd (1994, p. 5) emphasized the fact that, in myriad ways, British professions 'monopolise key knowledge, and...are then indispensable employees; but at the same time, they are subordinated to controls by other groups in organisational settings'. Professionals tended to be differentiated quite sharply from routine supervisors and administrators, from top managers, and from each other. In the public sector and manufacturing professional groupings competed with each other, while generally cooperating with top managers above, and routine supervisors and administrators below and around them. They generally did what top managers told them, and supervisors and administrators generally did what professionals told *them*. In most sectors one or more type of professional dominated others at any given time. Across commerce and finance similar patterns pertained except that professionals tended to be proportionally less numerous, and significantly weaker. However there is something else which is also very important to note. There is one grouping within UK private sector management which has been rather dramatically neglected by social scientific and management research. Engineers, accountants, research scientists and personnel/human resource managers have received copious attention. But the largest single grouping in UK management has not: that of marketing and sales specialists. This group has always been at the top (directoral) table in very significant numbers. Marketing, and sales before and with it, has probably attracted at least its fair share of the UK's abler school-leavers and graduates (Glover, 1978a; Leggatt, 1978; Swords-Isherwood, 1979; Handy et al, 1988).

The neglect of these people by most management researchers is both curious and unremarkable. They are so numerous and ubiquitous, and in some senses so commonplace, as to be almost invisible to people looking for the interesting and dramatic. They lack a coherent professional core and identity. Numbering over a million people, and truly the great unresearched, only a small fraction of them are members of the Chartered Institute of Marketing and other management and professional associations. In a nation of shopkeepers they are unproblematic compared with engineers, who often inaccurately tend to be seen as being hard done to; accountants who are also often inaccurately seen as both overprivileged and vaguely malevolent; and personnel mangers and R and D people, who in their different ways are (quite rightly) seen as fairly curious. Dominant without generally appearing to dominate, they only epithet that some of them, sales people, have attracted is 'the gin and tonic brigade' (Child, 1984). Yet they are important for this paper's themes because they form a major part of the context in which those who are partly, at least, genuinely professional specialists, such as accountants and engineers, operate in the private sector. They are also the natural advocates (like Chaston and Badger, 1993, quoted above) of customer and other commercial and organizational or managerial priorities, ones which are often at odds with the more practice-centred ones of professionals. Finally they are a major category of expert labour, one whose knowledge and skills overlap with and into those of counterparts in other specialisms.

In thinking of the possible subordination of professionals and of professionalism in management hierarchies, by the standard-bearers of commercialism and controlling managerialism, we are led inexorably to think about the part that accountants might play. Their concern with expenditure in particular, with control in general, and thus with managerial rather than more specialised priorities would seem to make them natural enemies of professional expertise and the development of professional 'priorities', and willing policers of professional activities. Yet, and although there is a great deal of evidence to support that view, accountants are professionals themselves, however commercial many of their concerns and interests might be, often with formal responsibilities of a public and semi-public type, however inadequately they may sometimes be fulfilled in practice. The fact is that, in the private sector, all professionals have much to gain from helping their employers to achieve their commercial aims and much to lose if they fail conspicuously to do so. In the public sector, too, irrespective of whether systems of internal markets exist, professionals normally need to serve the public and their organizational superiors more than their own personal ends, if they are to survive.

Armstrong (1989) has stressed the importance of accepting that 'the core feature of management within capitalist social relations of production is an agency relationship ... [which contains] contradictions between the inevitable dependence of employers and senior managers on trust and the fact that this is expensive, which gives them incentives to dispense with it ... in favour of deskilling and monitoring of management work'. For Armstrong this simple point helped us to understand the 'micro-political and historical dynamism within capitalist management organisation' (p. 307). Armstrong's position is compatible with that of Abbott

(1988) on how professions and professionals form a loosely knit open system of management-level occupation groups, who compete both within and outside employing organizations, for power, public esteem and legal and administrative support. Both Armstrong's and Abbott's can be used to underpin the discussion of contemporary relationships between private and public sector professionals and managers in the UK offered by Savage et al (1992). These latter authors distinguish between the late 1980s' emphasis on consumption in the life styles of many private sector commercial, financial and legal professionals, and the more 'ascetic' life styles of public sector ones in health, education and social services. They also note the 'undistinctive' life styles of many managers, civil servants and local government officials, and go on to describe how individuals move between professional and managerial jobs, and also to suggest how their life styles move with the times as economic conditions change along with the identities of those who need to be courted and impressed. These arguments parallel, in many ways, those of Crompton (1990) about how recent discussions of professions (e.g., Freidson, 1983; Abbott, 1988) have increasingly recognised their largely Anglo-American character and moved towards discussing them in a more general context of study of expert and managerial labour, and even of that of all occupations. She goes on to discuss the ending or reduction of several professional monopolies in the UK, either directly as with lawyers, opticians and dentists, and less directly through the introduction of quasi-markets in the public sector as in the NHS and higher education.

Crompton then becomes historical in her emphasis. Thus the aim of governments in the 1980s was to weaken the 'caring' public sector professionals and to strengthen the private sector ones which are seen as contributing directly to aggressive wealth creation, partly in reaction to the growth and subsequent - in their spheres - hegemony of the welfare state's 'helping' professions and Keynesian economic management after the Second World War. This suggestion that softer times favour the development of professions, whereas harder times tend to stifle their growth, is echoed over a longer time scale by Ackroyd (1994; 1996). His arguments suggest that when untutored entrepreneurship and rapid technical change are in the van of economic growth, professional growth tends to be in remission, whereas periods of social and economic consolidation and/or burgeoning large scale organization and management have tended to support the development of professions. Historical experience, at least that of the UK, broadly supports this kind of account, although its industrialization, and the development of many distinctively British institutions in the second half of the nineteenth century, the creation of the welfare state after 1945, and the programmes of deregulation and privatization of the Conservative governments of 1979 to 1997, are all virtually unique and probably unrepeatable events.

Du Gay (1994) and Brown (1995) have hinted powerfully at a number of contemporary managerial trends which clearly do threaten professionals directly. Du Gay criticized the 'populist "bureaucracy-bashing" of contemporary managerial discourse', and Brown noted how conventional middle class careers have increasingly been devalued. For both, the rapid international economic changes of the last two decades had generated considerable tension between those committed to liberal democratic societies sustained by efficient bureaucratic administration, and the desires to improve economic performance by introducing more flexible and more politicized and stressful patterns or organization and work and to bypass formal procedures of employment in order to 'extend social privileges to family members' (Brown, 1995). Such trends clearly threaten the employment situations of many organizational professionals, especially those in the public-sector. Brown notes how employees increasingly distinguish between two types of credentialled person: one who has invested in consumption so as to add value to their *curriculum vitae* as a 'rounded person', and another who has not been able to supplement their qualification with such 'charisma'. Intellectual ability plus technical expertise alone no longer equalled 'management potential'.

For Russell (1994) and Rothblatt (1994), arguing along similar lines in UK and US contexts respectively, state antagonism and indifference were combining with private greed to tear the traditional professions apart. Russell felt that, in the UK, professional autonomy was continually being invaded and abandoned by civil servants and politicians. As employers of professionals they had been letting their impatience override professional judgements because they were inconvenient, costly in the short run, or otherwise uncomfortable. Rather than bargain with professionals about their expert judgements they tried to control both the supply and demand for professional services by substituting their own often highly incompetent judgements. This was the route to a command economy. In the context of higher education it might soon be 'as unwise to attend a British university as to fly Aeroflot'. Fashionable buzz-words from management texts, like 'efficiency' and 'accountability' (cf. Ziman, 1994; chapter 9) were being applied in ways which threatened to wreck public services. 'Efficiency savings' being made were like those of the car owner who neglects servicing. 'Accountability' was far too often being implemented by processes of form-filling and points scoring by lay people, civil servants and members of the public, who were not competent to make the relevant judgements. The article by Rothblatt is primarily concerned with the recent large-scale commercialisation of medical services in the USA as a result of juries awarding massive damages in malpractice suits and the associated takeover of medical services across that nation by large insurance companies and a wide range of bureaucratic health maintenance organizations. 'Efficiency-minded' health management organizations or companies now employed doctors, controlling much of their work, so that medicine was no longer a practitioner-led profession. The same trends were discernible in the cases of the legal, engineering and academic professions.

However these rather pessimistic views from senior practitioners (including Ziman) contain significant blind spots. Crude indices of performance and sometimes heavy-handed bureaucratic controls have indeed been imposed on hitherto only vaguely accountable professionals. Yet, and as has been implied on several occasions above, this has generally been done in the expectation that the relevant professionals would take over the process of managing themselves more rigorously, and in due course refine both the indices and the controls at their leisure.

The numbers, relative to other groups involved, of professionals, and their indispensability, often make such a process look inevitable.

Further, in higher education, the law, the NHS and elsewhere the true character of the relevant changes has been confused by many factors. These have included changes in government; financial pressures of very varied kinds; expansion of the numbers of clients, patients, students, suppliers and so on; changes in the direction and content of provision; changes in the ownership and management of parent and related organizations; changing economic, social and political contexts and expectations; and so on. However, the following have *not* changed: doctors still treat patients, academics still write papers and give lectures, engineers still design products and develop processes, lawyers still advise clients and argue for them in court, architects still design structures, and accountants still audit accounts and construct and review budgets.

Professional producer-consumer relationships in different contexts

So far we have seen that professionals tend to be relatively more numerous and influential in public sector managerial hierarchies than in private sector ones, except when the latter consist of independent professional practices. We have noted how the growth and vocationalisation of higher education have been producing, by historic standards, large numbers of people with qualifications which are of a professional or near professional standard, without most of those involved being members of professional qualifying associations. We have discussed how deregulation and a wide range of 'new' and more commercial approaches to and techniques of management and consumerism have very often deliberately, and in most cases, in effect, been designed to undermine professional ideals and habits of relatively disinterested service and monopolistic practice. Further, we have noted the expansion of business and management education, training and practices which reinforce the positions and enhance the power of those who employ and manage professional expertise.

For independent fee-taking professional practices, traditional as in law, medicine, architecture, engineering, surveying, and newer as with information technology and management consultancy, the general trend has been in the direction of greater opportunities to make money, albeit in much more competitive and even turbulent commercialised environments than hitherto. In the public sector there have been many pressures to perform, often combined with less privileged, secure and respected experiences of work and employment. In the private sector strong commercial pressures and a wide range of managerial and organizational changes have generated an equally wide range of problems, threats, challenges and opportunities. Across most sectors professionals have increasingly been expected to work harder and more flexibly and often with less regard to conventional niceties of specialisation, monopolies of knowledge and skill, and even sometimes those of client care, confidentiality and so on.

In all of these broadly-defined sectors of professional employment there has been considerable organizational restructuring accompanied by all sorts of changes to expectations and working practices (Greenwood and Lachman, 1996). Some of the underlying forces are discussed by Ashburner, Ferlie and Pettigrew (1996). They focus on new public management (NPM) and start by noting how it has been a worldwide phenomenon since the 1970s. They explain how it alters the emphasis in public sector management from maintenance to change management through the development of 'quasi-markets' within and around public sector organizations, and they discuss the effects on professions and on the concept and practice of accountability. They are unsure about the extent to which NPM is likely to transform public sector management in the long term. However they are on firm ground in noting how most of its advocates have failed to develop coherent and cohesive philosophical, political, economic and sociological arguments and rationales in its favour, and how most of the relevant 'debates' have been conducted by politicians and authors of popular management texts. The authors ask whether NPM means convergence between private and public sector approaches to management or simply the latter borrowing from the former. They suggest that the truth lies between the extremes of incompatibility between private and public sectors and the notion of a generic approach to their management. In doing this they argue that before the introduction of 'reforms' and since in the mid-1980s, the idea of incompatibility was accepted too easily and that during and after the relevant changes, transfers of theory and practice from private to public sector have been too clumsy and accompanied by exaggerated presumptions of similarity.

An account of the continuing power of the professional ideal, broadly defined, in the UK, was offered by Ackroyd, also in 1996. He noted how the UK's professions have been periodically marginalized, with their growth suspended, but that they have shown a great capacity to adapt. Over a century ago a large number of what Ackroyd calls 'new model' professions had been constructed without government patronage or regulation. This had been achieved by combining control of the labour markets with informal control and cooperation within employing organizations of many kinds. Ackroyd calls this occupational 'double closure', whereby professional occupations become 'encapsulated groups' or 'quasi-organizations' within parent companies and public sector organizations. Ackroyd goes on to compare the perhaps surprisingly often very similar situations of professions in manufacturing and public services in the UK in the twentieth century. He discusses how commercial, consumerist, political and managerial pressures have recently created much stress for professional groups in these situations, but feels that they will endure. Thus he points out that reorganizations tend to take place around them, instead of engaging in their reconstruction. He also explains how, although superficial similarities exist, the management of traditional professional services and that of newer commercial ones are different. He accepts that the contemporary management of professional services is often difficult when it seeks to make them more accountable and efficient, but argues, too, that professional self-organization is too useful, rational and entrenched for it not to persist *and* expand into new services, notwithstanding current trends in their organization and control.

Professions and the future

Notwithstanding Ackroyd's optimism about the organizational and public sector professions, with which we broadly concur, an air of uncertainty has surrounded the UK's professions since the 1970s. There is for example widespread evidence of over-production of professionals in several traditionally key areas, with accountancy, architecture and law being among the more obvious examples. Further the rational economic 'prejudices' of many organizations and professional practices against older employees and practitioners have produced a quiet holocaust amongst such people (see for example Lyon, Hallier and Glover, 1998).

It is nowadays fairly widely accepted that the UK is a society which eventually became too successful for its own good, which spent too much effort and time in institutionalising and celebrating and living off its past successes. Decisions made and institutions created in mid-Victorian times programmed relative economic decline and numerous other unnecessary difficulties into its subsequent experience (Glover, 1985). It was not so much that it was 'an industrial country with an anti-industrial culture'. That perception of Wiener (1981) was a much exaggerated one. However the UK was and to a smaller degree still is an anti-industrial country in enough respects for it to matter (Glover, Tracey and Currie, 1998). The latter have included the status of various activities, occupations and professions; the content and organization of much education and training; views as to the usefulness of technical and scientific and other knowledge; and disjunctions between technical and social divisions of labour. Without going into specific details or developing a thorough analysis there has to be something 'distinctive' about a society which describes the rudiments of education as the 'three Rs' after having forgotten that there used to be fourth one - wroughting; which uses such *passive*, and in their conventional juxtaposition so status-concerned, terms as occupation and profession to describe work; which discusses 'the' manufacturing or engineering or services 'sector', when there are hundreds of each; which tends to eulogise services against manufacturing and *vice-versa* in an either-or fashion in the face of massive evidence about their complete interdependence and their *shared* bureaucratic, unproductive and menial elements; which is so lacking in confidence that its management practices have constantly aped those of an at least until fairly recently declining economy and society 3,000 miles away while displaying massive and massively unjustifiable scepticism towards lessons that could be learnt form an arguably, given the relative paucity of Germany's natural resource endorsement compared with that of the USA, a much more successful country a tenth of the distance away.

The UK did industrialize rather separately from, and yet also on the back of, commercial and imperial prowess. Also its system of matching education to work was designed more for an imperial, military, trading and financial power than for an industrial one because its preoccupations tended to be focused overseas and because its educated elite was metropolitan in type and small in number, and with those, upwards of 70 percent, of each age cohort who obtained few or no qualifications from full-time education tending to be defined as failures. The hard-nosed eighteenth century empiricism which made the nation successful appears to have been much diminished between mid-Victorian times onwards and about a century later, as institutions new and old took on a celebratory aspect. Divisions of labour in UK-based manufacturing and commerce tended to have an anomic quality, especially in the 1960s and 1970s, with those with crucial technical expertise lacking social and managerial weight.

As competitor nations overtook the UK and subjected it to particularly fierce competition, the country tended to regress, and to look to former strengths for its salvation. This involved, in the 1980s, strong elements of a reversion to a predatory and brute commercialism. The public services of a medium-sized and in some ways peripheral European power were much less prestigious to work for than when they were close to the heart of the world's largest empire, or that of the Empire that was shortly about to turn into the Commonwealth and which had earned a proud reputation in the Second World War.

Without a written constitution to provide a sense of security and in a period in which deference is conspicuous by its absence, great confusion has arisen about the nature of UK citizenship. Commercialism and lack of confidence in and around the public sector confused the issues still further so that individuals did not know whether to think of themselves as citizens, subjects or customers. A profession which has prospered conspicuously since the 1960s has been accountancy, which exists to pick up - but not so much to reassemble - the pieces following economic failure. Professions which have wanted praise for being creative, and which have not always earned it, like architecture, engineering and personnel management, have been criticized widely for their failures and occasional excesses. Further, in a partly hollowed-out society and culture there has apparently been a general loss of a sense of vocation, and indeed, of clear moral, political and public priorities (cf. Marquand, 1988). The society's habit of being world-open (as well, sometimes, as smugly racist and insular) currently makes it, in the above circumstances, unusually vulnerable to the influences of other cultures. No longer as influential, it has variously been perceived as being quaint and gullible. Such a general situation probably offers the UK's more resilient and/or ambitious and opportunistic professions more in the way of opportunities than threats. On the one hand they have practices which can be developed and applied to create wealth (broadly-defined). On the other, the strengths of their critics and opponents tend to be negative and unpopular: those of the bully, the cheat, and the carping critic.

It is important in this situation for professionals to take over whatever the bullies, cheats and critics do well, and to do it better by developing relevant commercial, financial and public relations skills. This means doctors and engineers, for example, taking more responsibility for the commercial and financial work of their employing units, and professional and expert labour of all kinds becoming much more involved than hitherto in all related aspects of management. This is the direction in which events, in the form of much employment and developments in state, professional, employer and other forms of education and training have, often perforce, been travelling for some time already.

Taken to their logical conclusion such developments could help to produce a sea change in the character of UK society. Burrage, Jarausch and Siegrist (1990, p. 209) noted how persistent professions were as institutions, and how consistent and uniform their goals have been, in the face of many major long-term changes in state institutions and policies. Professions socialized their new members so strongly, both formally and informally, and especially when practitioners retained full control over training, that professionals tended to be highly competent in a political and procedural sense, at manoeuvring around and otherwise circumventing attempts to change their practices, with would-be assailants usually no match for them. This, combined with the functional necessity of the work of key professions gives them economic and political strengths which few other institutions enjoy. By broadening their practices and their concerns, professions could help to bridge the historic gap between the two branches of the UK's middle classes, the existence of which distinguishes it somewhat from many of its foreign, notably its Continental, counterparts.

As Ackroyd (1994) noted, quoting Kocha (1990), there is little 'general conception [in the UK] of the "educated community" covering educated professional classes *and* educated business people'. Such people correspond partly to the popular English notion of 'herbivores' and 'carnivores', the 'caring' and 'tough' elements of the UK middle class (sometimes equated with *Guardian* and *Daily Telegraph* readers respectively), although there are similar subdivisions within professions (e.g., 'soft' and 'hard' human resource management) and between business concerns (compare the Roddicks of The Body Shop and Richard Branson with a wide range of openly abrasive and predatory business owners and leaders). Kocha (1990) discussed the relative homogeneity of Germany's *Bildungsburgertum* (educated middle classes) and the German notion of *Burgertum* or citizenship, which engages all the intellectually competent inhabitants of civil society, including the French *bourgeois* and *citoyen.* For Marshall (1950, published in 1963) 'citizenship and the capitalist class system have been at war' in the twentieth century. If we see professions as artefacts of citizenship (as well as in less rosy lights), as sources of freedom from civil, political and socio-economic oppression, we can see how they are indeed important components of civil society. We can also start to grasp how, if they do not abuse their monopoly powers and if they foster efficiency, they can be motors of economic development. We can imagine, too, how they are tempted to do the former in periods of social and economic complacency, and thus perhaps rightly attract the sort of opprobrium and action that the UK's professions did in the 1970s and 1980s.

Marquand (1988, pp. 7,8) argued that the communal ethic of pre-industrial times is much more suited to the late twentieth century and to later forms of industrial production and society than the rugged individualism of the seventeenth, eighteenth and nineteenth centuries. The communal ethic argued that 'property has duties as well as rights, that consumers owe producers a just price while producers owe consumers just dealing, that the community is greater than the sum of its parts, that high and low are bound together by a chain of reciprocal obligation, that man is placed by God on earth to serve greater ends than the satisfaction of his own wants', and so on. This is far from incompatible with professions performing key roles in a society, but it could be argued, albeit not willingly by us, that both society and professions are a little unwieldy and narrowly focused for the global economy which management writers, at least, want their readers to believe either exists or is forming. For Marquand, the UK recently had become addicted to rampant short term individualism because it was that which helped it to be successful before the twentieth century. Unfortunately the belief that society is no more than a collection of individuals pursuing their own goals had meant that few if any goals have been worked out for the public or private sectors. There was an intellectual and moral vacuum at the heart of the UK's political economy. This made retrenchment more painful than it need be when it was necessary. It hampered the search for ways to halt industrial decline, and for ways to share power with other countries.

The notion of active citizenship in a healthy economy and society and the existence of lively and thriving occupation-based practices like those of professions is compatible with the arguments of Marquand and others (Crouch and Marquand, 1993). These and other authors praise the relatively communal emphasis of Albert's (1993) Rhine Model of capitalism, which has been associated with the *Technik* approach to education, management, work organization and so on earlier in this chapter. Indeed the notion of 'practice' (as discussed by McNulty, Whittington and Whipp, 1993) and that of *Technik* (strictly 'engineering' but once better described as 'our word "technique" with a capital "t" and a knighthood') are very compatible. The main point to be learnt by English speakers when they consider the meaning of *Technik* is that it *includes* what they call 'management', that is, management is part of engineering and other *broadly*-conceived specialisms, not *vice-versa.* Technik is arguably the industrial heir of pre-industrial 'craft' as perhaps is the 'reflective' [meaning participative and supportive with clients as well as continually and openly self-reappraising] 'practice' of the professional work praised and discussed by Schön (1991) in the USA. It embodies all the *useful* arts *including* (in the sense of enclosing and using) the *useful* ones of 'management'.

The idea that professional-style expertise in the form of morally-guided practice should be at the core of societal development has an old and proud history (Dingley, 1996). The various critiques of managerialism of recent years (e.g., Locke, 1996; Enteman, 1993 and Aktouf, 1996) are strongly in tune with such a notion. So too was Dingwall's (1983) perception of the sociological study of the professions in the early 1980s, that it stood at something of a turning point. Dingwall suggested that functionalist and/or trait approaches had been allied to the 'pragmatic, utilitarian and atheoretical' in social science, and although such major theoretical contributions of the 1970s such as those of Freidson (1970), Johnson (1972, 1977, 1982) and Larson (1977) had reinvigorated debate, there was a need for theorising and research to be more comparative and historical (but see Maurice, 1972; Sorge, 1978; Fores and Glover, 1978; Glover, 1977, 1978b; Lawrence, 1980; Maurice, Sorge and Warner, 1980, and Child et al, 1983). Professions and their work had to be studied in their economic and social contexts. Professions were a category of occupations and this should be recognised more with the then-existing divisions of labour between sociologies of occupations and of professions being regarded as untenable. Also the importance of knowledge had to be re-affirmed continually: divisions of labour were also divisions of knowledge. They are also, of course, divisions of skill and, certain academic and managerial pretensions apart, and it is skill rather than knowledge which ultimately justifies the existence of any profession. Over the last fifteen or so years the development of understanding of professions has moved in the general direction indicated by Dingwall. Hence Macdonald's (1995) assertion that to understand a profession it is vital to understand its 'regulative bargain' with the state and its place in political culture and political power networks, its attempts to serve, defend and enlarge its jurisdiction, its altruistic and public spirited as well as its selfish characteristics (on the latter, see Saks, 1995, for example) and its strategies of social closure.

On the relationship between professional knowledge and power Corfield (1995) rejects both a downbeat Foucauldian (Foucault, 1980) view of knowledge simply serving the powerful and Bacon's (1598) more optimistic assertion that knowledge is power. She emphasises the variety and complexity of profession-public-state relationships in Britain between 1750 and 1800 and concluded (p. 250) that 'Pluralistic models of power and knowledge point to pluralistic linkages and pluralistic outcomes'. On professional power and the interdependence of professionals, employing organizations, clients, customers, managers and employees, the work of Etzioni (1969) on the semi-professions, the less entrenched, less established, less powerful professions, might be a useful starting point. So also, however, might the thinking of Lane (1996; also see Dingley, 1996) on the economic and social functions of apprenticeship in England between 1600 and 1914. The sources just quoted plus those concerned with managerialism (and professions), quoted earlier, are all relevant to creative thinking about how the positive features of professions might be made to extend usefully downwards as well as upwards and sideways.

An interesting paper on the construction professions by Leveson (1996) offers support to the possibly oxymoronic notion of sharing and democratising professional expertise. Leveson notes how the UK's construction professions have traditionally been hostile to the notion of multi-skilling, with architects, engineers, surveyors, planners and site managers (formerly known as site agents), traditionally keeping to themselves and learning little from each other. As a result departmentalism had long been rife in construction companies, with thinkers like architects and doers like surveyors and builders being particularly suspicious of each other. This inhibited teamworking and distracted attention from customers. However changes in construction markets had recently been demanding changes in professional attitudes and behaviour. Partnerships between companies and suppliers, using professional supplier agreements, and various kinds of project management, including management contracting, had been supplanting traditional adversarial relationships which has involved buying decisions being based on the lowest tender price. 'A modern external marketplace requires contractors to have a modern internal attitude' (p. 36). Leveson, a group personnel manager, goes on to explain how his construction company used project management, functional flexibility, elements of multi-skilling, recruitment, training, job rotation, management and continued professional development and continuous improvement, to integrate and develop the work and skills of its professionals. In doing so it had involved itself in developments in higher education for construction and with the professional construction associations which were moving down the same roads.

The construction professions are among the oldest. One of the newest is the information technology/management information services (IT/MIS) one. Some of the main reasons why tension and conflict between different professions are commonplace can be gleaned from a paper on IT and MIS work by Nicholson (1991). He demonstrates why, whenever a new body of expertise is built up, defensive attitudes develop amongst those who possess it as well as those who are threatened by it. In a partly similar vein Sturdy (1998) discusses the currently powerful normative pervasiveness of marketing ideas and of the 'discourse of enterprise' which define all people as 'sovereign consumers - patients, parents, passengers and pupils' (pp. 27, 27). This consumer orientation had a price: it tended to demoralise producers, such as employees who serve the public, because it demanded that they behave in 'false' ways. Sturdy describes situations in which customer 'needs' and management priorities like profitability are often in conflict. Such situations prevail at most levels of employment, including those of professionals, in highly affluent societies in which consumer choice is an increasingly salient and important feature of more and more areas of life (cf. Keat, 1994). For professionals this very broad and powerful development means that they increasingly need to be far more than mere providers of expert specialist services: they need to be actively engaged in reflexive discourse with clients, colleagues in other specialisms, administrators and managers, relevant (relevant for all sorts of often improbable notion) members of the general public, policy makers, and so on. This is only now, however, insofar as professionals increasingly operate in a democratic, deference-free, demotic and even populist political and socioeconomic climate. Sturdy's paper is a rich mine of ideas about the many issues of identity, power, service, citizenship, trust, control and social inclusion/exclusion associated with the power of consumerism in different societies. Van der Weyer (1996) discusses the way in which this power affects professionals who face the dilemma of either commercialising their operations and experiencing increasing discomforts of competition, or standing 'on their professional dignity ... [and being] accused of maintaining professional cartels and of failing to move with the times'.

In general, the future for professionals in the UK appears to be one in which producer domination of markets and relatively sheltered forms of employment increasingly belong to the past. Paradoxically in some respects, most professionals are experiencing some loss of power and status in a period in which their levels and breadth of skill and knowledge have rarely been greater. Other, younger, trees have grown up around them and they are no longer beacons in a sea of apparent mediocrity. On the other hand, they are not players in a zero-sum game. They and those with whom they compete and cooperate, be the latter other professionals, graduates and other managers, and so on, all stand to benefit and prosper more by working and learning together than by being adversarial.

Finally, and before we conclude this chapter with a brief discussion of the contents of the rest of the book, we will refer to a few sources which appear indicative of the kinds of direction in which future thinking about professions in and around management might most usefully go. One concerns the notions of thinking in organizations and of organizational learning (Senge, 1990). These concern such phenomena as strategic thinking, cognition in technical change and innovation, organizational discourses, belief systems and managerial agenda-building, decision theory, and so on. Obviously professionals make central contributions to these processes. Even broader considerations are however the focus of Aktouf (1996) who first offers a devastating moral, environmental and social critique of standard modern-cum-traditional management thinking, starting with classical economics, Fayol and Weber and working through Mayo, Simon and Mintzberg. Then Aktouf explores alternative approaches, from Germany, Japan, South Korea and Sweden. He finds elements of a more humane and responsible approach to management in these alternatives before going on to develop his thinking about what it might entail. He attacks a number of managerial(ist) clichés like the assumption that inequality, competition and soul-destroying divisions of labour are justified by greater efficiency, and unthinking faith in private property and in the rightfulness of territoriality. The notions favoured by Aktouf include cooperation, shared ownership, humility (especially), duty, obligation, self-organization and self-development. While Aktouf tends to exaggerate the degree to which managements actually perform in the ways that they appear and claim to, and also perhaps the degree to which organizations actually are manageable, while he neglects the power of consumption and consumers under conditions of high affluence, and while he neglects other writers in the critical management tradition, much of what he writes is very consonant with the notion of professional and other expert 'labourers' as democratically 'reflective practitioners' (cf. Schön, 1991).

Even wider but still relevant considerations are addressed by Bewes (1997), who attacks 'postmodern' cynicism as an originally subversive form of psuedo-critique which takes itself and its self-obsessed ironies too seriously. For Bewes, the self-consciously postmodern are the 'spoilt children of the crisis' who avoid hard-nosed rationality, conflict and suffering, at all costs, pursuing a soft kind of authenticity which is the cause of true authenticity's demise. While some of Bewes' writing tends to implode into its own kind of complex postmodern self-parody, the general thrust of much of it is applied effectively against the self-centred hypocritical pretentiousness of contemporary moral relativism. This kind of moral relativism is anathema to the essence of professional ethical concern (Dingley, 1996), and also a powerful element in the contemporary political and social climate.

The chapters

Here we will not describe the contents of the chapters which follow in detail. Instead we will simply outline the general character of each, while also picking out in each case one or more issue or other feature of it which is of particular relevance to the current situation and future role of professions in the UK.

The next part of the book contains chapters on three of the independent professions. The first and the third of these focus on lawyers and doctors, two of the three professions nurtured in the European universities in pre-industrial times, the other being the clergy. The second deals with management consultants, a profession currently of uncertain, albeit quite high, status which nowadays performs some of the functions once performed by the clergy in influencing and sanctifying actions of powerful individuals.

John Flood's chapter on corporate lawyers explores the changing organization and commercialization of corporate legal practice. Those who advise big business have profited greatly from the sea changes in government expectations of professions and in business activity in general of the 1980s, and from the growth in size of professional law firms since the Companies Act of 1967 allowed professional firms to consist of partnerships exceeding twenty persons. Corporate and other lawyers in the UK increasingly competed with accountants and with American and Continental lawyers for business. Their relationships with clients were increasingly transactional rather than long term. Yet partnership, which denoted collegiality and egalitarianism, persisted. Law was increasingly subservient to business, with this possibly most lucrative of the professions almost no longer a profession at all, and yet unavoidably, because of the nature of most of its tasks, of its jurisdiction and of the relationships with its clients and with the state, still the king of professions. Flood's concern is with large big city law practices. Deregulation has profited provincial lawyers far less, if indeed it has benefited them at all. This means that divisions between the more powerful and the weaker elements of the UK's legal profession have widened since the 1970s.

Timothy Clark and Graeme Salaman, in chapter three, discuss management consultancy, focusing on its performative character. They emphasize the orchestrated character of consultancy performance; the central, active role of the client 'audience' as the means of the performance; its risky, emotional and highly individual character; and its mysterious, paradoxical, surprising, threatening, intense and powerful essence. In a managerialist economic and political dispensation, with efficiency a powerful value (Enteman, 1993), management consultants had replaced religious leaders and soothsayers in offering advice and guidance to people who are powerful, albeit in some instances feeling threatened. As Clark (1998) has argued since, it is management consultants and gurus who many managers look to for inspiration and ideas, rather than to management researchers.

Chapter four, by Michael Kelly and Ian Glover, is concerned with the profession of medical doctors and with the effect of consumerism on their work in particular and on that of the National Health Service in general. They are concerned with the consequences which are likely to follow the elevation of the patient to consumer.

Doctors working in the NHS are, of course, only partly independent professionals. They are also public sector and also, in many respects, organizational ones. We have included them in the part of the book on independent professions partly because of their very long and extremely influential history as such, and partly because their employment and work situations, and their status, still retain many attributes of those of them. Kelly and Glover find the definition of patients as mere consumers or customers very inadequate, even puerile, in moral, practical and political terms. This is not because these authors venerate the status of medical doctors for its own sake. It is partly because patients are taxpaying citizens who collectively fund and who collectively and ultimately control the work of NHS doctors, partly because they are in certain key respects, the products of the NHS as well as its ultimate masters, and also because the medical expertise of doctors is in general so superior to theirs that they are generally not in a position to conduct transactions with doctors of the kind that they conduct in supermarkets, high street shops and showrooms and so on, although the vast majority of them are nonetheless certainly competent to make extremely pertinent contributions to discussions with doctors about their own health.

Chapter four also offers a number of thoughts about the theory of the professions, focusing mainly on what the authors see as being of value in Talcott Parsons' contributions of a half a century or so ago, contributions which have been unfashionable since the 1960s. Notwithstanding Parsons' superficially politically rather one-sided treatment of professions and his lack of understanding of the Anglo-Continental differences in the formation and character of higher occupations (cf. Fores and Glover, 1978; Fores, Glover and Lawrence, 1991), he made a major statement about the doctor-patient relationships in 1951 which, the authors argue, has great contemporary relevance. The authors also draw on the writings of Norbert Elias and Alfred Schutz to help explain how the roles of professions in society evolve and in doing this they are critical of some of the more sceptical elements of the well-known and influential views of Terence Johnson.

The three chapters in Part III, concerned with professions in the public sector, have a rather specialised character, which probably makes their discussion of the dilemmas that they address more insightful than they might have been otherwise. In the first, Charles Booth offers a brief but broad history and depiction of local government professions with an emphasis on the recent past and on the 'unprecedented attack' on them since the late 1970s which was attributable to a more critical public and to a sea change in national politics and economic policy. He also uses the leisure profession, as associated with the Institutes of Leisure and Amenity Management and of Baths and Recreation Management, as an important example of his arguments. However his main focus is on UK local government professional bodies' codes of ethics. He starts this with a general discussion of professional codes of ethics. Then he compares the main and the detailed attributes of the ethical codes of twelve public sector professions and compares them with those of two from Canada and two from the USA. He notes how UK professional bodies had been developing codes of ethics, in some cases from scratch, since the 1960s, in response to public and other criticisms. His research suggested that North

American codes were superior to UK ones, which tended to have been 'determined by professional self-interest rather than by ethical principles of altruism, collaboration and public service'. Booth appears to agree with the widespread criticisms of local government professions' competence and commitment. He thinks that they are unlikely to regain their previous dominance and that they do not deserve to do so. The character of their ethical codes showed the degree to which they had little intention of practising what they preached.

The museums profession and its management is the topic of the chapter by Stuart Davies. He is interested in how museums with their traditional professional values have been responding to the 'business managerialism' that has been introduced into public services management since the 1970s. He offers a fascinating account of how different kinds of museum, independent and public, have managed to survive and sometimes prosper in a more commercialised environment. Museum workers and managements tended to be professionals in a rather weak sense, but one that was generally quite effective in the sense of trading on a sense of shared culture, heritage and values. Museums and their staff tended to be value-driven. For a possibly uncertain future they needed to develop ('business') strategies which met the aspirations of their stakeholders like central or local government but which did not compromise their values. Challenges like this face most of the UK's professions.

The amusing title of Jane Goodsir's paper's borrows from that of a 1990 Audit Commission report of the financial costs of policing in England and Wales. In the late 1980s and early 1990s the Audit Commission and the Home Office produced six generally critical reports on the management and organization of policing in England and Wales. Goodsir explains how police officers form a 'non-traditional profession' operating as members of a state sanctioned monopoly in a context of great uncertainty. Recruits came from the skilled manual and lower middle classes. Only a small minority were graduates and far fewer of them had professional qualifications. Promotion was internal, and internal examinations tended to focus on practical issues of law and law enforcement. Senior police officers needed high-level skills in public governance and relations rather than those of low profile management or of entrepreneurship. On the other hand, police officers formed a cohesive and strong occupational community with its own strong formal and informal culture and systems of working, and they were entrusted by the state with responsibility for investigating abuses within their own ranks. In these ways they are not untypical of other professions which provide services under state mediation and control.

Public and expert criticisms of the police service had led it to try to reorient itself in the early 1990s. One way was to develop a calm, restrained, impartial, humane and fair way of going about its business and the other was to change its management and supervisory practices. Traditionally, police constables and other rank and file police officers were allowed considerable leeway in their interpretations of how the law should be enforced. 'Paperwork' had long been thought of, accurately, as interfering both with street level law enforcement and with its supervision. Demographic and other social changes had increased the need for officers at all levels to develop a wide range of practical and interpersonal skills. '"Management"... [was] now finding its way on to the police training agenda'. The increasing employment, still on a small scale, of such non-traditional recruits as women, graduates and members of ethnic minorities, and that of civilian office and technical staff, had also been complicating police management. The Sheehy Inquiry, reporting in 1993, had dealt extensively with personnel management in the police, and gave considerable attention to the notion of performance related pay. Cost and quality considerations had been made much more explicit and had been related directly to analysis of the levels of effectiveness of public support for different kinds of law enforcement. Major change was clearly both taking place and was likely in the future for the police. Pay, performance appraisal, discipline, and other reporting arrangements have already been changed, as have funding processes and priority setting. All these changes are relevant to the concerns of this book but the most interesting ones are probably those which concern changes in the most strongly traditional areas of police discretion: street-level autonomy and the investigation of complaints. And in a more general sense there is also the broad thrust of most developments in policing of the last generation, towards more 'management' and more 'technology', and towards less emphasis on and less respect for street level activity.

The chapters on the organizational professions deal with engineering, marketing, accounting, banking, personnel management, and information technology. On engineers, Tony Millman addresses the issue of their apparently low status and influence in industry and society relative to other types of manager and professional, and to engineers in other countries. His chapter suggests that engineers in the UK need to put more emphasis on improving their public image and less on such institutional changes such as revamping and rethinking of qualifications and re-organizing professional associations (Tracey, 1996). Work done at Stirling in the mid-1990s has suggested that both market repositioning as advocated explicitly by Millman and implicitly by others, and institutional changes, have already been helpful to UK engineers, and that Millman's alternatives are not incompatible. This research also suggests that parents who discourage their offspring from aiming themselves at careers in engineering and/or manufacturing are out of date, fighting battles of an earlier war, because they now appear to offer personally very rewarding and lucrative opportunities (Barry, Bosworth and Wilson, 1996; Glover, Tracey and Currie, 1998). However Millman's paper is of great value in the way in which it make explicit a tension in the debates surrounding engineering in the UK, a tension which in public debate had only previously been expressed implicitly, between advocates of top-down institutional change and advocates of the overlapping more democratic alternatives of market solutions, social movements, friendly persuasion and so on (Fores and Pratt, 1979; Glover and Kelly, 1993; Sorge, 1994; Glover and Tracey, 1997).

On marketing, Don Bathie's provocative chapter offers a thoughtful and trenchant critique from an experienced practitioner and academic advocate of marketing as an attitude and as an all-pervading philosophy, as opposed to marketing merely as a functional specialist professional activity. Bathie depicts marketing in the latter sense as a kind of 'art in a closed field', limited to the four standard P's of product, price, promotion and place. He also criticizes some postmodern depictions of marketing for treating it as an (almost) optional service function for core firms. He criticizes the Chartered Institute of Marketing for 'extreme functionalism and limited applications' and for pursuing an ideology of professionalism, not one of marketing. Of all of the functional specialisms in commerce and industry, marketing is of course the most historically and conceptually improbable candidate as a profession, because of its direct interest in the works of Mammon, because it is the most obviously commercial (cf. Dingley, 1996). On the other hand the ideal of marketing being a socially responsible and responsive activity in a civilised advanced social market economy is by no means an ignoble or unreasonable one.

On accountants, Roslender et al develop a line of thought first produced by them in the mid-1980s (Glover et al, 1986). This is that for all its 1980s' and subsequent prominence and even glamour, accountancy's future as an attractive professional and career option is far from guaranteed. The reasons for pessimism, according to the authors, include over-recruitment, the diminishing practical relevance of professional accountancy qualifications relative to those of sub-professional ones and of other specialists, the outmoded structure of the profession, and loss of public faith in it. The second of these reasons is, for us, the most threatening for accountants in the long run.

Barbara Paterson, formerly a senior personnel manager and now with her own thriving independent personnel consultancy, conducted a study of the work and the use of knowledge by 229 personnel specialists (of whom she interviewed 109) in Scotland is the mid-1980s. What was most interesting for us was her evidence on how her respondents tended to pursue managerialist aims through their involvement in political activity and, especially, by their instrumental and variable use of ideologies of professionalism, including the so-called 'soft' and 'hard' ones (cf. Legge, 1995). Thus personnel specialists appeared to cleverly exploit the ambivalence between emphasis on efficiency and in justice in their role, apparently at relevant different stages of business cycles. So they became tough minded fully fledged members of management teams in harder times, and more 'professionally' caring and considerate on behalf of employers in the good years. In the harder times, 'professionalism' tended to mean competence and, above all, credibility with top management. These points are massively significant for understanding the ways in which ideologies of professionalism and managerialism have been deployed for over a century in the UK.

As with the police as a 'hard' force or as a 'soft' service, and as with personnel, banking has also deployed hard and soft forces at different times. All three of these professions are not very strongly identified as such in the public mind. In his chapter Mark Hughes refers to his subjects as 'The Undisclosed Bankers' because of the paucity of empirical work on them, which he attributes to sociological antipathy to banks and their works as well as to something very much like the opposite, 'bankers' suspicion of public and social criticism. He discusses how UK high street banks appear to have changed from being professional, 'reliable' and 'courteous' to commercial, 'uncaring and selfish' since the 1970s. Before 1850 banking had been thought of as a trade rather than as a specialist profession. After joint stock banks were formed the old private banks were increasingly absorbed or displaced by them. Managers who could supervise head office departments and branch networks were increasingly needed, and in the 1870s a banking qualification was introduced by the Institute of Bankers.

The Institute had merged in 1993 with the 6,500-strong Chartered Building Society Institute, to form the Chartered Institute of Bankers (CIB), with just over 100,000 members. The CIB had the same aims as the old Institute, to further the study and interest of banking and to help its members acquire relevant knowledge and qualifications. Banks had always refused to recruit from each other, controlling the training and advancement of their staff closely, and the complexity of banking decisions, such as those concerned with loans, is not generally of the order of those made about products and processes, and the treatment of injuries and diseases, in engineering or medicine respectively. These facts, plus the relatively weak public identity of bankers as professional experts, had meant that bank staff tended to lack market power. Even so banking was generally thought of as a profession with professional examinations and careers. The culture of banking had been respectable, conservative, paternalistic and orderly. One researcher had described the culture of a major bank by using the following terms: highly structured, vertically differentiated, 'career-for-life', careerist, homogeneous, classless, cooperative, service sector personnel, 'conformist or unconventional?', status conscious, generalist, polite, literate, deliberate, orderliness, rationality, control oriented, and paternalist (Lawrence, 1987). However recent changes (of the last decade or so) in management had been in the directions of greater dynamism, creativity, riskiness, flexible matrix management, and market and profit and cost control orientation. The banks had remained secretive, with promotion processes typically subjective, informal and political, but they were becoming more outgoing and adaptable organizations, with more emphasis on employee abilities, commitment and effort, and less on bureaucratic role performance, loyalty and obedience.

The context for this change had been a breaking down of barriers between financial services and institutions in a general atmosphere, if not so much a reality, of deregulation. Hughes then goes on to consider whether bankers really do form a profession. He notes how they have a theoretical base for their work, but not a genuine licence to practice, and no code of ethics, although they did have an - increasingly tarnished - public ethical image, and not a professional culture insofar as bankers tend to relate primarily to their employers rather than to their professional body. Professionalization was in fact hard for bankers to achieve. Their knowledge base had never been very substantial and IT was currently helping to erode it. Management and work organization and performance evaluation and appraisal were largely in the hands of employers, not fellow professional bankers. Bankers had relatively little power and authority over clients, unlike, say, doctors, and the banks' activities have tended to be regulated by, rather than professionally independent of, the state. However Hughes admits that bankers do form an organizational profession, highly dependent on their employers for their often diverse work, but with some degree of control over a genuine if hardly very monolithic or complex knowledge base, with some real although limited autonomy at work within relatively complex and hierarchical organizations. For us the main question that Hughes' analysis raises is this. Has the fairly small but very real and genuine element of deprofessionalization in the recent experience of bankers been due to a major change in the nature of banking, involving much fiercer competition and ensuing commercialization, or were parts of the professional ethos of banking a long moribund inheritance from Victorian times, waiting to be swept aside by the first mild breeze of change from outside a notably smug and conservative sector?

The last two chapters, by six authors, one of whom contributes to both, are both concerned with information technology (IT) professionals or information systems (IS) specialists. The first, by Wendy Currie and Colin Bryson, focuses on the often serious problems of managing them. Is there anything specially new or different about their typically being employed 'on tap' or are they just like other 'technical specialists' in the UK in this respect? Currie and Bryson favour the latter view and there are analogies to be drawn with Millman's chapter in this regard. The second, by Stephen Ackroyd, Ian Glover, Wendy Currie and Stephen Bull, is more general by virtue of its interest in the character of their employment along a mixture of hierarchical and market principles, in their contested status as so-called knowledge workers, in the organisation and use of information and knowledge in the world, and in the role of IS specialists as the purported architects of much contemporary economic and social change through their key inputs to the creation of much new technology. The authors are also interested in the possibility of a shift from hierarchical, bureaucratic and formal work organisation to organisation of a more market based informal network type, facilitated by the use of IT in helping to coordinate work and in making communication and thus markets more efficient. In finding the arguments in favour of this possibility rather superficial, the authors suggest that what has really been happening is a recasting of patterns of *formal* organisation, and thus not a removal but a transformation of hierarchies. They also find the knowledge worker thesis facile: information (along with skills) people. They argue that the so far very weak (if real) professional organisation of IS specialists is simply a function of their newness; virtually all established professionals were originally entrepreneurial, like IS people today. Finally, they offer a general warning against millennialism, the belief that 'our age is like no other', in social science; see the end of the chapter and Figure 14.1 and the arguments linked to it there, on this point.

In the fifth and final Part of the book, in the concluding chapter, Glover and Hughes try to make sense of the preceding chapters with reference also to the concluding arguments and suggestions of *The Professional-Managerial Class* (Glover and Hughes, 1996b). They emphasize the ongoing power of most professional occupations, power which is rooted in the economic and social need for their specialist capabilities. They regard as chimerical and ultimately corrupt the notion that knowledge work and workers are coming to dominate employment, work, management, organization and society. However while much continuity is apparent in the story and the situation of the UK's professions, they are nonetheless often increasingly subject to strong external control and increasingly both encouraged and able to cooperate creatively with each other. As a result management teams and organizations are likely to become more efficient, it is suggested, but not much more democratic. Yet in the longer term better understanding of the nature and the strengths of professions should be used, the authors suggest, to help construct a more environmentally, morally and politically benign economic and social order.

References

Abbott, A. (1988), *The system of professions: an essay on the division of expert labour*, University of Chicago Press, Chicago and London.

Ackroyd, S., Hughes, J.A. and Soothill, K. (1989), 'Public Sector Services and their Management', *Journal of Management Studies*, Vol. 27, No. 6.

Ackroyd, S. (1994), 'Professions, their Organisations and Change in Britain: Some Private and Public Sector Similarities and their Consequences', paper presented to ESRC Seminar Series on Professions in Late Modernity, University of Lancaster, September 1994.

Ackroyd, S. (1996), 'Organization contra Organizations: professions and organizational change in the United Kingdom', *Organization Studies*, Vol. 17, No. 4.

Aktouf, O. (1996), *Traditional Management and Beyond: A Matter of Renewal*, Morin Editeur, Paris, Montreal and Casablanca.

Albert, M. (1993) *Capitalism versus Capitalism*, Whurr, London.

Armstrong, P. (1984), 'Competition between the organizational professions and the evolution of management control strategies' in K. Thompson (ed.), *Work, Employment and Unemployment*, pp. 97-120, Open University Press, Milton Keynes.

Armstrong, P. (1989), 'Management, Labour Process and Agency', *Work, Employment & Society*, Vol. 3, No. 3, pp. 307-22.

Ashburner, L., Ferlie, E. and Pettigrew, A. (1996), *The New Public Management in Action*, OUP, Oxford.

Bacon, F. (1598), 'Of heresies', in *Essays: Religious Meditations*, London.

Barnett, C. (1972), *The Collapse of British Power*, Eyre Methuen, London.

Barrett, P.S. (1993a), 'Business-Centred Practices or Practice-Centred Business: The Return Journey', paper presented at conference on Professions and Management in Britain, Stirling, 1993.

Barrett, P.S. (1993b), *Profitable Practice Management for the Construction Professional*, Chapman and Hall, London.

Barry, R., Bosworth, D. and Wilson, R. (1996), *Engineers in Top Management*, Institute for Employment Research, University of Warwick, Warwick.

Bathie, D.W. (2000), chapter 9 in this book.

Bewes, T. (1997), *Cynicism and Postmodernity*, Verso, London.

Brown, P. (1995), 'Cultural Capital and Social Exclusion: Some Observations on Recent Trends in Education, Employment and the Labour Market', *Work, Employment and Society*, Vol. 9, No. 1, pp. 29-51.

Burrage, M. (1973), 'Nationalization and the Professional Ideal', *Sociology*, Vol. 7, No.2, pp. 253-272.

Burrage, M., Jarausch, K. and Siegrist, H. (1990), 'An Actor-based Framework for the Study of the Professions', in (eds) M. Burrage and R. Tordenstahl, *Professions in Theory and History: Rethinking the Study of the Professions,* Sage, London, pp. 203-225.

Chaston, I. and Badger, B. (1993), 'The Professional - an Obstacle to Creating Customer-Oriented Public Sector Organizations?', paper presented at conference on Professions and Management in Britain, Stirling, 1993.

Child, J. (1982), 'Professionalism in the Corporate World: Values, Interests and Control', in D. Dunkerley and G. Salaman (eds), *The International Yearbook of Organization Studies,* Routledge and Kegan Paul, London.

Child, J. (1984), *Organization: A Guide to Problems and Practice*, Harper and Row, London.

Child, J., Fores, M., Glover, I. and Lawrence, P. (1983), 'A Price to Pay? Professionalism and Work Organisation in Britain and West Germany', *Sociology*, Vol. 17, No. 1, pp. 63-78.

Child, J., Fores, M., Glover, I. and Lawrence, P. (1986), 'Professionalism and Work Organisation: Reply to McCormick', *Sociology*, Vol. 20, No. 4, pp. 607-11.

Chisholm, A.W.J. (1975), *First Report on the Education and Training of Engineers on the Continent of Europe,* University of Salford, Salford.

Clark, T. (1998), reviews of M. Kubr, *Management Consulting: A Guide to the Profession* (third edition), International Labour Office, Geneva, 1996, and J. Micklethwait and A. Wooldridge, *The Witch Doctors: What the Management Gurus are Saying, Why it Matters and How to Make Sense of It,* 1996, Heinemann, London, *Human Resource Management Journal*, Vol. 8, No.1, pp. 93-95.

Clark, J. and Newman, J. (1992), 'Managing to Survive: Dilemmas of Changing Organisational Forms in the Public Sector', in R. Page and N. Deakin (eds), *The Costs of Welfare*, SPA/Avebury, Aldershot.

Corfield, P.J. (1995), *Power and the Professions in Britain 1750-1850*, Routledge, London and New York.

Crompton, R. (1990), 'Professions in the Current Context', *Work, Employment and Society*, Vol. 4, May (Special Issue), pp. 147-66.

Crouch, C. and Marquand, D. (eds) (1993), *Ethics and Markets: Cooperation and Competition within Capitalist Economies*, Blackwell, Oxford.

Dingley, J. (1996), 'Durkheim, professions and moral integration', in I. Glover and M. Hughes (eds), *The Professional-Managerial Class: Contemporary British Management in the Pursuer Mode*, Avebury, Aldershot.

Dingwall, R. (1983), 'Introduction', in R. Dingwall and P. Lewis (eds), *The Sociology of the Professions: Lawyers, Doctors and Others*, Macmillan, Basingstoke.

Dopson, S. (1996), 'Doctors in Management: a Challenge to Established Debates', in J. W. Leopold, I. A. Glover and M. D. Hughes (eds), *Beyond Reason: The National Health Service and the Limits of Management, Avebury, Aldershot.*

Du Gay, P. (1994). 'Making up managers: bureaucracy, enterprise and the liberal art of separation', *British Journal of Sociology*, Vol. 45, No. 4, pp. 655-73.

Engineering Council, The (1994), *The Engineering Profession*, The Engineering Council, London.

Enteman, W. (1993), *Managerialism: the Emergence of a New Ideology*, University of Wisconsin Press, Madison, Wisconsin.

Etzioni, A. (ed) (1969), *The Semi-Professions and their Organizations: Teachers, Nurses and Social Workers*, The Free Press, New York.

Fitzgerald, L. (1996), 'Clinical Management: the Impact of a Changing Context on a Changing Profession', in J.W. Leopold, I.A. Glover and M.D. Hughes (eds), *Beyond Reason: The National Health Service and the Limits of Management*, Avebury, Aldershot.

Flood, J. (2000), chapter 2 in this book.

Fores, M. and Glover, I. (1978), 'The British disease: professionalism', *The Times Higher Education Supplement*, 24 February 1978, p. 16.

Fores, M., Glover, I. and Lawrence, P. (1991), 'Professionalism and Rationality: A Study in Misapprehension', *Sociology*, Vol. 25, No. 1, pp. 79-100.

Fores, M., Glover, I. and Rey, L. (1976), 'Management versus *Technik*: A Note on the Work of Executives', Department of Industry, London.

Foucault, M. (1980), *Power/knowledge: selected readings and other writings, 1972-77,* in C. Gordon (ed), Harvester, Brighton.

Freidson, E. (1970), *Professional Dominance: The Structure of Medical Care*, Aldine-Atherton, Chicago.

Freidson, E. (1983), 'The Theory of the Professions: State of the Art', in R. Dingwall and R. Lewis (eds), *The Sociology of the Professions*, Macmillan, London.

Glover, I. (1977), *Managerial Work: A Review of the Evidence*, Department of Industry/The City University, London.

Glover, I. (1978a), 'Executive Career Patterns: Britain, France, Germany and Sweden', in M. Fores and I. Glover (eds), *Manufacturing and Management*, HMSO, London.

Glover, I. (1978b), 'Professionalism and Manufacturing Industry', in M. Fores and I. Glover (eds), *Manufacturing and Management*, HMSO, London.

Glover, I.A. (1980), 'Social Science, Engineering and Society', *Higher Education Review*, Vol. 12, No. 3, pp. 27-41.

Glover, I.A. (1985), 'How the West was Lost? Decline of Engineering and Manufacturing in Britain and the United States', *Higher Education Review*, Vol. 17, No. 3, pp. 3-34.

Glover, I. and Hughes, M. (1996a), 'British Management in the Pursuer Mode', in I. Glover and M. Hughes (eds), *The Professional-Managerial Class: Contemporary British Management in the Pursuer Mode*, Avebury, Aldershot.

Glover, I. and Hughes, M. (1996b), 'Towards a professional-managerial class?', in I. Glover and M. Hughes (eds), *The Professional-Managerial Class: Contemporary British Management in the Pursuer Mode,* Avebury, Aldershot, pp. 305-313.

Glover, I. and Kelly, M. (1987), *Engineers in Britain: A Sociological Study of the Engineering Dimension*, Unwin Hyman, London.

Glover, I. and Kelly, M. (1993), 'Engineering Better Management', in G. Payne and M. Cross (eds), *Sociology in Action: Applications and Opportunities for the 1990s*, Macmillan, Basingstoke.

Glover, I., Kelly, M. and Roslender, R. (1986), 'The Coming Proletarianization of the British Accountant', paper presented at the Fourth Annual International Aston/UMIST Labour Process Conference, Manchester.

Glover, I. and Tracey, P. (1997), 'In Search of Technik: Will Engineering Outgrow Management?', *Work, Employment and Society*, Vol. 11, No. 4, pp. 759-76.

Glover, I., Tracey, P. and Currie, W. (1998), 'Engineering Our Future Again: Towards a Long Term Strategy for Manufacturing and Management in the United Kingdom', in R. Delbridge and J. Lowe (eds) *Manufacturing in Transition,* Routledge, London, pp. 199-223.

Green, S.J.D. and Whitney, R.C. (eds) (1996), *The Boundaries of the State in Modern Britain*, CUP, Cambridge.

Greenwood, R. and Lachman, R. (1996), 'Change as an underlying theme in professional organizations: an introduction', *Organization Studies*, Vol. 17, No. 4. pp. 563-72.

Handy, C., Gordon, C., Gow, I. and Randlesome, C. (1988), *Making Managers*, Pitman, London.

Hutton, S.P. and Lawrence, P.A. (1981), *German Engineers: the Anatomy of a Profession,* OUP, Oxford.

Jarausch, K.H. (1990), *The Unfree Professions: German Lawyers, Teachers and Engineers, 1900-1950*, OUP, New York, 1990.

Johnson, T. (1972), *Professions and Power*, Macmillan, London.

Johnson, T. (1977), 'The Professions in the Class Structure', in R. Scase (ed) *Industrial Society: Class, Cleavage and Control*, Allen and Unwin, London, pp. 93-110.

Johnson, T. (1982), 'The State and the Professions: Peculiarities of the British', in A. Giddens and G. Mackenzie (eds), *Social Class and the Division of Labour,* CUP, Cambridge.

Keat, R. (1991), 'Consumer Sovereignty and the Integrity of Practices', in R. Keat and N. Abercrombie (eds), *Enterprise Culture*, Routledge, London.

Keat, R. (1994), 'Scepticism, Authority and the Market', in R. Keat et al (eds) *The Authority of the Consumer,* Routledge, London.

Kocha, J. (1990), '"*Burgertum*" and Professions in the Nineteenth Century: two Alternative Approaches', in M. Burrage and R. Tordenstahl (eds), *Professions in Theory and History: Rethinking the Study of Professions*, Sage, London.

Lane, J. (1996), *Apprenticeship in England 1600-1914*, UCL Press, London.

Larson, M.S. (1977), *The Rise of Professionalism: A Sociological Analysis*, University of California Press, Berkley.

Lawrence, P.A. (1980), *Managers and Management in West Germany*, Croom Helm, London.

Lawrence, P.A. (1987), 'Work and its context: senior managers in a clearing bank', Loughborough University Banking Centre Research Paper Series, No. 39.

Lawrence, P.A. (1992), 'German Engineers: A Study in Consistency', in G. Lee and C. Smith (eds), *Engineers in Management: International Comparisons,* Routledge, London.

Leggatt, T. (1978), 'Managers in Industry: their Background and Education', *Sociological Review*, Vol. 26, pp. 807-25.

Legge, K. (1995), *Human Resource Management: Rhetorics and Realities*, Macmillan, Basingstoke.

Leveson, R. (1996), 'Can Professionals be Multi-Skilled?', *People Management*, August 29, Vol. 2, No. 17.

Locke, R.R. (1984), *The End of the Practical Man: Entrepreneurship and Higher Education in Germany, France and Great Britain 1880-1940*, Jai Press, Greenwich, Connecticut.

Locke, R.R. (1989), *Management and Higher Education since 1940*, CUP, Cambridge.

Locke, R.R. (1996), *The Collapse of the American Management Mystique*, OUP, Oxford.

Lyon, P., Hallier, J. and Glover, I. (1998), 'Divestment or Investment? The Contradictions of HRM in Relation to Older Employees', *Human Resource Management Journal*, Vol. 8, No. 1, pp. 56-66.

Macdonald, K.M. (1995), *The Sociology of the Professions*, Sage, London.

MacIntyre, A. (1990), *After Virtue*, London, Duckworth.

McLelland, C. E. (1991), *The German Experience of Professionalisation: Modern Learned Professions and their Organizations from the Early Nineteenth Century to the Higher Era*, CUP, London.

McNulty, T., Whittington, R. and Whipp, R. (1996), 'Market Control: Work Experiences of Doctors, Scientists and Engineers', in J.W. Leopold, I.A. Glover and M.D. Hughes (eds), *Beyond Reason: The National Health Service and the Limits of Management,* Avebury, Aldershot.

Marquand, D. (1988), *The Unprincipled Society: New Demands and Old Politics*, Jonathan Cape, London.

Marshall, T.H. (1950), 'Citizenship and Social Class', reprinted in 1963 in *Sociology at the Cross-roads and Other Essays*, Heinemann, London.

Maurice, M. (1972), 'Propos pour la Sociologie des Professions', *Sociologie du Travail*, Vol. 13, pp. 213-25.

Maurice, M., Sorge, A. and Warner, M. (1980), 'Societal Differences in the Organization of Manufacturing Units', Organization Studies: A Comparison of France, West Germany and Great Britain', *Organization Studies,* Vol. 1, No. 1, pp. 58-86.

Nicholson, R. (1991), 'Facing the facts in a computer revolution', *Computer Weekly*, December, 12, p. 18.
Overy, R.J. (1992), 'German Professions: 1800-1950', *Business History*, Vol. 34, No. 1.
Paterson, B.E. (1991), *Personnel Specialists: A Study of Managerial Work and Knowledge Use*, unpublished Ph.D. thesis, University of Abertay Dundee, Dundee.
Paterson, B.E. (2000), chapter 11 in this book.
Roslender, R. (1992), *Sociological Perspectives on Modern Accountancy*, Routledge, London.
Rothblatt, S. (1994), 'Professions under fire', *The Times Higher Education Supplement*, 30 September 1994, p. 14.
Russell, C. (1994), 'Professions in the Firing Line', *The Times Higher Education Supplement*, 20 May 1994, p. 11.
Savage, M., Barlow, J., Dickens, P. and Fielding, T. (1992), *Property, Bureaucracy and Culture: Middle Class Formation in Contemporary Britain*, Routledge, London.
Saks, M. (1995), *Professions and the Public Interest: Medical Power, Altruism and Alternative Medicine*, Routledge, London.
Schön, D. (1991), *The Reflective Practitioner: how professionals think in action*, Avebury, Aldershot.
Scott, J. (1997), *Corporate Business and Capitalist Classes*, OUP, Oxford.
Senge, P. (1990), *The Fifth Discipline: The Art and Practice of the Learning Organization*, Doubleday/Currency, New York.
Smith, C. (1991), 'How are Engineers Formed? Professionals, Nations and Class Politics', *Work, Employment and Society*, Vol. 3, No. 4, pp. 451-70.
Sorge, A. (1978), 'The Management Tradition: A Continental View', in M. Fores and I. Glover (eds), *Manufacturing and Management*, HMSO, London.
Sorge, A. (1994), 'The Reform of Technical Education and Training in Great Britain: A Comparison of Institutional Learning in Europe', *European Journal of Vocational Training*, Vol. 3, pp. 58-68.
Sturdy, A. (1998), 'Customer Care in a Consumer Society: Smiling and Sometimes Meaning It', *Organization*, Vol. 5, No. 1, pp. 27-53.
Swords-Isherwood, N. (1979), 'British Management Compared', in K. Pavitt (ed.), *Technical Innovation and British Economic Performance*, Science Policy Research Unit, University of Sussex/Macmillan, Brighton, London.
Tracey, P.J. (1996), 'The Manufacturing Power Game: Market Repositioning and Institutional Change In and Around Engineering', paper presented to British Academy of Management Annual Conference, University of Aston, Birmingham.
Van de Weyer, M. (1996), 'End of the meal ticket mentality', *Management Today*, May 1996.
Watson, T. (1977), *The Personnel Manager*, Routledge and Kegan Paul, London.
Wiener, M.J. (1981), *English Culture and the Decline of the Industrial Spirit 1850-1980*, CUP, Cambridge.

Ziman, J. (1994). *Prometheus Bound: Science in a Dynamic Steady State*, CUP, Cambridge.

Part II

Independent Professions

2 The governance of law: the structure and work of corporate lawyers

John Flood

Introduction

An advertisement produced by a City of London firm of lawyers in the early 1990s read, in part: 'Frere Cholmeley Bischoff is a major player in the UK legal market with offices throughout Europe, the Middle East and recently Russia'. This is a firm within the top 25 law firms in the UK with over 150 lawyers, but if one were to look at such firms immediately after the second world war, a very different image would be seen. Law firms in 1945 were small, often with no more than 12 people, and conceived of themselves as an elite profession (Slinn, 1984). Terms such as 'major player' and 'legal market' are recent imports into the legal sphere. Such professionals eschewed personal glory - no profiles in the press - and kept quiet in the background. A tribute to Sir George Allen, a founding partner of Allen and Overy, on his retirement in 1952 said: 'He completely identified himself with his client ... always gave himself wholeheartedly to the client's interests' (Allen and Overy, n.d., p. 2). The period of business expansion since then has made calls on professional advice, whether law, accounting, or consulting, that has stimulated a tremendous growth by professional organizations themselves.

This chapter examines the changing structure and increasing commercialization of corporate legal practice. For law the Chinese curse is singularly appropriate: may you live in interesting times. Lawyers compete with accountants; they face competition from American and continental lawyers. Add to this the fact that long term relationships with clients are withering away in favour of more transactional relationships, and we can see that lawyers are being catapulted from the nineteenth straight to the twenty-first century.

Big business needs advisers. It expects to pay high fees for expert advice that covers all contingencies. Professional advisers in Great Britain command hourly rates of £300 or $600 or higher. And with successful deals premiums that boost the basic rates are often the norm. The key areas of professional advice required by business are strategy consulting (Gallese, 1989), accounting (Stevens, 1981), merchant and investment banking (Hobson, 1991) and lawyering (Stewart, 1983; Stevens, 1987; Flood, 1991, 1996). The first aims to direct business firms towards their most desirable goals; the second establishes the means by which goals can be measured; the third provides the finance; and the fourth copes with the regulatory and legal frameworks in which business functions. My central concern in this chapter is with the fourth group, but by necessity I will also refer to the others. Corporate professional services are not as easily and neatly divisible as I have outlined. Turf wars often take place over the perceived correct functions of, say, accountants and lawyers in tax work (Abbott, 1988). Even though professional bodies' rules proscribe illicit activities by their own members and others, these proscriptions are never completely effective. Attacks on restrictive rules come from bodies' own members and government. The Thatcher governments of the 1980s led forays against estate agents, lawyers, doctors, while accountants have also felt the push to external regulation. In a world where millions of pounds and dollars are made on international mega-deals, the expense of maintaining strict demarcations between professional spheres of work can be too high, and clients fail to understand their *raison d'être*. So we see law firms like Arnold and Porter of Washington DC establishing subsidiary companies which engage in consultancy for the financial industry and in real estate development (Fitzpatrick, 1989; Meeks, 1991); we see firms of conseils juridiques/avocats like FIDAL, employing over 1,000 professionals, which is part of the giant accounting group, KPMG (Travis, 1990; Dillon and Griffiths, 1991). We see English accounting firms setting up litigation support units to examine the figures when business deals go wrong or recessions intrude and to provide evidence in court (Fennell, 1991; Carr, 1991a).

The conventional approaches to professions too often fail to capture the ruptures, fractures, dissolutions, and transplants that occur most spectacularly among their elites. These changes may not always be revolutionary but they depend on plentiful revisionism to make them ideologically respectable and acceptable. Entrenched attitudes argue for practices being anchored in 'time immemorial'; radical changes are sought for practical reasons because the practices inveighed against were never securely moored in the professional ethos. Law perhaps more than the other groups faces problems which impose enormous constraints on its activities.

The law firm population

In order to understand what sorts of organization are being analyzed here it would help to describe the population. There are about 9,750 law firms in England and Wales (Chambers and Harwood, 1990, p. 5). They range in size from sole practitioners to firms with over a 1,000 fee earners. Unlike say the United States or Germany, Great Britain is tightly centralised in its commercial and political affairs. Virtually all institutions of influence are concentrated in London, e.g. the Stock Exchange, the Bank of England, Lloyds, Parliament. There are, in total, 57 firms with foreign offices, which collectively number 168 offices (The Legal 500, 1990).

These firms have between 1 and 14 offices each, with the exception of Baker and McKenzie which has more than 50. The firms with substantial overseas representation are essentially clustered in the top 20 law firms, which are more or less the key players in the elite legal field in the UK. This is demonstrated in part by the statistic that the 20 largest law firms in the UK employ over 12.5 percent of all solicitors in private practice (The Legal 500, 1991, p. 134).

What are these elite law firms? In spite of the simplicity of this question, it is not so easy to answer. And I will offer several interpretations of how we may examine this, mainly by comparing the English milieu to the American.

The American model

Some scholars have argued that what is taking place is the Americanization of professional practice and of lawyering in particular (Dezalay, 1991). While there is some substance to this charge, the isomorphism is not complete (Hodgart, 1991), especially in the area of international practice which English law firms exploited long before their American counterparts. Nevertheless, it is of value to understand the phenomenon of the big American law firm, because it is put forward as the exemplar of the large law firm, so that a valid comparison with Great Britain can be made.

The American law firm is composed essentially of two elements, namely, partners and associates. Obviously there is an extensive substructure bolstering the lawyers in the firms. Without paralegals, secretaries, messengers, proofreaders, etc., often in place 24 hours a day, 7 days a week, law firms would be unable to keep to the draconian 'drop-dead deadlines' often imposed on them in their work. The partners own the firm and employ the associates (Flood, 1985, 1987, 1988; Spangler, 1986; Hagan, Huxter and Parker, 1988; Galanter and Palay, 1991). The lynch pin of the American corporate law firm is the structure devised by Paul Cravath in the late nineteenth and early twentieth centuries (Swaine, 1948). In principle the firm would hire the best graduates from the top law schools, such as Harvard, Yale and Columbia, train them by giving them discrete parts of cases and transactions to work instead of handling entire small cases, and after a probation of roughly 7 years (now up to 9 or 10) decide whether to elect them to the partnership. If the decision was negative, the associate had to leave, often being placed in the corporate law department of one of the firm's clients. If the decision was favourable, the associate became an owner of the firm entitled to share in its profits. The system was very simple: up or out; Cravath loathed the idea of there being a cadre of disaffected permanent associates lingering around the firm. The result of Cravath's system was that the firm was imbued with a single culture, because of its organic growth, which would not be contaminated by lawyers being hired laterally out of that sequence (Fergus, 1989).

The partners generate their profits out of the associates, usually billing their time at a rate that is two and a half to three times their salaries (Stewart, 1983). The search for greater profits has led to two effects - leveraging and intensified demands on associates. The higher the partner to associate ratio, the further the partner's human capital can be stretched. In New York law firms ratios of 1:3 or 1:4 exist. While this benefits the partners, it becomes painfully obvious to the associates that their chances of making partner are being substantially reduced. It is a continuing tension. And in order to justify the large salaries paid to associates - New York firms often start their associates from law school with salaries of between $80,000 to $90,000 - partners demand high rates of billable or chargeable hours. Associates are expected to bill a minimum of 1,900 hours per year and up to 2,500 hours (and more) if they are seriously considering competing for partnership (Orey, 1990, p. 46). Stewart (1983) retails the myth of the machismo effect of billing hours. Two New York associates challenged each other to see who could bill the most hours in a day. One charged all 24 hours to clients; the other then flew from New York to Los Angeles and, with the benefit of travelling through three time zones, was able to bill 27 hours in one day. Apocryphal or otherwise, large law firms are exceptionally greedy institutions in what they demand of their associates. Nor is the move into partnership an escape from the relentless pursuit of profit. Partners are required to bill just as much as associates and to 'make rain' (bring in clients). Whereas partnership was believed to be a lifelong commitment by individual and partnership, that ideal dissolved in the 1980s (Brill, 1990). If partners fall below the standards set by management committees, they are sacked. Or, if partners fall out with each other, entire departments within firms will leave and move to other firms, often with substantial clients. Partnership as life long tenure is largely a myth among the American large law firms (Brill, 1990). Concomitant with the dissolution of the partnership myth is the collapse of the myth of democratic control of law partnerships. Partners are bound to share profits and losses, but the decisions on how they are apportioned are usually made by a small cadre of powerful lawyers within the firm (Tolbert and Stern, 1987; Lisagor and Lipsius, 1988; Eisler, 1991).

Perhaps the most sophisticated methodology yet developed for analyzing the successful law firms is that used by the American Lawyer (See Table 2.1). Each year it publishes league tables that rank the 'Am Law 100' according to various economic indicators. These are: gross revenues; revenue per lawyer; revenue profit; profits per partner; and the Am Law profitability index. Table 2.1 shows the top 20 law firms in the list ranked by gross revenues. Although these are large institutions, by staff and revenues, the 'Am Law 100' rankings do not merely depend on the actual numbers of lawyers - partners and associates - in the firms.

Table 2.1
Top 20 American law firms based on gross revenues from 'Am Law 100'

Firms by gross revenues	*Size lawyers/ partners*	*Gross revenues $m*	*RPL (Rank) $thou*	*PPP (Rank) $thou*
1 Skadden Arps	948/197	517.5	545 (9)	1195 (5)
2 Baker & McKenzie	1339/432	341.5	255 (90)	315 (67)
3 Jones Day	1052/369	320.0	305 (61)	350 (51)
4 Shearman & Sterling	487/123	281.0	575 (6)	800 (12)
5 Gibson Dunn	611/194	280.0	460 (15)	645 (19)
6 Davis Polk	380/96	240.5	630 (4)	1125 (6)
7 Sullivan & Cromwell	345/95	230.0	665 (3)	1210 (4)
8 Latham & Watkins	475/170	223.5	470 (14)	670 (16)
9=Cravath Swaine	288/64	213.0	740 (2)	1765 (1)
9=Fried Frank	368/104	213.0	580 (5)	815 (9)
11 Sidley & Austin	600/178	212.5	355 (33)	400 (35)
12 Simpson Thacher	384/95	201.0	525 (12)	1015 (7)
13 Weil Gotshal	457/113	200.0	440 (18)	690 (14)
14=Morgan Lewis	610/129	198.0	325 (48)	355 (49)
14=O'Melveny & Myers	449/145	198.0	440 (18)	615 (20)
16 Paul Weiss	366/82	195.0	535 (10)	915 (8)
17 Kaye Scholer	340/94	188.0	555 (8)	685 (15)
18 Millbank Tweed	398/98	187.5	450 (17)	665 (17)
19 Fulbright & Jaworski	582/10	183.0	315 (53)	340 (58)
20 Cleary Gottlieb	342/102	181.0	530 (11)	775 (13)

Key: RPL = revenue per lawyer PPP = profits per partner

Source: *American Lawyer (1990)*

For example, Jones Day Reavis and Pogue of Cleveland, Ohio, was the second largest law firm in the US in the late 1980s with 1,052 lawyers, and the third highest grossing with revenues of $320,000,000 (American Lawyer, 1990). The only firm with less than 100 lawyers in the 'Am Law 100' is Wachtell Lipton Rosen and Katz, with 94 lawyers, yet it ranked number 41 by gross revenues in 1989, with $115,000,000. However, gross revenues only tell part of a story. Instead if one takes the amount of revenue attributed to each lawyer, i.e. revenue per lawyer (RPL), then the highest ranking firm is Wachtell Lipton with an RPL of $1,225,000; Jones Day is ranked number 61, with an RPL of $305,000. The conclusion that can be drawn here is that Wachtell Lipton is more productive than Jones Day, despite being less than a tenth of the size and less highly leveraged, 1.8 to Jones Day's 2.8. This is reinforced when profits per partner are considered. For Wachtell Lipton they are $1,590,000, the second highest figure; and for Jones day they are $350,000, resulting in a rank of number 51 in the league. The key figure is undoubtedly revenue per lawyer as it measures lawyers' business from the demand side. Because Wachtell Lipton is one of the market leaders in mergers and acquisitions work it commands high fees, a function of demand. Jones Day is a general practice firm and therefore is forced to support some areas of work that will be less remunerative than others. Although Wachtell Lipton is markedly successful, it is subject, because of its focus, to the vagaries of the markets and the states' legislative manoeuvres on mergers and acquisitions.

The British model

At the basic structural level the British large law firm is not significantly different from the American (Flood, 1989, 1996), despite there being no direct equivalent to Cravath in Great Britain. There are essentially the two same elements, partners and assistants (associates). There is a third category, not found in American firms, that of trainee solicitors (formerly articled clerks). This two year trainee period is a form of indentured apprenticeship imposed on all entrants to the solicitors' profession. Nevertheless, they are classified as fee earners. In the large firms, after passing the Law Society examinations, the partnership track is roughly 8-10 years to full equity partnership. Most American law firms have a basic binary divide between salaried associates and the equity partners. In such cities as Chicago - and increasingly New York - the large firms have traditionally operated a two-tier partnership system. Incongruous as it appears the associate is promoted to a salaried partnership for a period of up to 4 years, and then perhaps promoted to a full partnership. Fundamentally, the two-tier system is a means of extending the partnership track, but since the value of partnership is being devalued, expectations might not be severely dented. In the UK the two-tier partnership is standard, although not every City firm uses it. A study of the staff structure of London law firms showed that equity partners were leveraged at a rate of between 1:2 to 1:5 (equity partners to assistants and salaried partners), which is roughly comparable to the US (CIFC, 1991). Four of the top five firms, namely, Clifford Chance, Linklaters and Paines, Slaughter and May, and Freshfields, have purely equity partnerships. One senior partner who expressed dissatisfaction with the idea of salaried partnerships, told me how junior partners, however, must buy into the capital. This charge is subtracted from the first 4 years' earnings as partner then returned when the capital is sold back to the firm on retirement (c.f. Dobkin, 1986a; 1986b). The upshot is that one way or another entry into partnership incurs penalties or costs that favour the senior members: in other words junior partners have to pay their dues.

Furthermore, most UK large law firms use a lockstep system of partner remuneration rather than the American 'eat what you kill' method. Lockstep rewards seniority and longevity without accounting for client-getting (Carr, 1991b): 'eat what you kill' benefits those lawyers who bring in the most clients, without regard to seniority (Flood, 1987). The argument is that lockstep fosters collegiality whereas 'eat what you kill' promotes intense competition that could lead to the partnership rupturing (Brill, 1990). As a not uncommon view by a senior partner from a large UK law firm put it: 'I don't like "eat what you kill"; it ruins the *esprit de corps*. It just isn't feasible here'.

The American Lawyer is extremely fortunate in having access to the types of data that promote these analyses. Unfortunately, data are less plentiful and less reliable in the UK. But there are some useful measures. The most obvious means is to study size: size, wealth and power are usually associated.

Table 2.2
Fifty largest London law firms based on numbers of fee earners and plcs as clients

Firm	*Tfe*	*Ptr*	*Ass*	*Plc*	*Pr*
1 Clifford Chance	1092	208	666	148	3
2 Linklaters & Paines	652	122	342	154	2
3 Lovell White Durrant	596	119	260	70	9
4 Slaughter and May	556	93	295	186	1
5 Freshfields	530	97	277	82	6
6 Allen & Overy	502	98	228	69	10
7 Norton Rose	439	89	250	76	8
8 Herbert Smith	432	84	225	113	4
9 Simmons & Simmons	431	108	195	62	11
10 Denton Hall	410	103	167	27	23
11 Nabarro Nathanson	408	96	153	46	14
12 McKenna & Co	329	68	163	78	7
13 Richards Butler	291	79	137	13	=31
14 Cameron Markby Hewitt	270	69	126	14	30
15 Stephenson Harwood	253	78	136	40	=17
16 Clyde & Co	239	75	95	4	=41
17 Wilde Sapte	237	59	109	7	=38
18 Turner Kenneth Brown	230	67	77	56	12
19 Theodore Goddard	206	60	110	40	=17
20 Taylor Joynson Garrett	204	68	90	18	27

Key: Tfe = total fee earners; Ass = assistant solicitors,
Ptr = partners, Plc = public limited companies,
Pr = rank by number of plc

Source: The Legal 500 (1991); Crawford's Directory (1991)

Table 2.2 shows the 20 largest law firms in London. The figure for total fee earners includes, besides partners and assistant solicitors, trainee solicitors and paralegals. So, for example, Clifford Chance, the largest law firm in the UK, has

1,092 fee earners of which 874 are actual qualified lawyers. The firm at position number 20 has 204 fee earners, 158 of which are qualified lawyers.

English law firms are smaller than their American counterparts. In the early part of the twentieth century, the American press had already coined the term law factory for corporate law firms and one Julius Henry Cohen published in 1916 a book titled, *Law: Business or Profession*? (Flood, 1985). American law firms resulted from the confluence of certain forces: among them were the rapid growth of capital between 1870 and 1920 (Friedman, 1985; Hobson, 1984), the development of the case method in law schools (Stevens, 1983), and the creation of the bipartite structure of associates and partners by Paul Cravath (Swaine, 1948). Thus the megalaw firms of today, such as Jones Day mentioned above and Shearman and Sterling, with 487 lawyers, were fostered in this ferment. Later the New Deal entrenched American lawyers firmly in the regulation of commerce and finance.

English firms were also heavily involved in the development of capital at home and abroad (e.g. Slinn, 1984). But the ancillary structures of the law school and the Cravath method for organizing law firms never evolved in a similar fashion. Professional firms remained small and until the passing of the Companies Act of 1967, partnerships could not exceed twenty persons (Flood, 1989). Slinn notes that even after World War II, 'there were 7 partners [in Freshfields], fewer than at least 2 of the other leading City firms, Linklaters and Paines, and Slaughter and May, each of whom had 12 partners' (Slinn, 1984, p. 159). But during the 1970s and 1980s, nurtured by the Big Bang in the City of London (McCullough, 1988), the large English law firms flourished. One American technique the English law firms have borrowed is the merger. Clifford Chance, Lovell White Durrant, Norton Rose, and Denton Hall, for example, have all grown through mergers with other firms. The desire has been to grow rapidly to compete in the international legal market place, especially with the American firms. Indeed, a former senior partner of Clifford Chance was reputed to have claimed that the reason for the merger between Coward Chance and Clifford-Turner was so that Clifford Chance would be big enough to merge with one of the big accounting firms. Most of the other firms in the top 20 have fuelled their growth internally and organically. There are dangers attached to merging. In the late 1980s the then American firm of Finley Kumble Wagner Heine Underberg Manley and Casey, which had grown extremely rapidly by cherry-picking lawyers and entire departments from other law firms, was casting about for a London outpost. Berwin Leighton had just associated itself with the American firm when Finley Kumble imploded and disintegrated (Flood, 1989; Eisler, 1991). It was an embarrassing time for the English firm, as Finley Kumble was shown to have engaged in dubious and unethical practices about which many partners had no knowledge although they had to suffer the liability. The litigation between the partners continues still. One result of this debacle is that in conversations among lawyers about firm mergers, the name of Finley Kumble is always raised. It has a perverse fetishistic effect. Finally, although size could stand as a proxy for levels of activity, it lacks refinement and particularity for such a task. Instead, we can look to involvement with clients and work.

The last decade was one of enormous activity in corporate acquisitions and restructuring, known as M&A (mergers and acquisitions) work (Hirsch, 1986), for example the Guinness bid for Distillers (Hobson, 1991), often financed with junk bonds (Bruck, 1988; Burrough and Helyar, 1990), requiring the extensive involvement of lawyers (Hermann, 1989), who were sometimes depicted as entrepreneurial as their clients (Auchincloss, 1986). One proposal for identifying involvement with clients and gauging a law firm's attractiveness or demand function is to count the number of public limited companies (plc's) that indicate a particular law firm as adviser in *Crawford's Directory of City Connections* (1991). Table 2.2 shows how many plc's each of the 20 largest London law firms has as clients. The numbers of plc clients do not comport precisely with size as measured by total fee earners. The numbers in the far right column of Table 2.2 show the ranking according to plc's instead of firm size. Even though the rankings have changed, we are still involved with approximately the top 20 firms. These rankings would suggest that such firms are more intensively involved with corporate Britain than others. The firms with fewer than 5 plc's tend to be specialist firms in such areas as shipping or insurance.

Since the 'Am Law 100' attempts to construct an index for productivity, I carried out a similar formulation creating a ratio of plcs to total fee earners. Those firms with the highest ratios could be classified as the most efficient in corporate practice. Table 2.3 illustrates the results of the exercise. Here the rankings move more dramatically than in Table 2.2. Ashurst Morris Crisp is clearly the front runner with a figure of 0.55, compared to Clifford Chance which ties at number 16, with Allen and Overy, with a ratio of 0.14. Despite Allen and Overy's weak showing here, it has compensations in that its banking practice is strong. The results of Table 2.3 are probably at best suggestive, because at bottom, Crawford's Directory, fails to inform us of how truly involved various plcs are with their advisers.

Table 2.3
Ratio of plcs to total fee earners for top 20 law firms based on number of plcs

Firm rank by number of plcs	*Ratio of plc/tfe*	*Firm rank by ratio*
1 Slaughter and May	0.33	3
2 Linklaters & Paines	0.24	=8
3 Clifford Chance	0.14	=16
4 Herbert Smith	0.26	=6
5 Ashurst Morris Crisp	0.55	1
6 Freshfields	0.15	15
7 McKenna & Co	0.24	=8
8 Norton Rose	0.17	13
9 Lovell White Durrant	0.12	19
10 Allen & Overy	0.14	=16
11 Simmons & Simmons	0.14	=16
12 Turner Kenneth Brown	0.24	=8
13 Macfarlanes	0.28	=4
14 Nabarro Nathanson	0.11	20
15 Travers Smith Brtwte	0.39	2
16 Baker & McKenzie	0.28	=4
17=Theodore Goddard	0.19	12
17=Stephenson Harwood	0.16	14
19 Berwin Leighton	0.21	11
20 Alsop Wilkinson	0.26	=6

Key: Tfe = total fee earners; Plc = public limited companies

Source: Crawford's Directory (1991)

We do have some data compiled by a business consulting firm, Databank, on gross fees of the top 20 law firms for 1989. Table 2.4 ranks the firms by market share. The result here is a ranking that corresponds closely to the American firms in Table 2.1 - size and gross fees correspond closely. Given these data in Table 2.4 it is neither possible to calculate revenue per lawyer nor profits per partner, as the table uses total fee earners and fails to provide net operating income. But we can compute analogously, by developing a 'revenue per fee earner' statistic.

Table 2.4
Top 20 law firms in England and Wales by market share based on gross fee income in 1989

Firm	*Market share %*	*Gross fees £m*	*Total fee earners*
1 Clifford Chance	4.2	163.8	996
2 Linklaters & Paines	2.9	113.1	623
3 Lovell White Durrant	2.5	97.5	555
4 Slaughter and May	2.2	85.8	515
5 Freshfields	2.1	81.9	480
6 Allen & Overy	1.9	74.1	461
7=Herbert Smith	1.8	70.2	400
7=Simmons & Simmons	1.8	70.2	403
9=Denton Hall	1.7	66.3	387
9=Norton Rose	1.7	66.3	390
11 McKenna & Co	1.4	54.6	324
12 Nabarro Nathanson	1.3	50.7	353
13 Richards Butler	1.2	46.8	287
14=Cameron Markby Hewitt	1.1	42.9	242
14=Evershed Wells & Hind	1.1	42.9	249
16 Wilde Sapte	1.0	39.0	216
17=Stephenson Harwood	0.9	35.1	212
17=Clyde & Co	0.9	35.1	200
17=Turner Kenneth Brown	0.9	35.1	205
20 Alsop Wilkinson	0.8	31.2	187
Total for top 20	33.4	1,302.6	
others, 9,795 firms	66.6	2,597.4	
Total all firms	100.0	3,900	

Source: Databank (quoted in International Financial Law Review [1990, p.5])

What the data tell us is that today's City law firms are big institutions - though not as large as the big accounting firms - that engage in transactions where large sums of money, millions of pounds, are at stake, where each fee earner generates between £1.5 million to almost £2 million a year, and where the partners can earn up to or beyond £750,000 a year. And the English legal press now writes similar profiles to those in America. Legal Business described a planning lawyer, David Cooper, at Gouldens, thus:

> 'All my friends are my clients', he claims. 'I don't have a private life'. That is the only possible explanation for the fact that he personally billed £1.75m last year ... That means that Cooper's department ... billing £2.4m, was

> responsible for more than ten percent of ... Goulden's gross fees last year ... Cooper claims that he probably works 4,500 and 5,000 billable hours a year - which boils down to between 12 and 13 hours every single day of the year - and an average of nearly £400 an hour if based on a strict hourly basis. 'Work it out', he challenges, 'I start at 7 am and start charging, charging, charging' (Dillon, 1992, p. 25).

The business of these firms is to satisfy the demands of the international corporate marketplace. These demands too in turn impose demands on the means of delivering professional services.

City lawyers' work

The work of corporate lawyers is based on the demands of their clients. Law is different from other occupations, e.g. medicine, where practitioners select a specialty for its intrinsic interest. In law the field is picked because the biggest and most powerful clients want those services. It is the client not the speciality per se that gives status to lawyers.

Corporate clients consume a wide range of services from their lawyers, not all of which is legal. The following list gives some idea of the range: international and domestic banking and finance, securities issues, mergers and acquisitions, general corporate and commercial advice, intellectual property, litigation and arbitration, shipping and international trade, aviation, financial services regulation, information technology and telecommunications, insurance, natural resources, property, taxation, environmental and EU law. In their publications law firms tell the public world what it is they do and how they go about it. Law firm brochures came into existence in 1984 when restrictions on lawyer advertising were relaxed. It is obvious that large corporate clients already knew what their lawyers could do for them, yet the firms went to great expense to produce these descriptions of firm work and life. In addition to the general brochures, firms now produce booklets dealing with the work of their foreign offices, specialty groups, and with current issues they think will affect clients' interests, for example joint ventures in Poland. Clients also request information about the types of services which law firms might deliver, for which firms put together 'proposals for legal services', especially for clients who are thinking of appointing law firms as legal advisers. These are less glossy, more elaborate and detailed than the brochures, including such information as billing rates. Such information is demanded, for example, when a firm wants to participate in a 'beauty parade', i.e. tender for a project. During the 1980s there was intense competition among the City firms for the privatization work that the government was distributing. A senior partner of one of the top 5 firms said:

> The work has particular problems. First, there is a beauty parade when a budget has to be given, the [government] department wants to know how many

partners will be involved, who they will be, how many assistants. The work is not so well paid as ordinary private work, but the prestige is enormous. We must be doing a good job otherwise they wouldn't keep coming back to us. We don't like having to fix a budget because one doesn't know what it will cost until its done, but we are pretty good at getting the range right. There has to be an appreciation of costs, knowing what is the right amount of effort to invest in a matter - a question of judgement.

Without doubt the largest sections in the City firms are the company/corporate and commercial departments - sometimes known as 'CoCo' work (The Legal 500, 1991, p. 139); this is the core of their expertise. For example, out of 856 lawyers based in London in Clifford Chance, over half are involved in the corporate department (Clifford Chance, 1991). The firms take pains to try to distinguish themselves from the others when describing their work and firm philosophies, and in attempting to do so provide insight into what it is they do. When describing the company/commercial area Allen and Overy write:

> In broad terms, our work can be seen as falling into three principal categories: corporate finance, banking (including restructuring and insolvency work) and international capital markets ... Recent years have seen remarkable and exciting developments in the corporate finance area. Not only has there been an extraordinary amount of new legislation and regulation but there have been radical changes in the types of businesses and transactions carried on by our clients. Our corporate finance practice involves advising on take-over bids, Stock Exchange flotations, governmental privatizations and private company acquisitions and disposals. We have been particularly pleased by the continued expansion of our mergers and acquisitions and new issue work and there has been dramatic growth in the demand for our special skills in relation to management and leveraged buy-outs, which have included many complex transnational buy-outs (n.d. p. 14).

Simmons and Simmons says:

> Major corporate transactions have never been more complex. It is a serious intellectual challenge to create a structure which delivers the transaction within the timetable, the regulatory framework and our clients' commercial requirements. Our objective is to design the deal in the most practical and sensible way and then to execute it, as a team, on time and at a reasonable cost. That takes knowledge, hard work, experience and efficiency (n.d.a. p. 3).

In the areas of international finance and banking, Herbert Smith state: 'Our ... service is driven by the philosophy that lateral thinking is the key to helping our clients find solutions for difficult and complex propositions; commonsense and simplicity are our aim in the expression of these solutions' (n.d.a. p. 1).

Corporate and finance work have to a large extent always had a coherent structure for the law firms, but rapid developments in technology and international finance have begun to pull at traditional divisions of labour with the result that new areas of work have emerged. Denton Hall says of its communications group:

> Communications are developing with breath-taking speed. Recent years have seen the evolution of a truly global industry, driven by technological advances, and equally rapid development of the national and international framework of regulation. We at Denton Hall have been at the forefront of these changes ... The Group has prepared submissions to the European Commission ... on a range of telecommunications matters including the INTERSTAT, INMARSAT AND EUTELSTAT Treaties ... We are involved in lobbying during the progress of the 1990 Broadcasting Bill through Parliament, and have advised a number of clients on its implications ... Our experience includes advising one of the five successful applicants for UK mobile data licences ... (n.d.a. pp. 1-6).

Besides the influence of technology on change in work practices there are changes in the political topography of the world. The transformation of the nations of Eastern Europe into fledgling democracies has altered the ways in which professional services are delivered for corporate clients. Theodore Goddard (at position number 19 in Table 2.2) has joined with one of the big accounting firms, Ernst and Young, and an investment bank, Midland Montagu, to form an investment advisory service for clients who want to do business in the Soviet Union. In effect, they have created a multi-disciplinary practice (MDP). They put forward a list of questions they can answer for their potential clients:

> How do we start in this new market?
> What laws govern foreign investment?
> What procedures need to be followed?
> What taxes apply to profits earned locally and remitted overseas?
> How can roubles be exchanged for hard currency?
> What sources of finance exist?
> What new culture do we need to learn? (Midland Bank, n.d.)

Together the advisers constructed a fixed planning stage, then if the deal was to go through there would be a variable rate implementation stage. It is not only the culture of the USSR that is new and strange, but also the culture of the deliverer, the MDP. City lawyers are on the whole ambivalent about this concept, believing it to be a subterfuge by the accounting firms in order that they might take over the law firms.

Another area of work in which boundary disputes have been common with accountants is corporate tax. All corporate transactions, national and international, have tax ramifications (Picciotto, 1993). Freshfields describes itself as giving advice on:

> the taxation of domestic and international groups of companies, partnerships, joint ventures and financial institutions, their directors and employees the tax implications of financing, leasing and property transactions the structuring of mergers, acquisitions and company flotations and reorganisations (Freshfields, n.d.).

The tax department is usually the smallest in the constellation of law firm departments (c.f. Page, 1991). For example, Allen and Overy, with 496 fee earners, has 214 involved in company and commercial work, and if we include corporate finance the figure is 309, but only 17 fee earners in corporate tax (Chambers, 1991, pp. 78-97).

Commercial property transactions have always been a staple of City lawyers' work because buildings, plant, and land are large parts of companies' assets. And these are areas where several kinds of expertise need to be coordinated. As Ashurst Morris Crisp point out: 'the issues facing the property industry have become increasingly more complex, requiring the integration of separate specialist skills to provide planning, construction, environmental and tax advice in support of general property advice' (Ashurst Morris Crisp, 1991, p. 19). A firm like Ashursts lists itself as adviser to developers, such as Trafalgar House, major space users, such as Allied-Lyons plc, funding institutions, such as British Airways Pension Fund, and public authorities, such as the London Docklands Development Corporation and the Cardiff Bay Development Corporation (Crawford's Directory, 1991). Denton Hall adds:

> We talk the language of property, not 'legalese', and so can communicate across both professional and national frontiers. We can coordinate the work of multi-disciplinary teams including accountants, architects, surveyors and other experts. In addition to our London base, we have offices in Milton Keynes, Brussels, Hong Kong, Tokyo, Bangkok, Singapore and Los Angeles, and close links with lawyers in other major overseas commercial centres particularly in the European Community. We are able to offer a truly international property service (Denton Hall, n.d.b. p. 2).

Property work has given rise to subspecialties. Two especially are development and construction, and environmental law. Herbert Smith notes: 'Major construction projects, whether relating to commercial, industrial or public works - and particularly those with an international element - give rise to increasingly complex and sophisticated legal and financial issues' (Herbert Smith, n.d.b. p.1). Simmons and Simmons writes:

> The Development and Construction Law Group includes specialists on all aspects of a development including tax planning and funding, planning and environmental matters, site acquisition and assembly, development, construction and engineering agreements, professional appointments,

> warranties, insurance, dispute resolution and the impact of 1992 and the single European Market (Simmons and Simmons, n.d.b.).

The new dimension added to the property lawyer's work is that of dealing with the environmental issues. As Simmons and Simmons point out: 'During the 1990s no business will be able to afford the luxury of ignoring the environmental aspects of its operations' (Simmons and Simmons, n.d.b). Both of these subspecialties cross over into the area of dispute resolution because neither exists without the potential for conflict.

The types of task I have outlined here are essentially facilitative, that is they are concerned with the creation and implementation of transactions. And this constitutes the bulk of City lawyers' work. Yet many consider the central role of lawyers to be conflict resolvers, that is, being involved in litigation and other forms of dispute resolution. Osiel phrases it as 'the possibility of litigation casts such a long shadow over the rest of lawyers' work' (1990, p. 2066). Certainly litigation is an important part of lawyers' work, but the warrants for claiming it as the core are few (c.f. Abel and Lewis, 1989, p. 508; Mackie, 1989; Flood, 1991).

Under the Solicitors Act of 1974, solicitors had a monopoly on starting litigation. That has now been modified under the 1990 Courts and Legal Services Act and others may initiate court actions (Merricks and Wallman, 1991, p. 18; c.f. MacErlean, 1989). Evidence from the United States suggests businesses are now resolving more disputes by litigation since the 1960s, when Macaulay suggested businessmen were keen to avoid being formally embroiled in disputes (Galanter and Rogers, 1988; Macaulay, 1990. See also Economist, 1990; Mackay, 1991). It appears that the same trend has been occurring in the UK. Chambers (1991), p. 7) asserts: 'The rise in litigation in some parts of the country has been staggering … Medium-to-large London firms had an average growth of 43 percent in litigation, with one medium-sized specialist litigation practice reporting a 47 percent growth in work'. In both mergers and acquisitions and restructuring work the stakes can be high (Connon, 1991), which makes litigation or arbitration real possibilities, so the City firms commit substantial resources to dispute resolution. Freshfields says:

> Much litigation and arbitration has an international element involving a multiplicity of jurisdictions. It is often technical and complex, frequently involving the collation of large quantities of documents and other evidence. The department has more than 60 staff (Freshfields, n.d.).

And Cameron Markby Hewitt notes:

> We take a positive lead in all disputes and seek to adopt a constructive and efficient approach. We act speedily to obtain or respond to applications for injunctive relief to protect our clients' interests, and have particular knowledge in Mareva (attachment) and Anton Piller (search and seizure orders). Our

objective is to obtain a commercially favourable outcome with the client's interest uppermost (Cameron Markby Hewitt, n.d. p. 16).

All City firms will do litigation, but not all are renowned for it. Two firms - Simmons and Simmons and Herbert Smith - are reputed to have the busiest litigation practices, although Lovell White Durrant and Freshfields have the largest departments with 116 and 93 litigators, respectively (Chambers, 1991, p. 57). These firms also become involved in what one partner called 'semi-litigation'. It includes appearing in enquiries before the Monopolies and Mergers Commission, the Department of Trade and Industry, the Office of Fair Trading, and before Lloyds when underwriting syndicates are investigated.

The City is noted for one particular area of work in litigation which is shipping. Charter party agreements always contain a clause specifying 'arbitration London'. As a shipping firm partner said, 'London is the main shipping centre in the world, though New York is muscling in'. He went on to say that many shipping arbitrations can be done quickly in 'evening arbitrations'. The solicitors often act as advocates in these, using counsel only for the bigger arbitrations.

The final area of work in this brief survey is insolvency and corporate reconstruction, which booms as recessions deepen. As Chambers puts it, 'The recession has its compensations. The high rate of business failure means that insolvency lawyers are busier than they have been for almost a decade' (1991, p. 7). Herbert Smith describes it this way:

> The (1980s) have seen a major increase in the number of personal and corporate insolvencies. The rapid expansion of business into unfamiliar markets, financial over-extension and instability in exchange and interest rates have brought many more businessmen, partnerships and companies to a position where intervention has been required by banks, trade creditors and others, sometimes outside and sometimes through the Courts (Herbert Smith, n.d.c. p. 1).

Insolvency is not the sole preserve of lawyers, there now being a distinct group of insolvency practitioners which includes lawyers and accountants. And indeed, accountants have by far the greatest share of the work, monopolising the appointments as receivers and administrators (Waller, 1991, p. 16).

Although I have described these areas of work as separate activities, they are often integrated into transactions which require elements from all. For example, in depicting the privatization work done by Slaughter and May, Page writes: 'most departments within Slaughters experience knock-on-effects from the work generated (ranging from complex tax issues to questions of leasing)' (Page, 1990, p. 25). Similarly, Allen and Overy writes of itself:

> We have always been aware of the benefits to be gained from combining our individual strengths, and these resources are tapped through our 'know-how'

groups - people brought together to pool the particular expertise they have on individual topics. Some of the 'know-how' groups concentrate on highly specialised, self-contained areas of law whereas other, including those dealing with employment, construction law, the EC 1992 programme and intellectual property, cross traditional departmental boundaries. In order to develop and maintain a broad view, all lawyers, partners and staff alike, are encouraged to belong to more than one 'know-how' group (Allen and Overy, n.d. p. 8).

Discussion

I have laid out some of the dynamics that drive the large modern elite law firm: its structure and its work. Without doubt the structure is under strain. What sufficed for small groups of people is finding difficulty satisfying the large numbers who wish to join the legal profession. How does a law firm with a flat profile maintain the type of growth into which it appears locked? To some degree accountants with their multiple levels of grades within the firm structure have evolved a method to cope. But still the essential bargain is that the good associate will be rewarded with partnership (i.e. membership) after a lengthy probation. Two other problems emerge from this tension. First lawyers have flirted with the idea of incorporating with limited liability; it cuts across the professional ideal, even though many would say that ideal is subservient to business. Second, as firms grow, nationally and internationally, their clients encounter the difficulty of conflicts of interest, which in the modern era are almost impossible to avoid.

Corporate law is struggling to come to terms with globalization and the increased commercialization and entrepreneurial approach to legal practice. It is a strain. Partnership denotes collegiality and egalitarianism; but these do not necessarily obtain any more. If a law firm needs to 'downsize' to increase productivity it will lay off surplus partners and assistants. At one time this required the partnership agreement to be dissolved and restructured. This is no longer true. Partnerships are elastic, meaning different things to different constituencies. If we add to this the fact that professional partnerships, whether in accounting or law, are under attack from liability suits from aggrieved clients and government regulators, professional services begin to look less and less distinctive. The tradition of law speaks to law as a liberal profession. For some, say, those that combine academic and practising careers, that may be so: for most, however, law is a hard grind where productivity targets, billable hours, and fees are constantly chased.

This emphasis on the economic affects the social aspect of the legal profession. Globalization forces English lawyers to compete with American and other lawyers. Ascriptive ties as ways of hiring new staff thus diminish in effectiveness and more meritocratic means come into play. The field of practice begins to change and with it its rules, both constitutive and regulative, leading to more unknown changes. Traditions are abandoned and the social structure of professions is reformulated.

Law has always had a problem of definition, more so than other professions. What does it do? Both Bourdieu (1987) and Abbott (1988) have emphasised the permeability of professional boundaries. Law is now at a stage where it is in competition with legal professions from other cultures and with other professions. Can it capture the field?

References

Abbott, A. (1988), *System of The Professions: An Essay on the Division of Expert Labor*, University of Chicago Press, Chicago.

Abel, R. and Lewis, P. (1989), 'Putting Law Back into the Sociology of Lawyers', in R. Abel and P. Lewis (eds), *Lawyers in Society: Comparative Theories*, University of California Press, Berkeley, CA.

Allen and Overy (n.d.), 'Allen and Overy', London.

American Lawyer (1990), 'Am Law 100', American Lawyer (Special Report), July, p. 1.

Ashurst Morris Crisp (1991),'Proposal for Legal Services', London.

Auchincloss, L. (1986), *Diary of a Yuppie*, Houghton Mifflin, Boston.

Bourdieu, P. (1987), 'The Force of Law: Toward a Sociology of the Juridical Field', (1987), *Hastings Law Journal*, Vol 38, p. 817.

Brill, S. (1990), 'The Changing Meaning of Partnership', *American Lawyer* (Supplement), March, p. 1.

Bruck, C. (1988), *The Predators' Ball: The Junk Bond Raiders and the Man who Staked Them*, The American Lawyer/Simon and Schuster, New York.

Burrough, B. and Helyar, J. (1990), *Barbarians at the Gate: The Fall of RJR-Nabisco*, Arrow Books, London.

Cameron Markby Hewitt (n.d.), 'Cameron Markby Hewitt', London.

Carr, J. (1991a), 'Numbers Men Gear Up to Enjoy the Court Feast', *Evening Standard,* 25 November, p. 36.

Carr, J. (1991b), 'City Lawyers Clock up over £250 an Hour', *Evening Standard,* 14 June, p. 39.

Chambers, M. (1991), (ed.), *Chambers & Partners Directory: A User's Guide to the Top 1000 Law Firms in England and Wales and All Barristers' Chambers,* Chambers, London.

Chambers, G. and Harwood, S. (1990), *Solicitors in England and Wales: Practice, Organisation and Perceptions: First Report: The Work of the Solicitor in Private Practice*, Law Society, London.

CIFC (1991), *National Summary Report*, Winchester.

Clifford Chance (1991), 'Press Information': Background Briefing, London.

Connon, H. (1991), 'From Boom to Bust in Three Easy Stages', *The Independent*, 5 January.

Crawford's Directory (1991), *Crawford's Directory of City Connections*, Economist, London.

Denton Hall Burgin and Warrens (n.d.a.), 'The Communications Group', London.
Denton Hall (n.d.b.) 'Property', London.
Dezalay, Y. (1991), 'Marchands de Droit', PhD thesis, Paris.
Dillon, K. (1992), 'Profile: Top Billing', *Legal Business*, April, p. 22.
Dillon, K. and Griffiths, C. (1991), 'KPMG FIDAL: The Largest Law Firm on the Continent', *Legal Business Magazine*, July/August.
Dobkin, R. (1986a), 'Why Law Firms Face a Capital Crisis', *International Financial Law Review*, April, p. 37.
Dobkin, R. (1986b), 'Easing the Capitalisation Burden for Partners', *International Financial Law Review*, October, p. 21.
Economist (1990), 'Corporate Law: The Defence Rests', *Economist,* 10 November, No. 9.
Eisler, K. (1991), *Shark Tank: Greed, Politics and the Collapse of Finley Kumble, One of America's Largest Law Firms*, Plume, New York.
Fennell, E. (1991), 'Accountants Cut Soaring Claims Costs', *Times,* 21 May, p. 30.
Fergus, C. (1989), 'Lateral Hiring: The Key to US Law Firm Expansion', *International Financial Law Review*, 12 May.
Fitzpatrick, J. (1989), 'Legal future Shock: The Role of Large Law Firms by the End of the Century', *Indiana Law Journal*, Vol. 64, p. 461.
Flood, J. (1985), *The Legal Profession in the United States*, American Bar Foundation, Chicago.
Flood, J. (1987), 'Anatomy of Lawyering: An Ethnography of a Corporate Law Firm', PhD thesis (Evanston).
Flood, J. (1988), 'The Changing Face of American Corporate Law Practice', *Revue Francaise D'Etudes Americaines*, No. 35, p. 55.
Flood, J. (1989), 'Megalaw in the UK: Professionalism or Corporatism? A Preliminary Report', *Indiana Law Journal*, Vol. 64, p. 569.
Flood, J. (1991), 'Doing Business: The Management of Uncertainty in Lawyers' Work', *Law & Society Review*, Vol. 25, p. 41.
Flood, J. (1996), 'Megalawyering in the Global Order: The Cultural, Social and Economic Transformation of Global Legal Practice', *International Journal of the Legal Profession*, Vol. 3, p. 169.
Freshfields (n.d), 'Freshfields', London.
Friedman, L. (1985), *A History of American Law*, second edition, Simon and Schuster, New York.
Galanter, M. and Palay, T. (1991), *Tournament of Lawyers: The Transformation of the Big Law Firm*, University of Chicago Press, London.
Galanter, M. and Rogers, J. (1988), 'The Transformation of American Business Disputing? Some Preliminary Observations', unpublished paper.
Gallese, L. (1989), 'Counselor to the King', *New York Times Magazine*, *Part 2: The Business World*, 24 September.
Hagan, J., Huxter, M. and Parker, P. (1988), 'Class Structure and Legal Practice: Inequality and Mobility among Toronto Lawyers', *Law & Society Review*, Vol. 22, p. 9.

Herbert Smith (n.d.a.) 'International Finance and Banking Law', London.
Herbert Smith (n.d.b.) 'Construction Law', London.
Herbert Smith (n.d.c.) 'Insolvency Law', London.
Hermann, A. (1989), *Law -v- Business: Business Law Articles from the Financial Times 1983-1988*, Butterworths, London.
Hirsch, P. (1986), 'From Ambushes to Golden Parachutes: Corporate Takovers as an Instance of Cultural Framing and Institutional Integration', *American Journal of Sociology*, Vol. 91, p. 800.
Hobson, D. (1991), *The Pride of Lucifer: The Unauthorised Biography of Morgan Grenfell*, Mandarin, London.
Hobson, W. (1984), 'Symbol of the New Profession: Emergence of the Large Law Firm, 1870-1915', in G. Gawalt (ed.), *The New High Priests: Lawyers in Post-Civil War America*, Greenwood Press, Westport, CT.
Hodgart, A. (1991), 'Choosing Between US and UK Firms', *American Lawyer*, November.
International Financial Law Review (1990), 'Comment', *International Financial Law Review*, p. 5.
Lisagor, N. and Lipsius, F. (1988), *A Law Unto Itself: The Untold Story of the Firm of Sullivan and Cromwell,* Morrow, New York.
Macaulay, S. (1990), 'Long-term Continuing Relations: The American Experience Regulating Dealerships and Franchises', Madison, Wisconsin.
MacErlean, N. (1989), 'The Accountant as Advocate', *The Accountant,* August.
Mackay, Lord. (1991), 'Litigation in the 1990s', *Modern Law Review*, Vol. 54, pp. 171.
Mackie, K. (1989), *Lawyers in Business: And the Law Business*, London.
McCullough, V. (1988), *Economist Pocket Guide to the New City*, Economist, London.
Meeks, M. (1991), 'Alter[ing] People's Perceptions: The Challenge Facing Advocates of Ancillary Business Practices', *Indiana Law Journal*, Vol. 66, p. 1031.
Merricks, W. and Wallman, R. (1991), *The Courts and Legal Services Act A Solicitor's Guide,* The Law Society, London.
Midland Bank (n.d.) 'Investment in the Soviet Union', London.
Orey, M. (1990), 'No Longer Risk Free', *American Lawyer*, December.
Osiel, M. (1990), 'Book Review: Lawyers as Monopolists, Aristocrats, and Entrepreneurs', *Harvard Law Review*, Vol. 103, p. 2009.
Page, N. (1990), 'A Private Function', *Legal Business*, April.
Page, N. (1991), 'Taxing Times: Quality versus Quality?', *Legal Business Magazine*, July/August.
Picciotto, S. (1993), *International Business Taxation*, Butterworths, London.
Simmons and Simmons, (n.d.a), 'Simmons & Simmons', London.
Simmons and Simmons, (n.d.b), 'Environmental Law Department', London.
Slinn, J. (1984), *A History of Freshfields*, Freshfields, London.

Spangler, E. (1986), *Lawyers for Hire: Salaried Professinals at Work*, Yale University Press, New Haven, CT.
Stevens, M. (1981), *The Big Eight*, Simon and Schuster, New York.
Stevens, M. (1987), *Power of Attorney: The Rise of the Giant Law Firms,* Simon and Schuster, NewYork.
Stevens, R. (1983), *Law School: Legal Education in America from the 1850s to the 1980s*, University of North Carolina University Press, Chapel Hill, North Carolina.
Stewart, J. (1983), *The Partners: Inside America's Most Powerful Law Firms,* Simon and Schuster, New York.
Swaine, R. (1948), *The Cravath Firm and Its Predecessors, 1819-1947*, two volumes, Ad Press, New York.
The Legal 500, (1990), Legalese, London.
The Legal 500, (1991), Legalese, London.
Tolbert, P. and Stern, R. (1987), 'Clans and Hierarchies: Governance Structures of Major Law Firms', unpublished paper.
Travis, G. (1990), 'FIDAL: The Largest Law Firm in Europe?', *Lawyers in Europe*, p. 6.
Waller, D. (1991), 'Accountants: Growing Places', *Legal Business Magazine*, July/August.

3 Understanding consultancy as performance: the dramaturgical metaphor

Timothy Clark and Graeme Salaman

Introduction

Conventional views of the consultant activity envisage it in terms of a variety of roles or metaphors. Tilles (1961) identifies three roles - seller of services, supplier of information and business doctor dispensing cures. The first is regarded by those involved in terms of a conventional sales-purchase transaction; the second in terms of the flow of information between the parties; the third in terms of patient and doctor. Schein (1969) distinguishes between three types of consultancy in terms of their impact on the respective roles of the consultant and client, these are the purchase of expertise, doctor-patient and process models (pp. 5-12). Blake and Mouton (1983) identify five 'consulting modes' which differ in terms of the way the consultant relates to the client, i.e. in terms of theories and principles; prescription; confrontation; catalytic and acceptant (p. 14). Nees and Greiner (1985) identify and discuss the implications of five types of management consultant: mental adventurer; navigators; management physicians; systems architects; and friendly co-pilots (pp. 69-70).

Many of these metaphors are flattering to the consultant, and it is likely that consultants would be likely to adopt and, when possible, to impose a conception of their role and function in terms analogous to the doctor or therapist. These roles emphasise professional status, professional autonomy, and assume a major and acknowledged body of specialist knowledge. Yet it is our contention that these metaphors are inadequate in three main ways. First, many of them assume precisely what is *missing* from the relationship between consultant and client - an agreed, accepted, authoritative and relevant body of knowledge - in which the consultant is accomplished and expert, but which is denied to the client, and which can be used as a basis on which to build the nature of the client-consultant relationship. As a number of commentators have noted whilst there is consultancy knowledge it lacks the status and authority of other professional knowledge, and does not supply a basis for occupational qualification and certification (see Oakley, 1993; Whitley, 1991). There is no *agreed* body of managerial expertise with the consequence that there is no single recognised body of knowledge for management consultancy. Furthermore, as Freidson (1970) has argued, the two essential conditions of occupational security or professional monopoly are not met in the case of occupations such as management consultancy: the occupation has not gained exclusive competence to the control and performance of the task; and the occupation is not in control of the process of entry, membership and qualification (p. 11).

Secondly, these images of the client-consultant relationship are excessively embedded in a focus on the rationality of modern organizations and modern industrial society. The metaphors assume the same 'celebration of rationality' within organizations as noted by Weber. 'When Weber wanted to contrast the organizations of industrial capitalism with those of other civilizations he identified their most distinguished characteristic as a belief that their affairs were conducted legally, reliably, consistently, calculatingly, and predictably, magic having been banished from their procedures' (Turner, 1990, p. 83). The views of the consultants' work and relationships mentioned earlier draw upon the same rationalistic, utilitarian, formalistic, hard-headed assumptions. We suggest that the actual nature and focus of much consultancy activity deliberately opposes these values, and succeeds because of it.

Thirdly, in our view, the distinguishing qualities of the client-consultant relationship lie less in the currently available metaphors for institutionalised/professionalized assistance, counselling or exchange, and more in the nature of the interaction between these two parties. While supporting the value of metaphorical conceptualizations of the relationship between the parties (although wishing to move beyond the rational, secular, industrial context used by most commentators) we wish to use metaphor to capture the key features of what actually happens when clients and consultants meet and 'work' together. Oakley (1993) has usefully noted that a distinguishing feature of consultancy is that, unlike a profession, people cannot become qualified as consultants through 'rigorous and long training that leads to certification or licensure' (Blau, 1984, quoted in Oakley 1993, p. 4). The point is not that such training is unavailable but it is irrelevant for the key to consultancy success lies more in the *consultancy activity as a dramatic event* than in the mastery of any esoteric theory which might underlie it. Oakley (1993) notes that one of the characteristics of 'knowledge industries', such as management consultancy, is that the knowledge which underlies success 'resists complete codification of a formal kind but ... is dependent on the appreciation of complex relationships and the practice of craft skills embedded in systematic, reflective understanding' (p. 6).

Given the previous argument we wish to suggest in the paper that the most appropriate metaphor for understanding and analysing the activities of management consultants is that of performance. This portrays the consultant as a performer working with an audience (i.e., a client). During the course of this presentation the consultants are depicted as rehearsing and constructing their performance in private space prior to using 'scripts', 'scenes' and 'props' and other theatrical devices. The aim of this paper is to explicate this metaphor so that it may be subsequently applied to the activities of management consultants. To achieve this the paper is organized as follows. The first section examines the nature and key features of metaphor in general. This is followed by an elaboration of the key elements of performance emanating from the work of three writers in the 'dramaturgical school': Kenneth Burke, Erving Goffman and Iain Mangham. In the final section the dramaturgical metaphor is applied to two consultancy activities - executive search and management gurus.

The nature of metaphor

We concur with Ortony's (1975) remark that metaphors are necessary, not just nice. Any understanding of the world in general is inherently metaphorical. In this sense, our theories and explanations of social and organizational life are underpinned by metaphorical structuring. Following Morgan (1986), we would argue that 'the use of metaphor implies *a way of thinking* and *a way of seeing* that pervade how we understand our world generally' (p. 12). Metaphor is essential to our everyday language, thinking and expressive abilities, for 'our conceptual system, in terms of which we both think and act, is fundamentally metaphorical in nature ... the way we think, what we experience, and what we do every day is very much a matter of metaphor' (Lakoff and Johnson, 1980, p. 3).

This argument is hardly new. For instance, Stephen Pepper in his book *World Hypotheses* (1942) argued that western philosophers organize their knowledge of the world in terms of four world hypotheses (Formism,.Mechanism, Contextualism, Organicism) and that each of these is generated and determined by a separate *root metaphor* (Similarity, Machine, Historic event, Integration). He wrote that each world hypothesis is a complete and coherent world-view in that they can 'handle fairly adequately any fact that is presented to them' (p. 98). World hypotheses are therefore all-encompassing in their explanatory scope. Each has a similar degree of exegetic power, but draws attention to, and therefore obscures, certain features of the social world. In other words each world hypothesis is equally capable of explaining the world in general but in its own terms.

More recently, Gareth Morgan (1980, 1986) has examined the way in which organization theory is imprisoned by its metaphors. He develops an hierarchical link between 'paradigms', 'metaphors' and 'puzzle-solving activities'. Building on the work of Kuhn (1970) he suggests that organizational studies is comprised of a number of paradigms or 'schools of thought'. These are distinctive ways of seeing the world and are therefore alternative views of social reality. As with Pepper's world hypotheses, each paradigm is a relatively coherent system of ideas which is based on a shared metaphor. The relevant research areas and methods (i.e., puzzles and puzzle-solving activities) are suggested by the metaphorical imagery underpinning a particular school of thought. As Morgan (1980) writes 'The use of a metaphor serves to generate an image for studying a subject. The image can provide the basis for detailed scientific research based upon attempts to discover the extent to which features of the metaphor are found in the subject of inquiry' (p. 611).

Metaphor is used whenever we understand and experience one thing in terms of another. Thus, metaphor proceeds from the assertion that A is (or is like) B, where A and B were previously classified and understood as different entities. This combination or juxtaposition of A and B creates new meaning which is absent until the two elements are joined. As Schön (1979) writes 'It is the restructuring of the perception of the phenomenon named by *'A'* and *'B'* which enables us to call 'metaphor' what we might otherwise have called mistake' (p. 259).

An important feature of metaphor is its selective focus. Metaphor highlights certain aspects of a phenomenon and hides others, for when we comprehend one phenomena in terms of another we tend to develop a lopsided understanding. In highlighting certain features metaphor forces others into the background, or even conceals them altogether. As Ortony (1979) writes 'metaphors result in a sort of cognitive myopia, in which some aspects of a situation are unwittingly (?) emphasised at the expense of other, possibly equally important, ones' (p. 6). For example, we might describe an athlete as being like a leopard on the track. In choosing the term leopard we draw attention to, and conjure up, specific images of an animal moving with explosive speed, power, strength and grace. At the same time this metaphor requires that the athlete possesses selected features of a leopard. We ignore the fact that a leopard is a wild animal with feline features, yellow and black spotted fur, four legs, claws and a tail. Instead we concentrate on those features that the athlete and leopard have in common. In this way metaphor presents a partial truth. It gives a distorted image in which certain aspects of the phenomenon are selected in whilst others are selected out. Metaphorical comparison is therefore necessarily selective.

The root, or primary, metaphor which structures the argument in this paper is that of 'consultant as performer'. This is a dramatic metaphor in that it depicts consultancy as a theatrical event involving activities which are inherently dramatic. Thus a consultant performs to an 'audience' (e.g., a client). During the course of this presentation the consultant is pictured as rehearsing and constructing their performance in private space prior to using 'scripts', 'scenes' and 'props' as well as using a number of other theatrical devices when performing 'in front' of an audience. In this respect the consultant is a social actor within an organizational setting.

As with any metaphor 'consultancy as performance' is a selective and compact image in that it draws attention to specific properties of consultancy. For, in arguing that consultancy is a dramatic event in organizational life, those features associated with other metaphors of consultancy such as 'consultant as advocate/lawyer' or 'consultant as evangelist', are forced into a background role. In emphasising a dramaturgical metaphor certain features of consultancy are highlighted whilst others are hidden. When we use the theatrical metaphor we think of the consultant as an 'actor', performing to an 'audience' in an 'improvised' manner according to a number of 'script headings' whilst utilising 'props' and 'cues' in an organizational 'setting'. By way of contrast when a consultant is likened to an advocate/lawyer we might focus on the consultant as a 'professional' with 'technical expertise', working to a 'brief' from a client when arguing a 'case' in front of a 'judge and jury'. When we think of a consultant as an evangelist our attention turns to religious imagery. In doing so a consultant may become viewed as a 'guru' who 'preaches' a message from a 'divine text' to 'followers' and potential 'converts' who then 'sign up'. In this sense the consultancy market is comprised of a number of competing 'sects'.

However, a critical feature of the dramaturgical metaphor is its broad scope. Its limits are wide enough to incorporate the imagery associated with the other two metaphors. Both the 'consultant as advocate/lawyer' and 'consultant as evangelist' metaphors can be viewed as alternative types of performance. Each of these metaphors is innately theatrical. Thus, a lawyer performs to a brief (script) in a court-house (stage/setting), to a judge and jury (audience), using 'cues' from witnesses and pieces of evidence (props). Similarly, an evangelist's performances are tempered by their interpretation of a religious text (script), often delivered from a pulpit in a church (stage) to followers and churchgoers (audience) to the accompaniment of music and the singing of hymns (props). Furthermore, both performances are conceived and prepared in a private space prior to enactment in front of an audience. In this respect, just as the machine and organism are structural metaphors in organization studies (Morgan, 1980) the dramaturgical metaphor may be considered the primary metaphor of consultancy. We now turn to a discussion of the central features of the dramaturgical metaphor. This focuses on the key elements of performance as propounded by Kenneth Burke, Erving Goffman and Iain Mangham.

The dramaturgical metaphor

The theatrical analogy (i.e., all the world is a stage), or dramaturgical metaphor, has been around for some considerable time. More recently in the social sciences one of the most influential and profound developments of this argument was propounded by Kenneth Burke in his book *A Grammar of Motives*, first published in 1945. In this, and subsequent work (e.g., 1969), he attempts to answer two questions 'What is involved when we say what people are doing and why they are doing it?' (1945, p. 17). Therefore, his interest is in seeking to understand how people interpret and make sense of their social world. He argues that when people seek answers to these questions they perceive, interpret and describe the behaviour of others in theatrical terms. For Burke it is inevitable that people come to understand their social world by employing the principles of drama since human behaviour is inherently theatrical. When we engage in social intercourse 'we each know and understand each other's actions because each of us has to *act them out* or dramatize them' (Perinbanayagam, 1974, p. 536). In other words, we employ the principles on which we base our own social action in order to understand the social behaviour of others. So, as people engage in social action, they come to conclusions on the aforementioned questions, and are forced to do so, by the employment of dramatic principles. In this sense drama is not a mere analogy for social action - it is at the very heart of its generation and interpretation. The principles of theatre - words, actions, settings, scripts, scenes, cues, props, etc. - underpin our interaction with other people and the way in which we come to comprehend this. In this way, social action is generated within the same constraints as drama. Hence, to use Burke's terminology, the grammar of drama is also the grammar of social intercourse.

Burke terms the method he is employing as 'dramatism'. This proceeds on the basis that:

> for there to be an *act*, there must be an *agent*. Similarly, there must be a *scene* in which the agent acts. To act in a scene, the agent must employ some means, or *agency*. And it can be called an act in the full sense only if it involves a *purpose* (1969, p. 446).

At the centre of his 'dramatistic' approach are five 'generating principles' known as the Pentad. These are - Act, Scene, Agent, Agency, Purpose. Any complete account of social behaviour he argues, will '... offer *some kind* of answer to these five questions: what was done (act), when or where it was done (scene), who did it (agent), how he did it (agency) and why (purpose)' (1945, p. 15).

There are two useful features of Burke's approach. First, Burke describes his approach as 'dramatism' since it focuses on the '... intentions and purposes we read into other's actions, *as if we were members of a critically aware theatre audience*' (Burns, 1992, p. 109, our emphasis). Thus, Burke draws attention to the value of the dramaturgical metaphor in understanding organizational events and in so doing the significance of regarding any form of social action as a performance. Secondly, the focus is on understanding what *actually happens* when individuals interact. His dramatic schema lays bare the foundations upon which social intercourse is built. This provides a structure for understanding and analysing social action. Similarly, in focusing on consultancy as a *performance* our aim is to draw attention to what happens when consultants and clients meet thereby providing a framework to assist in understanding the nature and dynamics of this form of interaction.

Perhaps the most influential work in the dramaturgical analysis of social action is Erving Goffman's *The Presentation of Self in Everyday Life*, first published in 1959. In this he compresses Burke's dramaturgical Pentad (Act, Scene, Agent, Agency, and Purpose) into two basic notions: (1) there has to be an audience to which performances are addressed, and that the part played by the audience is critical; and, (2) any performance is comprised of two regions, a front stage and a backstage .

Goffman (1990) defines a performance as 'all the activity of an individual which occurs during a period marked by his continuous presence before a particular set of observers and which has some influence on the observers' (p. 32). Any performance is a 'dramatic realization' in which the performer conveys to an audience that which they wish to express. In this sense a performance is a managed event in which the performer consciously attempts to influence the response of other interactants. Through a performance an actor seeks to manipulate the situation for their own ends. To effect this Goffman suggests that the actions contributing to and defining a performance tend to be idealised in that they conceal and underplay those aspects which are inappropriate and therefore inconsistent with the impression an actor is seeking to generate in the audience. Furthermore, in order to relate more closely to an audience a performer may give the idea that the 'routine they are presently performing is their only routine or at least their most essential one' (pp. 56-57). To sustain this a performer may use a number of techniques. One is to segregate the audience to ensure that different routines are not seen by the same individuals. For instance, an actor may maintain a screen *persona* which varies significantly from their roles in theatre. Another way of making an audience feel special is to foster the impression that a particular performance is unique. This is achieved by obscuring the routine features of a performance and emphasising the spontaneous aspects. A performer may use a variety of techniques, such as speaking without notes, seeking participation from the audience and personalising the presentation in some way (e.g., the inserting of the bride and groom's names during a wedding service), so as to convey the impression of spontaneity and uniqueness.

The second feature of Goffman's dramatistic schema is the distinction between the front stage and backstage activity of every performance. The front stage region refers to that part of the performance which is visible to, and at which, the audience is present. This is the permanent, or fixed, part of an individual's performance which defines the situation for the audience. This region has two aspects. The first is the 'setting' which amounts to background items such as scenery, furniture and any other visible equipment (i.e., props). The second is 'personal front' which in turn has two aspects: 'appearance' refers to those features of an individual which inform the audience of the performer's social status such as sex, age, clothing, size and looks, and so forth; 'manner' are those personal features which indicate the role the performer is intending to play, they include posture, demeanour, facial expression, speech pattern, etc. All three elements should be congruent. Indeed, social interactions occur in settings which are appropriate for them. This is similar to the relationship between scene-act-agent proposed by Burke at the beginning of his *Grammar of Motives*:

> Using 'scene' in the sense of setting, or background, and 'act' in the sense of action, one could say that 'the scene contains the act'. And using agents in the sense of actors, or actors, one could say that '"the scene contains the agents'.
> It is a principle of drama that the nature of acts and agents should be consistent with the nature of the scene (p. 3).

In other words, our behaviour, purposes and feelings are composed so as to be consistent with the manifold settings which frame our social intercourse. A scene prompts and encourages appropriate kinds of action for which it was designed and discourages actions which are considered inappropriate (i.e., incongruent). For instance, a confession box or doctor's surgery are two settings which prompt the divulgence of intimate details concerning a person's life. However, the information which is imparted during interaction is appropriate to the setting since in one a person seeks forgiveness whilst in the other they seek a cure. Hence, the setting both determines and encloses (i.e., frames) the appropriate behaviour contained within a person's performance. As Goffman writes 'The decorations and permanent fixtures in a place where a particular performance is usually given, as well as the performers and performance usually found there, tend to fix a kind of spell over it' (p. 126) - in this way a place tends to retain some of its character so that once we have entered a particular setting we tend to adapt our behaviour 'naturally' (Burns, 1992, p. 118).

The backstage region is defined by Burns (1992) as 'some time and space for the preparation of procedures, disguises or materials, essential to the performance, or for the concealment of aspects of the performance which might either discredit it or be somehow discordant with it' (p. 112). In this region the audience is excluded enabling the performer to relax 'drop his front, forgo speaking his lines, and step out of character' (Goffman, 1990, p. 115). The conduct of any performance is therefore characterised by a considerable degree of risk and danger. Should the veil drop and the 'backstage' be revealed to the audience, the performer is exposed with the consequence that the audience may reconceptualise the role of the performer. Hence, any performance is highly risky since it may go disastrously wrong. The individual is in constant risk of being discovered with the consequence that character is gambled.

Goffman's (1990) use of the dramatic, or dramaturgical, metaphor focuses brilliantly on the heuristic advantages that accrue from conceptualising organizational and social life as if people were playing out roles, scripts and parts to audiences. The model of performance we are seeking to elaborate draws on three features of Goffman's dramaturgical model. First, in consultancy the audience (i.e., the client) is central to, becomes involved in, and, as a result of their participation, transformed by the event. Subsequently, the nature of client participation is managed by the consultant through the unfolding of the consultancy script. Second, all performances involve risk since a crack may appear at any moment which permits the audience a glimpse of the back-stage. To use a theatrical example, there is a constant danger that the scenery may collapse at any time to reveal the back-stage crew working the pulleys, trapdoors and other mechanisms which are used to maintain a sense of reality and the quality naturalness. Third, a performer stresses the unique, spontaneous, features of their performance to the audience. In this way a performer attempts to particularise their actions in order to create an event which has a special resonance for the audience.

More recently the work of Iain Mangham (1978, 1987, 1990; with Overington, 1987), building on the writings of Burke and his followers, argues that life is not *like* theatre, but life *is* theatre. For instance, in arguing that management is a performing art he compares an organizational performance by Lee Iacocca, President of Chrysler, with a theatrical performance of *Richard III* by the great nineteenth century actor Edmund Keane and concludes:

> I am not arguing that Iacocca's performance is *like* a performance of Edmund Keane. I am claiming that it *is* isomorphic: his performing, like yours or mine *is* theatre (1990, p. 107).

For Mangham, then, we are all performers strutting on different stages. This is similar to Goffman's view of the individual as an institution managing a whole set of roles and social selves. According to Burns (1992), Goffman presents the individual as 'a series of selves, one 'inside' the other, after the fashion of a Chinese box, or Russian doll. There is an inner self lurking inside the self which is present, or presented, to the outside world of others' (p. 107). This division of selves contains the possibility that during an encounter an individual may function as playwright, director, audience, and critic (Mangham, 1978, p. 27). As playwright the individual fashions a script thus determining the overall setting and script headings within which social intercourse takes place. As director they assist both in the initial construction and interpretation of the roles that the players will act as well as orchestrating the nature of their interaction (i.e., the movement of the actors on stage). As an audience an individual is aware of the performances given by others, whilst as a critic they monitor and evaluate these.

In applying the theatrical analogy to organizational life Mangham (1978) argues that 'The dramaturgical model of man is based upon the idea that man improvises his performance within the often very broad limits set by the scripts his society makes available to him' (p. 25). This definition emphasises two central features of any performance - *script* and *improvisation*. Much of what passes as everyday social intercourse, he argues, regardless of the context, is structured around the interplay between three different types of scripts: *situational*, *personal* and *strategic*. The first two concepts are derived from Schank and Abelson (1977) who define a *situational script as:*

> a structure that describes appropriate sequences of events in a particular context. A script is made up of slots and requirements about what can fill those slots ... Scripts handle stylised everyday situations. They are not subject to much change, nor do they provide the apparatus for handling totally novel situations. Thus, a script is a predetermined, stereotyped sequence of actions that defines a well-known situation (p. 41).

They occur when the situation is clearly specified, where several actors have interlocking roles to follow, and where each of the actors shares an understanding of what is supposed to happen. Thus, actors 'assume and enact relatively clearly defined roles within the confines of the anticipated sequence of events' (Mangham, 1978, p. 34).

When a performance is constructed to achieve some personal goal the actor is following a personal script. A personal script generally exists solely in the mind of its initiator. Unlike situational scripts the actors may not share an understanding of what is supposed to happen. In such instances, the actors who are being duped may be unaware that they are participating in a personal script and therefore have little congniscance of the role they are playing. Indeed, they may only discover their role some time after the event. Such scripts may be played out by confidence tricksters, fraudsters, con artists, and so forth. However, there are a number of personal scripts which are common enough for them to have become stylised events. Examples include the performance of a second-hand car salesman, insurance salesmen, a jealous spouse and the circumlocutory politician.

The last type of script is termed a strategic script. This refers to a performance where the actor is seeking to initiate certain behaviours from those with whom they are interacting. These are particularly manipulative in that the performer is only too well aware of what they are trying to achieve. The actor consciously attempts to influence the response of others by planning and then invoking a strategic script. Such performances differ from personal scripts in that the actor is pursuing a private agenda rather than a personal goal. Examples include a manager attempting to persuade colleagues, a therapist questioning patients, a football manager motivating their players etc.

In developing the concept of a strategic script, Mangham (1978) is seeking to emphasise the 'creation and management of impressions as an important feature of social interaction' (p. 28). This view of performance has its conceptual roots in the dramaturgical metaphor developed by Goffman which was elaborated earlier. Implicit within this conception of performance is the view that social actors, consciously or unconsciously, seek to create, sustain, and transform the impressions of their audience. For Mangham, therefore, a central feature of performance is the art of impression management.

Improvisation is critical to the achievement of any performance since according to Mangham (1990) a 'script has nothing more than potential: the performer's text is an abbreviated and necessarily incomplete version of a possible work of art' (p. 107). For a performance to be fully realized we need to know the character to be played and the script headings. Put differently, the position (i.e., their role) of an actor, relative to other participants in any interaction, is determined by the script headings. The actor then improvises their character within the broad constraints of the script headings. A character is defined as the distinctive characteristics with which an actor imbues a particular role through the attachment of certain mannerisms, habits, inflections, actions, etc.

In developing our argument of consultancy as performance we wish to draw on two useful features of Mangham's approach to the dramaturgical metaphor. First, social action of all kinds, and therefore including consultancy, proceeds according to script headings. A whole host of writers have already conceived of the consultancy activity as being comprised of a number of stages (e.g. Beckhard, 1969; Kakabadse, 1983). These are the script headings for a situational script - that of consultancy. Second, clients and consultants then improvise their performances around this structure. Within the broad parameters provided by the script headings they may fashion their personal or strategic scripts and in so doing cast not only their own role but also that of their fellow actors. These may be modified as a consultancy assignment progresses. Furthermore, since clients and consultants both function as playwrights, directors, audiences and critics personal goals may not be realized. As Mangham (1978) writes 'In such circumstances, for interaction to proceed at all, the person must take account of their expressions, their purposes, and intentions and seek to align his activities with theirs, and, likewise, they with his' (p. 27).

In summary what is meant when we say that the essence of consultancy is performance? In broad terms we would agree with Goffman's definition of performance, but wish to go beyond it more explicitly. He defines performance in terms of the presence of an individual before a group of observers which has an impact on observers. We wish to strengthen and broaden this definition by drawing on a number of the points emanating from the previous discussion of the dramaturgical metaphor. The basic elements of the model of performance suggested by the writings of Burke, Goffman and Mangham are presented in Table 3.1.

Table 3.1
The derivation of the typology of consultancy performance

	The nature of performance
Burke	Social action is inherently dramatic Act, Scene
Goffman	Audience Backstage and Front stage
Mangham	Script (situational, personal/strategic) Improvisation

Dramaturgical metaphor and consultancy

The discussion in the previous sections has identified the main elements of the performance metaphor. The purpose of this section is to apply this metaphor to the activity of management consultants. Two types of consultancy activity are discussed - executive search (colloquially known as headhunting) and management gurus. In applying the metaphor to such diverse types of consultancy we aim to demonstrate the inherent flexibility of this metaphor in that it can be applied to a wide range of consultancy activities. The applications of the metaphor are only described in brief here; they are developed further in other writings (Clark, 1995; Clark and Salaman, 1996a, 1996b, 1998).

Executive search

The role of search consultants ('headhunters') is to find suitable candidates for senior level organizational roles; primarily board-room appointments. Ostensibly this can be conceived of as a purely rational and clear cut services: developing and using networks of contacts to carry out a preliminary search and identification of potential candidates. Yet we maintain that even here the dramaturgical metaphor allows unexpected insight into the dynamics of the process.

Essentially the headhunter (itself of course an interesting metaphor which common usage has caused almost to lose its bite) acts as impresario to the key event - the meeting between the sponsors and backers (i.e. the clients) with potential members of the cast (i.e. the candidates).

The headhunters manage the audition, that crucial, fleeting performance where would-be members of the cast display their qualities supported behind the scenes by the advice and instruction of the headhunter (who also has something to lose if the auditions fail). During the audition the candidates display themselves in terms of the roles and characters required by the selectors, showing mastery of themselves under trying conditions, mastery of the situation and most importantly mastery of the organization they aspire to join. Mastery, in short, of a script they have not been allowed to see but must infer competently and thoroughly. Candidates must show they always wanted to play Hamlet, and are wonderfully prepared to do so; but the final qualification is that they know the script for a Hamlet which has never been written but is simply daily enacted, largely unknowingly, by the selectors. The competent candidate is familiar with the organization routines that underpin the script. They know the play better than the selectors. They are assessed as much for their knowledge of a script that does not exist as for their mastery of performance in the script. The headhunters manage this process through a careful process of selection, coaching, preparation, stage management and the management of presentations. Mangham's remarks, quoted earlier of strategic scripts, that they emphasise 'the creation and management of impressions ...' (Mangham, 1978, p. 28) is highly pertinent to headhunters' role.

The assignment process is inherently volatile and dangerous. Most of the danger attaches to the candidates: they are frequently of a level of seniority where their continuing public mastery of their senior roles would be seriously damaged if it were known that they had been rejected elsewhere. Poor reviews affect performers' confidence; they also affect the confidence of others around them. Given the fragile nature of senior executive reputation, public rejection would impact on their capacity to carry off their roles with conviction. The essence of the headhunter role is that they limit this danger. Furthermore, the danger is not only to candidates; too many rejections also means that the headhunter is losing touch with the needs of the recruiting organization. The headhunter too is on test.

Thus, in executive search activities the headhunter manages the audition to minimise the risk to participants not simply by coaching and preparation but also in a sense by ensuring that the entire process remains backstage - hidden. For those who fail the process, it never occurred: character, reputation remain intact; confidence will not be affected. The headhunters' impression management is so total that for many participants there is no public awareness of the event at all. Headhunters, therefore, can usefully be seen as impresarios, arranging and directing a certain sort of audition performance, managing impressions, and limiting the dangers associated with 'risking character' - the candidates' and their own.

Management gurus

We also maintain that some consultants - management gurus - achieve success and reputation by the nature and quality of their public performance - but these are not 'like' actors with an audience. The point about these gurus is that their performance (as much as the content of their message) is the key to their impact and influence.

A number of writers have attempted to account for the success of management gurus such as Tom Peters, Rosabeth Moss Kanter, Chris Argyris and John Harvey-Jones by reference to the content of the ideas they promulgate, noting important connections and affinities between this material and the values of those to whom it is addressed (Guest, 1990, 1992), the nature and appeal of their 'products' and marketing (Alvesson, 1990), or the social-political values of the society within which they occur (du Gay and Salaman, 1992).

However, while recognising the importance of these analyses of the ideas themselves, we wish to draw attention to aspects of the performances of those who initiate, represent and promulgate this material. To an extent the impact of the material derives from the power and impact of the way in which it is delivered in public. Such analyses, on their own, fail to recognise the extent to which organizations - and the consultancy activities which contribute to, and benefit from, organizational life are '... a sensual and emotional realm, replete with its own ceremonies, rites and drama' (Turner, 1990, p. 85) and thus fail to attend to the role of performance as an important arena where this emotional realm is manipulated.

We maintain that the key to understanding the power of such management gurus and their message is to focus on the gurus' performance. What do we mean by this term? Goffman defines performance in terms of the presence of an individual before observers which has an impact on the observers (Goffman, 1990). We wish to extend this definition in the following ways:

1 It depends on the 'performer', and on the performer's behaviour, not on other resources or bodies of knowledge or positions or accoutrements. The performer may create supportive *accoutrement*, out of everyday materials, but s/he does not depend on them. Rather the relationship is the other way around; their role

and importance is defined by the consultant's performance. In the same way, when a magician pulls something from a hat it does not matter whether it is a scarf, a bird, a dove or something else. Rather the roles of these props is to support and sustain the magician's actions which comprise their overall performance. Similarly, a consultancy report, the candidate shortlist, the results from psychometric tests all have relevance in that they assist the consultant both to maintain and realise a performance. Their relevance and role in the creation of the performance is orchestrated by the consultant. Care has to taken when using materials and props since as Mangham and Overington (1987) write 'When attention focuses not upon the work in its entirety but upon the materials or techniques which have been used to create it, the frame is likely to break' (p. 102). Put differently, once the audience's attention switches from the realization of the performance to the way in which it is put together the theatrical reality is undermined.

2 A consultancy performance is not of the normal type - where the performance is conceptualised as simply theatrical - as involving performers performing at, and to, a largely passive audience. In a theatrical performance the audience retains a distance from that which is enacted in front of them. They do so in the belief that the theatrical is 'an abstraction from the blooming, buzzing confusion of actuality' (Mangham and Overington, 1987, p. 103). Witnessing the murder of a character on stage does not cause anyone to call the police or for a doctor. In the consulting performance the 'audience' is not the same as a theatre audience, it does not simply listen to and observe a representation of reality, rather it is *central* to the performance itself. The audience is the *means* of the performance, its accomplice and its measurement. This conception of performance enlarges its meaning beyond its normal theatrical sense to include other sorts of performance where the focus is less on the performer realising a performance for an audience, and more on the 'performer' managing the whole event so that the audience has a positive experience. The latter relates both to the audience's experience of participation as well as the outcome resulting from the interaction. To achieve this the performance is created, adapted and realised so as to meet the needs of a particular audience. Yet without the consultant clients are unable personally to re-create the event. As in the theatre, once the curtain is down and the actors have left the stage the audience are helpless. They are reduced to a loose assembly of individuals who were once participants in the realization of a theatrical event. They may want more, and indicate this by shouting vociferously at the end of a performance, but without the actors on stage they are unable to recreate the event in which they have just participated.

3 Building on the previous point, the duration of a performance depends upon the actions of the performer. It ends when they bring it to a close. Once they disconnect from the audience the performance is over. The interaction, and

therefore the event, is at an end. The audience is left with memories and impressions of an experience from which they may attempt imperfect and partial recreations. Yet without the central catalyst (i.e., the performer) there is no performance. As a consequence a performance perishes once the final curtain calls are taken and the performer leaves the stage.

4 A consultancy performance is highly risky. It may go disastrously wrong. It involves the manipulation of techniques and materials of an unusual kind, and in an unusual way.

5 It generates remarkable tension, excitement, energy, which cannot be derived simply from an account of the event or from its formal content (or from those sad and often empty souvenirs - offprints, copies, handouts) but has to be 'experienced' directly. It is thus highly dependent on the individual consultant.

6 The event deals in emotion. Regardless of the cognitive content of the performance, the power and effects of the performance *qua* performance, are inherent in the emotion it generates and displays, and therefore success occurs as much (if not more) on the emotional level than on the rational, cognitive level. This is because emotion can at best be described to others but cannot be experienced directly. As Goffman puts it 'there is an expressive rejuvenation and reaffirmation of the moral values of the community' (Goffman, 1990, p. 35).

7 The event is characterised by mystery, by riddle, the world turned upside down, paradox, amazement, surprise, and threat. Consciousness, expectation, normality, are turned upside down. Statuses are at risk, identities can be undermined, relationships questioned, convictions unsettled.

Schechner (1977) has characterised the essence of this sense of performance in terms of five critical features: '(l) process, something happens here and now, (2) consequential, irremediable, and irrevocable acts, exchanges or situations; (3) on test, something is at stake for the performers and often for the spectators; (4) initiation, a change in status for the participants; (5) space is used concretely and organically.' The first four of these catch very accurately the intensity, power, danger and impact of consultancy performances.

Luckily there are examples of the performance of management gurus that have been publicly displayed - for example, the public or televised performances of Tom Peters, John Harvey Jones and others. Peters is a particularly good example, and although - as with all successful consultants of this *genre* - his performance is unique and uniquely idiosyncratic - it demonstrates the key characteristics common to such performances: demonic energy leading to near exhaustion; a powerfully physical presentation with a great deal of restless energy; high levels of commitment and passion which generate an intensity of experience - for audience and presenter; challenge, threat, confrontation. The audience is not allowed simply to sit and receive information, to spectate passively. It is brought into the event by challenge and attack.

A Peters' session is not going to be a bland, calm neutral presentation of options and possibilities: there will be conviction, certainty. The presenters will show - must show - absolute certainty and conviction. If they falter, we falter. They must believe in themselves and we will believe in them the presence of danger, risk, surprise. It's not safe. We might be exposed, caught out. There will be threat and danger -for all parties - presenter and audience. Things could go wrong. It might be embarrassing; in fact it almost certainly will be since anything may happen, but he will get away with it - although only just.

The message is posed in riddles, in dilemmas, in mysteriously gained insights which leave the 'audience' impressed by the performer's knowledge of them and their experience; the presenter 'knows' them; 'knows' their problems, 'knows' their subterfuges and tricks. They are open to him.

This is what consultants' performances look like. We have seen them. Some of us may have even experienced them. They are strangely powerful and impressive; very different from the conventional academic presentation of data, theory, conclusions, etc. But how do they work? What actually happens? Where is the source of their power?

The performance of the consultants in question - Tom Peters and many others - the management gurus - also displays many significant features: the strenuous efforts, by one device or another - to reawaken, to generate fundamentally transformed 'consciousness' of self, organization, priorities; to see new patterns, and new possibilities which ordinary life, before the performance had not made available or obvious. The focus on the emotional and irrational, with all the fear and anxiety that this occasions for audience and performer, is also similar. (And surely one's first impression on witnessing a consultant performance is anxiety that the performance is so extravagant, so melodramatic, that it will appear absurd; but slowly this risk, being overcome by the performer, actually adds to his/her stature). But there is also risk for the audience. No-one is safe. Those who hope that they can remain immune and detached as observers soon find that by a variety of devices they are drawn into the session, become the focus of the session in which strange things happen to them - they may exposed to combative questions; publicly posed with riddles, forced to reveal their ignorance which is then immediately exposed, required to participate in role plays - a battery of destabilising techniques are used which move the content of the event from a safe, cerebral level to the level of 'here and now', with egos, identities and pride at stake, with potentially significant alterations in status (e.g., senior manager to public incompetent, etc.).

The focus of this type of performance is on the emotional, the generation of threat and risk for all parties, the de-stabilising of identities, allied to the repetitive emphasis on simplified, action-focused ritualistic nostrums, all presented in a style where 'confidence dominates over doubt, steadfastness over vacillation, optimism over pessimism' (Malinowski) create an environment where the consultants are able to generate a collective sense among the managers not only of power and impact, but also of truth and relevance. As Goffman puts it, (of performances) '... reality is being performed' (Goffmann 1990, p. 35).

Conclusion

This article attempts to illuminate the work and role of consultants, in particular the activities of headhunters and management gurus, in terms of the dramaturgical metaphor. It does so by offering a model of consultancy which presents consultants as responsible for the successful 'bringing off' of performances. Our focus is on the nature and quality of the interaction between consultants and audience. At the heart of the performance there lies a concern for, and an emphasis on, the irrational, emotional symbolic aspects of organization. Such a focus is not only the key to understanding consultancy - it is also the key to the consultant's success. Successful consultants have always known, and exploited, what this article is arguing: that success and reputation depends on the magic and mystery of the performance.

Furthermore, given the constraints and characteristics of the consultancy industry (i.e., the absence of an exclusive knowledge base on which to establish a professional monopoly) the management and achievement of an impressive performance is the only possible way in which continuing personal success can be established and maintained. Hence, performance is central to both the effectiveness of the consultant within the organization and to their competitive success within the industry.

References

Alvesson, M. (1990), 'On the Popularity of Organizational Culture', *Acta Sociologica*, Vol. 33, No. pp. 31-49.

Beckhard, R. (1969), *Development Strategies and Models,* Addison-Wesley, Reading, Mass.

Blake, R.R. and Mouton, J.S. (1983), *Consultation: A Handbook for Individual and Organizational Development*, Addison-Wesley, Reading, Mass.

Blau, J. (1984), *Architects and Firms,* MIT Press, Cambridge, Conn.

Burke, K. (1945), *The Grammar of Motives,* University of California Press, Berkeley.

Burke, K. (1969), 'Dramatism', *International Encyclopedia of the Social Sciences*, Vol. 7, Macmillan, New York.

Burns, T. (1992), *Erving Goffman,* Routledge, London.

Clark, T. (1995), *Managing Consultants,* Open University Press, Buckingham.

Clark, T. and Salaman, G. (1996a), 'Management Gurus as Organizational Witchdoctors', *Organization.*, Vol3. No. 1. pp. 85-107.

Clark, T. and Salaman, G. (1996b), 'Telling Tales: Management Consultancy as the art of story telling', in D. Grant and C. Oswick (eds), *Metaphor and Organizations*, Sage, London, pp. 166-84.

Clark, T. and Salaman, T. (1998), 'Telling Tales: Management Gurus' narratives and the construction of managerial identity', *Journal of Management Studies*, Vol. 35, No. 2, pp.137-61.

Du Gay, P. and Salaman, G. (1992), 'The Cult(ure) of the Customer', *Journal of Management Studies*, Vol. 29, pp. 616-33.

Freidson, E. (1986), *Professional Powers: A Study of the Institutionalization of Formal Knowledge*, University of Chicago Press, Chicago.

Goffman, E. (1990), *The Presentation of Self in Everyday Life*, Penguin, London.

Guest, D. (1990), 'Human Resource Management and the American Dream', *Journal of Management Studies*, 27, pp. 377-97.

Guest, D. (1992), 'Right Enough to be Dangerously Wrong', in G. Salaman (ed.) *Human Resource Strategies*, Sage, London.

Kakabadse, A.P. (1983), 'How to Use Consultants', *International Journal of Manpower*, Vol. 4, pp. 3-20.

Kolb, D.A. and Frohman, A.L. (1970), 'An Organizational Development Approach to Consulting', *Sloan Management Review*, Vol. 11, pp. 51-65.

Kuhn, T.S. (1970), *The Structure of Scientific Revolutions*, 2nd Edition, University of Chicago Press, Chicago.

Lakoff, G. and Johnson, M. (1980), *Metaphors We Live By*, Chicago, University of Chicago Press.

Lawrence, P. and Lorsch, J. (1969), *Developing Organizations: Diagnosis and Action*, Addison-Wesley, Reading, Mass.

Mangham, I. L. (1978), *Interactions and Interventions in Organizations*, John Wiley, Chichester.

Mangham, I.L. (1987), 'A Matter of Context', in I.L. Mangham (ed.) *Organisation Analysis and Development*, John Wiley, Chichester.

Mangham, I.L. (1990), 'Managing as a Performing Art', *British Journal of Management*, Vol. 1, pp. 105-15.

Mangham, I.L. and Overington, M.A (1987), *Organisations as Theatre: A Social Psychology of Dramatic Appearances*, John Wiley, Chichester.

Morgan, G. (1980), 'Paradigms, Metaphors and Puzzle Solving in Organizational Theory', *Administrative Science Quarterly*, Vol. 25, pp. 605-22.

Morgan, G. (1986), *Images of Organization*, Sage, London.

Nees, D.B. and Greiner, L.E. (1985), 'Seeing Behind the Look-alike Management Consultants', *Organization Dynamics*, Winter, pp. 68-79.

Oakley, K. (1993), 'Management Consultancy - Profession or Knowledge Industry?', paper presented to Conference on Professions and Management in Britain, University of Stirling.

Ortony, A. (1975), 'Why Metaphors are Necessary and Not Just Nice', *Educational Theory*, Vol. 25, pp. 45-53.

Ortony, A. (ed.), (1979), *Metaphor and Thought,* Cambridge University Press, Cambridge.
Pepper, S.C. (1942), *World Hypotheses*, University of California, Berkeley, CA.
Perinbanayagam, R.S. (1974), 'The Definition of the Situation: An Analysis of the Ethnomethodological and Dramaturgical View', *Sociological Quarterly*, Vol. 15, pp. 521-42.
Schank, R.C. and Abelson, R.P. (1977), *Scripts, Plans, Goals and Understanding,* Laurence Erlbaum, Hillsdale, New Jersey.
Schechner, R. (1977), *Performance Theory*, Routledge, New York.
Schein, E.H. (1969), *Process Consultation: Its Role in Organization Development,* Addison-Wesley, Reading, Mass.
Schön, D.A. (1979), 'Generative Metaphor: A Perspective on Problem-setting in Social Policy' in A. Ortony (ed.) *Metaphor and Thought*, pp. 254-83, Cambridge University Press, Cambridge.
Schön, D.A. (1983), *The Reflective Practitioner,* London, Temple Smith.
Tilles, S. (1961), 'Understanding the Consultant's Role', *Harvard Business Review,* November-December, pp. 87-99.
Turner, B. (1990), 'The Rise of Organizational Symbolism', in Hassard J. and Pym, D. (eds), *The Theory and Philosophy of Organizations*, Routledge, London.
Whitley, R. (1989), 'On the Nature of Managerial Tasks and Skills: Their Distinguishing Characteristics', *Journal of Management Studies*, Vol. 26, pp. 209-24.

4 The doctor-patient relationship: an essay on the theory of the professions

Michael Kelly and Ian Glover

Introduction

In 1951 Talcott Parsons' The Social System was published (Parsons, 1951). Although it is primarily a work of sociological theory, one of the things that it is best remembered for is the section or essay dealing with the doctor-patient relationship in which Parsons combines an example and a theoretical statement. It might even be suggested that this was the start of medical sociology. Certainly there is a sense in which medical sociology may be seen as a continuing debate with this theoretical statement by Parsons. The essay on the relationship between the doctor and the patient also has much to say to contemporary audiences about the nature and the role of the professions. This chapter reviews this Parsonian contribution and examines the relevance of Parson's work to the contemporary study of professions.

In the nearly fifty years since the original publication, much has been written about the sick role and the doctor role as outlined by Parsons. In the last forty years or so most of what has been written has been critical. This is especially so in the case of British writers. It is perhaps time to reappraise this important contribution, not least because in a post-modern climate in social theory in which the presumed certainties and other errors of structural-functionalism appear no more heinous than the exaggerated claims of Marxism, so that the alleged political biases of Parsons' work can be laid aside and the real purchase of the ideas be considered in detail. The task will be made more interesting by considering the implications of Parson's work for some of the theories of Norbert Elias and Alfred Schutz. We will suggest that between them this trio of writers have provided a means of understanding contemporary developments better than some influential competing ideas.

The Parsonian formulation

The formulation of Parsons' ideas about the sick role and the doctor role are themselves premised on the certain key ideas about professions which in turn form part of a broader account of social systems. For Parsons, the project of *The Social System* was a unified one, so that, for example, he presented his ideas about medicine as an example of the value of his theoretical scheme. The theoretical ideas are complex and are themselves derived from Parsons' understanding of nineteenth century social theory and in particular the work of Pareto, Marshall, Durkheim and Weber (Parsons, 1937). From his interpretations of Durkheim and Weber in particular, Parsons was in a position, in The Social System, to argue that there were a number of patterns of human conduct which allow the analyst to make sense of any human interaction. Parsons called these patterns, which he saw as the things which give society its shape, the pattern variables. The easiest way to think about the pattern variables is to begin by envisaging them as a set of questions which can be asked about any social situation, with the answers to the questions providing a clear theoretical description of the phenomenon from a sociological point of view. Thus the pattern variables are a toolkit which allow the observer of social arrangements to describe them theoretically.

The questions are actually sets of opposites. The questioner asks how much is the phenomenon like one or other of the pair of opposites. This then allows for effective description of real world phenomena which are neither one thing nor the other. However by asking and answering the question the pattern is revealed. There are five pairs of opposites. The first is affectivity versus affective neutrality. This acknowledges the importance of human emotion in social intercourse. The theoretical question is how much is emotion and feeling a part of what is being observed. The second pair is called collectivism versus individualism. This is about the recognition that human social arrangements may be organized for the benefit, however that may be defined, of the many or for the benefit of individuals at the expense of others. People's reasons for doing things may likewise be oriented in one or other of these directions. The third pair is called particularism versus universalism. This is concerned with the fact that some things which humans do have very localized applicability in space, time and culture. Other things that humans become involved in seem to occur wherever societies exist. For example, religious belief is a universal feature of all known societies, although that does not mean that all members of a society hold the same religious beliefs, or indeed any religious beliefs at all. Thus the form and content of religious beliefs vary dramatically across cultures and time and are very specific to particular types of social configuration. The fourth pair are ascription and achievement. They are concerned with the idea that the ways in which people enter into various roles and statuses in any given society may either be on the basis of something they have or have failed to do, that is that it is achieved in some way, while other social positions are attained by virtue of a set of personal characteristics which in some sense are outwith the person's ability to change. Thus one's gender or ethnic group membership are largely given, while one's qualifications are something either attained or not as a consequence of the engagement with the educational system. Finally, social activities and arrangements may be very specific, that is organised towards a very clear end or goal, whereas other actions and arrangements may be much more diffuse in orientation, not so much with no goal or end state in view so much as being related to a variety of end states and goals which may themselves be contradictory. This pair is simply known as specificity versus diffuseness.

Armed with these five pairs of opposites, we can assess any set of human arrangements and make sociological sense of them. In passing, it should be noted that this is but one way of doing sociological analysis, and that there are a large number of other ways of achieving a sociological understanding. However Parsons' theoretical toolbox does provide us with some very interesting insights into the nature of social life, a set of insights which have not infrequently been overlooked, probably because of the ideological nature of some of Parsons' later writings. The central point of The Social System is indeed the section where he turns his attention to the case of modern medicine to demonstrate the power of his ideas.

The discussion of the medical profession in the Social System is itself premised on one other very important assumption which Parsons makes quite explicit. This is that in the contemporary division of labour, professions occupy a particular position by virtue of the technical competence that doctors have in respect of their area of activity. Modern societies are based on the principles of specialisation and competence, and in many of them the professions are a, often the, signal example of this principle. It is also very important to note that the discussion is not just about the medical profession. Parsons is insistent that the relationship between the doctor and the patient that is the focus for this relationship is a social system or rather a sub-system within a broader set of sub-systems and systems, which together make up the whole system of a human society. In this very important sense, the concern is with something dynamic and interactive.

Parsons on the doctor-patient relationship

By using the five pattern variables, the following observations may be made about the doctor-patient relationship. First, the contrast between affectivity and affective neutrality points us to the fact that for the person who is ill the sickness will be invested with a great deal of emotion. They may be in pain or suffering in some other sense, and they may indeed be in fear for their life. For the doctor, however, the relevant phenomena constitute his or her work. The doctor's involvement must be with the pathology rather than with the person's feelings about their illness. The technical competence is protected as the doctor retains an objective detachment from the patient's subjective involvement. By the same token, social distance must be maintained, and the doctor's professional integrity is undermined once the boundary between the doctor and patient changes to that of friend or intimate. This is especially important because medical consultations and medical interventions not infrequently require that patients remove their clothing and that the doctor reaches through internal examination of parts of the body which, if such acts were carried out in other circumstances, could only be defined, at least in Western culture, as sexual acts or as physical assault, or as both. Medicine, both as it was practised when Parsons wrote, and now, breaches social and physical boundaries of the body in ways that are very special and which because of the intimacy involved carry a weight of meanings about privacy and intimacy and indeed sexuality. To protect the patient from abuse and to protect the doctor from the consequences of what they do in the name of medicine, a variety of techniques and meanings are used. The purpose of these is to manage the affectivity-affective neutrality issue.

Parsons made the case that the profession of medicine is organised for the good of society as a whole rather than for the good of individual practitioners. The profession is in this sense outward looking and its activities work on the principle of doing good rather than harm. The practical interventions may be at the individual level, but the end result is the utilitarian one of the greatest happiness of the greatest number. This is the way in which the idea of the collectivism-individualism pair is handled.

The particularism-universalism pattern offers some helpful insights into the doctor-patient relationship. Sickness is a universal feature of all human societies. To be sick is to be human. How particular illnesses are named and the explanations for this deviation from biological normality have very particular cultural and historical content. Likewise the healer role is something which seems to be found universally, but it can nevertheless take a wide variety of historical and cultural forms. The form that the doctor or healer role has taken in modern societies was, and indeed has become increasingly universal through the twentieth century, and this Parsons attributed to the technical efficacy of medicine itself.

The doctor role is an achieved status. Thus in virtually all modern societies there is a very well defined system or systems of medical education and training which are subject to the most exacting standards of control and licensing, and these define who may and who may not practice medicine. Further, there are very strict controls of alternative practitioners or quacks who might attempt to assume knowledge and understanding of the human body and its ills. In modern societies the doctor role is not inherited or a birth-right. Similarly, Parsons argues that being sick is also an achieved status, albeit a negative one. So although the sick role is universalistic and therefore in theory could happen to anyone, becoming sick involves losing something, that is one's health.

Finally, the doctor role is functionally specific rather than diffuse. This means that the things over which the doctor exercises control are specified rigidly through the definition of what is and what is not pathology, and his/her powerful position is guaranteed and because it is based on proven ability and high levels of technical competence, all guaranteed by the role of professional training and licensing. When Parsons was writing there was not, he suggested, an imperative for the medical profession to stray very far outside the boundaries of the pathological in body and mind in order to conduct its work. The limits of medicine were clear and were related to the locatedness of pathology in a clearly delimited sphere.

It is important to note that the doctor role and the sociological implications of it are not to be understood in a vacuum. The doctor role is half of a system and a process of interaction. To appreciate the complexities of the role fully it is important to locate it in this system. The sick role, according to Parsons, has four components in the institutionalized form that it takes in contemporary society. These four elements are two pairs of rights and obligations. The rights are, first, exemption from normal social responsibilities and second, exemption from responsibility for the condition. The exemption from normal social responsibilities is most obvious in respect of the right which is given to workers to absent themselves from occupational duties when sick. Likewise children are allowed to be absent from school if they are unwell. However, there is a more subtle sense in which the exemption applies. This relates to allowances that will be made in respect of ordinary social conduct and assumed social competencies. For example, if someone has a gastric disorder then repeated bouts of vomiting might, indeed will be, seen as an acceptable albeit unpleasant symptom of the condition. Similarly if someone has a head injury, then some disorientation and confusion might well be entirely routine sequelae. However, if someone who is otherwise quite healthy, vomits and appears to be disoriented and confused, and we discover that they have consumed a large quantity of beer, then the same allowances are unlikely to be made. In other words, the person who is sick has certain privileges, which are not granted to others who are not sick, and those privileges are institutionalized in the way in which the care of the sick is organized in modern societies. It follows, of course, that in the case of the head injury or the gastric problem, then no blame for the state of affairs will be applied, whereas the drunk is seen to be culpable and to a large degree responsible for the state of affairs themselves.

In most specific instances it is in many ways a great deal more complicated than that. The head injury might have been caused while the patient was engaged in a robbery and could be the result of a fall from a roof during the crime, the gastric episode may be the result of an action of deliberate self-harm, and if the beer drinker joins Alcoholics Anonymous he or she will learn that alcoholism is a disease and that he or she is sick and in need of help. However the general principle of exemptions allows a clear view of the first of the ideas that Parsons put forward about the sick role.

The second pair of elements relating to the sick role deals with the obligations of those involved. Parsons assumes that the being sick is undesirable. It is unpleasant and painful, or at least uncomfortable. Ordinarily therefore no one would want to be sick. Therefore the first obligation is to want to get well. Unfortunately, argues Parsons, we cannot make ourselves well by an act of will. So we need the expert help of the physician to accomplish that end. So the second obligation is to co-operate with the physician in order to achieve this.

Having set up this ideal of a system to analyze the doctor-patient relationship, Parsons then extends the discussion to consider how the interaction occurs. Two things need to be borne in mind here. First, the pattern variables and the social system of doctor and patient are not to be understood as descriptions of reality. Instead they are constructs which allow an analytic purchase to be made on what is a complex and changing set of relationships. Thus to say simply that the world is not the way that Parsons describes it is an invalid criticism. Parsons' use of these ideas comes much closer to Weberian ideal type analysis, in which the exaggerated elements of a phenomenon are presented to help us to reason about the ways in which real social actors behave, bearing in mind that those social actors have in their minds' eyes sets of constructs to which they orient their actions. The ideal type facilitates the process of verstehen. Verstehen was never a substitute for reality, but Weber (1930) believed that by constructing ideal typifications it was possible to get as close as was analytically possible to actors' motives and understandings. In related vein, when Schutz (1967) referred to the question of shared meanings and to the recipes which people use to understand the world and to act upon, he was assuming an approach to human interaction which acknowledges that people carry round in their heads all kinds of structures and meanings and that the sociologist's task is to articulate these things. Arguably Parsons is engaged in a very similar exercise, and although his pattern variables are not the constructs which people have in their heads, how they should behave when they are ill, and what they can expect from a doctor clearly are a part of their taken for granted worlds. Schutz (1967) argued that the task of the social sciences was to make clear those recipes that people lived their every day lives by, not to create obfuscation. The constructs that give the world meaning to ordinary people he called first order constructs. The doctor role and the sick role are of this order. Where Parsons goes further than Schutz is that he shows how the second order constructs, that is those that only have an existence in the discourse of expert scientists (the pattern variables) generate the first order constructs. Parsons' theoretical tour de force is to bring together two elements in structure and agency and to show how these interrelate. He was of course very familiar with the work of Weber and his account of Weber's ideal types as outlined in The Structure of Social Action (1937), Parsons' other early major theoretical text, was influential in his own analytical thinking.

The second important thing to recognize is that the doctor and sick roles should be read non-normatively. A case can be made that Parsons was running a moral agenda in favour of a conservative medical profession and that his constructs were ideal in the sense of describing how he would like the world to be. Attempts might also be made to dismiss the theoretical schema on the grounds that the ideal types are supportive of the status quo and therefore uninteresting in terms of contemporary theorizing. It should however be the case that if the ideal types are treated as ideal only in the sense of their being theoretically so, then the schema can be used very productively. This will be demonstrated below.

It is important to consider, then, some of the likely points of deviation from the theoretical ideal. It is important to note that Parsons himself was very well aware of these difficulties, and indeed the section of The Social System on the doctor-patient system devotes a great deal of space to these issues. In the first place Parsons notes that although the basis of the professional task, and therefore the underlying need in the relationship, is the technical competence of the doctor, the functional specificity of the role derives from the expertise of the doctor which in turn devolves from the nature of the division of labour in the modern world. Much of the doctor's work is naturally routine and during it the professional task consists of applying routine sets of criteria to well defined problems. However, in some cases the technical expertise is useless. Certain disorders such as degenerative diseases and terminal illness are simply not amenable to any kind of intervention. It is ironic that since Parson's work on the subject, this tension in the work of doctors has become more pronounced. The control of infectious disease has allowed a greater proportion of the population than ever before to survive into old age, and this means that more and more patients present with complaints that medicine as a whole, not just the individual practitioner, but the profession as a whole cannot cure. At the same time the pressure on doctors to 'be able to do something', and the expectation that they will, has entered the common sense assumptions of modern people. Meanwhile the ability of medicine to do much more than to provide palliative care becomes less and less. Medical knowledge is finite at any given time, although constantly changing. Therefore periodically the doctor will run into the limits of medicine. In these cases it is not so much what is written in the textbook which is important, but what is not written in the book. If all that being a member of a profession involved was remembering the large amounts of information in a text, then entry to it would be difficult but subsequent involvement relatively simple. On the other hand, being a useful member of a profession entails being able to apply years of experience to a wide range of different similar cases. In this sense what being a professional is all about is continually, learning and re-learning the ropes at particular points in time. Above all it means being able to work with the presentation of a patient that does not fall into some well defined category, that marks out and defines professional expertise. It is knowing, through years of experience, what is not in the book that is crucial (Fores, Glover and Lawrence, 1991).

The kinds of issue that might arise, therefore, are cases where the patient's condition is uncontrollable and nothing can be done. In these cases it is not so much the limits of medicine, as the limits of the human body itself, that the medical practitioner has to confront. Medicine is not like magic, although we might all at times want it to be. There are limits both to the amount of damage that the human body can sustain, and there are limits to the capacity of the human body that arise as a consequence of the vagaries of the ageing process. There will be gaps in the ability of medicine to deal with that which confronts it. The gaps may be closing, but for the foreseeable future some gaps will remain.

However there is another area where boundary problems arise which are neither contingent on the limits of medical knowledge, nor the limits of the human body. These are the limits of what is medicine at all! The most obvious problematic here is the boundary between psychiatric illness and social deviance. Certainly there are many mental illnesses which are organic in origin and there are many other phenomena which are sometimes called mental illnesses for which drug treatments are said to be effective. The question which arises is: where is the boundary between that which is truly medical, and that which is simply behaviour out of context? Since the publication of The Social System it is certainly the case that the boundary has been pushed further outwards, as the number of mental states which may come under the purview of medicine has grown. All manner of treatments exist for everything from sex changing to unhappiness, from eating disorders to dyslexia. The medical profession and its allies in psychology and counselling have been resoundingly successful in defining all sorts of social phenomena as medicine. But even at these outer reaches of medical imperialism the question must be asked as to the appropriateness of the kinds of expertise that doctors have for this kind of thing. This tendency reaches its most extreme in health promotion in which anything just about can be defined as a health issue and therefore of particular interest to those who might wish to interfere. Health promotion has a profoundly moral, not to say moralistic, approach to these things, and no doubt the world would be a great deal healthier if people did not smoke, if they drank less, and if they took a bit more exercise. At the very least we would have to acknowledge that medical knowledge of these matters is at best uncertain and that medical expertise is no better than say, relevant sociological expertise. So in the sense that to see the doctor as someone whose technical competence is central to his/her role, and whose central role in the affairs of patients is assumed to be appropriate, and whose patients respond and enter the sick role on the basis of trust in this technical competence, is fine so long as the technical competence can be assumed. If it cannot for the good reason that it is just plain uncertain, then a core element in the ideal type is under threat.

Another problem which attaches to the interaction between the doctor and the patient relates to the affectivity of the process. The ideal type assumes that the doctor will maintain an emotional detachment from the patient and their problems. This is linked to the technical side of the occupation. The decision making process is governed by rationality not emotion. On their side of the relationship the patient is strongly involved at an emotional level in what is going on because while for the doctor the interaction is work, for the patient it is their life and their body! As well as the strongly negative affectivity on the part of the patient linked to the undesirability of the patient role itself, to being in pain and discomfort, there are other forces at work which add another level of complexity. This relates to the strength of the attachment that the patient may form for their doctor. This may have its origins in the dependency and helplessness of the patient, or as Parsons himself thought, in the psychodynamics of the encounter. In either case the relationship is not generally a neutral one and therefore real problems of real people interfere with the operation of the ideal.

Of course the assumption that the status of being a patient is in and of itself undesirable, is only absolutely true in the ideal as opposed to the real world of human conduct. As Parsons himself noted, the sick role conferred certain benefits and these might be seen as desirable in themselves. To be exempted from normal social role responsibilities is a favoured status, and one which we might all wish to make use of from time to time. At a more complex level, people might be motivated to achieve the sick role in order to procure other benefits or to manipulate others in their family circle. This too is a very dynamic and complicated set of interactions which the ideal serves to show the potential possibilities. In other words even the anchor point assumptions have to be examined and their typicality considered.

As stated in several places in this chapter already, the system which Parsons described was an interactive one in which the position of the patient was critical. In ideal typical terms, the sick role was institutionalized so as to consist of two rights: not to be held responsible for the condition, and exemption from normal social responsibilities; and two obligations: the obligation to want to get well, and the obligation to cooperate with the physician. The professional is of course in a set of relationships which correspond broadly to this institutionalized set of elements. But the medical practitioner is also in a set of relationships which is broader than that. Medical science addresses the population of people who have a morbidity. Medical science can say something of significance to a whole raft of pathogens and their links to the human body. However it is not possible to match the population of the persons experiencing morbidity to the group of people who are receiving treatment. That is a range of social processes become operative which determine the nature of the entry to the relationship and to the Parsonian system, which are not necessarily linked in a cause and effect way with the technical potential of medical science, with the patient's compliance with the medical regimen, with the desire to get well, or indeed with the likelihood of success of the intervention. These social processes are to a large degree overlooked in Parsons' account. But they do require some further elaboration in order to focus on the modern professional role. So while in any given population there will be a group of persons who are in the institutional sick role, who have a well defined pathology and who are receiving treatment, there will also be other groups who have a pathology who are not receiving treatment, as well as those who are receiving treatment, and who are in the sick role but where no observable pathology exists. In the same population there will be those who have problems which they believe to be serious, but who delay in seeking the available technically competent help. There will be still others who do not immediately present for treatment because their disease is asymptomatic.

There is a large, respected, if rather dated, literature bearing on this issue. It has examined the relationship between seeking help and the presence of symptoms and shown that it is complex. The fact that efficacious treatments exist and that doctors can deploy them is in large measure beside the point. The literature has also shown that the precise point at which a person becomes a patient, the point at which the medical practitioner legitimizes the help seeking rather than treating it as trivial, is a social process as well as a process of diagnosis. Lay people bring all sorts of beliefs and ideas to a consultation, and their help-seeking is guided as much by those beliefs as by any other rationality, including a clinical one or a technical one.

There are two sub-issues here. First, help-seeking as a route to medical treatment involves people taking deliberate actions or deliberately doing something. In doing so they actively promote a particular definition of themselves as in need of care. They have recognized at the common sense level that they cannot do much else about the problem without some technical assistance. This definition does not form an administrative nor a managerial category. It is part of the self-concept of the person seeking help. They are experiencing their own subjectivity as an object outside of themselves, which is not entirely under their control. Therefore help is required. This is a subjective phenomenon which draws upon a set of recipes for action which include the institution of the sick role. Where subjective state meets the formal organization which provides the help-seeker with the label patient, the sick role is formed.

The second sub-issue is that the subjective health and illness experiences which drive the relationship from the patient's perspective are very different to objective clinical measures of pathology. Subjective experience of pain and suffering has personal meanings for the individuals involved and is expressed in a language appropriate for lay people describing subjective feelings. It is very different to the precise language of clinical science. To try to find some common ground as a means delineating the sick role or the doctor role is meaningless. However the attempts to re-order professional practice in a way that is based on the idea of an equality of meanings in a shared discourse is precisely the line of reasoning of much of the UK's Patients' Charter, for example. Much of the criticism of the dominance and power of the medical profession, and that of other professions for that matter, is based on a notion of shared meanings that simply do not stand up to any kind of empirical test.

There is another group of people which do not fit easily in to a simple idea of the relationship between the professional and their client. These are those people who are clinically ill, but who are also well. The person with well-managed diabetes or asthma would fall into this category. In these cases the person has the disease, is fully aware of the fact, and has had to alter their lives accordingly. Thus they have to take their medication, they perhaps have to make special dietary provision, and so on. They visit their medical advisers periodically for repeat prescriptions and routine check-ups. Yet while these people are clearly patients because their doctor is providing care for them, aside from their direct contacts with their medical advisers are they patients at all? They play a variety of social roles, which as long as their diseases are under control, are more important than their occupation of the sick role.

There is a very useful body of knowledge about people with chronic illnesses and the ways in which they interact with medical services. It reveals how some people who have chronic illnesses try to minimise their effects on their lives. In social-psychological terms, the idea of patienthood, and therefore of reliance on or even involvement with the professionals, has very limited salience indeed. It is as if they are saying 'I am me and I happen to have diabetes, but the most important thing about me is the fact that I am a father, a rugby player and someone who enjoys listening to jazz'. The diabetes is incidental to the rest of the person's life. Their social identities beyond their patient status such as father, sister, worker, for example, are much more important than their identity as diabetic. They are someone who, amongst other things, has diabetes. Such studies have also shown that some people let their illnesses flood their lives. For these individuals their sense of who and what they are becomes inextricably bound up with their illness and their patient status. They are Diabetics. In these cases they seem to say, 'I am a diabetic, and the most important thing about me is my diabetes, and I only want to interact with you on the basis of my diabetes'. The key point here is that it is the recipient of care who defines what they are in a process that is to a considerable extent independent of the labels applied by professionals or anybody else for that matter. That process is a social-psychological one. In other words the issue is one of human agency as much as structure with the human agency being shared between the partners involved, but where the meanings and the discourse of the partners may not be shared other than at the intersect of the social construction of the disease itself. Therefore those pundits who have viewed the patient as the powerless dupe of professional conspiracy have missed an important element in the nature of the client-professional relationship. It is not so much that there are different types of relationship between doctors and patients which may labelled as more or less equal, as the parties involved have quite different reasons for being in the relationship at all and that this is the governing factor in the way the patient approaches their engagement with their physician. This is not either a feature that arises as a consequence of the rise of Patient Charters, consumerism or any of the other relatively recent manifestations of the client-professional relationship. This ability of the patient to define the relationship in any away they choose to, is a feature of this institution since the emergence of the medical profession itself. It had to fight to obtain its legal monopoly powers, it was shunned by all but the weakest and poorest in society for generations, and a private world of scepticism and downright hostility to the ministrations of doctors is a thread running through fiction and working class life for at least the last couple of hundred years. The general public has not on the whole been naively manipulated by a powerful profession and probably most lay people most of the time keep a healthy distance from their doctors until they have no alternative but to seek assistance, and even then it is a highly contingent assistance. Of course the problem of non-compliant patients, for which read sceptical patients, is well documented in the literature, as is the submerged portion of the clinical iceberg who do not seek out treatment when they have some kind of pathology. Medical sociology and health psychology have constructed these people as problems. The sceptical enquirer should perhaps ask for whom do such people cause problems?

The next related point concerns so-called appropriate and inappropriate patients. This has been a long-running theme in the medical sociological, psychological, general practice and nursing literatures (Kelly and May, 1981). The original argument was that lay health beliefs did not correspond to medical ones. Consequently some patients defined themselves as ill when they were not and presented 'trivia' or 'rubbish' to their medical practitioners and wasted much valuable medical time (Jeffrey, 1979, Balint, 1957). There have been several responses to this view. Some sociologists have regarded patients being labelled in this way as a not very subtle and rather disagreeable form of social control (Lorber, 1975). Some nurses have taken a high moral tone, and condemned the apparent lack of professionalism involved in negative patient labelling (Armitage, 1980). Still others have seen it as little more than more and better patient education being required.

However each of these responses is beside the point in some way. Inappropriate presentations will always be part of medical practice, whatever sifting mechanisms are devised to ration the number of such consultations. This is because the practitioners' tasks diagnostically are precisely those of discriminating between the important and the trivial and making some sense of patient behaviour that does not correspond to the ideal type descriptions of pathology found in medical textbooks (May and Kelly, 1982). Moreover good preventive care is to a large extent based on the idea that by screening a group in the population cases will be identified. There will be many more negative than positive cases and so by definition preventive work involves seeing many people who have nothing wrong with them. The same principle applies in reverse in the patients who seek reassurance when there is no pathology present. In any case the fact is that in any people processing organization, be it a hospital or a supermarket or a school, the people, the employees of the organization, have to employ various devices to organize and to prioritise their work. There may well be procedures like triage, with very clear protocols as to how the prioritisation should be done, but inevitably informal systems of organizational management will come into play. The labelling of patients is one such device, and is an inevitable part of the organizational dynamics of a medical setting. To criticise it as unprofessional is to miss one of the most significant things about the nature of any work that involves dealing with the general public.

This reaches its most difficult problem with health promotion. Here the object is to get people who think that they have nothing wrong with them, to attend a health check session and to act as if they were a patient. Some of those attending will indeed be identified as having medical problems and will assume the sick role proper. The doctor carries out the doctoring function on non-patients. This is a rather odd way for the professional to behave. After all, what other professional group actually spends time and effort in trying to stop people using their services? Health promotion is of course a relatively modern phenomenon at least in the way described here. However the role of the physician as the preventer of illness is actually a very old one indeed.

Patienthood, as opposed to the ideal typical sociological concept of the sick role, is not synonymous with the presence of symptoms and signs of disease, the experience of illness, or trivial presentations. Well people make use of the health services. This is especially and appropriately so in the fields of disease prevention and health promotion. Thus someone who attends a clinic to be immunized, or someone who attends for screening or a health check is a patient, strictly speaking. But they are also all the other roles that they occupy in life and the patienthood will have a very low salience for them so long as the check does not reveal anything serious. In trying to think of a different word to describe the other half of the relationship with the doctor the term client is a possibility. But even this does not capture the intrinsic nature of the issues involved. There is an interesting curiosity about the patient in this situation. Not only are they not in the sick role, they are in a kind of anti-sick role in the sense that the objective of their being in the relationship at all is that they are trying, or the medical services are trying on their behalf to prevent them occupying the role in the first place. There can be few other professional roles where the professional activity of the professional, or at least some of it, involves trying to stop that which defines the professional role in the first place. The professional as anti-professional is the outcome. Of course the argument can be made that the preventive role has always been part of the doctor role, it is just that it has expanded and professionalised a great deal since Parson's original essay, and that this preventive function and the patient involvement with it, can be encompassed within the theory. Alternatively the argument can be made that this anti-professional role is a fundamental departure, at least in its contemporary scope and scale, and that a new role is required to encompass what the patient is involved in during such a relationship.

Perhaps the key to understanding this is to consider the patient's perspective on this. Do they feel like patients? Does the setting of health promotion work, where the preventive work usually takes place, make the person feel like they are a patient after all? Does the whole paraphernalia of health promotion create legions of the worried well? To what extent does the user of health promotion services take advantage of them by saying, metaphorically at least, 'While I'm here doctor, would you mind having a look at ...?'.

The archetypal doctor-patient relationship, as depicted in the medical and social scientific literature, is that of a sick person dependent on expert doctors. This indeed is at the very heart of the Parsonian system, and is central to most understandings of professional engagement with clients across a broad span of occupations. It is argued that such relationships may be authoritarian or they may be more like a partnership between equals, but in the final analysis, it is the doctor's expertise and the patient's need of help which is the defining characteristic of the relationship. Very clearly the kinds of relationship which exist between customers and vendors, consumers and providers, or even between such clients and professionals as house purchasers and solicitors, are rather different to this. There are elements of dependence in all of these relationships. However they tend to be of different orders of magnitude and quality to that between the doctor and patient, not least because they are dominated and mediated through a cash nexus. There is usually a much greater degree of emotional involvement, at least from the recipient's point of view, in the doctor-patient relationship than in the other types of relationship mentioned here.

Consumer organizations and movements, including those given public and administrative form in the Patient's Charter, make strong cases for greater equality between doctors and their patients. There is a strong sense in which much of this smacks of middle class articulateness and a pseudo-sociological critique of doctors. The extent to which the population at large wants to be an equal with their doctor in matters of medicine, as opposed to matters of politeness and civility, is an empirical question. It is certainly clear in this context that Parson's ideal type as a representation of people's experience of social reality, and their aspirations in dealing with their doctor, has enduring theoretical relevance. Where some additional thought needs to be given to the theoretical constructs relates to the familiar issue of the presence of professional within a bureaucracy.

In the United Kingdom, and in most advanced societies, health services are delivered in public or private bureaucracies. These are set up and they function along the principles of internal differentiation and specialization. There is a division of labour within which there are relatively clear lines of authority, responsibility, command and authority. This was true of the UK's National Health Service and it remains true in the reformed post-1990 Health Service. It is also true of individual hospitals. Like any other organizations, they are more or less efficient in what they do.

However, there are some tasks which bureaucracies are quite good at, at least in Western societies. The processing of large numbers of people who have a vast range of different individual and often idiosyncratic characteristics is something which bureaucracies handle quite well. If nothing else, the sheer size and the need for virtually universal territorial coverage, makes bureaucracy the logical, rational and necessary system of organization for a health service or, on a smaller scale, a hospital. This is not to say that bureaucracies do everything well, but it is to say that they are the most appropriate form of organization for many of the functions required in a modern society.

However, it is also inevitably the case that at the point at which bureaucracies intersect with the general public there is always and inevitably a tension. This is between the rules and rationalities of the bureaucracy and the lay ideas of the members of the public. In some cases this does not matter. For example, the Armed Forces have a code enforceable by law which renders their bureaucratic rules supreme. Thus in the days of conscription, just because the recruit did not accept that the army had rights to conscript him, did not stop the Army from so doing. In contrast, it is not usually like that with medical services. With the exception of certain areas of psychiatric, geriatric and paediatric medicine, there is an assumption enshrined in practices such as informed consent, that while the bureaucracy may have certain rules and procedures, users are only bound by them if they voluntarily submit to them. It is, in other words, a relationship of legitimate authority with the patient acknowledging explicitly, in informed consent, or implicitly, by allowing medical treatment to continue, the right of the bureaucracy to exercise superordination.

This is the key dilemma or issue that concerns us here, and for which Parsons' approach is so relevant. The doctor is the expert, and has considerable authority vested in his or her role, but the patient is, in the final analysis, if not in most everyday instances of doctor-patient interaction, a free and equal agent who can almost always choose to disobey 'doctor's orders'. This much is apparent from what we have written so far, drawing on Parsons' explanations of the doctor-patient relationship.

The sociology of the professions

Traditionally, the sociology of occupations (that of professions) has tended to see an occupation as something determined by and intrinsic to the nature of its tasks. Thus train drivers drive trains. However a different emphasis was introduced by Johnson (1972) when he argued that the control and organization of tasks defines the nature of occupations and professions – a more politicized and ostensibly more subtle emphasis. Nevertheless both the traditional approach and Johnson's modification of it use a very modernist emphasis on task, function and structure.

A genuinely alternative approach or strand in the sociology of occupations and professions has long co-existed with the traditional one. This draws partly on the Chicago approach to the sociology of occupations and partly on phenomenology (cf. Schutz, 1967, and Peter Berger's *The Human Shape of Work*, 1964). This argues that the nature of occupations is based much more on that of the relationships, especially the face to face ones, that people experience as they go about work. So occupations and professions differ because shop assistants, dentists, prostitutes, doctors, architects and so on and their customers or clients act in specific different ways towards each other. So it is not only selling goods, drilling teeth, lying on beds and so on, which ultimately determine the nature of occupations, but also what passes between all of the people involved in general, and by what passes between people as insiders and as outsiders in particular. Examples of insiders would be dentists and dental nurses, and managers and secretaries.

With professional occupations in particular, individual practitioners such as doctors or engineers, identify themselves very strongly as such, and it is their relationships with colleagues, peers, patients, and so on which distinguish their activities most powerfully. This viewpoint is not only, following Johnson (1972) about control, it is also, and far more importantly, about 'being', about concepts of self in the heads of participants. This 'life world' (Schutz, 1967) contains a series of concentric circles, like layers, with the inner ones those of immediate relevance, for example doctors dealing with patients and nurses or engineers working with technicians and secretaries. The outer zones of relevance are the farther concentric circles, containing such phenomena as professional associations, media portrayals, politicians interested in the National Health Service, and so on. The micro world of the professional is the inner layers, and the outer ones link him or her to their macro world or social structure.

Here lies the important link referred to at the start of this chapter, with the ideas of Elias (1994). In *The Civilising Process* Elias argued that it is changes in the micro world that lead to changes in the macro social structure, that it is generally mistaken to look for the origins of social change and development in broader social-structural and socioeconomic forces, and that it is much more sensible to look at changes in the everyday social behaviour of individuals and in the meanings of the occupations and professions that they inhabit to them. How, we should ask, following Elias, do particular professionals and others render what they do meaningful? How do occupational members construct and reconstruct their social worlds over time? Exploring these small-scale worlds helps us to interpret the broader process of social change.

Discussion and conclusion

The arguments outlined above help us to understand how recent changes in the doctor-patient relationship are affecting the meanings of the activities of being a doctor, patient or other person involved in a professional-client relationship. Parsons' theorizing is particularly important for understanding them as evolving relationships and types of interaction, rather than in the technologically determinist sense used by Johnson and the more traditional writers on professions and occupations.

The relevance of all of the above for understanding the broader implications of the changes to the doctor-patient relationship in the UK's National Health Service (NHS) in recent times concerns our concepts of the public and the private. Parsons stressed the central importance and the variability of this relationship in health care. Schutz helps us to understand how shared and other meanings influence action and how both evolve in everyday life and Elias tell us how powerful the effects of such apparently small scale events and forces can be in the context of grand social change.

In his well-known and popular account of professions and of the social conditions that give rise to them, Johnson (1972, p. 45) argued that a 'profession is not, then, an occupation but a means of controlling an occupation'. We understand his emphasis but find it misplaced. We think of a profession both as a senior or higher-status type of occupation and of professionalism (notably in the main English-speaking countries) as a means of controlling and developing such occupations and their relationships with their clients, customers, patrons and others involved with them. We think that Johnson's account of professions thus tends to be one-sided through its desire to downplay the value of earlier and politically more uncritical (from a left-wing perspective) accounts such as those of Parsons, which had tended to go towards the opposite extreme by implicitly exaggerating the cooperative features of professions and professionalism. We find the essence of both Johnson's and that of Parsons' approaches to be both acceptable and compatible.

Regarding the medical profession in the NHS in the UK, Johnson (1972, pp. 77-78) uses arguments which would appear to define its clients and the consumers of its services on the basis of their citizenship. We find the notion of citizenship by far the most satisfactory for defining and understanding the role of the consumer of NHS services in general and of the patient of the NHS doctor in particular. We see the patient as citizen, as an active, functioning member of society, as the ultimate, or near-ultimate, depending on one's theology, source of medical authority. However we also see the citizen as rationally and/or perforce submitting himself or herself to that authority at appropriate times in order to be cured and/or cared for. As a citizen the patient is the equal of the doctor, but he or she is not a doctor and the exercise of authority in the doctor-patient relationship is inevitably a variable feast, as Parsons explained.

Johnson (1972, p. 89) also suggested that mass affluence and mass consumption were major threats to collegial professional authority and that consumer movements and 'communalism' would exert 'client control' over professions. Such trends might swamp the gentlemanly ethos and image of the more collegial professions like those of academic, doctor or lawyer. We suspect that this argument was also taken a little too far by Johnson, with form being overemphasized at the expense of substance. We regard the imposition of managerial(ist) controls over doctors in the NHS in and after the 1980s, through general management, the assertion of patients' rights, and the development of internal markets and the purchaser-provider split, as something of an over-reaction to the excesses of medical dominance and as somewhat excessive in themselves. As we have argued elsewhere (Kelly and Glover, 1996) doctors and other NHS professionals ought to learn how to manage the Service themselves in a different kind of socioeconomic context to that of the 1940s and 1950s, rather than submit to management by the fashionably expert but medically inexpert.

References

Armitage, S. (1980), 'Non-compliant Recipients of Health Care', *Nursing Times*, Vol. 76, pp. 1-3.

Balint, M. (1957), *The Doctor, The Patient and the Illness*, Pitman, London.

Berger, P. (1964), *The Human Shape of Work*, Collier-Macmillan, New York.

Elias, N. (1994), *The Civilizing Process: The History of Manners and State Formation and Civilization*, Trans. G. Jephcott, Blackwell, Oxford.

Fores, M., Glover, I. and Lawrence, P. (1991), 'Professionalism and Rationality: A Study in Misapprehension', *Sociology*, Vol. 25, No. 1, pp. 79-100.

Glover, I.A. and Lawrence, P.A. (1998), 'In Search of Mediocrity: Historic Antecedents of Managerial Incompetence', conference on The History of British Management 1945 to 1990, Business History Unit, London School of Economics.

Jeffrey, R. (1979), 'Normal Rubbish: Deviant Patients in Casualty Departments', *Sociology of Health and Illness*, Vol. 1, pp. 98-107.

Johnson, T. (1972), *Professions and Power*, Macmillan, London.

Kelly, M.P. and Glover, I.A.(1996), 'In Search of Health and Efficiency: the NHS 1948-94', in J.W. Leopold, I.A. Glover and M.D. Hughes (eds), *Beyond Reason? The National Health Service and the Limits of Management*, Avebury, Aldershot.

Kelly, M.P. and May, D. (1982), 'Good and Bad Patients: A Review of the Literature and a Theoretical Critique', *Journal of Advanced Nursing*, Vol. 7, pp. 147-56.

Lorber, J. (1975), 'Good Patients and Problem Patients: Conformity and Deviance in a General Hospital', *Journal of Health and Social Behaviour*, Vol. 16, pp. 313-25.

May, D. and Kelly, M.P. (1982), 'Chancers, Pests and Poor Wee Souls: Problems of Legitimation in Psychiatric Nursing', *Sociology of Health and Illness*, Vol. 4, pp. 279-301.

Parsons, T. (1937), *The Structure of Social Action*, Free Press, New York.

Parsons, T. (1951), *The Social System*, Routledge & Kegan Paul, London.

Schutz, A. (1967), *The Phenomenology of the Social World*, Trans. G. Walsh and F. Lehnert, North Western University Press, Evanston, Illinois.

Weber, M. (1930), *The Protestant Ethic and the Spirit of Capitalism*, Trans. T. Parsons, Unwin, London.

Part III

Public Sector Professions

5 Public professionals or public servants? Making sense of UK local government professional bodies' codes of ethics

Charles Booth

Introduction

Since the 1960s, an unparalleled growth has occurred in the number of professional codes of practice, conduct and ethics (Harris, 1989). This has been due to a range of factors, including a growth in the number of professions, a growing interest in the fields of business, professional and administrative ethics, and increasing public and political criticism of some professions. As a result of this last factor in particular, there has arisen an unprecedented level of tension between the demands for professional accountability voiced by the public and the quest for autonomy pursued by professions (Frankel, 1989). The response to increasing criticism of the professions is arguably the most powerful driving force behind the move to codify professional values in this way, and this criticism has been mirrored by a sustained attack on the management of the public sector in general and of local government in particular. Given the high incidence of professional specialization in local government it may be expected that the relevant professions will respond to these criticisms through their codes, as well as seeking other means of lobbying for the causes which, arguably, justify their existence (Taylor, 1992).

The literature contains little empirical research on professions in local government (Laffin, 1986), and even less on their professional codes. The relevant literature that does exist is mainly concerned with establishing the theoretical principles which surround the ethical management and provision of public services, with considering how best these might be expressed, and with arguing whether or not professional codes are an appropriate forum for such expression. This paper seeks to extend empirical knowledge, while remaining firmly rooted in this theoretical hinterland.

The paper briefly reviews the position of the professions in UK local government, and as an example includes a short case study of the leisure profession. The literature on professional codes is also reviewed, with specific reference to public sector professions. A number of research questions and hypotheses are derived from these introductory reviews and are explored further in the empirical section of the paper, which reports the results of a content analysis of selected UK local government codes. To develop the analysis further, some of these codes are then compared with codes for public service professionals in the US and Canada, with a view to determining whether other professional bodies have adopted different principles and approaches, and whether there exists scope for mutual learning. In order to fulfil the stated purpose of developing the theoretical literature while also advancing empirical knowledge, the paper concludes with a series of broad recommendations for the revision of UK local government professional codes and highlights areas for further research.

Professions and professionals in UK local government

Local government in the United Kingdom, unlike some other areas of the public sector, has a long history of professionalism. Professionalism has been described as one of the 'most significant features of British local government' (Laffin, 1986, p. 1). While in the Civil Service specialist professionals have always been regarded with some suspicion and have traditionally been marginalized (Metcalfe and Williams, 1990), the local government officer cadre continues, although to a lesser extent than previously, to be dominated by professionals.

At the risk of being simplistic, it may be as well to rehearse the most important functions of UK local government. Despite very significant recent changes, the primary function of local authorities continues to relate to their service responsibilities. These may be discharged in a number of different ways: by provision, by purchase, by regulation and by facilitation. Thus, a local authority may directly provide a housing service, may purchase a refuse service from a contractor, may regulate the behaviour of other agencies in the provision of goods and services (under environmental health legislation, for example) and may facilitate via grants, loans or other means the provision of a service by voluntary agencies or the private sector (for example, loans to housing associations). Secondary functions, often but not necessarily undertaken in order to support primary service responsibilities, include planning (strategic or service), resource acquisition, internal organization and management, and accountability and review (Leach and Stewart, 1992). Professionals will be involved in all these functions.

It is, however, unhelpful to assume that all these professions are homogeneous. Henry (1993, pp. 110-12) distinguishes between what he terms 'liberal welfare semi-professions', such as social work, planning and teaching, from 'industrial semi-professions', such as accounting, engineering and surveying. Laffin (1986, p. 23) similarly distinguishes between 'public service' professions and 'technobureaucratic' professions, with the former mainly concerned with the front-line delivery of services to clients, and the latter with the management and administration of large public bureaucracies.

Neither view adequately captures the richness and diversity of reality, and should be overlaid with the realization that street level bureaucrats, whatever their profession, may have more in common with each other than with their professional colleagues managing them, and vice versa. Thus, a surveyor dealing directly with council tenants is likely to have more affinity with her housing management colleagues than with the Chief Surveying Officer. Similarly, a Director of Social Services may very well have more in common with the Director of Finance than with her front line social workers. This position is underlined by the development of associations outwith the main professional bodies whose membership is determined by status rather than profession (such as the Society of Local Authority Chief Executives), or by status as well as profession (such as the Society of County Treasurers). Nevertheless, it is appropriate to hold on to the notion of a broad distinction between professions whose purpose is directly to serve a client public (such as housing, social work, teaching and so on), and others to whom the link is less direct and whose primary function is to serve the employer authority (accountants, lawyers, administrators, etc.).

From whence do these local government professions derive their position? Professionalism first arose in local government during the nineteenth century, partly as a deliberate counterweight to local corruption and to what was felt to be the pernicious effect of local interests. As services accrued to local authorities, the growth of professions continued in parallel, with, for example, the creation of the Association of Women Housing Managers in 1916, the Town Planning Institute in 1919, and the Institute of Baths and Recreation Management in 1921. With the creation of the Welfare State, major new responsibilities attached to local government such as planning, education and so on, and new professional bodies accompanied this growth. During the 1960s, the professions, although challenged by the new impetus towards local corporatism, came to dominate policy making in local councils; a position assisted by such diverse influences as service growth, cental government sponsorship, and the growing stability and influence of the two-party political system, which provided ideological clarity and helped to remove, or at least insulate local policy making from, uncertainty and disruption in the local political environment (Laffin and Young, 1990).

This growth of influence depended on the acceptance of professional power by national, and particularly, local politicians. This acceptance was premised on the reconciliation of two factors; the exclusive competence claimed by the professions, and the countervailing commitment made by professionals to the public good - in other words a tension similar, but not identical, to that between the professional's demand for autonomy and the public's demand for accountability. These notions of competence and commitment have been interpreted in a number of ways by professionals themselves. Competence implies not only the notion of exclusive professional knowledge, but also a claim to managerial and political competence. Similarly, commitment implies not only a commitment to the public interest in a general sense, but commitment to a particular service, such as housing or planning. In addition the notion implies commitment to local democracy and this element underlies the rhetoric of political neutrality and responsibility towards the authority as a whole rather than solely to members of the majority group (Laffin and Young, 1990).

However, despite these arguments, professionals in local government have faced an unprecedented attack since the late 1970s. The reasons for this are complex and it is intended here to give no more than a brief outline. They include: the increasing polarization of political parties and the change in membership of parties at a local level; changing demands and approaches of the new local authority members; changing ideologies in British politics; and demographic and cultural changes among the British population.

Further reasons include: the growth of new policy areas in local government towards which traditional professional skills and approaches were deemed to be unsuited; the patent failure of some policy solutions advanced by professionals in the 1960s; the change in approaches to recipients of services from clients to customers, and the rise of consumerism; the increasing rigidity of professional boundaries leading to inflexibility, lack of mutual learning and glaring problems of coordination of services; the increasing disparity between professional accountability mechanisms and those demanded by politicians and the public; the implications of public expenditure constraints, increased visibility of policy making, and an increase in the number (and degree of influence) of stakeholders, and the consequent risks of implementation failure; and the questioning of professional solutions and claims to competence from within the professions themselves (Elcock, 1983; Gyford, 1991; Laffin and Young, 1990; Towey, 1985).

The professions were therefore assailed from several different directions - government, clients, employers and internally - and their claims to both competence and commitment severely challenged. It is unlikely that they will ever regain their previous dominance, and it is difficult to find any support for the argument that they should do so. It can be argued that the single most important factor underlying this decline, apart from the fundamental policy mistakes that raised very severe questions as to competence, was the fundamental disparity between professional values and those of their various publics. In fact, the policy mistakes themselves were a product of this problem.

In order to highlight some of the more useful issues concerning professionalism, professionalization and professional values, it is intended to present a short case study of the leisure profession in local government.

The leisure profession - a brief case study

In many respects, leisure is the newest local government profession. Although the Institute of Baths and Recreation Management was founded in 1921, it was not until 1983 that a broadly coherent and unified professional body of leisure managers was created, with the formation of the Institute of Leisure and Amenity Management - although it should be noted that the Institute of Baths and Recreation Management continues to resist calls for amalgamation and remains the Institute of Leisure and Amenity Management's main competitor. Newer local authority services that developed in the 1980s have remained unprofessionalised (for example, economic development services), and, given the present political climate, it is possible that leisure will remain the 'youngest profession' for the foreseeable future.

To what extent, however, is leisure a 'typical' local government profession? On the one hand, the range of local authority services and the *ad hoc* nature of their development over time, has meant that the status and nature of local authority professions differ enormously.

The leisure profession may therefore be agreed to be as typical as any other - in other words, it is typical because it is atypical. On the other hand, it does appear that the profession shares certain broad characteristics with some, if not all, other local government professions. Henry (1993) argues that the development of the leisure profession mirrors that of other liberal welfare models, although as the market orientation of leisure provision has become more important, the identity of the profession has become the subject of tension and ideological struggle. Similarly, of the two groups identified by Laffin (1986), the leisure profession qualifies as a public service profession rather than otherwise, although it should be noted that the distinction, never clear cut, is becoming increasingly blurred with the growing trend towards financial decentralization and the designation of individual facilities as profit-centres.

Prior to the establishment of the Institute of Leisure and Amenity Management in 1983, there existed a variety of professional bodies in the leisure field (Bacon, 1989), notably the Institute of Baths and Recreation Management (founded in 1921), the Institute of Parks and Recreation Management (1926), the Institute of Municipal Entertainers (1947), the Association of Recreation Managers (1969) and the Institute of Recreation Managers (1969). Most of these bodies had a membership of less than 2,000, and in some cases much lower. In addition, a myriad of even smaller bodies and associations represented members working in even more tightly defined specialist fields.

The reasons for amalgamation are varied and complex (and as has been noted, insufficiently persuasive to ensure that a completely unified professional body was established). First, it was considered that economies of scale could be achieved through amalgamation, particularly as the fragmentation of the profession meant that it was largely unrepresented in policy-making at a national or local level. This was not necessarily perceived as a critical issue prior to the 1960s, when there was little sustained political interest in leisure issues. However, this changed as leisure became an important social activity, and as competition for resources and influence among interest groups generally became more intense. The fragmentation and insularity of the leisure profession prevented appropriate or effective engagement in the political debate (Bacon, 1989).

Second, prior to the reorganization of local government in 1974, the provision of leisure facilities by local authorities primarily took place under the auspices of other, larger, departments. The leisure profession was usually defined in terms of its technical characteristics (Houlihan, 1988). The 1973 Cobham Report recommended the bringing together of the disparate leisure, baths, parks, and sports activities under one departmental roof, and most district authorities chose to do so during the 1974 reorganization (Henry, 1993).

Third, the late 1970s saw the formation of the Yates Committee, which was set up to investigate ways of improving the quality of recreation management generally and the training and career development opportunities of recreation managers generally. The Committee was critical of the fragmentation of the profession and recommended that the existing bodies should attempt to establish a single professional institute for leisure and recreation managers (Houlihan, 1988), with a view to supporting the evolution of a 'comprehensive, unified and multi-disciplinary profession', and a 'credible profession with status' (Recreation Management Training Committee, 1984, p. 96). The final report was, ironically, published a few months after the formation of the Institute of Leisure and Amenity Management.

The historical background of the amalgamation and the processes of professional formation give rise to a number of interesting issues. It seems clear that the complex and politically charged process of amalgamation absorbed an enormous amount of energy, with the effect that policy issues were neglected. This is highlighted by a statement by a leisure professional given in Bacon (1989, p. 71), which is worth quoting at some length:

The big problem is that we already seem to have lost out on the big issue:

> 'What business are we really in?' The overriding emphasis has been a constitutionalism, of getting the legalities and mechanisms of the Institute together, and of late on training and education, and of deciding how to allow new members in the club and who to keep out. The problem has been that other key questions concerning the role of leisure in society, 'What are we really trying to do in our job?' have been omitted or addressed at a relatively superficial level.

Second, the main reasons and advantages for amalgamation put forward by the Yates Committee (and presumably advocated by professionals themselves) concern the meeting of professional needs, rather than the needs of national leisure policy, the general public, or of the clients and customers of the leisure service (Houlihan, 1988). Third, while the leisure profession has generally avoided the public and political obloquy attached to other professions, notably planners, engineers and architects (indeed, it appears remarkable that the strengthening of professional power seems to have been accepted if not welcomed by central government), it has not been able to escape the effects of the financial and ideological constraints placed on local government. As local authorities have been forced to embrace (some more willingly than others) a more explicit market orientation, so the funding, nature and rationale of leisure provision has shifted.

Henry (1993, pp. 24-25) describes the policy succession: from leisure as a welfare service and mode of social consumption in the 1960s and early 1970s; to the emergence of leisure as a tool for economic rather than social transformation, with provision dominated by market forces and the private sector in the late 1980s. As a result, the profession is struggling to contain the tension between its heritage as an instrument of social provision, and its environment dominated by economic rationality and efficiency - 'it remains to be seen whether such a tension can be managed within a single organization' (Henry, 1993, p. 113).

Fourth, successive writers have pointed to the failure of the Institute of Leisure and Amenity Management to express any 'clear sense of morality and mission in providing recreational objectives' (Bacon, 1989, p. 78), largely because of the difficulties of doing so and of simultaneously satisfying a diverse and powerful set of stakeholders. Coalter (1986) refers to the need (and hitherto, by implication, the failure to do so) for the profession to establish a social purpose. The Yates Committee argued for the importance of developing a coherent philosophy and set of values for the leisure service. On a slightly different point Houlihan (1988) raises concerns regarding the diminution of the role of the public in professionally dominated policy areas, and points to the potentially very damaging tensions between professional and client definitions of need. The clear implication is that a strong sense of values is not enough, particularly if those values are to be determined by professional self-interest rather than by ethical principles of altruism, collaboration and public service. One way in which professions might seek to enshrine such principles is through the adoption of codes of ethics, practice and conduct.

Professional codes

On one level, it is useful to use the term 'professional codes' as a shorthand for codes of practice, conduct and ethics established by professional bodies. However, some conceptual clarity in defining such codes is also required. Unfortunately, such clarity is not easily to be found in the literature. For example, Hendler (1991, p. 157) distinguishes between codes of ethics, which comprise 'visionary statements regarding the normative and ethical aspects of the profession'; and codes of conduct, which contain more detailed guidelines for appropriate professional behaviour, including professional competence and conflicts of interest. This distinction is absent from other treatments, such as Kernaghan (1980), where conflict of interest is seen as a primary ethical issue confronting public administrators, and is therefore at the heart of effective public service codes of ethics. Indeed, he refers elsewhere (Kernaghan, 1993) to the conflict of interest question being the *sole* issue in some US codes.

Harris (1989) points out that professional bodies themselves are apt to use the different terms interchangeably and in overlapping ways. However, he claims to discern some broad patterns, in that codes of ethics generally consist of brief statements of normative ethical principles, and codes of conduct refer to more detailed and specific statements, sometimes expanding or clarifying the application of ethical principles in specific circumstances. Codes of practice, on the other hand, often contain a more detailed description of technical standards to which professional work is to conform, and it is suggested that these codes are primarily for the benefit of the client rather than the guidance of the professional, in that they establish what the client may have a right to expect. This approach is echoed by L'Etang (1992, p. 737), who states that codes of ethics are 'easily distinguished from the more legalistic prudential/technical codes of practice and conduct'.

This is all rather unsatisfactory, particularly given the actual use of the terminology by the professions themselves. While the sample taken for the purposes of this research is too small to permit generalization, it may very well be the case that these kinds of conceptual definitions represent an exercise in futility. Among the organizations contacted for the purposes of this research, only one termed its professional code a code of ethics (or rather a 'Guideline on Ethics for Institute Members'). Again, only one professional association called its code a code of practice. One body had two codes: a 'code of ethics' solely focused on the conflict of interest question, and a 'code of conduct' dealing with other issues. One body had a 'code of conduct' for individual members and a 'code of practice' for corporate members.

It may be more useful, therefore, to distinguish between codes in other ways, for example by using the continua developed by Kernaghan (1980) and by Frankel (1989). Kernaghan depicts codes as lying on a continuum represented at one end by what he calls 'The Ten Commandments Approach' and at the other by 'The Justinian Code Approach'. The former approach represents a brief statement of broad ethical principles, without any provisions for monitoring or enforcement. The latter approach, on the other hand, represents a comprehensive and detailed coverage of both principles and administrative arrangements. Most codes will combine elements of both models.

Frankel's approach is rather more sophisticated. He identifies three conceptually distinct types of code along a continuum, while acknowledging that individual codes may include features of all three types. The first type of code is aspirational, comprising a normative statement of ideals towards which professionals are expected to strive. The second type he terms educational, and this type attempts to develop and interpret key ethical statements by including detailed commentary on the principles expressed by the code. The third type is regulatory, with detailed provisions regarding the conduct of members of the profession, backed up by an explicit system of sanctions.

The model may be further developed, however. It may be expected that codes will differ in their primary focus - in other words whether they are primarily aimed at promoting or safeguarding the interests of the client, community or general public; of the employer or of colleagues; or of the profession itself. By combining these elements with the Frankel continuum, it is possible to construct a matrix upon which professional codes may be plotted (see Figure 5.1). It should be acknowledged that the model has some shortcomings - particularly in the case of those professions who operate in private practice, or who are self-employed. In other cases; the employer will also be the client. Nevertheless, it is considered that the model is sufficient to bear the analysis. It is not expected that professional codes will be evenly distributed across the matrix. By definition, regulatory codes may be expected to have as their primary focus the interests of the profession, or perhaps of the employer, although it is possible that the public interest may also be a focus. Aspirational codes, on the other hand, are far more likely to focus on the client or the public interest. The type and focus of professional codes, however, begs the question of their function and purpose. It is useful to distinguish here between explicit purposes and implicit, perhaps unstated, functions, although one profession's function may be another's purpose. This distinction is often ignored in the literature (see for example Frankel, 1989; Harris, 1989; Taylor, 1992) but it is worth making in order to distinguish, in some cases, voiced rhetoric (means) from unvoiced reality (ends).

Professional codes may have a number of different purposes, some of which may be explicit in the codes themselves. It should be stressed that not all have equal weight as far as individual professions are concerned, that some overlap, and that some may be mere window dressing. They include: the promotion of ethical, and deterrence of unethical behaviour; the governance of professional conduct generally (implying technical and prudential standards); the provision of a written benchmark against which ethical or other professional problems may be measured, and the provision of assistance to professionals in making ethical judgements; the legitimation of the imposition of sanctions for unethical or unprofessional conduct; the making of a commitment to professional and moral development; the establishment of common (or explicitly differentiated) rights and responsibilities among the members of a profession; the provision of mechanisms for adjudication and resolving disputes, for example between a professional and a client; and the statement of principles, mission or purpose of a profession - or in other words the cause it professes to serve (Frankel, 1989; Harris, 1989; Kernaghan, 1993; Taylor, 1992).

Underlying functions of codes include the development of protective mechanisms against public criticism; the creation of a social contract between the profession and its publics (clients, employers, fellow professions and so on); the communication of expectations of professional roles and responsibilities to clients and employers; the expression of professional identity, allegiance and solidarity; the enhancement of the profession's reputation and thereby its status and autonomy; the legitimization of professional norms; the preservation of professional bias via the socialization function represented by the code; and the creation of a support system for individual professionals to resist, for example, unreasonable or vexatious claims from employers or clients (Fischer and Zinke, 1989; Frankel, 1989; Hendler, 1991; Kernaghan, 1980). Interestingly, these functions may also be adopted as explicit reasons underlying the adoption of a code - as part of their response to the research project the Chartered Institute of Public Finance and Accountancy cited increasing public criticism and increasing vulnerability of individual professionals as the two main factors informing the Institute's decision to develop a code.

The benefits of developing a professional code derive from the effective performance of these functions and purposes. Thus, the achievement of benefits for the profession, for its members and for its clients, depends not only on the contents of the code, but upon the processes involved in its development and the effectiveness of its monitoring and enforcement.

For example the function of a code as creating a social contract requires the code to be developed in an accountable and participatory manner. If it is developed and imposed solely by an elite caucus within the professional body, it is unlikely to function effectively in this way. Few long term benefits will derive from a code that has no meaning for the members of the profession, that provides no accountability, that does not respond to the concerns of the profession's publics, that is not honoured by the profession, or that is not enforced or is seen to be unenforceable.

So far as problems and pitfalls relating to an adoption of a professional code are concerned, the issues of form and content are seen as crucially important. Short, aspirational codes are criticised because they offer little or no guidance to professionals faced with complex ethical problems (Kernaghan, 1993), or because they may offer a simplistic view of the world (Lucy, 1988). On the other hand, codes following the Justinian model (see above) may be cumbersome, overlong and still fail to provide coverage of every dilemma a professional may face (Kernaghan, 1980). Regulatory codes which emphasise enforcement may be inappropriate if there is nothing ethically substantive to enforce, but on the other hand, aspirational codes which lack enforcement mechanisms can be criticised as 'paper tigers' (Hendler, 1991, p. 165).

Other problems may arise from the processes involved in developing the code. Rather than expressing professional ethics, a code may represent the professionalization of ethics (Frankel, 1989), whereby ethical or moral principles may be subsumed by the profession's norms.

Hence Houlihan's (1988) uneasiness at the call for a clear set of professional values to guide the leisure profession: whose values and needs are to inform such a guide - those of the profession or those of its clients? The necessity for the participation of the professions' stakeholders in developing, monitoring, reviewing and evaluating codes has been pointed out (Hendler, 1991; Taylor, 1992), especially if the code is to express principles of public service, participation, democracy and client-centredness.

Code development may bring other problems. Professions are broad churches, and there is a danger that in attempting to formulate codes that can be accepted by a majority of the profession's members, professions may end up with codes that are anodyne, unenforceable and virtually meaningless, or which fail to engender the commitment of the different groups of members they are designed to appease. Alternatively, powerful sets of interests within the profession may attempt to influence or 'capture' the code to serve their own ends (Frankel, 1989). It is also necessary to consider more closely some of the ethical issues concerning the public sector professions, and it is to this area that we now turn.

Professional codes and public ethics

Unlike the United States and other countries, Britain has no professional body representing a public administration profession. The nearest equivalent to US bodies such as the American Society for Public Administration, or the National Academy of Public Administration, was the Royal Institute of Public Administration, which failed in July 1992. The US institutions are incorporated as professional bodies, with codes of ethics established, and are closely identified with senior career elites in American public service (Fischer and Zinke, 1989).

Similarly, while US public administration journals regularly carry important articles on public administration ethics, similar journals in Britain seem mostly to ignore the topic. This means that the existing literature on public service ethics is predominantly American and Canadian, which raises problems in view of those countries' different constitutional arrangements. Encouragingly, there are signs that growing attention is being paid to ethical issues in this country (see Chapman, 1993; Thomas and Healey, 1991; Taylor, 1992). However, it is inevitable that any exploration of professional ethics and the public sector is rooted in a literature that largely stands at a remove from contemporary British experience.

In discussing public sector professional ethics one principal issue presents itself - what important principles or issues might be of concern to public sector professionals? A key approach here is that of Denhardt (1989), who distinguishes between the substantive values of individual rights, liberty, justice and equality underlying the democratic ideal, and the more instrumental values expressed by bureaucracy, such as impartiality, accountability and due process; in other works, ideals relating to objectivity and fairness. Other approaches promote the Rawlsian notion of 'Justice' as an appropriate overarching principle (Pavlak and Pols, 1989; Stackhouse, 1989).

Rawlsian justice encompasses notions of equality, truth-telling and promise-keeping, human rights, and freedom. It also allows the important distinction between individual ethics (which may include professional ethics) and organizational ethics (the values of the employer). Similarly, Lundquist (1993), in mapping the ethical standpoint of the bureaucrat, distinguishes between bureaucratic ideals and personal ideals (although he explicitly distinguishes professional ideals from either).

Although the conceptual difference between these ideals may be perceived as clear cut, socialization processes will inevitably mean that the individual and the organisation will each affect each other (Winn, 1989), and it may not be helpful to try to parcel up one set of values and label them 'organizational' and another set 'personal' (or 'professional'). We must bear in mind, however, that some aspects of personal ideals (for example, those informed by religious belief) will not be explicitly subscribed to by either the organization or the individual's profession.

What does appear important is to clarify what values might be expressed in a code adopted by a profession whose expressed aim is to serve the public interest. It seems clear that any such values need to be informed by universal (rather than relativist) and objective (rather than subjectivist) principles. To run the risk of flippancy for a moment, it is unlikely that a professional code would have endorsed bribery in the Middle East, or racism in South Africa. Nor will the decision as to what constitutes (un)ethical behaviour be left entirely to the individual.

Further, although the notion of public service or serving the public interest is notoriously woolly, we feel it must include values such as objectivity, impartiality, promise-keeping, truth-telling, due process, respect for individual and collective human rights (including liberty and equality), accountability and fiduciary honesty. If these values are not made explicit, we would argue, serious questions should be raised about the weight attached to public service by the profession, as well as about the likely effectiveness of any such code as a guide to moral behaviour and development. We also think it likely that public profession's codes will carry considerable stress on the professional's duty to the employer, as well as to the public good, particularly given the (fallacious but nevertheless widely cited) dichotomy between policy and administration in the public service.

Are these values likely to be expressed in these terms? Given the comparatively low profile issues of business and administrative ethics are accorded in the British literature and in public sector professional discourse, we think it unlikely. This creates problems for analysis as far as coding is concerned, especially when carrying out a comparative analysis. Which of these values are likely to be given the most weight? It would be tempting, but misleading, to accord the same weight to standard, if vaguely worded, clauses regarding bringing the profession into disrepute to aspirational or educational clauses expressing moral purpose.

On the other hand, a woolly phrase concerning serving the public interest in a code which is otherwise crammed with technical regulations should not be allowed to disguise the basic nature of the code. We must therefore aim to adopt a pragmatic if 'unscientific' approach and to relate weighting to context. Transparency and rigour should avoid or minimise methodological problems.

What research questions and hypotheses arise from this brief review of the literature? Key research questions include: to what extent are professional codes a response to public criticism? If distinctively public professions attempt to codify certain values, to what extent is a genuine 'public service ethic' reflected in their codes? To what extent do professional codes embrace ethical principles? Do codes amount to a robust defence of professional and public service values, or are they merely the justification of self-serving interest groups? What are the expressed purposes of the codes? Can their other functions be reliably established?

How have the codes been developed? What are the types of code adopted by public professions? Is there any substantive difference between the codes of British and other public professions? It is acknowledged that the research project can only provide a partial answer to these questions, and that a far more substantial project including professions from other parts of the public sector, is required to do the subject justice. Nevertheless, it is possible to derive a number of modest hypotheses:

Hypothesis 1 Most British code are regulatory in nature and have their primary focus the employer or the profession itself.

Hypothesis 2 Most British codes do not express substantive ethical content.

Hypothesis 3 Most British codes are not developed consultatively or participatively, either internally or externally.

Hypothesis 4 Most British codes do not provide guidance for professionals faced with ethical dilemmas.

Hypothesis 5 Most British codes do not contain provision for monitoring and evaluation.

Hypothesis 6 American and Canadian codes differ from British codes in all of the above respects (except for hypothesis 3, where no information is available).

Research findings

It was considered that the most appropriate approach to the project was to carry out a content analysis of the codes themselves.

Standard reference texts indicate that there are over 70 institutions currently existing in the UK which represent members of the local government workforce. The majority of these were immediately eliminated from the enquiry, such as trade unions, associations which represented a discrete geographical part of the UK, associations which represented particular tiers of local government, bodies with a tiny membership, bodies whose membership was derived from status rather than profession and professional bodies whose majority of members were drawn from workers in other sectors.

The professions that remained (and the relevant professional bodies) were:

Public sector accountants	Chartered Institute of Public Finance and Accountancy (CIPFA)
Social workers	British Association of Social Workers (BASW)
Housing officers	Institute of Housing (IOH)
Leisure/Recreation managers	Institute of Leisure and Amenity Management (ILAM)
	Institute of Baths and Recreation Management (IBRM)
Environmental health officers	Institute of Environmental Health Officers (IEHO)
Trading Standards officers	Institute of Trading Standards Administration (ITSA)
Planners	Royal Town Planning Institute (RTPI)
Librarians	The Library Association (LA)
Museum profession	The Museums Association (MA)

Of these, BASW and ITSA failed to respond to requests for information. In addition, valuers, surveyors, lawyers, and architects were ruled out as either no association existed for members in local government, or local government members were governed by the codes of the generic professional bodies. Other groups were eliminated as they possessed no professional code, or because their code applied only to a particular issue, for example the Society of Education Officers, whose code is solely concerned with the application for grant maintained status for schools. In the case of highways engineering, although a number of different bodies existed, all who responded made it clear that they followed the generic code of practice of the Engineering Council. Lastly, in the case of teaching, no professional association appears to exist, with trade unions (whether affiliated to the Trades Union Congress or not) partially fulfilling the role.

As well as the codes themselves, institutions were requested to provide details of the development procedures involved. The primary focus of the research was the codes themselves, which were coded and analysed so as to establish the type, focus and substantive ethical content.

The type and focus of individual codes are shown in Figure 5.1, where they have been plotted against the matrix developed earlier in the paper. The majority of codes were regulatory, with the primary focus being the employer or profession itself. Where there existed substantive clauses which stressed other elements, this has been indicated with an arrow. Thus, the primary focus of the IEHO is the profession, but the code does contain substantive clauses concerning the interests of the public and of the employer.

Two codes were classified as educational (MA and CIPFA), as these contained detailed guidance on interpretation and use. The code of the Libraries Association also provided guidance for members, but was plainly intended as, and shared many features with, a regulatory code. Only one code was apirational (IBRM), containing statements of broad values and principles towards which members were encouraged to strive.

		Public	Employer	Profession
		F O	C	U S
T		ASPA		
	Aspirational	IBRM>		
		APA		
Y				
	Educational		<MA>	<<CIPFA
P				<<LA
			<TPIC>	
E		CIP>	<RTPI	
	Regulatory		ILAM>	<<IEHO
			<IOH	

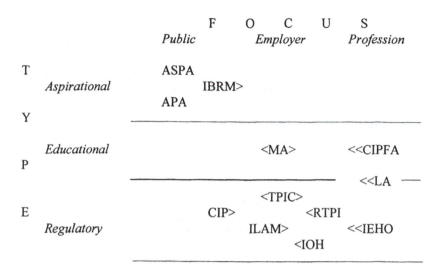

Figure 5.1 Public sector codes - type and focus
See the next section for descriptions of the APA, ASPA, CIP & TPIC.

As far as ethical content was concerned, a series of key principles was derived and applied to the codes (see Table 5.1). Individual clauses were coded and analysed to establish the substantive 'ethical' content of each code. Some of these principles may require clarification. The principle labelled 'collaboration' refers to the commitment made in some codes to the principle of working collaboratively, either with colleagues, or with the wider community, to serve the public interest. Three broad categories of conflict of interest were established - those were, that in case of a conflict between the demands of the employer and the public interest the latter should prevail; that in case of a conflict between the demands of the employer and professional standards, the latter should prevail; and that in the case of a conflict between the interests of the employer and the interest of the employee, the former should prevail. Lastly, while most codes had a clause requiring members to try to maintain professional competence, only a few contained a requirement to strive to develop oneself or others.

It should be noted that codes differed in their implied or express commitment to some of these principles, and in these cases the spirit as well as the letter of the codes have been acknowledged.

Comparative analysis

The same analysis was also applied to a very small number of American and Canadian codes. No pretence of scientific rigour can be made regarding the selection of these codes, but it is considered that their inclusion contributes to the analysis. The professional bodies concerned were the American Planning Association (APA), the American Society for Public Administration (ASPA), the Canadian Institute of Planners (CIP) and the Town Planning Institute of Canada (TPIC).

Table 5.1
Breakdown of professional codes
(S = stated, I = implied; Com = developed by committee, Mem = developed by membership, Public = developed through public consultation)

	CIPFA	*IBRM*	*IEHO*	*ILAM*	*IOH*	*LA*	*MA*	*RTPI*
%age membership in local government	53	50+	64	N/K	50	N/K	50+	60
Code development	Com	N/K	Mem	N/K	Mem	N/K	N/K	Public
Key principles								
- promote equality		S	S		S	S		S
- eliminate/not knowingly promote discrimination					S	S	I	S
- serve public interest	S	S	I	I	S	S	S	S
- honesty and integrity	S	S	S	S	S	I	I	S
- impartiality	S	S	S		S	S	S	I
- collaboration		S		S			S	
- protect environment		S		S				
- conflict of interest (employer/public)		I			I	S		
- conflict of interest (employer/profession)	S				I	S		
- conflict of interest (employer/individual	S	S	S	S	S		S	S
- value colleagues/staff		S					I	
- develop self/others		S		S		S	S	

Table 5.2
Comparative analysis
(S = stated, I = implied)

	APA	*ASPA*	*CIP*	*TPIC*
Key principles				
- promote equality	S	S	S	
- eliminate/not knowingly promote discrimination		S	S	
- serve public interest	S	S	S	S
- honesty and integrity	I	S	S	S
- impartiality	I	S	S	S
- collaboration	S	I		S
- protect environment	I			S
- conflict of interest (employer/public)	I	I	S	S
- conflict of interest (employer/profession)				I
- conflict of interest (employer/individual)	S	S	S	I
- value colleagues/staff		I	S	S
- develop self/others		S	S	S

The type and focus of these codes has also been plotted on Figure 5.1, and it can be seen that the codes are either more strongly aspirational, or are focused more emphatically on the public interest, than most British codes. Their substantive ethical content is shown in Table 5.2, and again it is considered that they score more highly than most of their British counterparts.

Conclusions

It is readily admitted that the size of the research sample severely limits broad and generalisable conclusion. Nevertheless, given this significant caveat, some tentative conclusions may be drawn concerning the hypotheses stated above.

Hypothesis 1 Most British codes are regulatory in nature and have as their primary focus the employer or the profession itself.
The research would tend to bear this out.

Hypothesis 2 Most British codes do not express substantive ethical content.
This hypothesis is not proven by the research findings. What is clear, however, is that there are some important ethical principles that individual codes signally fail to address.

Hypothesis 3 Most British codes are not developed consultatively or participatively, either internally or externally.
As some bodies failed to supply information on this point, no conclusions may be drawn, although it may be of interest to note that the RTPI is currently undertaking a public consultation exercise regarding a major revision of its code.

Hypothesis 4 Most British codes do not provide guidance for professionals faced with ethical dilemmas.
On the limited evidence available, this would appear to be the case. Even the codes which do have significant guidelines incorporated do not claim that the guidelines should necessarily be used for this purpose.

Hypothesis 5 Most British codes do not contain provision for monitoring and evaluation.
The research would tend to bear this out.

Hypothesis 6 American and Canadian codes differ from British codes in all of the above respects (except for hypothesis 3, where no information is available).
The research would tend to bear this out in the case of Hypothesis 1. In addition, the ethical content of the foreign codes studied appears generally to be more substantive.

So far as broad conclusions and recommendations are concerned, we would make the following comments:

1 British local government professions generally need to rethink their approaches to professional codes. An explicit commitment needs to be made to a rigorous and transparent ethical stance, which is informed by the choice of appropriate ethical principles. In short, professions need to consider what precisely they are here for, to rediscover their sense of purpose and embrace these purposes explicitly and wholeheartedly.

2 These ethical foundations, and the detailed wording of the codes that are constructed upon them, need to be developed in partnership with the profession's key publics.

3 Provision should be made for regular monitoring, evaluation and review, and again these processes need to be undertaken in conjunction with key stakeholders.

4 It may be appropriate for professions to develop different codes in tandem. While there is a need for codes in order to regulate the conduct of members, broad aspirational codes which establish the highest ethical principles of the profession are also required. Returning to the categorization dismissed earlier in the paper, it may be useful for professions to develop aspirational codes of ethics alongside, regulatory codes of conduct. This, however, ignores the value of educational codes, where detailed ethical guidance may be given.

So far as further research is concerned, the project described in this paper is acknowledged barely to have scratched the surface. All the research questions identified above require further attention and, indeed, elaboration. In addition, the questions should be broadened out. Is the matrix developed in this paper a useful tool for conceptual analysis, or can it be improved? What other conceptual tools might be appropriate and how might they be developed? In what ways are local government professional codes similar to those of other professions, in the public sector and elsewhere? Are American codes generally superior to British codes, as this research tentatively suggests? More fundamentally, perhaps, and totally outwith the scope of this paper, do codes work? How do we know? How can we find out?

References

Bacon, W. (1989), 'The vulnerable profession? An analysis of the structure and role of the Institute of Leisure and Amenity Managers in Post- Keynesian society', *Local Government Studies*, Vol. 15, pp. 65-79.

Chapman, R A. (ed.), (1993), *Ethics in Public Service*, Edinburgh University Press, Edinburgh.

Coalter, F. (1986), 'A Leisure Profession? Definitions and Dilemmas', *Local Government Policy Making*, December, pp. 40-48.

Denhardt, K.G. (1989), 'The management of ideals: a political perspective on ethics', *Public Administration Review,* Vol. 4, pp. 187-93.

Elcock, H. (1983), 'Disabling professionalism: the real threat to local democracy', *Public Money*, June, pp. 23-27.

Fischer, F. and Zinke, R.C. (1989), 'Public administration and the code of ethics: administrative reform or professional ideology?', *International Review of Public Administration*, Vol. 12, pp. 841-54.

Frankel, M.S. (1989), 'Professional codes: why, how and with what impact?', *Journal of Business Ethics*, Vol. 8, pp. 109-15.

Gyford, J. (1991), *Citizens, Consumers and Councils: Local Government and the Public*, Macmillan, Basingstoke.

Harris, N. (1989), *Professional Codes of Conduct in the United Kingdom: A Directory*, Mansell, London.

Hendler, S. (1991), 'Do professional codes legitimate planners' values?', in *Dilemmas of Planning Practice: Ethics, Legitimacy and the Validation of Knowledge*, H. Thomas and P. Healey (eds), Avebury, Aldershot, pp. 156-67.

Henry, I.P. (1993), *The Politics of Leisure Policy*, Macmillan, Basingstoke.

Houlihan, B. (1988), 'The professionalization of public sector sport and leisure management', *Local Government Studies*, Vol. 14, pp. 69-82.

Kernaghan, K. (1980), 'Codes of ethics and public administration: progress, problems and prospects', *Public Administration*, Vol. 59, pp. 207-23.

Kernaghan, K. (1993), 'Promoting public service ethics: the codification option', in *Ethics in Public Service*, R. A. Chapman (ed.), Edinburgh University Press, Edinburgh, pp. 15-29.

Laffin, M. (1986), *Professionalism and Policy: the Role of the Professions in the Central-local Relationship*, Gower, Aldershot.

Laffin, M. and Young, K. (1990), *Professionalism in Local Government: Change and Challenge*, Longman, Harlow.

Leach, S. and Stewart, M. (1992), *Local Government: its Role and Function*, Joseph Rowntree Foundation, York.

L'Etang, J. (1992), 'A Kantian approach to codes of ethics', *Journal of Business Ethics*, Vol. 11, pp. 737-44.

Lucy, W.H. (1988), 'APA's ethical principles include simplistic planning theories', *Journal of the American Planning Association*, Vol. 54, pp. 147-49.

Lundquist, L. (1993), 'Freedom of information and the Swedish bureaucrat', in R. Chapman (ed.), *Ethics in Public Service,* Edinburgh University Press, Edinburgh, pp. 75-91.

Metcalfe, L. and Williams, S. (1990), *Improving Public Management*, Sage, London.

Pavlak, T.J. and Pols, G.M. (1989) 'Administrative ethics as justice', *International Review of Public Administration*, Vol. 12, pp. 931-48.

Recreation Management Training Committee (the Yates Committee), (1984), *Final Report*, HMSO, London.

Stackhouse, S.B. (1989), 'Upholding justice in an unjust world: a practitioner's view of public administration ethics', *International Review of Public Administration*, Vol. 12, pp. 889-911.

Taylor, N. (1992), 'Professional ethics in town planning: what is a code of professional conduct for?', *Town Planning Review*, Vol. 63, pp. 227-41.

Thomas, H. and Healey, P. (eds), (1991), *Dilemmas of Planning Practice: Ethics, Legitimacy and the Validation of Knowledge*, Avebury, Aldershot.

Towey, J. (1985), 'Professionalism: when officers are amateurs', *Local Government Policy Making*, March, pp. 29-31.

Winn, M. (1989), 'Ethics in organizations: a perspective on reciprocation', *International Review of Public Administration*, Vol. 12, pp. 867-87.

6 Victorian values in Victorian buildings? The museums profession and management

Stuart Davies

Introduction

Despite a virtual revolution over the last twenty or more years in presentation methods and services to their customers, museums still struggle to shake off the popular image of being 'dingy places with different kinds of bits' (Trevelyan, 1991) or 'worthy but dull' (Audit Commission, 1991). Regular museum users would have no problem in refuting this image, but they do not yet constitute a sufficiently large group to completely dispel this piece of heritage mythology.

The people who work within museums have fared even less well. Society has few role models from literature or the media and those which it does have are not notably flattering. In Mervyn Peake's Gormenghast, for example, the treasures are housed in the Hall of the Bright Carvings.

> This hall which ran along the top storey of the north wing was presided over by the curator, Rottcodd, who, as no-one ever visited the room, slept most of his life in the hammock he had erected at the far end. For all his dozing, he had never been known to relinquish the feather duster from his grasp; the duster with which he would perform one of the only two regular tasks which appeared to be necessary in that long and silent hall, namely to flick the dust from the Bright Carvings (Peake, 1946).

The popular image of the curator is that of a scholarly but odd person, distinctly unworldly, whose principal task is labelling and cleaning the objects in his or her care, perhaps answering the occasional question from a visitor.

Reality is of course somewhat different. Museums, art galleries, historic house museums and numerous other 'attractions' make a significant contribution to the heritage of this country, to its tourism potential and, indirectly, to local economic development. Many are operated as small businesses and virtually all have had to adopt business and management methodologies in order to survive the squeeze on funding which has been for many years the norm in the heritage and arts industry. 'Curators' actually make up only a small proportion of those working in museums, albeit an influential one. Other 'professionals' from the worlds of conservation, education, design, marketing and security (to name only a selection) have applied their skills and disciplines to the museums sector.

The UK museums sector is divided into three parts: the national museums which are about 75 percent funded by central government, local authority museums (about 85 percent funded by local taxation) and independent museums which are independent in terms of governance but still rely heavily on local authority grants for their survival. Each of these three parts is broadly equal in terms of the number of museum sites, staff employed and visits made to them. It is claimed that the sector employs about 40,000 people (Klemm and Wilson, 1993) and about 78m visits are made to museums each year (Myerscough, 1991).

The sector is one of enormous contrasts in scale and operational complexity. At the one end of the spectrum are the great national institutions like the British Museum, the Natural History Museum and the Victoria and Albert Museum. At the other end is a myriad of small museums opening only seasonally and often run entirely by volunteers. It is important to realise that even in the local authority public museums (which many would regard as 'typical' of the industry), 65 percent have less than 10 employees (Klemm and Wilson, 1993).

One thing, however, which all but the very smallest have experienced since at least the 1970s has been the encroachment of 'management' on to an intrinsically conservative and quite unscientific world. In the public sector this accelerated appreciably after 1979 with the introduction of a much more strident 'business managerialism' into all areas of subsidised public services. The language of strategic management, business planning, performance indicators and marketing, for instance, has increasingly been heard by curators and museum managers.

This process has been encouraged by an increasing insistence by funding agencies (and especially the Museums and Galleries Commission (MGC) and the Area Museums Councils (AMCs)) that museums should be able to demonstrate good management practice (at least at a strategic level) as a prerequisite to funding in the future. The MGC's national Registration scheme requires the production of basic policy documents and indications that their responsibilities are being taken seriously by governing bodies. Indeed, there has been increasing pressure from stakeholders at all levels in the sector to be assured that the public subsidy is yielding an acceptable return.

This paper examines how museums are responding to these challenges and seeks to critically evaluate whether or not its traditional professional values are incompatible with the rigours of goal-orientated business managerialism. It has evolved out of earlier research into strategic management within local authority museums (Davies, 1993) which raised the possibility that professionalism might be an impediment to the introduction of, and subsequently a genuine commitment to, strategic management in the museums sector.

Methodology

The findings outlined in this paper are derived from three principal sources. The first is a detailed literature search of the museums press, in particular the *Museums Journal*, published by the UK Museums Association, but also a range of American trade press as well. Secondly, a study of strategic planning in UK local authority museums conducted in 1992, using questionnaires and a series of qualitative interviews with professional museum managers, sought to identify the barriers to strategic planning in the sector, including 'professionalism'.

Finally, in 1993, a questionnaire survey (followed up by qualitative interviews) targeted at experienced museum professionals, specifically examined the relationship between the museum professional and the requirements of modern museum management. This survey, which achieved a response rate of 34 percent, originated as a pilot study to determine the potential usefulness of a full survey of the Museums Association's membership.

Professional values

To achieve an understanding of the values which are the driving force behind the museum professional, one has to examine the origins of museums in this country. An identifiable concept of 'the museum' had emerged out of private 'cabinets of curiosity' by the seventeenth century, the British Museum was founded in 1753 and many Literary and Philosophical Societies established museums in Georgian and early Victorian England. But it was not until the second half of the nineteenth century that a recognisable modern museum movement exploded upon the scene. It has been suggested that before 1850, Great Britain possessed 59 museums, but between 1850 and 1914 a further 295 were added (Wittlin, 1949: 136). This enormous growth accounts for the influence of Victorian values and also why the overwhelming majority of museums are housed in pre-1914 buildings.

The motivation for founding museums did of course vary considerably. But this period was the great time for municipal foundations and they shared much in common, not least of all as being perceived as part of the Victorians' passion for 'improvement'. Dr Dale, a prominent figure in the pursuit of Birmingham's 'civic gospel', in later life recalled the beginning of the 'civic revolution' in Birmingham:

> Towards the end of the sixties a few Birmingham men made the discovery that perhaps a strong and able Town Council might do almost as much to improve the conditions of life in the town as Parliament itself ... They spoke of sweeping away streets in which it was not possible to live a healthy and decent life; making the town cleaner, sweeter and brighter; of providing gardens and parks and music; of erecting baths and free libraries, an art gallery and a museum; ... Sometimes an adventurous orator would excite his audience by dwelling on the glories of Florence, and of the other cities of Italy in the Middle Ages and

> suggest that Birmingham too might become the home of a noble literature and art (Davies, 1985, p. 16).

Asked 'why should every town have a museum?', one Victorian commentator replied:

> Because a Museum and a Free Library are as necessary for the mental and moral health of the citizens as good sanitary arrangements, water supply and street lighting are for their physical health and comfort (Greenwood, 1888).

Other reasons were to be found in the municipal museum legislation of the period; museums were to be '... for the instruction and recreation of the people' (Lewis, 1989).

There was certainly a strong educational mission among those who founded and advocated the first public museums. The 1880s and 1890s in particular were an age of enthusiasm for education and many commentators believed that museums offered an opportunity for people, who had perhaps not had the benefit of formal education, to make up for lost time. One publication in the 1880s, for example, urged people to 'visit the nearest Museum periodically, and let it be to you an advanced school of self-instruction' (Hudson, 1975 p. 64).

By and large this enthusiasm for the civilising and educational role of museums came from liberal commentators and advocates of museums as part of broader cultural development in late Victorian England. What of the curators themselves?

> It would be impossible to draw a profile of a typical Victorian curator. Those engaged in museum work were an incongruous mix of academics, pseudo-academics, amateurs, visionaries and elevated town hall clerks. The national museums curators aligned themselves with university scholars. Curators of large provincial museums aligned themselves with national museum curators. Curators of small museums aligned themselves with just about anybody (Kavanagh, 1991, p. 44).

There was from the beginning a distinction between the nationals and large provincial museums and the rest. James Paton described in 1894 how he saw the curators:

> divided into two great classes: the specialist who belongs to the great public and nationalist museums, and the provincial curator who has to be everything and to do everything in his own much-embracing institution (Paton, 1894, p. 97).

But there was also some measure of agreement about the purpose of curators:

> it is our business to accumulate material, preserve it, and render it accessible to everyone who wishes to study it (Howarth, 1915).

Free access to collections gathered for the benefit of present and future generations was an important Victorian museum value, often embodied in foundation statements by the industrial philanthropists often associated with the origins of public museums in the Midlands and the North. The Mappin Art Gallery in Sheffield, for example, was founded on the understanding that the corporation would ensure that it was 'to be open to the public in perpetuity and without any charge' (Brears and Davies, 1989, p. 49). The fact that many of the early curators of the major museums were in post for extraordinary lengths of time (Teather, 1990), implies considerable commitment.

In his presidential address to the Museums Association in 1893, Sir William Henry Flower (1898, p. 31) described the 'first duty of museums' as being 'to preserve the evidence upon which the history of mankind and the knowledge of science is based' but also that the 'value of a museum will be tested not only by its contents, but by the treatment of those contents as a means of the advancement of knowledge'. This purpose for the museum is supported by the value system of their curators, who believe that the understanding and appreciation of objects and works of art is an important part of the cultural and intellectual well-being of the nation. The strong belief in the necessity of maintaining museum collections, in perpetuity for the benefit of the present public and for future generations, without direct charge to the beneficiaries, was the bequest of the founding fathers of the profession. Most of it does not appear to have been seriously challenged throughout the twentieth century.

In an attempt to more closely identify the issues which curators feel museums should be addressing now, respondents were offered a list of twelve objectives commonly found in museum service strategic plans and they were asked to select five of them. The results, presented in Table 6.1, reveal both consistency across the sector and some significant variations between different types of museum.

Table 6.1
Objectives for a museum and art gallery
(respondents were asked to select five from a list of twelve)

	Local Authority museums n = 39	National museums n = 28	Independent museums n = 15	Total n = 82
To educate and entertain all visitors	24	22	11	57
To maintain the professional standards detailed in the Museums Association's codes	14	2	4	20
To provide a service which promotes the locality	11	1	2	14
To provide a service which is customer-orientated, accessible and available to everyone	28	14	7	49
To maintain, develop and conserve collections held in trust for future generations	29	23	13	65
To encourage participation rather than merely observation	11	4	4	19
To demonstrate the unique contribution of museums to society	1	2	1	4
To develop facilities for their social value as well as aesthetic enjoyment	9	6	3	18
To manage the museum and art gallery services efficiently and effectively	24	12	9	45

To provide a service to the highest possible professional standards	20	17	7	44
To add to knowledge by carrying out and promoting research	11	21	9	41
To attract financial support from the private and public sector and through other forms of income generation	3	10	5	28

If we assume that selection of objectives reflects the values underpinning the curators' thinking, then some useful conclusions may be drawn. Firstly there is general agreement on two areas; museums should 'maintain, develop and conserve collections held in trust for future generations' and that they should 'educate and entertain all visitors'. Thereafter there is less agreement. Rather surprisingly, perhaps, only the local authority curators placed a high priority on providing a service 'which is customer-orientated, accessible and available to everyone'. The nationals, as might be expected, ranked research highly (third in fact), while the local authorities and independents gave precedence to managing services 'efficiently and effectively'. All of them ranked providing a service 'to the highest possible professional standards' fourth or fifth. Once again, then, a measure of commonality of values can be identified where collection care and education are involved, but thereafter the different parts of the sector focus on their priorities; customer-orientation for the local authorities; research for the nationals and managing efficiently for the independents.

In recent years local authority museums have largely abandoned any pretensions to being research institutions and have re-positioned themselves by adopting a customer-orientation stance, both through their exhibits and their involvement with local communities. The independents have always needed to manage efficiently and effectively but operational pressures show no sign of driving them to abandon the core values of collection care, education and entertainment. What differentiates them from theme parks and heritage centres is that they recognise that they have, in their collections, a long term asset for which they are responsible for, but also need to care for in their own interests. The nationals retain their support for scholarship as they have done since the nineteenth century.

As part of this research project, respondents were asked to identify the distinctive contribution of 'professionals' to museums. The responses from the local authority curators were generally consistent, a number of key attributes appearing frequently: understanding; experience; training; knowledge; commitment; standards and ethics. The point that many of them made was that the professional, as a consequence of his or her commitment, knowledge experience and training had an understanding of museums and the issues associated with them (including the important areas of standards and ethics) which could not be replicated by a non-professional, or (crucially) professionals from other disciplines such as librarianship or leisure and recreation. It was upon this distinctive understanding that the case for drawing museum managers from the ranks of professional curators largely rested.

There were some voices of dissent who felt that the professional had little or nothing to offer that others could not. One even went as far as to say that 'many museum professionals have alienated their communities with their entrenched attitudes'. There was not the same degree of consensus among staff from the national and independent museums, but all of the elements described above were present. To these should be added 'academic' or 'specialised' knowledge frequently stressed by the national respondents.

The museums profession

Few who work within museums would today deny that a museums profession exists. It is not the intention of this paper to explore that proposition in any depth, but a brief description of the profession's development is necessary to understand the relationship between profession and management in the 1990s.

The formation, by a handful of curators, in 1889 of the Museums Association might suggest that a profession was recognised sufficiently long ago to be now unequivocably established. In reality it grew only relatively slowly. It gradually increased its membership from 27 institutions and 50 individuals in 1890 to 472 institutions, 347 individuals and 7 life members in 1945, and to 620 institutions, 2,319 individuals and 403 others by 1993. There were some inherent problems from the outset. Firstly, the Association included the parallel membership of institutional and individual members. Because it embraced both employer and employee this necessarily limited its ability to develop as a professional body determined to establish an autonomous power for its members. The very agencies from whom this autonomy needed to be won were powerful forces within the Association. Secondly, membership has tended to be concentrated in the local authority part of the museums sector, leaving the national museums and independent museums relatively under-represented (Teather, 1990, pp. 26-7). In 1982 the Association's own President described it as 'a local authority club' (Cossons, 1982).

From the very beginning the Association focused on such issues as the interchange of duplicate and surplus specimens; labelling; collection typologies; indexing of collections and the preparation of small educational loan collections for circulation among schools. This in part reflects the strong natural history bias among the Association's founding members but also the fact that its preoccupation was with the technical rather than the political (Lewis, 1989, pp. 9-11). Some have gone so far as to see this early preoccupation with technical matters as putting museums on to an unfortunate development path.

> It is open to speculation whether the progress of the profession might have been different if the Museums Association had concerned itself more with the founding of a profession from 1889, with all that implied for salaries and standards, and less with swapping information about desk cases and labels for lepidoptera (Kavanagh, 1991, pp. 46-7).

It is perhaps significant that today's museum workers still identify 'professional' issues as, broadly, being those relating to collections and their care, rather than wider philosophical, political or managerial issues.

Even within these terms the 'professionalization' of museums proceeded slowly, and fragmentation remained a strong characteristic. By the 1920s four museum curator orientations were easily recognisable: amateur or honorary; the full-time paid curators; the scholar and the scientist. It should be emphasised that in 1928 only 14 percent of museums in the United Kingdom had full-time paid curators (Teather, 1990, p. 30). The national museums were developing a specialization in scholarship (or scientific research) which ensured that they continued to differentiate themselves from most of the rest of the sector. The sudden increase in small independent museums in the 1970s and 1980s only exacerbated this situation.

The issue of 'fragmentation' within the 'profession' may be discussed with reference to Table 6.2.

Table 6.2
Proportion of total full-time staff employed in each activity by type of Museum

Activity	Type of Museum National %	Local Authority %	Other %
Management and Administration	12.2	12.1	19.8
Curatorship	9.9	19.6	11.1
Research	9.8	1.4	1.2
Conservation	7.7	4.3	3.2
Education	1.8	3.6	2.1
Security, attendant and warding duties	34.9	32.6	16.4
Other	23.7	26.4	46.2
Total	100.0	100.0	100.0
	n = 3758	n = 3462	n = 1739

Source: *Prince and Higgins-McLoughlin*, 1987, p. 81

If one allows for the vagaries of definition (in small museums, for example, it might be difficult to determine whether an individual is a curator or a manager) then there are broader similarities between the types of museum than those who lay emphasis on the fragmentation of the profession might allow. It is of course true that the nationals put a far higher emphasis on research, while the independents have more managers and administrators, perhaps reflecting their greater attention to visitor management. They certainly have more retail sales staff (6.6 percent compared with less than 3 percent in the national and local authority museums), but far fewer security and warding staff, a reflection of their usual emphasis on interpretation rather than the housing of treasures.

The number of staff in local authorities who see their principal activity as 'curatorship' is paralleled by the distribution of those holding the Museums Association's Diploma, the only widely recognised professional qualification. While comprehensive reliable figures are still difficult to find, the broad picture is clear. By the mid-1980s, 43 percent of local authority museum directors held the Diploma, but less than 10 percent of other directors (Prince and Higgins-McLoughlin, 1987, p. 84). A much more recent survey suggested that no more than 28 percent of curators and managers in local authority museum services held the Diploma, while in all museums with more than 10 employees, (in itself the minority) no more than 13 percent of curators and managers held the Diploma (Klemm and Wilson, 1993, pp. 16,33). The professional heartland clearly focuses on the local authority museums.

It is, of course, also interesting to note that only a minority of those who work in museums actually hold the recognised professional qualification. Even when security, attendant and warding staff are excluded (about 30 percent of the workforce), those who have the Diploma (and those who aspire to) are still fewer than those who do not. By March 1993 only 546 out of the Museums Association's 2,319 individual members held the Diploma. This perhaps represents, at best, less than 5 percent of the potential membership among managers, curators, conservators and educators working in museums. This situation exists partly because the Diploma has always been curator-focused, but more and more other 'professionals' have come to work in museums in recent years. But it is also because many of the more research-orientated scholars and scientists working as curators within the national museums have never seen the value in holding a qualification which in essence is supposed to indicate that the holder is competent to manage a small to medium sized museum and its collections.

Respondents to a questionnaire survey were asked to indicate what they considered themselves to be. Sixty-four percent of the local authority people described themselves as managers, while the rest said they were curators. All of them, in fact, were managers, but those from the smaller museums in particular insisted that they were primarily curators (i.e. museum professionals) who were obliged or expected to carry out managerial functions. The responses from the independent museums were in exactly the same proportions. Most of the national respondents described themselves as curators or according to their particular occupation, such as scientist or conservator. This may reflect a lower expectation of carrying out managerial duties even among quite senior staff in the much larger national organizations. Equally it might say much about their perception of their primary function.

The same sample (n = 82) were asked if they thought they belonged to a profession, and 90 percent of them said that they did. However, only 70 percent of all respondents said that that was the museums profession, 85 percent of the local authority and independent respondents and 44 percent of the nationals. The 15 percent of the local authority and independent respondents generally offered a combination of museums with a specialist discipline. The nationals offered a range of specialist disciplines revealing that they considered themselves first, for example, a geologist, but only second a museums professional.

The focusing on collection issues, the fragmented nature of museums, and the perception of being an amateur (not to say eccentric) non-essential vocation have all contributed to the general low status, reflected in the salary structure of workers in the sector. Gladstone's view may still be held by many today. He said that he 'would never be a party to increasing the salaries of the gentlemen of the British Museum; for he could imagine no more delightful existence' (Kenyon, 1927, p. 27). Is it then at all reasonable to even count museum workers as belonging to a profession?

It would be very easy to get into a very tedious debate about whether or not museum workers, and perhaps particularly curators, are really a 'profession' or whether they simply belong to an occupation which is aspiring to being a profession. The following discussion is intended simply to establish what the perceptions of those that work within museums is, on the basis that perception may be more important than reality when one is considering the relationship between professionalism and management.

Goode (1969) argued that society was becoming more professionalized in the 1950s and 1960s only in the sense that a higher percentage of the labour force began to call themselves professions. He believed 'that many aspiring occupations and semi-professions will never become professions in the usual sense: they will never reach the levels of knowledge and dedication to service that society considers necessary for a profession'. Members of any occupation also give it a higher prestige ranking than the rest of society, but ultimately it is society that determines their worth in terms of money, status, power and legislative protection. In all these respects museum workers are lowly valued by society and seem to rest very firmly among Goode's 'aspiring occupations' or 'semi-professions'. This view has been confirmed by a study of American museum workers (Mariner, 1974).

Museums fare better from the attributes approach to defining a profession. They have acquired many of the trappings of professionalization. The Museums Association was established in 1889, followed shortly by the Museums Journal. A university-based training system exists, ethical codes of conduct have been drawn up and, at least through the Museums and Galleries Commission's registration scheme, there is a recognised body of standards.

However, the attributes approach has fallen out of favour, and then replaced by concepts of power. This exposes museums, as a profession, to where they were in any case weakest in the attributes of professionalism. They have not been able to establish autonomy over museum work and certainly do not enjoy any significant legislative protection.

The role of the professional association is not that of a regulator, ensuring that the professionals control activities and protecting its members, interests against outside threats by using the power created either by legislation or some sort of deference invested in it by society. This does not exist. The Museums Association has certainly developed its professional role considerably since 1889, but it does still retain the function of acting as a focus for the 'exchange of information' on curatorial issues. What it has added is the role of trying to guide museums and their governing bodies towards coordinated action and to represent the interests of museums at national level, and especially to government. The profession therefore derives such strength as it has from its ability to 'influence' rather than to wield real 'power'. This does not, however, necessarily mean that it is any less of a 'profession'. Certainly it cannot meet the sort of criteria which might be drawn up based on the law or medicine. But what is most important is that most of its practitioners believe that they are part of a profession and act as such. They often mix a missionary zeal (often found in minority or threatened groups) with a sometimes little concealed disdain for other groups which they may come into conflict with.

There is also evidence that some degree of power over at least the contents of service delivery is enjoyed by the profession. More interestingly, it is possible, as Weil (1988) has suggested, that the pursuit of 'professionalism' has itself led to the raising of standards and may gradually raise the standing of museums in the eyes of society.

One way of determining the 'power' of the museums profession is to gauge the influence that various stakeholders have in determining which services are provided, as perceived by the curator-managers. Table 6.3 shows the considerable influence of staff in this area.

Table 6.3
Analysis of those stakeholders who were perceived by curator-managers as being influential in determining the provision of museum services

	Local authority museums	National museums	Independent museums	All museums
	%	%	%	%
Volunteers/'Friends'	41	7	43	30
Visitors/Users	77	68	71	73
Professional Curators	92	75	93	86
Other museum staff	87	82	71	82
Other managers	46	61	50	52
The governing body	67	75	86	60
	n = 39	n = 28	n = 14	n = 81

There appears to be a consensus about the relative influences of the stakeholder groups. What is important to note is that with the exception of volunteers in the Nationals, all groups make a significant impact in all sectors, underlining the necessity of recognising the power of stakeholders. However, it is also clear that the professional curators have the major influence in determining the delivery of services. While this may be interpreted as indicating professional power, it could equally represent a weakness. The failure to allow (either intentionally or otherwise) powerful stakeholders to have a greater say in what services are delivered might actually be harmful to museums.

By the 1980s the Museums Association found that it needed to define exactly what a museum is. After consultation with its membership, it came up with:

> A museum is an institution which collects, documents, preserves, exhibits and interprets material evidence and associated information for the public benefit.

In effect this is a mission statement for the museums profession. Three quarters of a sample of museum staff from the whole sector (n = 82) agreed that this accurately reflected what today's museums were trying to achieve. The only serious dissent came from among the local authority curator-managers, 20 percent of whom could not agree that this was so. One felt that it was 'the wrong way round', while to another it was incomplete, saying 'nothing about activities and public involvement'. There was an interesting correlation between those who dissented and respondents known to be considered at the leading edge of new thinking about the role of museums in society. Follow-up enquiries confirmed that most of them considered the definition to be too narrow, introspective and giving insufficient weight to either the customers or wider social benefits. They were, in other words, concerned that the mission statement did not adequately reflect the needs of all the stakeholders. Their interests might be represented by the phrase 'for the public benefit' but this was not explicit enough for some respondents.

Management

In the course of interviewing and while observing professional meetings, it has become clear that there is a common perception that 'management' has become an increasingly prominent (and, some would feel, intrusive) element in museums in recent years. This may actually be identified with the new management methodologies which gradually appeared from the United States in the 1960s and were picked up and trumpeted by the more far-sighted museum professionals at an early date (Cossons, 1970).

But these concepts of strategy, performance, value-for-money, efficiency and effectiveness perhaps only really gripped the museums world after 1979, when they became a significant aspect of government initiatives to expand the role of the market throughout society and, in particular, to reduce public expenditure. It is what has come to be known as 'business managerialism' (Pollitt, 1990; Gunn, 1988) that has formed museum curators' perceptions of what modern management is all about. It is also seen as an important element in what is perceived as both a significant challenge to the museums' profession's right to manage itself and as a barrier to having the freedom to manage according to the means most appropriate to the sector. One distinguished professional, for example, has spoken of 'the harm which has been done, at considerable expense, by the imposition of unacceptable management practices' (Robertson, 1985).

A major issue concerning local authority museums since the nineteenth century has been where in the organised hierarchy of the authority should they be placed. Museum professionals have agreed strongly that museums can best serve their publics (and themselves) by being a stand-alone department with their own Chief Officer reporting directly to a Museums Committee. The local government reorganization of 1974 saw many museums subsumed within Leisure Services directorates and most have followed in the years since until there are now very few museum Chief Officers remaining. This has raised doubts about the suitability of local authorities to be entrusted with the care of museums (Boylan, 1988).

The impact of these developments was brought home to the local authority museums world in the Audit Commission (1991) report, *The Road to Wigan Pier?* This critically reviewed the current state of museums and made recommendations for the establishment of clear policies, strategies, marketing plans and a performance culture.

Although this has not necessarily been the disaster that some have implied (Davies, 1990), about one quarter of a sample of local authority senior museum professionals still consider that it is preferable that museums should be stand-alone institutions, if still within the structure of local government. One quarter of the sample also report frequent or a great deal of 'interference' from non-museum personnel, presumably justifying the call for more autonomy. Over 50 percent do not believe local authority museums should be more independent of their host organizations, presumably either recognising the advantages that integration within the authority can bring or at least accepting the reality of the situation that museums find themselves in.

The issue of where museums should get their managers from has been frequently debated within the profession. It has perhaps been felt most acutely in the local authority museums which are more exposed to Librarians or Leisure Officers coming forward with the belief that 'a good manager can manage anything' and the head of a museum service need not have a professional background in museums.

Respondents to a questionnaire were asked to rank a series of statements about professionalism, curators and managers, between 'strongly agree' and 'strongly disagree'. Table 6.4 summarises the results. There seems to be strong support for the concept of an active professional association from about two thirds of the respondents with 10 percent or fewer seriously dissenting. There was also a general rejection of the proposition that professionalism is a barrier to good management.

The respondents were, however, divided over whether or not professional curators make the best managers, the non-curatorial professionals in the national museums particularly strongly disagreeing with this suggestion. Most respondents agreed that the best museum managers had also been good curators and disagreed with the suggestion that finding both qualities in the same person was necessarily rare. Similarly they rejected the idea that professional curatorship and good management have little in common.

Table 6.4
Responses to a series of statements about professionalism, curators and managers

	Local authority museums		*National museums*		*Independent museums*		*All*	
	Strongly agree or agree (%)	Strongly disagree or disagree (%)	SA or A (%)	SD or D (%)	SA or A (%)	SD or D (%)	SA or A (%)	DS or D (%)
'We must fight as a profession to protect museums'	71	16	65	4	60	7	66	10
'Good professional curators make the best museums managers'	34	29	23	46	40	27	32	34
'Professional curatorship and good management have little in common'	16	74	19	65	0	53	14	67
'Professionalism is a barrier to good management'	8	79	8	85	0	93	6	84
'It is rare to find a good curator who becomes a good manager'	8	60	19	69	20	60	14	63
'An adequate manager who has been a curator is preferable to a good manager who has had no previous museum experience'	29	50	27	50	33	40	29	48
'The best museums managers have also been good curators'	63	11	38	23	47	20	52	16
'It is essential that those working in museums should have their own professional association'	76	5	73	15	60	7	72	6
		n = 38		n = 26		n = 15		n = 79

Finally, nearly one half of the respondents disagreed with the suggestion that 'an adequate manager who has been a curator is preferable to a good manager who has had no previous museums experience', but nearly one third agreed with it. The responses were similar across all parts of the sector. They reveal a significant body of support among curators for the primacy of the curator-manager in museum management.

One of the most important developments within museums over the past twenty years has been the introduction of modern management methodologies, often drawn from private sector practice. An understanding of professional curatorial attitudes to managerial methods was sought by asking respondents to record their responses to a series of statements on a scale from 'strongly agree' to 'strongly disagree'. The results are contained in Table 6.5.

Table 6.5
Curator-managers' perceptions of the benefits of introducing new managerial methods into museums

Respondents strongly agreed or agreed with the following statements about management methods	Local authority museums (%)	National museums (%)	Independent museums (%)	All museums (%)
been beneficial to museums	84	74	71	79
helped improve museums	81	78	79	80
increased museums' credibility	81	55	43	66
made museums more efficient	76	70	71	74
made museums more effective	66	67	57	65
been essential to museums' survival	76	67	64	71
Respondents strongly disagreed the following statements about management methods:				
wasted valuable resources	68	55	79	66
distracted curators from real tasks	68	59	64	65
diverted funds needed for other things	66	52	64	61
imposed an alien culture on museums	58	33	43	47
put too much power in the hands of 'managers'	74	59	29	61
made museums over-bureaucratic	53	30	50	44
led to few benefits	74	67	71	71
	n = 38	N = 27	n = 14	n = 79

The first, and very positive, point to observe is that the great majority of curator-managers have recognised the value to museums of introducing modern management methods. More than two-thirds believed that these had been beneficial to museums and had helped to make them more efficient and effective. On the whole the local authority respondents were slightly more positive than those from the nationals and independents. The only serious difference of view appeared to be over whether or not new management methods had increased the credibility of museums. The local authority curators were enthusiastic in their agreement but the others were distinctly lukewarm, probably reflecting different perceptions of what constituted 'credibility' in the eyes of their different stakeholders.

At least two-thirds of local authority and independent curators rejected the suggestion that new management methods had wasted valuable resources, distracted curators from real tasks, diverted funds needed for other things, or put too much power in the hands of managers. However, once again the national curators did not disagree as strongly as the others. And when it came to whether managerial methods had made museums over-bureaucratic, 46 percent of national curators agreed or strongly agreed, while only 30 percent disagreed or strongly disagreed. The local authority curators (33 percent of whom agreed or strongly agreed) and the independents were also ambivalent about this one. Similarly 37 percent of national curators agreed or strongly agreed that these new management methodologies had imposed an alien culture on museums while only 33 percent disagreed or strongly disagreed. Local authority curators (and less so the independent museum curators) were inclined to reject this proposition but not in overwhelming numbers. It is in the responses to these two questions that one sees professional conservatism resisting the introduction of methodologies with which there is less than full sympathy or accord.

The overall message from the responses to this question is that there is a large measure of acceptance that museums have to apply appropriate modern management methodologies and that these have been generally beneficial. There is some resistance to them on the basis that they are alien to the museum culture and lead to increased bureaucracy. 'Management' has been embraced enthusiastically by many curators but to a significant minority it is still regarded as a 'necessary evil'. This feeling is strongest in the national museums, although the sample (drawn not from the Directors but their senior staff) may to some extent (though not all) account for this.

A further test of curator-managers' response to management methodologies was to ask them what they thought of the usefulness of a range of common techniques, ranked from 'very useful' to 'irrelevant'. The results, in Table 6.6, reveal (again) a large measure of consistency throughout the sector.

Table 6.6
Curator-managers' perceptions of usefulness of management tools and techniques
(percentage finding them very useful or useful)

	Local authority museums	National museums	Independent museums	All museums
Strategic planning	100	100	93	98
Total quality management	53	46	60	52
Performance indicators	89	71	73	80
Mission statements	87	75	67	79
Stated objectives	97	100	100	98
Budget forecasts beyond This year	87	100	93	92
SWOT analysis	93	32	47	64
Stakeholder analysis	39	32	7	31
Business planning	84	82	87	84
Corporate plans	89	86	80	84
PEST analysis	18	14	7	15
Collection management Plans	100	96	93	97
	n = 38	n = 28	n = 15	n = 81

What emerged, not entirely unexpectedly, was low awareness of what 'stakeholder analysis' and 'PEST' were among all respondents. More surprisingly, SWOT analysis does not appear to be well known in the national museums. Additional comments suggest that TQM's perceived usefulness is partly the result of ignorance but also because its usefulness has not been widely tested in museums yet.

A previous study (Davies, 1993) asked a sample of managers (n = 77) to indicate how they had, or would, go about making budget cuts. The intention was to test how well strategic planning held up as a meaningful process when put under the pressure of reductions in financial resources. It was also hoped to achieve an indication of the strength of professional attitudes and its influence over strategic decision-making at times of organizational stress. The results revealed a considerable reluctance to have to cut in areas which may be considered the 'professional heartland'. The broad pattern would seem to be that the more enlightened managers prioritise their activities, seek to generate additional income, then reduce expenditure in either the 'soft' area of the operational budget or by reducing the quantity of service available to the public. Only after this will the professional core of the service be cut. It is suggested that this may represent unwritten strategies based on organizational culture which supersede the 'up-front' strategies at times of crisis.

Professionalism and management

Fragmentation, or perhaps one could say diversification, within the museums world has usually been seen as a barrier to full professionalization (and therefore as unhelpful) but it possible has had its merits. The national museums have never fully subscribed to the notion of a museums profession because so many of its workers see themselves as primarily something else (for example a scientist or scholar) before being a museum worker. As we have seen, some of the nationals have had to take quite drastic steps to resolve the tensions between the research and management objectives, but there is little reason to suppose that a stronger sense of 'a museums profession' would have helped.

Similarly, the concept of 'a profession' is underdeveloped in the independent sector. But it is here that the very existence of 'non-professionals' (by which the 'professionals' usually mean people without a curatorial background) has ensured that the independents have been more customer-orientated, essential, of course, to their survival. Indeed, as a result of this the independents have frequently been cited as role models for the rest of the sector when it comes to introducing new ideas (Boylan, 1992, p. 39). So there is little evidence that the absence of a strong 'museums profession' has been anything other than beneficial to the independents.

This leaves the local authority public museums which have always provided the core of the 'museums profession' and have had the greatest influence in the Museums Association. Curators from this part of the sector have arguably had the leading role in developing collection management techniques, professional standards and codes of practice. At the same time their museums enjoy perhaps the least autonomy of action in the whole sector, being normally part of much larger organizations (museums typically account for 1 percent or less of a local authority's expenditure) and usually occupying a low position in the hierarchy, with the strategic direction of the service frequently being in the hands of a non-museum professional (such as a Leisure Services Officer or a Librarian). Under these circumstances perhaps what is most remarkable is how museums have retained a distinctive professional existence at all. The tensions between museum professionals and others in the larger organization seems to be more about a conflict of values than a simple manager and professional conflict (Raelin, 1992). Many museum professionals consider themselves as much managers as those 'above' them in the local authority hierarchy.

Advocacy, and defending their right to exist, consumes a great deal of time and energy of individuals, the Museums Association and supportive bodies such as the Museums and Galleries Commission and the Area Museum Councils. Advocacy is a key skill in an area of activity which is perceived as being low in social importance, albeit rated high in terms of satisfaction by customers as shown by a number of surveys.

The strength of the museums world lies in the values widely held in common by curators and other 'professional' workers. A basic belief in the importance of art and heritage to society underpins their commitment to the necessity of conserving and interpreting collections for their aesthetic and educational worth. It may be that these values are the 'glue' which helps their advocacy role and their frequently defensive posture.

But they have little power in the accepted sense. Without this their value system can easily be marginalized (or even ridiculed) by far stronger players in the organizational contexts (such as government or local government) in which they operate or the heritage and tourism market places. To survive they rely heavily on influencing their stakeholders' attitudes and actions, and especially on trying to persuade these stakeholders to adopt their values. To be effective in this they need sound strategies.

Unfortunately, although there is ample evidence that strategic management, as a concept, has been at least superficially embraced, there remains the probability that at least in a significant minority of museums the very values held by the professionals which are perhaps the museums' major asset, also incline them to be resistant to goal-orientated management methods, especially when these are perceived as being externally imposed by organizations (such as the local authority or the Department of National Heritage) which do not necessarily share the values of the museum curators. It is under these circumstances that conflict may arise or, at least, museums may be reluctant to adopt business managerialism enthusiastically.

Those who staff museums, and especially the curators, who form a patrician class within them, have a strong sense of belonging to a profession which upholds values which should transcend the organizational requirements of those who are responsible for governing museums. They have therefore been traditionally resistant to stakeholder influence, relying heavily on the fact that within their host organizations (whether it be the state or a local authority) they have been tiny operations, regarded as vaguely eccentric but something which the host organization 'ought to have'. The harsher economic climate in the public sector in the 1980s seems to have reduced this significantly as a tenable strategy for survival and museums have had to face up to being challenged to justify their existence and to demonstrate that they are capable of being well managed within their traditional value structure.

If 'professionalism' is in any sense a barrier to 'good management' it is not because of any realistic ambition among museum workers to become a profession in the traditional sense of the word. Rather it is because 'professionalism' is actually a facet of the culture of museums.

Museums, and the people who lead them, are value-driven. But, as Campbell and Yeung (1991) suggest, they may not achieve the strong mission necessary to influence stakeholders, unless both values and strategy are given appropriate weighting. Strategies which meet the aspirations of their stakeholders should be devised which do not compromise their values. When that happens, Victorian values may regain respect in a post-Thatcher goal-orientated society.

References

Audit Commission (1991), *The Road to Wigan Pier?*, HMSO, London.

Boylan, P. (1988), 'The Changing World of Museums and Art Galleries', in J. Benington and J. White (eds), *The Future of Leisure Services*, pp. 128-34.

Boylan, P. (ed.) (1992), *Museums 2000: Politics, People, Professionals and Profit*, Museums Association/Routledge, London.

Brears, P. and Davies, S. (1989), *Treasures for the People*, Yorkshire and Humberside Museums Council, Leeds.

Campbell, A. and Yeung, S. (1991), 'Creating a Sense of Mission', *Long Range Planning*, Vol. 24, No. 4, pp. 10-20.

Cossons, N. (1970), 'McKinsey and the museum', *Museums Journal*, 70/3, pp. 110-13.

Cossons, N. (1982), 'A New Professionalism', *Museums Journal*, 70/3, pp. 110-13.

Davies, S. (1985), *By the Gains of Industry*, Birmingham City Museum and Art Gallery, Birmingham.

Davies, S. (1990), 'Living with Leisure Services: The Kirklees Experience', *Transactions of the Museum Professionals Group*, pp. 18-22.

Davies, S. (1993), *Strategic Management in the Public Museums Sector*, unpublished University of Bradford MBA thesis.

Davies, S. (1994), *By Popular Demand : A strategic analysis of the market potential for museums and art galleries in the United Kingdom*, Museums & Galleries Commission, London.

Flower, W.H. (1898), *Essays on Museums*, Books for Libraries Press, New York.

Goode, W.J. (1969), 'The Theoretical Limits of Professionalisation', in A. Etzioni (ed.), *The Semi-Professions and Their Organisation*, pp. 266-313, The Free Press, New York.

Hanna, M. (ed.), (1993), *Sightseeing in the UK 1992*, British Tourist Authority, London.

Hudson, K. (1975), *A Social History of Museums*, Macmillan, London.

Kavanagh, G. (1991), 'The museums profession and the articulation of professional self-conscious mess', in G. Kavanagh (ed.), *The Museums Profession: Internal and External Relations,* pp. 39-55, Leicester University Press, Leicester.

Kenyon, F. (1927), *Museums and National Life*, London.

Klemm, M. and Wilson, N. (1993) *An Analysis of the Workforce in the Museums,Galleries and Heritage Sector in the UK*, Museums Training Institute, Bradford.

Lewis, G. (1989), *For Instruction and Recreation: A Centenary History of the Museums Association*, Quiller Press, London.

Mariner, D. (1974), 'Professionalising the Museum Worker', *Museum News,* (April), p. 52.

Myerscough, J. (1991), 'Your museum in context', in Ambrose, T. and Runyard, S. (eds), *Forward Planning*, Routledge, London.

Paton, J. (1894), 'The education of a curator', in *Report of the Proceedings of the Fifth Annual General Meeting of the Museums Association.*
Peake, M. (1946), *Titus Groan*, Penguin, London.
Prince, D. and Higgins-McLoughlin, (1987), *UK Museums Database*, Museums Association, London.
Raelin, J.A. (1992),'Cross-Cultural implications of professional/management conflict', *Journal of General Management*, Vol. 17, No. 3, pp. 16-30, Spring.
Robertson, I. (1985), 'Financing Museums: The View of the Professional', *Museums Journal*, December, Vol. No. 3, pp. 125-29.
Teather, J.L. (1990), 'The Museum Keepers: The Museums Association and the Growth of Museum Professionalisation', *Museum Management and Curatorship*, 9, pp. 25-41.
Trevelyan, V. (1991), *Attitudes Survey of Non-Museum Visitors*, Area Museum Service for South Eastern England, London.
Weil, S.E. (1988), 'The Ongoing Pursuit of Professional Status: The Progress of Museum Work in America', *Museum News*, November/December, pp. 30-34.
Wittlin, A.S., (1949), *The Museum: Its History and its Tasks in Education*, Routledge & Kegan Paul, London.

7 Footing the bill: professionalisation and the police service

Jane Goodsir

Introduction

In 1990, the House of Commons Home Affairs Committee expressed concern about the 'ineffectiveness and inefficiency of an archaic police system'.

Audit Commission reports normally seek to illuminate by looking at matters of detail in the way that business is done. In a series of reports on the Police produced between 1988 and 1991 the Commission raised numerous matters of concern. Its findings were fairly damning. Comparing the Police with sister services such as the Fire and Ambulance services, the Commission concluded that Police had failed to set key measurable service standards. At a higher level, the Commission reported on a number of significant strategic and management failures, indicating a determination to alert policy makers to deficiencies in Police management nationally.

In summer 1992 the Home Secretary announced the 'Inquiry into Police Responsibilities and Rewards', chaired by Sir Patrick Sheehy (Sheehy Report, Home Office, 1993a). Terms of reference were wide ranging. The report, together with the government White Paper *Police Reform* (Home Office, 1993b) was published in June 1993, facilitating substantial change in police service management.

The Sheehy Report proposes major changes in police resource management and staffing structures. Building on Audit Commission Reports describing underdevelopment of strategic 'people' management systems within the police, it makes a series of recommendations concerned with personnel issues. Taken with the 'Police Reform' White Paper, the police face root and branch reform of management, imposed by the Home Secretary through Parliament.

The findings of the Royal Commission on Criminal Justice published in summer 1993 are concerned with the operation of the Criminal Justice system in general. But some of its recommendations relate to police conduct in investigating crime.

The Commission's work was carried out against a background of public dissatisfaction with police conduct and discipline in investigating offences.

This paper examines the police as a professional group, and outlines some key debates concerning police management over the past three years. As managers and politicians seek to reconceptualise the role of the police as a service, and not a force, the changing role of the police is examined. Rethinking the role of the police involves moving away from the military model of organisation. It implies a process of restructuring, negotiation with different interest groups, a search for new shared understandings, and the promotion of a new message to the public. One may assume that the process will involve the debate and discussion within the service, and beyond. The paper deals briefly with prospects for research.

Police - power and control

Culture

Much research since the 1960s has been concerned with police culture. It may be seen as a culture in which achievement in high profile operational matters (fighting crime and keeping the peace) has been segregated from 'mundane' matters like efficient personnel and information management, carried out by relatively low status civilian staff.

Power and control currently lie in the hands of Chief Constables, who started their careers 'on the beat', and progressed through the ranks. From a managerial point of view until recently, senior police officers may have been relatively unsophisticated and isolated from current managerial and personnel practice. From a legal and political viewpoint, Chief Constables have enjoyed considerable autonomy, and have been able to exploit complex funding arrangements with relatively little direct accountability. At a lower level, the historic office of constable carries considerable autonomy, the legal capacity to exercise wide discretion, and to determine a street level view of the 'public interest'.

Police work takes place in a world of 'dirty realism' (Dorn, Murji and South, 1991), in which the members of the public are classified as the 'roughs' and the 'respectables'. According to McConville and Shepherd (1992), police occupational culture at street level is - 'a white, male, action centred sense of mission, underpinned by substantial internal solidarity and the stereotyping of individuals and groups who are 'outsiders'. Moreover, it is said that there is a considerable gap between junior officers and the 'butterfly men' - the liberal, well educated and mobile senior officers responsible for developing modern post-Scarman policing perspectives. Given the autonomy of junior officers, we may assume that the influence and effectiveness of junior managers (sergeants, inspectors) is of critical importance in shaping police policy as it implemented on the streets.

Conflict and authority

Police powers are extraordinary. With a monopoly on the use of legitimate force, policing requires an exceptionally high level of integrity. In consequence, the behaviour of police officers is highly regulated, by, for example, the Police and Criminal Evidence Act (PACE 1984). 'Doing things by the book' - a display of adherence to the letter, if not the spirit of the law is a significant, occasionally overriding concern in the service. Yet under PACE, research indicates significant police deviations from legal obligations after an initial period of compliance.

Contact with the legal system, with lawyers, and exposure to cross examination in court may have significant influence on police approaches to conflict resolution. According to Stephenson (1992), 'the police role in the adversarial sytem places them at the heart of a win-lose conflict that seems to generate antagonism to their opponents'.

Unlike most other occupational groups, police are 'on the record' when dealing with high conflict situations - violent arrest, for example. This is undoubtedly desirable. Yet reliance on the 'Book', legal powers, experience of adversarial legal process, means that police have a high awareness of legal authority as a symbolic (and real) source of power. Ideas of authority and 'force' are intrinsic to the police, giving rise to a culture that D. Elliott, HM Inspector of Constabulary has described as 'confrontational and adversarial' (Elliot, 1993).

Occupational experience of external confrontation, and emotional public demands can give rise to emotional numbness, estrangement, and cynicism, according to Hochschild (1983), writing about staff in service industries. The particular work context and adversarial experience of the police gives rise to significant management problems, with consequences that we shall examine later.

Police as professionals

With falling crime clear up rates, and concern about police effectiveness and efficiency, it is not so surprising, perhaps, that over the next few years, this public sector service is likely to experience substantial change imposed through external agencies. A range of professional groups experienced government sponsored change and reduced autonomy during the 1980s. As an occupational group, police are a non-traditional profession, operating in a context of great uncertainty, and with a state sanctioned monopoly (namely, legitimate use of force).

'Professionalisation', of course, has been seen as a successful ideology providing group mobility through occupational upgrading (Johnson, 1972). While state mediation undoubtedly reduces overt autonomy in relation to service priorities and delivery, it is clear that at street level police constables are expected to use 'subjective common sense' (Brogden, Jefferson and Walklate, 1988). But compliance with overall police objectives may be complicated by the capacity of street level officers to resist organisational pressures with their own resources (Lipsky, 1980).

At a higher level, senior police officers, as public sector managers, work in a highly political arena in which an illusion of operational autonomy and policy making is constrained by legislation, social context, and the need to satisfy different influence groups (Harrow and Willcocks, 1990). Senior managers in the public sector, not least those in the police service, must account for their decisions in a context of intense media interest. The need for public sector senior managers to demonstrate skills in public governance rather than low profile industrial style managerial and entrepreneurial effectiveness has been discussed by a number of writers.

Professional recruitment in the police service takes place against a background of tests and examinations, reflecting traditions analogous to civil service competitive entry. Subsequent internal competition for promotion meets standards determined internally, or in conjunction with the Home Office. For lower ranks, promotion examinations traditionally have been concerned with technical issues relating to the law and law enforcement. Under proposed legislation, the curriculum will be extended to cover managerial topics. The elite passes through courses at Bramshill, which according to Reiner, are valued as much for the hidden curriculum - communing with other movers and shakers in government agencies - as for their formal content.

Policing - a gentleman's profession?

Police recruits are drawn from the skilled manual and lower middle classes, with higher and lower classes poorly represented, according to Reiner. Promotion comes from within. Even 'fast stream' officers move through all the junior ranks. In 1988 only 6 percent of the police establishment were graduates. While 40 percent at Chief Officer level had degrees, police officers are not members of the kind of gentlemen's profession described by Burrage (1993) in his account of the legal professions.

It is not a profession that favours women. According to Brown (1992), the service continues to subject women to differential deployment and tasks, and only made significant moves to implement Equal Opportunities policies after the appearance of Home Office Circular 87/1989 *Equal Opportunities Policies in the Police Service*. Ethnic minority officers, like women, are underrepresented in the service.

Professional expertise

The police operate in an environment of uncertainty affecting the behaviour of both service providers (the police themselves) and service users (the public). The police exercise individual discretion and varying levels of diagnostic skill in carrying out their duties. Police are subject to intensive formal and informal internal education, and possess considerable expertise in the exercise of power within a strong legal framework.

Police are not overtly concerned with market closure, autonomy, and the monopolistic application of recognised expert knowledge. But manifestations of police culture - identification with the occupational community, and degree of formal and informal programming, for example, are characteristic of other professions providing services under state mediation and control (Johnson, 1972). Frequently police are concerned with controlling and ordering duties, often working in collaboration with other social service providers.

Yet within the service the presence of an increasing number of 'other' professionals - accountants with chartered status, for example, are employed to impart expert advice. According to Brown (1992), relations are not always happy, as civilian staff are poorly integrated within the police service, particularly at senior level, reflecting traditional divisions. One may speculate that increasing 'professional' administration within the police and in contracted out services may involve the employment of high status professional 'outsiders', carrying the possibility of conflict between police and other professional groups with competing occupational ideologies.

The need for change

Returning to Audit Commission Reports on the Police Service, key areas identified for development included accountability and funding, resource management, and performance indicators. The publication of the reports heralded a new dawn for many police managers, with the prospect of imposed radical reform of the service. By 1992, the Sheehy Inquiry into Police Pay and rewards was working to terms of reference determined by Home Secretary Kenneth Clarke. This signalled the beginning of the end of the historic 'Edmund-Davies' principles under which Police had secured favourable treatment on the basis of non-comparability of their work with other employment sectors.

Sheehy - imposed change?

Emphatically rejecting Edmund-Davies this summer, the Sheehy Report (Sheehy) recommends a series of structural changes to police pay and service conditions, eliciting outrage in police ranks. 'The Sheehy report reduces the police service from being a dedicated vocation to being just another job ... Sheehy has devastated police morale ...' observed Alan Eastwood, of the Police Federation, representing junior ranks in the service.

In a very detailed report, Sheehy argues that police have become top-heavy and over-managed, recognising that some work on restructuring has already taken place. Police pay is not sufficiently linked to roles, responsibilities and performance. Conditions of service and allowances are outmoded. Fixed tenure agreements are needed to provide greater flexibility. A detailed plan for uprating basic pay while abolishing allowances is set out, together with a strategy for setting up performance related pay elements. Linking police pay with the median of private sector pay, many of the Sheehy recommendations are clearly designed to provide long term savings on policing costs.

In setting out detailed implementation arrangements, as well as broad principles of policy, Sheehy provides a national framework for action, potentially precluding creative application of the policy by senior police managers. Some detailed recommendations of the Report have come under sustained attack from those officers likely to be responsible for its eventual implementation.

Police change in the 1990s

A number of police scandals surfaced in 1989 raising questions about continuing effectiveness of the police without reform. The wholesale collapse of prosecutions based on evidence from officers in the West Midlands Crime Squad raised the prospect of continuing public suspicion about police malpractice. Acting on Audit Commission findings, the police service has been engaged in a significant reorientation. Independently of Sheehy and legislative pressures, senior police managers determined to embark on a process of strategic change and reorientation.

This reorientation has been particularly concerned with 'professionalising' strategies. These relate to both professionalisation of management approach, and the promotion of a professional policing 'ethos'.

Communicating change

The Metropolitan Police Force, under the leadership of Sir Peter Imbert, has set the agenda for police led change during the past 5 years. The Met PLUS programme has been a significant attempt to influence the culture of the police. Consultants Wolfe Olins concluded that profound cultural change in the service was needed to reinforce managerial changes in the Metropolitan Police.

Given the size and nature of the police service, this has been a substantial and costly undertaking. Brown (1992) has speculated on implementation difficulties, suggesting problems relating to a proportion of middle ranking officers apparently blocking change. Elliott, of the Inspectorate of Constabulary, observes that resistance to change among senior officers may arise through perceptions that the new policing ethos undermines their power to manage effectively (Elliot, 1993).

An outstanding feature of the reconceptualisation process is a concern to change the nature of communication with the public. As one senior officer put it:

> Our ideal is the constable on the beat. The 'community police officer' is how we would like you to think of us. The actual perception is more often of us as dressed in police riot order kit. There is a real tension between these two roles.

> You can't get away from the fact that we are the embodiment of legal force in society. We are part of the enforcement strategy. The theory for this problem is for the police to help communities tackle their own problems. Schools, the education authorities, and others in health education are an embodiment of the community; they should be identifying priorities that I should then be helping you to solve (Grieve, 1992).

Two significant promotional initiatives concerning professionalism and change have emerged in the past 3 years. The Police 'statement of Common Purpose and Values' promoted by Sir Peter Imbert, former Commissioner of the Metropolitan Police, set out the policing 'mission' in 1990. It is now adopted nationally. While the overriding aim of the police is 'to uphold the law' the statement goes on to deal with *how* policing is to be conducted. Key phrases include '... acting without fear or prejudice to the rights of others ... professional, calm and restrained ...'. In acknowledgement of ongoing difficulties, the police 'must respond to well founded criticism with a willingness to change'.

A draft Statement of Ethical Principles followed in December 1992, setting out 11 points relating to the conduct of policing. These include upholding human rights; acting with impartiality; taking responsibility for individual acts and omissions. HM Chief Inspector of Constabulary, Sir John Woodcock commented

> As a profession, we need it because we need to assist officers to take difficult decisions ... the world of policing is one of considerable uncertainty in which there are many conflicts between, for instance, the rights of suspects and the requirements of effective criminal investigation (Woodcock, 1993).

Taken at face value, the production of an ethical code and a statement of purpose reflect a post-Scarman concern to improve policing services as they are conducted by officers, experienced on the streets and perceived by the public. They indicate a preoccupation with the management of criticism and difficult relationships externally and internally. They may also be seen as an occupational organising strategy, mobilising a new 'professional' ideology to preserve autonomy in the face of threatened state intervention and control.

Ideological shifts within the police service have been developing for some years. A number of factors have given rise to re-evaluation of the policing and police management. Brunson argues that radical changes have to be preceded by and initiated through ideological shifts. Moreover, he maintains that where old and new ideologies are competing, and old values retain some allegiance, then the context for change is poor. The communication of new (professional) corporate values externally may be seen as an attempt to 'symbolically frame the context' - potentially an efficient but indirect way of influencing human resources internally. Communicating a powerfully coercive 'partly false' image might be one way of purposely changing corporate behaviour (Alvesson and Berg, 1992).

This symbolic approach to change within the police is unlikely to succeed unless underpinned by a link between image and observable change in behaviour patterns. In practice, this may be difficult to achieve. Day to day experience of police work seems to undermine desired new 'open' attitudes. It appears that authoritarian attitudes among new police recruits rise as they experience real policing work. Training has a temporary, liberalising effect on officers, who then revert to old occupational assumptions and beliefs. The assumption that control of image and policy will lead to the internalisation of values, and thus bring control of police work on the ground, may well be misplaced.

Professionalisation in management

The imperative of professionalism in managerial work - as understood in industry - is relatively new to the police service. There is relatively little research on police management *per se*. Rather police research has focused on policy oriented issues such as police accountability.

Like many organisations subject to strong external control, the police service is centralised and relatively formalised. This implies that responsibility for the service is removed from the individual officer and placed in the administrative structure. In a context in which changing standards are imposed externally, and from above, lower ranking officers may fear loss of control, and become passive (Mintzberg, 1979).

Leadership and implementation of change implies a need to manage a series of interrelated processes and systems innovations, according to Pettigrew et al (1992). Judging by the recent literature produced by police themselves, there is keen interest in developing new managerial practice in a number of areas. Yet there are clearly difficulties in changing systems and attitudes within the current formalised organisation.

According to Sheehy,

> The service would also benefit from the use of civilian professionals and from redistribution of responsibilities within senior management teams in such areas as finance, personnel, information systems, procurement, training and management services (Home Office, 1993a, 3.43).

> Overburdened with paperwork, middle ranking officers are limited in the degree of attention they can devote to leading their officers. Specialist units dedicated to particular concerns have developed their own management infrastructures creating confusion about acountability and poor internal communication. Officers themselves will be expected to improve management efficiency with line managers having greater control of resources.

Supervisory work

Complex legal considerations as well as cultural traditions give rise to difficulties in supervising police work. Reiner maintains that the

> autonomy of rank and file culture is created by self abrogation of police elites who see explicitly and authoritatively binding policies for handling discretion as contrary to the basic legal conception of the constable's duty of law enforcement (Reiner, 1992b, p. 486).

Indeed, this aproach to the office and its discretion was endorsed in 1993 by Paul Condon, the new Metropolitan Commissioner:

> The office of constable is not about being any kind of worker: it's about the oath of allegiance, the use of discretion, and responsibility under the law. As Commissioner, I cannot say 'officer, arrest that man'.

Yet this approach brings problems in supervisory work. Lord Scarman commented on the 'dangerously low level of supervision of the processes of arrest, interrogation and charge' in 1986. In that year the Police and Criminal Evidence Act (PACE) was implemented, with all its controlling and checking provisions relating to arrest and detention.

Controlling mechanisms on police imposed through legislation tend to rely on the processing of paperwork. Most recently, S. 95 of the Criminal Justice Act 1991 (CJA), has imposed a duty to maintain information on aspects of policing relating to gender and race. In addition, the legislation enables those engaged in the administration of criminal justice to become aware of the financial implications for their decisions. Chatterton (1987, 1989) found that lower level supervisory ranks spend much of their time processing paper, interfering with street level supervisory work. Supervisory work on the streets often resulted taking over and directing things.

Police training has been updated to take account of the need for more practical and interpersonal skills, as well as legal knowledge. The White Paper *Police Reform* of 1993 endorses new management development initiatives, and skills based assessment of managerial competence in promotion examinations. However, given the complex legal basis for autonomy at street level, questions remain about the control and supervision of police work within such a formalised structure. 'Management' is now finding its way on to the police training agenda.

Personnel and recruitment

Equal Opportunities has become a growing challenge within the service. The Inspectorate of Constabulary has adopted the issue as one of their reporting points.

In consequence equal opportunities have a high profile with senior officers. There is speculation that women, for example, may bring different styles and approaches to conflict resolution. Yet the possible influence of non-traditional police recruits - graduates, women, ethnic community officers - in changing police culture is limited by continued under- representation.

Loveday (1993) has examined the work of civilian staff in the police service concluding that (sworn) police officers have refused to take direction from highly competent technical staff, and civilian experts have been denied opportunities for wider managerial development. At present, the recruitment of finance staff can be determined by inexpert police officers in the absence of expert civilian staff.

During the Sheehy Inquiry, many questions were raised about the police approach to personnel matters. While appraisal systems exist, the effectiveness of the current system has been challenged in relation to performance related pay. One can speculate that problems may arise if assessment and appraisal procedures are influenced by the police approach to discipline issues and the current complaints procedures. Following the criminal justice system model, simple criticisms by the public - about rudeness, for example - must be substantiated to a high (legal) standard of proof, rather than dealt with on an informal basis.

Financial awareness and resource management

Awareness of policing costs has been an objective of recent legislation (CJA 1991). Performance agreements for Chief Officers should focus *inter alia* on cost effectiveness in terms of resources according to Sheehy. Senior officers have been active in seeking out cost effective measures in operational matters. Police priorities have changed as police analyse the effectiveness of and levels of public support for certain types of law enforcement. Informal processing of offenders through cautions has risen dramatically as officers seek cheaper disposal of criminal cases.

For example, policing of certain minor drugs offences has been downgraded as costs have been assessed. Use of the official caution as a means of disposing of relatively serious adult offences has cut legal paperwork and police attendance time in court. This trend is reflected in other areas of policing activity.

Streamlining of management to devolve resources and responsibility has already led to restructuring in which local commanders take primary responsibility for local policing, and the management of local police budgets. More flexible shift systems have been introduced, allowing for deployment of officers at peak demand times.

The White Paper proposes the extension of compulsory competitive tendering in a range of areas. This brings the need for police to manage service relationships with a diverse network of contractual suppliers, rather than through internally controlled services.

There may be police anxieties about certain strategic facilities being put out to contract. But on an operational level, there may also be public resistance to the targeting of police resources to set priorities. For example, the police have a role as peace keepers and social service providers of last resort, deploying some resources in response to local public demands.

Quality

The idea of 'Total Quality Policing' has emerged as a strategic and social marketing tool. While some 'quality' thinking is concerned with internal police management issues, most is concerned with identifying and measuring public needs, preferences, and satisfaction levels.

Greater attention to independent quality assurance is recommended in Sheehy, (1993a, 3.43). The White Paper with its emphasis on 'Partnership' and quality of service issues proposes that the police 'concentrate their effort on the policing tasks regarded as priorities by the society they serve' (1993b, 7.2). Working to secure policing Charters in response to the Citizen's Charter is becoming as endorsed as a quality of service initiative (1993b, 7.17).

There are of course difficulties relating to customer care and policing. With offenders (and many victims of crime) engaged in an involuntary 'consumer' relationship with the police, perceptions of quality may be somewhat jaundiced. Nonetheless, attention to the needs of detainees, anti discriminatory practice in relation to particular communities, and a range of consultative measures could produce raised standards in areas in which traditionally there has been concern over police performance.

Prospects for the police

It is clear that senior police are adopting some industrial management ideas and techniques as they seek to manage strategic change in the service. Performance indicators have been introduced. The signs are that change is a complex and intensely political process. Management of change often implies a temporary dip in performance as reforms are worked through and staff come to terms with new processes. Criminal statistics for 1991 show falling clear up rates for reported criminal offences.

Legislation this Autumn is likely to consolidate some changes already introduced, and to take some matters very much further. The main thrust of the legislation is to streamline police reporting arrangements, provide greater freedom and personal accountability for Chief Constables to manage, devolve responsibilities, and introduce new pay, performance and discipline arrangements.

Historic funding processes will be abandoned. The Home Office is likely to set policing priorities centrally with a local consultative element. Information about the performance of different forces will be standardised. Some long awaited IT initiatives are likely to be implemented, presenting additional systems change. A range of control mechanisms will be introduced.

Opposition to reform within the police has recently focused on Sheehy. Given the range and depth of other initiatives designed to change policing and its management, there has been little publicly expressed opposition to reform. Rather, opposition seems to have taken the form of slow compliance with good practice initiatives, expressions of anxiety, and the continued exercise of discretion in the old manner.

In a climate where the arming of the police is a distinct possibility, influencing the behaviour and judgement of individual officers will continue to be the greatest challenge in police management.

Opportunities for management research

The substantial body of research on the police carried out in the 1980s by researchers in universities, the Home Office and elsewhere has, according to Reiner (1992b), been predominantly policy oriented. Much work has been concerned with police culture and organisation theory. Research on management has been more concerned with constitutional, legal and governance issues than with management within the police service.

Areas for development could include exploration of personnel practice within the service, ethical dimensions of police work, different individual policing styles, police civilian staff, the work of supervisory and senior ranking staff, trade unions within the police service, police public relations and marketing practice.

While police management represents an interesting area for research, access has occasionally proved difficult. As the service employs new types of staff in new working relationships, it will be interesting to see whether the new police values of openness to criticism lead to new opportunities in management research.

References

Alvesson, M. and Berg, P. (1992), *Corporate Culture and Organisational Symbolism*, Walter de Gruyter, Berlin.

Audit Commission for Local Authorities and the National Health Service in England and Wales (1989a), *The Management of Police Training,* HMSO, London.

Audit Commission for Local Authorities and the NHS in England and Wales (1989b), *Effective Policing*, HMSO, London.

Audit Commission for Local Authorities and the NHS in England and Wales (1990), *Footing the Bill,* HMSO, London.

Audit Commission for Local Authorities and the NHS in England and Wales, (1991), *Reviewing the Organisation of Provincial Police Forces*, HMSO, London.

Bradley, D., Walker, N. and Wilkie, R. (1986), *Managing the Police - Law, Organisation, Democracy*, Wheatsheaf, Brighton.

Brogden, M., Jefferson, T. and Walklate, S. (1988), *Introducing Police Work*, Unwin Hyman, London.

Brown, J. (1992), 'Changing Police Culture' in *Policing*, Vol. 8, pp. 307-22.

Brunsson, N. (1982), 'The Irrationality of Action and Action Rationality: Decisions, Ideologies and Organisational Action', *Journal of Management Studies,* Vol. 19, No. 1, pp. 29-44.

Burrage, M. (1993), 'Looking Backwards and into the Future: From a Gentleman's to a Public Profession', unpublished paper, London School of Economics and Political Science, London.

Chatterton, M. (1987), 'Front line Supervision in the British Police Service' in G. Gaskell and R. Benewick (eds), *The Crowd in Contemporary Britain*, Sage, London.

Chatterton, M. (1989), 'Managing Paperwork' in M. Weatheritt (ed.), *Police Research: Some Future Prospects*, Avebury, Aldershot.

Cherrett, M. (1993), *Performance Indicators Policing*, Vol. 9, pp. 40-53.

Dorn, N. and Murji, K. (1992), 'Low Level Drug Enforcement', *International Journal of Sociology of Law*, Vol. 20, pp. 159-71.

Dorn, N., Murji, K. and South, N. (1991), 'Mirroring the Market? Police Reorganisation and Effectiveness against Drug Trafficking' in R. Reiner and M. Cross (eds), *Beyond Law and Order: Criminal Justice Policy and Politics in the 1990s*, Macmillan, London.

Elliott, D. (1993), Unpublished address to Metropolitan Police Service 'Fairness-Community-Justice', Conference, 27 February 1993.

Etzioni, A. (1969), *The Semi-professions and their Organisation*, Free Press, New York.

Foucault, M. (1979), *Discipline and Punish - the Birth of the Prison*, Penguin, Harmondsworth.

Grieve, J. (1992), 'The Police Contribution to Drugs Education: a Role for the 1990s', in R. Evans and L. O'Connor (eds), *Drugs Abuse and Misuse: Developing Educational Strategies in Partnership*, pp. 53-64, Fulton Press, London.

Harrow, J. and Willcocks, L. (1990), 'Public Services Management: Activities, Initiatives and Limits to Learning', *Journal of Management Studies*, Vol. 27, No. 3, pp. 281-304.

Hoschschild, A. (1983), *The Managed Heart: Commercialization of Feeling*, University of California Press, Berkeley.

Home Office (1978), Committee into Police Pay and Negotiating Machinery, Report, Cmnd 7283, (Chairman, Lord Edmund-Davies).

Home Office (1993a), Inquiry into Police Responsibilities and Rewards, Report, Vols. 1 and 2, Cmnd 2280.I and 2280.II (Chairman, Sir Patrick Sheehy), HMSO, London.

Home Office (1993b), *Police Reform: A Police Service for the Twenty-First Century*, Cmnd 2281, HMSO, London.

Johnson, T. (1972), *Professions and Power*, Macmillan, London.

Kirby, T. (1993a), 'Police Solve Fewer and Fewer Crimes', Report in *Independent*, 24 February.

Kirby, T. (1993b), *Independent*, 1 July.

Lipsky, M. (1980), *Street Level Bureaucracy*, Russell Sage Foundation, New York.

Loveday, B. (1993), 'Civilian Staff in the Police Service', *Policing*, Vol 9, pp. 117-35.

Lukes, S. (1974), *Power*, Macmillan, London.

McConville, M. and Shepherd, D. (1992), *Watching Police, Watching Communities*, Routledge, London.

Mintzberg, H. (1979), *The Structuring of Organisations*, Prentice Hall, Englewood Cliffs, N.J.

Morgan, R. and Smith, D. (eds) (1989), *Coming to Terms with Policing*, Routledge, London.

Pettigrew, A., Ferlie, E. and McKee, L. (1992), *Shaping Strategic Change*, Sage, London.

Reiner, R. (1992a), *Chief Constables*, Oxford University Press, Oxford.

Reiner, R. (1992b), 'Police Research in the United Kingdom: A Critical Review' in M. Tonry and N. Morris (eds), *Modern Policing*, Chicago University Press, Chicago.

Royal Commission on Criminal Justice (1993), Report, Cmnd 2263, Chairman Lord Runciman, HMSO, London.

Scarman, Lord (1986), Letter to *Times*, 7 October.

Smith, R. and Perry, J. (1985), 'Strategic Management in Public and Private Organisations: Implications of distinctive contexts and constraints', *Academy of Management Review*, Vol. 10, No. 2, pp. 276-86.

Stephenson, G. (1992), *The Psychology of Criminal Justice*, Blackwell, Oxford.

Stewart, J. and Ranson, S. (1988), 'Management in the Public Domain', *Public Money and Management*, Spring/Summer, pp. 13-19.

Woodcock, J. (1993), *Police Review*, 1 January, p. 27.

Part IV

Organizational Professions

8 Restructuring and repositioning of the UK engineering profession

Tony Millman

Introduction

The UK engineering profession currently comprises 42 Institutions/Societies, representing 300,000 registered members, under the general umbrella of the Engineering Council.

The Engineering Council was established by Royal Charter in 1981. Its main role is to maintain a register of qualified engineers and technicians; accredit and monitor courses at universities, and colleges; approve programmes of training and experience; and launch a range of initiatives to promote and advance the profession. The Engineering Council has undoubtedly found it difficult to coordinate the activities of such a large number of autonomous Institutions located at split sites throughout the country.

In an attempt to unify the profession, the Chairman of the Engineering Council, Sir John Fairclough, took the bold step of calling for a comprehensive restructuring which will radically affect the organization and operation of member Institutions. His vision is that of a new 'overarching body', with the existing role of the Engineering Council subsumed into the new body. To this end, a Steering Group was set up to consider the formation, role and organization of such an integrated body to act as a focal point for the profession. At the time of writing, the Steering Group had published its proposals in an interim report and a series of regional meetings were being held as part of the consultative process.

While being generally supportive of the Engineering Council and the achievements of member Institutions, Fairclough (1992) has openly criticized their limited success in achieving recognition on a broad front. He has, for example, made the scathing comments that 'engineering is a fragmented profession which lacks focus, status and influence' in the UK; requiring greater lobbying power on big issues, ... with Government, with education and training, with industry and commerce, and with Europe and beyond'. Not surprisingly, this has sparked an intense debate within the profession - releasing pent up feelings among individual members and blatant posturing among the major Institutions.

This paper examines the pros and cons of unification, focusing on two interrelated issues that need to be addressed by the engineering profession: restructuring and repositioning.

Restructuring is largely an internal matter for the profession with the prime aim of achieving the highest quality service to the profession at the lowest delivered cost.

Repositioning of the profession is about relationship marketing and should focus on both internal and external constituents. It must be based on recognition that the profession is competing for the attention of individuals and groups within engineering companies and throughout the economy and society at large.

Restructuring and repositioning are intertwined because external public credibility and standing is dependent on member satisfaction and the quality of relationships within. A prerequisite, however, is for the profession to know where it is going and a willingness to get its own house in order before telling the world that it has arrived. There is no point whatsoever, for example, claiming an integrated profession possessing a shared vision of the future, a service orientation and contributing to the quality of life, if it is obvious that nothing has changed. The general public and those whom the profession serves directly, have an uncanny knack of being able to separate shadow from substance!

This chapter cannot be regarded in any sense as written by a detached observer. The author is a Chartered Engineer. To use a footballing metaphor, he has some difficulty in separating the roles of spectator, player and referee. For the most part, the text moves from the descriptive to the analytical and explanatory; but there are numerous occasions when it is unashamedly prescriptive and promotes the case in favour of unification. The engineering profession needs to be constantly reminded that the current proposal is the third time in thirty years that it has played the unification game. The overwhelming need now is for an unambiguous and workable result.

Historical background

It is not intended in this chapter to trace the early history of individual professional Institutions. Nor is it appropriate to dwell on the role of engineers in the alleged drift from a pro-industrial to an anti-industrial culture (see, for example, Hobsbawm 1968; Wiener 1981; Rubinstein 1993). It is sufficient here to note that most Institutions began by providing an independent forum for learned discussion. Gradually, as their number expanded in line with industrial specialization and development, they found themselves setting more stringent standards for membership and operating increasingly at the policy interface between Government and the engineering industries.

By the early 1960s, there was widespread recognition of fragmentation. The number of Institutions exceeded fifty and a general desire for greater cooperation and coordination led to formation of the Council of Engineering Institutions (CEI), incorporated by Royal Charter in 1965.

Throughout the 1970s, the CEI made substantial progress in achieving common standards of education/training; but there were acrimonious debates concerning constitutional issues, pay and status; and serious doubts were expressed about its effectiveness in promoting the profession. This prompted the Labour Government to set up a Committee of Inquiry in 1977 under the Chairmanship of Sir Monty Finniston.

Finniston reported in 1980. Despite good intentions and eighty recommendations related to his core theme of enhancing 'the engineering dimension', Finniston's proposal to set up a new statutory Engineering Authority received a remarkably hostile response. The Institutions resented Finniston, partly because that he was not an engineer (i.e. a metallurgist), but mainly because his Inquiry was imposed by Government and some of his proposals were perceived to threaten their continuing independence. Additionally, and more influentially in the end, the newly elected Conservative Government was reluctant to support anything that smacked of regulation or intervention. Both sides prevaricated for many months. What emerged in November 1981 was a compromise chartered body - The Engineering Council - without statutory powers.

The Engineering Council has had over a decade to build its credibility. Some observers argue that it has been slow and has achieved little, whereas others believe that it is under-resourced and that it has been frustrated by its terms of reference. By the late 1980s, reform of some kind seemed inevitable.

Salient details of Engineering Council membership during 1992 are shown in Table 8.1, from which it should be noted that the top three Institutions (i.e. the Electricals, Civils and Mechanicals) account for over one half of registered members. Moreover, the top three also represent two thirds of the 199,000 Chartered Engineers, giving them a dominant voice in current activities and any future reforms. This concentration of power is a recurring theme throughout this paper.

Table 8.1
Membership of the major UK professional engineering institutions 1992

Institution	*Registered membership*	*Total membership*
Institution of Electrical Engineers (IEE)	58,780	134,270
Institution of Civil Engineers (ICE)	49,083	79,211
Institution of Mechanical Engineers (IMechE)	46,395	75,616
Institution of Marine Engineers (IMarE)	13,061	16,861
Institution of Structural Engineers (IStructE)	12,707	21,678
Royal Aeronautical Society (RAeS)	10,307	17,883
Institution of Electronics & Electrical Incorporated Engineers (IEEIE)	20,528	28,019
Other Institutions	89,290	204,281
Total	300,151	577,819

Notes: 42 Institutions have nominated or affiliated status with the Engineering Council.
Over 28,000 registrants belong to more than one Institution.

Source: *The Engineering Council*

Table 8.2
A comparison of chartered engineers with other UK professional bodies

Professional Body	*UK Membership (as at mid 1992)*
Chartered Engineers	199,000
Chartered Accountants	116,000
Medical Doctors	97,300
Barristers/Solicitors	77,600

Sources: *The Engineering Council, Institute of Chartered Accountants, The British Medical Association, The Law Society, The Bar Council*

The Fairclough initiative

The recommendations of the Council of Presidents' Steering Group (1993) are set out in its lengthy interim report entitled: 'Engineering into the Millennium'. Three components form a central part of these recommendations: first, the Engineering Council should be reformed and not abolished. Second, the creation of a *New*

Relationship between the reformed Engineering Council and the Institutions. Third, the proposal to move towards a *Single Institution.*

The notion of a New Relationship is likely, in itself, to be welcomed by the Institutions. Unfortunately, tied to it is a proposal to group Institutions with common interest into 6 *Colleges*, thereby introducing an intermediate layer of organization in a system already heavily criticized for its bureaucracy. The proposed Colleges are: Electrical, Mechanical, Civil, Extraction and Processing, Transport, and the rather odd grouping of Pan-disciplinary Support and Services. Existing Institutions will be invited to join *one* College. Given the current composition of the profession, it is hardly surprising to find the first three Colleges named in the proposal!

By far the most controversial recommendation, however, is that of progress towards a Single Institution. This involves the reformed Engineering Council, existing Institutions and new Colleges eventually transferring all their functions to a new Single Institution. It is envisaged that Colleges might then evolve into *Divisions* of the Single Institution. Further definitions were deferred to the next stage in the Steering Group's deliberations, as was consideration of whether the profession should seek statutory powers.

Time scales for the reforms are ambitious: a programme for creating the New Relationship to be drawn up by the end of 1993; and by the end of 1995, a proposal to be established, on which the whole profession would then be invited to decide, to move in a series of steps towards a Single Institution.

Internal restructuring

Differentiation versus integration

The age-old trade off between differentiation and integration continues to pervade most technology-driven organizations, including the professional institutions. The purpose of discussion under this subheading is to address the key strategic question:

How far should the profession go along the continuum from its current position as a loose federation of highly differentiated Institutions/Societies, towards total unification in name and operation?

As currently constituted, the Engineering Council provides a useful, if underdeveloped, umbrella for the profession. In the absence of hard survey data, it is difficult to say with confidence whether it is the Engineering Council or member Institutions which attract the most personal affiliation and loyalty. On the one hand, it can be said that since its inception, the title CEng has gathered a certain cachet of respectability which has become much sought after by some young graduate engineers and others in the early stages of their training. Yet there is the worrying estimate that only about one quarter of engineers achieving the requisite academic qualification each year go on to train and gain experience for registration.

On the other hand, engineering degrees have carried the labels 'mechanical', 'electrical', 'civil', 'aeronautical', etc., making it reasonable to conjecture that these routes to CEng have reinforced identity with individual disciplines and Institutions. Somewhat belatedly, as degree courses have become more inter-disciplinary, the boundaries are being breached and integrative skills are gathering greater credibility. Witness the increased inputs to engineering project work from industrial/graphic design and business management now found in courses in the more progressive universities.

The author wishes to note, with some gratification, this trend towards integrative teaching - though overcoming the 'specialist' mind set of engineering lecturers (at a Polytechnic) in the mid 1980s seemed an uphill struggle. Running integrative topics was initially regarded as the way forward, but always 'someone else's job' and hardly the fast career track for academics in engineering departments! This is why the Engineering Council's early initiatives in schools and institutions of further/higher education will eventually pay off.

Such recent developments will not, however, affect the vast majority of managers and engineers who passed through the higher education system at a time when integrative teaching, especially the inclusion of business management topics, did not appear in the core curriculum. It is here that resistance to change may well prove difficult to overcome. Chartered Engineers, for instance, will almost certainly wish to retain their identity as specialists in particular fields of engineering activity. This is mainly covered by the 'learned society' role and must continue to be accommodated as it is the *raison d'être* for professional institutions.

The same cannot be said of the many other coordinative and administrative functions performed by Institutions such as setting and monitoring standards of performance, accreditation of degree courses, handling membership matters, promotion of the profession, publishing activities, organizing conferences, seminars, and so on. Clearly, these are common across all member Institutions. With careful attention to the division of responsibilities, it should be possible, within a reasonable time frame, to identify common functional requirements so as to gain economies of scale and scope in an integrated operational framework.

The logic of splitting up the learned society role from administrative support is hard to fault, but it pales into insignificance when compared with the daunting task of negotiating higher levels of integration or unification in the form of a Single Institution.

Incremental versus radical change

Incremental change through mergers or absorption may, at first sight, appear attractive as the least disruptive form of rationalization. Experience has been mixed. There are recent examples to support this approach (e.g. IEE/IERE, IEE/IMfgE). Equally, the aborted IEE/IMechE 'amalgamation' provides a salutary experience of what can go wrong despite the claim of the IMechE President that the two Institutions were 'convergent, not divergent bodies'. An editorial in the IMechE's Engineering News

(Farmer 1991:2) at the time captured the mixture of scepticism, inertia and depth of feeling surrounding the proposed IEE/IMechE merger:

> Had talks progressed further, it should have become clear to both parties that they had strayed some way from their original declared mutual aim of one year ago, to create a new organization ... better equipped to serve the needs of the modern engineer.
>
> Draft proposals have indicated that the merging institutions, far from reaching out and grasping the challenge, excitement and opportunity for innovation implied in their stated ideal, would merely reinvent themselves on a grander scale.
>
> Intending to be a chartered, learned society, building on two long established professions, the evolving body would have just one option for a title: the Institution of ... and ... Engineers. Given the scale of pride and sentiment embodied in both memberships, the ranking order may never have been agreed.

Radical change under the banner of say a single Institution of Professional Engineers implies an 'all or nothing' approach. The half way solutions adopted at present, whereby the names of larger Institutions survive while others are in most respects relegated to subgroup status, may emerge as ends in themselves rather than providing a useful interim step towards unification. Rationalizations such as the IEE's 'acquisition' of the Institution of Manufacturing of 1992, (formerly Production) Engineers (IMfgE) are recipes for cynicism and simmering discontent. At worst, they risk the unwelcome spectacle of the Engineering Council as 'pig in the middle', while other Institutions poach disaffected members and compete for new graduates.

The formation of a Single Institution would provide the only true 'amalgamation' implying 'round table' status of all specializations within the profession. The new Institution would then assume responsibility for overall strategy in full consultation with the various Divisions. The names of all member Institutions would disappear under this proposal, but the various grades of membership could be retained (i.e. Fellow, Member, Graduate) along with the titles: CEng, IEng and EngTech. No comment is offered at this stage as to where the Royal Academy of Engineering might fit into this revised schema.

A major sticking point in any negotiation leading to unification is likely to be site rationalization. Herein lies the dilemma: the marbled halls and prestigious addresses of Birdcage Walk, Savoy Place and Great George Street, are part of the ethos of individual Institutions and there will be enormous pressure to retain them to fulfill the learned society role. Some Institutions also operate regional offices. Split sites are not conducive to integration and a certain sense of history may well have to be sacrificed as colocation becomes the preferred option on grounds of cost and communication.

Poor utilization of assets is one manifestation of the wider problem of the deteriorating financial situation facing some Institutions. Given the number of qualified UK engineers who have not sought membership, increasing fee income by boosting recruitment offers a partial answer and there is some scope for developing commerical activities. But recession has exacerbated the problem and some Institutions will undoubtedly find it difficult to remain viable. If one or two Institutions falter and receive a bad press, then the standing of the profession might plummet to a level from which it may never recover. Financial pressures alone are sufficient to justify the drive towards unification.

And finally, returning to the issue of differentiation, it must be remembered that the branch network of all Institutions provides the main point of contact for most members. To some, the branch *is* the Institution. Branches survive and prosper on the voluntary efforts of a few dedicated members. It will be essential that these people buy in to the reorganization.

Self or statutory regulation?

Professional engineers have long craved for higher status. The pages of professional Institution magazines and newsletters regularly feature correspondence from members bemoaning their apparently deteriorating status in society and low pay.

There is a substantial body of opinion in the engineering profession which feels that the route to enhanced status lies in some form of delegated power to operate within a quasi-legal framework. Professions such as medicine and law offer useful analogies and it is easy for proponents to argue that engineering demands similar levels of expertise and judgement. Just as the 'distinctive competence' of professionals in medicine is about researching disease or diagnosing and treating illness, so it could be cogently argued that engineers are concerned with diagnosing and solving problems.

The engineering profession also has similar opportunities to cocoon itself in a code of ethics, recruitment standards, registration and disciplinary procedures. However, while these trappings of autonomy and self-regulation may be necessary for enhanced status, they are seldom sufficient to achieve the privileged position currently enjoyed by medicine and the law. For unlike the last two professions, engineering rarely touches the lives of members of the general public in such an emotional and direct way. A comparison of Chartered Engineers with membership of other professional bodes is to be found in Table 8.2.

For further clues regarding what it takes to achieve and sustain a privileged position it is worth briefly examining the meaning of the word 'profession'. According to Freidson (1975), the word has dual meaning: first, it is a species of a generic concept, namely 'occupation'; and second, an avowal or promise. The first is well understood. The second is of particular interest in the context of this chapter and spawns a few fundamental questions for the engineering profession:

What role do engineers currently play in society?
What role do engineers want to play in the future?
What skills and benefits are most valued by different sections of society?
What promises have been made?

> Have these promises been delivered?

Ultimately, as will be argued later, it is powerful groups in society who make judgements about integrity and accord professions the degree of exclusivity they are deemed to deserve.

The problem of the engineering profession is captured in the words of Freidson (1975, p. 73):

> If a profession's work comes to have little relationship to the knowledge and value of its society, it may have difficulty in surviving. The profession's privileged position is given by, not seized from, society, and it may be allowed to lapse or may even be taken away.

Few professional engineers need reminding of the persistent problem of defining the term 'engineer'. It appears that everyone from car mechanic to television repairer, and from software designer to the head of the engineering function in a large multinational company can use the title. This is unlikely to change and can only be tackled via differentiation.

From the foregoing it should be apparent that this chapter is less concerned with the pursuit of statutory organizational arrangements than with *earning* legitimate acceptance by society. Since the days of the Great Engineers the profession has allowed its position in society to lapse. It now needs to mount a campaign of organizational renewal and repositioning.

Repositioning

Internal marketing

Repositioning of the engineering profession must start with careful attention to internal marketing, by identifying meaningful communications platforms within the profession and in the organizational setting in which engineers operate.

Most professional engineers work in medium/large organizations. This means that they operate in a political system in which pecking orders and power structures impact on decision making. There is considerable evidence to suggest that executive decision making at corporate level in large groups of companies is dominated by financial considerations and at divisional level by attention to products/markets/technologies. In some extreme cases, this has led to a schism in which corporate boards have become so preoccupied with the City and 'short termism' that their dialogue with divisional boards is increasingly restricted to reviewing business plans, proposals for capital expenditure and applying tight controls based on financial performance ratios. This is consistent with 'hands off' corporate/business unit approaches to organization structure commonly found in conglomerates. To improve top-down and bottom-up communication, some enlightened engineering groups invite heads of business units to sit on corporate boards; and they encourage synergistic horizontal communication through various committees dealing with organization-wide issues such as: new products, process engineering, quality management, information technology, and so on.

Where do professional engineers fit into such hierarchies? Examination of the composition of boards and the distribution of engineers throughout organizations reveals that while they are thin on the ground at corporate level, they are relatively well represented at divisional level and among functional managers and specialists.

A more penetrating question is: how well prepared are engineers to move from specialist to functional manager and director roles, and from functional director to managing director, and so on, right up to the top echelons of corporate management?

Cranfield University's experience shows that these critical transitions are poorly managed by most companies and the problem is exacerbated in business units where directors/managers heading up the three key functions of marketing/sales, manufacturing/production and engineering/technical have mostly trained initially as engineers of one kind or another. Such organizations often pay scant attention to developing general management capability and succession planning.

Cranfield University is not alone in identifying this shortcoming in the development of engineers and in calling for stronger links between technical disciplines and general management training:

> There are still too many British boardrooms within which those with the technological capability to understand and shape direction of the business are unable to make a full contribution to policy and strategy debate because they are simply not well enough grounded in the disciplines of business (Hood, 1991, p. 13).

> The necessary psychological condition is for directors to be willing to start letting go of some of their deeply learned specialist thoughts and behaviour, to allow time and space for learning of new attitudes, knowledge and skills (Garratt, 1987, p. 45).

Clearly, there is a strong case for developing professional engineers: first, to help them reframe the way they see their business and its external environment; and second, to enable them to make early and more 'rounded' contributions to corporate/business strategy. These are minimum requirements for gaining the respect of colleagues.

By reforming, rather than abolishing the Engineering Council, the Fairclough initiative has resisted jettisoning its most important achievement - the national system of *Continuing Professional Development* (CPD).

CPD should be made the 'Unique Selling Proposition' for internal marketing within the engineering profession. To quote an Engineering Council Newsletter (1991, p. 1): the CPD system was set up to '... enable individuals to update and develop their knowledge and skills and help industrial companies to improve their performance'.

There is no better platform for intervention and from which to launch a repositioning campaign than CPD.

In operationalizing CPD, any new professional body must restrict its role to encouraging, promoting and facilitating management development programmes. Short updating courses in technical areas are a different matter and many Institutions have a successful record of income generation. In contrast, management development is very personal and contextual, requiring the kind of commitment over time that emerges from partnerships between client company, individual delegate and the organization providing training. Ultimately, management development takes place when delegates return to work and put into practice the concepts and ideas that have been developed during the programme. It would not be reasonable to expect a professional engineering body to acquire the staff and facilities to conduct such training. A more cost effective route would be to appoint top class CPD liaison officers to forge links with companies, business schools and management development organizations.

Persuading employers to accept the logic of CPD will be easier than securing the time for delegates to devote to it. The Engineering Council's recommendation of a minimum 35 hours per year CPD is probably about right as an initial target, though suggestions that it should be mandatory deserve wider debate. In reality, time allocations are meaningless unless considered alongside programme content, level and quality of training, and the receptivity of individuals to particular types of training. Beyond this, generalizations become difficult and more detailed comment is outside the scope of this chapter.

Turning now to the burgeoning field of formal management education, the stance of the engineering profession is unclear. Take, for example, the Diploma in Engineering Management (DipEM). Even though the DipEM is currently sponsored by four Institutions and endorsed by around 25 companies, the number of completions is very low. As a late entrant, the DipEM appears to be swimming against the tide. The new professional body would be better occupied in embracing long established, nationally recognized qualifications such as the Certificate/Diploma in Management Studies (C/DMS) and internationally recognized qualifications such as the Master of Business Administration (MBA) which already attract a high proportion of engineers.

To further muddy the waters, there is what has become known as the Management Charter Initiative (MCI), which grew out of the Handy Report (1987) and Constable & McCormick Report (1987). These reports greatly stimulated the debate on management education and working parties were formed by the Foundation for Management Education in an attempt to examine and define multi-level management competencies. MCI has had greater success in defining competence-based management qualifications at middle and supervisory level than at top management level. At one stage the notion of a 'Chartered Manager' emerged. Fortunately, this was shelved as unworkable.

CPD in the engineering profession is clearly part of a much wider scene. In some cases, the profession may wish to make its own distinctive contribution; but in most cases, external developments will force the pace and members will increasingly rely on their professional body to represent their interests. Only two further requests stem from highlighting this dynamic situation: first, the new professional body should ensure that the trainers' net be cast over all three grades of registration (i.e. CEng, IEng and EngTech); and second, due consideration be given to working within the new framework for National Vocational Qualifications.

International orientation

Most policy prescriptions for restoring national and corporate competitiveness emphasize awareness of the international dimension. This has serious implications for the profession. Exhortations to the membership to become more internationally orientated will have little impact unless the new professional body is itself seen to be internationally oriented.

One of the cornerstones of the Engineering Council's international initiatives has been its links with the Fédération Européenne d'Associations Nationales d'Ingénieurs (FEANI). Many UK professional engineers feel intuitively that moving towards some form of pan-European registration is the way forward, yet the benefits often seem remote and FEANI has been slow to establish itself.

Total FEANI registrations passed the 11,500 mark in mid 1992, of which 87 percent were from the UK. Superficially, this remarkable statistic suggests that UK professional engineers are to be commended on their commitment to Europe. But this is difficult to reconcile with knowledge that FEANI has existed for over 40 years and claims to include the national engineering bodies of 21 European countries!

Why is it that the total number of registrations is so low? Why are the other 20 countries so laggardly? What is the perception of FEANI held by say German, French and Italian engineers? Is it that our European counterparts are less concerned with professional status?

If the new engineering body wishes to reaffirm its commitment to FEANI, then it should be reminded that *positioning by association* is important, i.e. you are judged by your friendships. Given the relatively high UK membership, the profession has a vested interest in seeing FEANI succeed.

Apart from affiliation with FEANI, evidence of the Engineering Council's international orientation is difficult to find. Take, for example, the Director General's Report (Filer, 1992, p. 6) of the seven key areas in which he highlighted 'excellent progress' and four others in which he saw 'solid and sustained progress', none mentioned international activities. This is not to denigrate the achievements listed, especially initiatives on education/training and recruitment of women. These are all of national importance, but they urgently need supplementing by a range of international initiatives.

At Institution level, evidence of international orientation is patchy. On the positive side, the larger Institutions have, either individually or jointly, run a number of very successful conferences, often tied to major exhibitions and with industrial sponsors (e.g. Autotech, Aerotech, Eurotech Direct). On the negative side, some Institutions are ploughing ahead with international cooperation agreements and networking arrangements at an alarming rate. First, insufficient thought seems to have been given to *selectivity* among relationships. This may work against favourable repositioning. Second, even if the right partnerships can be struck, it is doubtful if the critical mass of skills and resources is available to support efficient networking.

The larger Institutions are also conscious of the need to cater for the interests of their overseas membership, which in some cases is of the order of 15 percent of total membership. Herein lies a further glaring example of the potential for costly fragmentation. As individual Institutions exploit and expand their overseas branch network, they will each continue to build on their own administrative staff and overseas affairs committees. In short, there are overwhelming opportunities to gain economies of scale in international activities.

This chapter does not pretend that an internationally oriented professional body can bring about attitudinal change in the short term, or for that matter, bring about lasting change. As argued earlier, true management development takes place in the work setting. Urging companies to expose their engineers to international business should, therefore, be an integral part of the new professional body's remit and preferably built into the CPD initiative.

External relationship marketing

Repositioning of the profession in society is firmly in the area of external relationship marketing. This would normally involve extensive market research to ascertain the current position owned by the profession and to characterize the ideal position it would like to own. At some stage, it would be useful to ask members of the profession: How would you like an informed outsider to describe you? This and other questions would almost certainly reveal: mismatches between the profession's perception of itself and those held by society; the nature of attributes/benefits most valued by key groups, and appropriate platforms for repositioning.

In the absence of comprehensive research and analysis of this kind, it is still possible in this chapter to speculate, albeit crudely, on the outcome because in the real world there are only a few positions worth striving for. Here, by way of example, are a few core themes around which positioning statements for the profession might be developed:

(a) contribution to wealth creation;
(b) working in the national interest;
(c) engineering products/processes that have changed the world;
(d) great achievements in engineering;
(e) applying engineering know-how to make life easier;
(f) what a chartered engineer could do for your company and,
(g) insights into the world of engineering, etc.

Above all, the choice of platform and associated messages must be credible. The new professional body should avoid the temptation to adopt the kind of hollow political slogans typified by the 'white heat of technology' and 'enterprise culture', or anything that smacks of a crusade against the ingrained attitudes of an anti-industrial society. As alluded to earlier, the more the messages touch the lives of individuals, the better. Note how, for example, ICI cleverly used cataract treatment, hip replacement and seed technology to enhance their image through an 'ICI World Class' corporate advertising campaign.

Unfortunately, the engineering profession is unlikely to possess the budget of an ICI or DTI for mass advertising. The expenditure would be impossible to sustain and might well provoke an adverse reaction from fee paying members. A more subtle and direct way of exploiting core themes can be developed by using public relations campaigns. This would involve targeting selected reference groups and opinion leaders, perhaps starting as follows:

(a) *Human resource managers* influence recruitment and have a strong say in salary grading. It is they who interpret 'equivalence' of qualifications and status across a wide range of occupations. It is essential that they know precisely what a CEng, IEng and EngTech can do for their company and it is likely that they would also be very receptive to the new professional body taking the lead in CPD.

(b) *Chief executives* are concerned with measurable outputs, e.g. improving profitability, productivity, cost reduction and competitiveness generally. Campaigns such as 'design for profit' and 'design for economic manufacture/assembly', spring to mind as successful examples in the mid 1980s. When combined with competitions on design, manufacturing and/or marketing excellence, they can generate considerable interest and prestige for the winners beyond the initial campaign. Advertising and editorial comment placed in selected management journals provide the main media channel.

(c) *Individuals in society who are predisposed to engineering excellence* These people may not be engineers themselves, but they are reachable via the magazines they read and the places they visit. The power of journalists writing for lightweight magazines is underrated.

All three of the above audiences require first class copywriting skills, supported by a coordinated effort to put forward speakers with good communication skills. Institution news sheets are packed with good stories being told at branch meetings. These need to be packaged for external consumption under a strong corporate brand image for the profession.

Concluding remarks

The Fairclough initiative provides a timely trigger for change and deserves serious consideration by every stakeholder in the profession.

At the time of writing (July 1993), it would be dangerous to adjudge response to the Steering Group's interim report based solely on opinions expressed in Institution news sheets and from regional discussion meetings. News sheets tend to reflect the opinions of Institution officials who have a vested personal interest in the outcome. Such opinions are important because they become, through editorial policy, a kind of quasi-manifesto on key issues facing the profession. Radical reorganization will almost certainly involve relocation among full time officials and job losses in the medium/long term; and substantial change in committee structure at branch level.

Interpreting the sentiments of the mere 1,500 or so members attending the 22 regional meetings conducted in June/July 1993 is equally problematic. These meetings comprized a fair proportion of past/current committee members who have lived thorough previous attempts to restructure the profession. A certain sense of *déja vu* pervaded most meetings and the poor attendance, particularly by younger members, is hardly encouraging to those leading the initiative. Does this reflect lack of support for Fairclough or general apathy within the profession, or both?

The most visible posturing so far has come from the Institution of Electrical Engineers. It has already rejected the move towards a Single Institution and has signed a memorandum of understanding with the Institution of Mechanical Engineers and the Institution of Electronics & Electrical Incorporated Engineers for further collaboration. The Institution of Chemical Engineers claims to have also rejected a single Institution, though its survey of members was conducted before the Steering Group's proposals were published. Other major Institutions are noticeably reticent in supporting the Steering Group of which they were either an integral part or to which they provided a substantial input.

And finally, some officials are clearly using the term unification in a pejorative way, preferring to speak of an 'evolutionary approach' and 'networking' as a way forward. If these attitudes prevail and win the vote of the whole membership, then the most likely outcome will be mergers built around the big three Institutions, to the exclusion of minority interests, thereby undermining the spirit of the Fairclough initiative.

References

Constable, C.J. and McCormick, R. (1987), *The Making of British Managers,* British Institute of Management, London.

Council of Presidents (1993), *Engineering into the Millennium,* Interim Report of the Steering Group, April.

Engineering Council (1991), *CPD System Gets Go-Ahead,* Newsletter, Issue No. 13, April.

Fairclough, Sir John (1992), Chairman of the Engineering Council, Special Meeting of the Council of Presidents of Member Institutions, January.

Farmer, M. (1991), *Life After the Broken Engagement,* Engineering News, The Newspaper of the Institution of Mechanical Engineers, August, No. 78.

Filer, D. (1992), *Excellent Progress in Key Areas,* The Engineering Council Newsletter, No. 15, May, pp. 5-8.

Finniston, Sir Montague (1980), *Committee of Inquiry into the Engineering Profession,* HMSO, Command Document 7794, January, London.

Freidson, E. (1975), *Profession of Medicine: A Study of the Sociology of Applied Knowledge,* Dodd, Mead and Co., New York.

Garratt, R. (1987), *The Learning Oganisation,* Fontana Collins, London.

Handy, C. (1987), *The Making of Managers,* Report sponsored by the National Economic Development Council, Manpower Services Commission and British Institute of Management, HMSO, April.

Hobsbawm, E.J. (1968), *Industry and Empire,* Pantheon, New York.

Hood, N. (1991), Professor of Business Policy, University of Strathclyde, Letter to the Financial Times, 12 April.

Rubinstein, W.D. (1993), *Capitalism, Culture and Decline in Britain 1750-1990,* Routledge, London.

Wiener, M. (1981), *English Culture and the Decline of the Industrial Spirit 1850-1980,* Cambridge University Press, London.

9 Marketing: the limits of professionalism

Don Bathie

Introduction

The discussion presented in this paper is an explicit critique of the drive for professional status by marketers, or at least organizations representing marketing. While the discussion is obviously focused on marketing there are enough points of general applicability to make the discussion relevant to other business-related professions (established or emergent). The critique presented has several dimensions and the discussion concentrates on identifying the bases for thinking about and criticizing marketing as a profession. While each dimension is identified and discussed there is considerable scope for the refinement of the discussion. This critical approach is based on two perspectives.

Firstly, that the natures of organizations and organizational environments are changing and that the professional concept of marketing is a limiting factor in the adoption of marketing in such circumstances. The dimensions of this, illustrated in this paper, include the description of marketing as the practice of 'art in a closed field' (where the professional view of marketing limits marketers to the continued remixing of the same standard 4P's of marketing activities), and; the presentation of a post modern description of organization structures which would (does) limit the relevance of professional marketing to an optional, service function.

Secondly, the discussion describes the changes and developing views as to the nature of marketing itself - in particular the movement of marketing out of the formal, functional arena to the organizational - cultural arena. From marketing as activity, to marketing as attitude. The paper presents two related points with regard to this development. The first concerns the broadening of ideas about marketing to the description of it as an orientation rather than a function. It is argued that the definitions and activities of marketing as a profession have, and continue to, constrained the applicability and application of marketing. The discussion goes on to develop this point by contrasting the marketing profession with the most basic characteristics of professionalism - expertise and ideology - and finds that in terms of the current practice of the marketing profession, it only meets some of the needs of professions and appears to be making little effort to develop the others.

The justification for adopting a critical approach to the marketing profession is twofold. At one level it is an application of the academic paradigm that nothing is unquestionable and that marketing contains its own share of questionable characteristics:

> not to forget to ask, re-ask and rephrase obvious questions about the longitudinal management of the marketing mix and its results, and the complex processes involved (Vink, quoting Savitt, 1992).

On another, more personal level the presenter of this paper has struggled long to match the requirements and characteristics of purported professionalism with the practices of marketers and the developments in marketing ideas and practices. This paper represents elements of that struggle.

The marketing profession

Professions and professionalism have been the subject of much work in social and organizational research. While this work has ranged across a series of characterizations and descriptions the idea of the 'profession' used in this paper concentrates on the characteristics and activities of an organized group of labour. In terms of Millerson's description of a profession, is taken to be 'a comparative status level attained after deliberate action by an occupation' (1964).

The process of achieving the comparative status level of a profession results in

> a structured form of work which institutionalises aims of interactive competence, consciousness of responsibility, empathy and acquired practical experience (Offe, 1985).

Millerson (1964) expanded on the characteristics of a profession by identifying and describing their qualifying associations. His analysis identified the most the general qualifying associations as:

- Skill based on theoretical knowledge
- Provision of education and training
- Testing the competence of members
- Formal organization
- Professional code of conduct and adherence to it
- 'Service to Society'

The main features of professionalism as a structural form were later described by Waters (1989) as:

- Theoretical knowledge
- Professional career- vocational commitment to supra-personal norms.
- Formal egalitarianism
- Formal autonomy - subject to internal regulation
- Scrutiny of product - subject to peer review
- Collective decision-making.

Such structural definition and analysis of a profession serves well to describe the characteristics and process of qualification of the marketing profession in the UK. This process has been defined and driven by the (now) Chartered Institute of Marketing (CIM). Their success in developing the professional status of marketing is undoubted, at least in terms of the structured sense.

Evidence of the this success was presented recently at the 'Rethinking Marketing' conference in a paper by Peter Simcock (1993), in his paper *Marketing as a Profession.* He noted the achievements of the marketing profession, as characterized by the CIM, in terms of the perceptions of marketing as a profession and in terms of its ranking on a scale of professionalization. His presentation showed that in terms of the following:

Perceptions. Marketing's ranking along a spectrum of professionalization gave it a rank of 7. This compared with a ranking score of 12 for the Royal College of Obstetricians and Gynaecologists and the Royal College of Surgeons - and scores of 4 for the Institute of Industrial Managers and the Society of Chiropodists. It gave the Chartered Institute of Marketing equal ranking with the Inns of Court and the (then) Institution of Production Engineers.

Professionalization. Using a thirteen point scale, derived from a Millerson approach to analysing professions, marketing had progressed greatly in the years between 1969 and 1993. While in 1969 the marketing profession had only two of the defining characteristics of a profession, by 1993 it had achieved seven of the characteristics, including that of the all important Royal Charter of Incorporation.

There is little doubt that the driving force in this professionalization of marketing has been the work of the CIM. The roots of the institute that represents the marketing profession lie in the Sales Managers' Association of 1911, which developed into the Institute of Marketing which was awarded a Royal Charter in 1989. Many of the characteristics of a profession are enshrined in the documents of the CIM including - codes of practice, ethics of confidentiality, professional qualifications and professional discipline.

A critique of the profession

While the CIM is not the sole focus for a critique of the marketing profession it represents many of the problematic areas associated with professionalism in marketing. As such it is a useful and valid proxy for the profession. The critique offered in the discussion concentrates on the structural/functional characteristics of the marketing profession. These are seen as valid characteristics for discussion given their importance as defining characteristics of professionalism and the significance of the resultant effects of possession of and emphasis on these characteristics.

Art in a closed field

The first dimension of this critique of professions in marketing relates to the definition of an area, or field, that is an essential part of the process of professionalization and to the limits that such definition has placed on marketing practice. In progressing this approach the idea of exhaustion is used to describe how the limits of professional marketing have acted to functionalise marketing practice. Exhaustion relates to:

> The exhaustion, in a systematic way of all the possibilities of action calculable given a certain restricted set of objects and states (McHale, 1992).

McHale uses an example from one of Beckett's plays to illustrate 'art in a closed field' where the exhaustion derives from the closed field of a room that a character negotiates and renegotiates.

> Here he moved to and fro, from the door to the window, from the window to the door, from the door to the window; from the fire to the bed, from the bed to the fire, from the fire to the bed ... from the door to the window, from the window to the fire; from the fire to the window, from the window to the door (Beckett, 1953).

The parallel in a marketing context is that the definition of marketing currently advanced by the profession narrowly defines the field of marketing and leaves the marketer in somewhat the same position as the character in Beckett's play. The closed field of marketing as represented by definitions such as the CIM's -

> The management process responsible for anticipating, identifying and satisfying customer requirements profitably (Chartered Institute of Marketing, 1993)

leaves the marketer to move unceasingly from product to price, price to place, place to product, product to promotion, promotion to price ... In terms of organizational behaviour the professional definition of marketing limits the field of marketing to that worst case scenario as described by McIver (1987):

> The worst outcome for those who believe in the marketing philosophy is that marketing practitioners should be penned in their small back room, increasingly introverted and subservient to the self-interested money makers and politicians, and applying their technical expertise in the realms of persuasion to the ultimate destructive end of making the worse appear the better cause.

The relative lack of development of what is recognisably an extended field for the marketing professional is evidenced not only in the definitions of professional bodies. It is also extensively characterized by the contents of marketing texts, at both general and specialist levels; the contents of marketing journals and the sameness of the topics researched and re-researched; and the nature and content of marketing development courses and programmes. The closedness of the marketing field as defined by the profession rapidly engenders the feelings expressed by Colvina (1978):

> It was absurd to waste any more time on an operation whose implicit possibilities I had by now explored completely, an operation that made sense only as a theoretical hypothesis.

Professions in a postmodern configuration of production

The idea of exhaustion that initiated the discussion in the previous section has been used extensively in discussions of the demise of modernity and the rise of postmodern society. While it is difficult to uncritically and wholeheartedly adopt a postmodern approach to business, organizations and the market place, there is certainly enough in the idea to give reasonable pause for thought among marketing professionals. Descriptions and predictions of the nature of commercial organizations, their environments, their structures and their ways of working in postmodern society are characterized by a picture

> of the familiar post modernizing one of fluid shapelessness driven by shifting tastes on the one hand and localized decision-making on the other (Crook et al, 1992).

Crook, Pakulski and Waters (1992) build on this postmodern landscape (or more appropriately, seascape) to suggest the likely nature of the production systems.

Figure 9.1
The differentiation of production systems

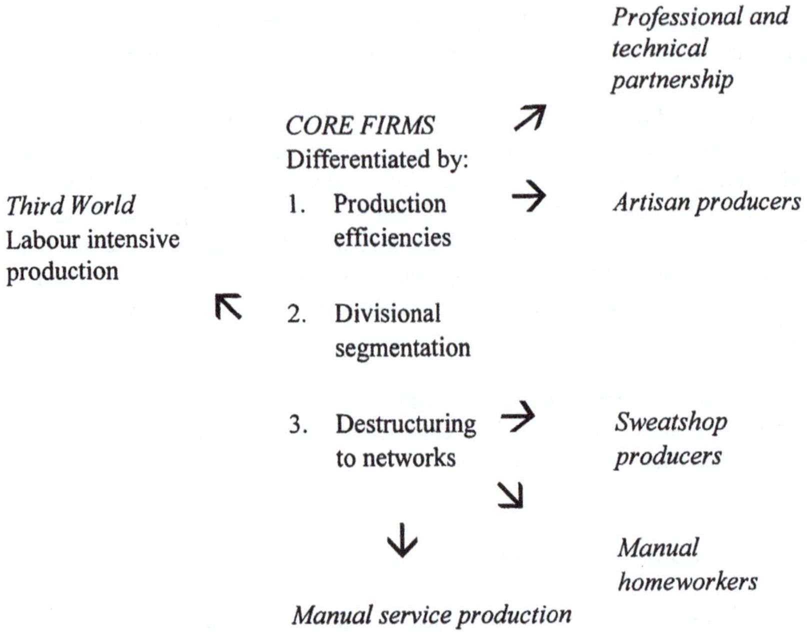

Source: *Crook, Pakulski and Waters 1992*

In this scenario marketing as a profession is placed clearly among that group of services that are almost optional for the core firms. What is required of the marketing profession is its expertise and skills in support of the objectives and values of the core firms, in return for fees of course. McIver's worst case becomes reality. Marketing practitioners and professionals:

> ... become subservient to the self-interested money makers and politicians ... (McIver, 1987).

While historically such a position in the production system would have seemed appropriate and desirable for marketing - this is no longer the case. Current wisdom regarding marketing presents marketing as an orientation vital for the core business and for organizational success. The customer/market focused orientation of marketing is not paid service provision - it is rather a defining characteristic of the organization's culture. The marginalizing of marketing implied in such a production system is the result of characterizing marketing as a profession dominated by expertise and functional skills rather than an ideology.

For the current marketing profession the question becomes one of:

> what if the best should happen and the managers who make the decisions at all levels should themselves become, if not marketing man in the full sense, at least involved with the marketing philosophy? It might mean that marketing would cease to be regarded as a distinct discipline and be merged into general management. But that would be a small price to pay (McIver, 1987).

A focus on functions

As has been suggested in the previous discussion, marketing has gone through a process of development with regard to definitions of the discipline and with regard to the meaning of practising marketing. While there is still debate and doubt about the nature of marketing it is now clear that descriptions of marketing that are dominated by functional activities and limited applications (as exemplified by the CIM definition quoted earlier), are too limited and limiting to be effective. In describing the apparent loss of power of the functional marketer in consumer products companies, the commentator Roger Cowe shows how this extreme functionalism of the marketing profession can work against marketing.

> In one sense, the decline of marketeers is a kind of victory; their creed has permeated most companies, which have now become 'market oriented' rather than being dominated by technology, product or even bureaucratic demands. To some extent, this systematic approach has undermined the importance of functional marketing departments (Cowe, 1993).

Marketers and marketing academics might disagree with Roger Cowe's generalization about the extent to which the marketing 'creed' has permeated companies. However, the view expressed shows that there is a difference between the idea of marketing and the practice of marketing as a function (however professionally it is practised).

The emphasis of the marketing profession on functional skills and expertise is almost total. The most recent evidence of this domination of function is contained in the programme offered by the CIM for Continuing Professional Development (CPD) - launched in 1993. The CPD programme defines three levels and general types of course provision:

- Implementation and Practice
- Advanced (managerial skills)
- Strategic

The actual course programme describes seven sets of courses:

> Management Theory and Practice - seventeen courses which are all either skills based or describe the application of skills in specific contexts.

Selling Theory and Practice - twelve courses, all skills based.
Marketing Specialisms - thirty courses, all skills based.
Sales Specialisms - six courses, all skills based.
Sales Management - three courses, all functional management. Management Development - four courses, all strategic management skills.
Business Skills - twenty one courses, all skills based.

It may be that the courses, while being overwhelmingly skills/functionally - based in description, do contain orientation and ideological bases and components. However, there is room for certain doubt in this, given the nature of the profession's definition of marketing as a management process and its other characteristics. Nor is the CIM alone in this functional emphasis, the content of other programmes in marketing are equally functionally - based.

For example, in article entitled 'The Education and Training of Marketing Managers', Thomas (1984) identifies sixteen skills '... the bedrock of effective marketing management in the 1980s'. He identifies these skills as:

- Planning skills
- Environmental awareness
- Organizational ability
- Segmentation - product development skills
- Behaviour analysis skills
- Market research commissioning skills
- Information analysis skills
- Innovation management skills
- Strategic thinking skills
- Sales and advertising management and productivity management skills
- Marketing mix optimization skills
- Interdepartmental cooperation and conflict resolution skills
- Financial management skills
- Systems thinking skills
- The ability to comprehend the long term interests of the company
- The ability to 'market' marketing enthusiastically.

With the possible exception of 'marketing marketing' there is little evidence here that the marketing manager and by implication the marketing professional is anything more than a functional specialist with a functionally - defined set of skills.

The argument against such an emphasis is that marketing as an orientation requires significant and (more than) equal development, if the full potential of marketing is to be realized. While professions such as marketing require a base of expertise they also require an ideology. In the sense that:

ideology refers simply to that level of reality, at once individual and collective, subjective and objective, at which people orient meaningfully to their world. (Wernick, 1991).

Training in, development of, support of, emphasis and communication of this ideology is as important as the functional skills. Given the historic, and current, lack of emphasis on such an ideology in the marketing profession it might be argued that now is the time to give such development even greater emphasis than function development.

Structure and function: culture and beliefs

The idea of marketing as an orientation in a business/organizational context, as promoted in this paper, goes beyond that view expressed by writers such as Pearson:

> Orientation is therefore a question of degree - the degree to which one function (or object) orientation dominates the way of thinking in an organization and consequently the way decisions get taken and the way people do their jobs (Pearson 1993).

In the sense that orientation is used by Pearson the emphasis is still placed on function and the domination of one function in an organization. The idea that specific functions can/should dominate is too problematic in the organizational context. Domination in this sense is situation specific and dependent on the nature of the organization's skills, resources, market situation and competitive environment.

> Consequently, it may be sheer arrogance to suggest that marketing, as a function, must dominate. Better to reserve that judgement for its philosophy [that] a customer/market orientation should permeate every corporate function. Arguably, it's not marketing but its pursuits - customers and their retention that should transcend all interests of all aspects of the business (Wong, 1993).

The focus of the argument in this paper is that marketing has attempted, with varying degrees of success, to dominate as a function. The professionalization of marketing has consciously aided this attempt at domination. Such attempted domination has however resulted in and will predictably continue to result in negative effects on marketing's progress.

It is argued that the professional emphasis on function has closed the field of marketing's perceived applicability. Further this closed field has concentrated marketers' thinking and actions on a narrow range of activities which appear to be only partly what is required for successful marketing.

The adoption of a marketing orientation may be more fundamentally what is required for effective marketing and organizational success. The efforts of the marketing profession in changing organizational orientations have concentrated on functional dominance. While this may be necessary it may not (will not) be sufficient for effective marketing. Wholesale changes in culture and belief in organizations require more than functional dominance:

> ... breaking loose from so long established a mind-set is not easy. It requires a change in culture, in habits, instincts and ways of 'thinking and reasoning' (Skinner, 1986).

While functional domination may effect, ways of 'thinking and reasoning' changing culture, habits, instincts will require the communication of and the generation of a commitment to an ideology of marketing. Such an ideology is not apparent in the work of the marketing profession.

In Wong's terminology (1993), it is not the marketing function but its pursuits that should be dominant The dominant ideology of the marketing profession, as represented by the Chartered Institute of Marketing, is an ideology of professionalism, not an ideology of marketing.

While such an ideology prevails the emphasis of the profession will remain on structure and function and the lack of an appropriate marketing ideology will continue to restrict marketing's applicability and continue to marginalise the marketing function. What is required in marketing is an idea of marketing that is powerful enough to realise marketing's role as a builder of organizational culture.

Conclusion

It is probably dangerous to draw conclusions in any work that contains elements of postmodernism. However, there is a least one tentative conclusion to be drawn from a critique of the marketing profession. The application of a professional ideology to marketing has resulted in an artificial narrowing of the ideas and applications of marketing. The dichotomy between academic and practitioner ideas of marketing and the definition and structures of the profession will only grow greater while the profession pursues a professional ideology over a marketing ideology.

> The conquest of the earth ... is not a pretty thing when you look into it too much. What redeems it is the idea only. An idea at the back of it; not a sentimental pretence but an idea; and an unselfish belief in the idea - something you can set up, and bow down before, and offer a sacrifice to ... (Conrad, 1988).

An ideology of marketing would have very different characteristics from a professional ideology and a shift from one to the other will involve significant changes in emphasis for the marketing profession and for professional organizations. Some of what is needed can be expressed thus:

From a *Professional* to a *Marketing* Ideology

Expertise	-	Ideas
Function	-	Culture
Marketing	-	Customers
Service	-	Core
Specialized labour	-	General competency

References

Beckett, W. (1953), *Watt*, Grove Press, London.

Chartered Institute of Marketing, various publications.

Colvina, J. (1978), *The Castle of Crossed Destinies*, Pan, London.

Conrad, J. (1990), *Heart of Darkness*, Penguin, Harmondsworth.

Cowe, R. (1993), 'Marketeers branded as has-beens', *The Guardian*, August.

Crook, S., Pakulski, J. and Waters, M. (1992), *Postmodernization*, Sage, London.

Hickson, D.J. and Thomas, M.W. (1969), 'Professionalization in Britain: A Preliminary Survey', *Sociology*, Vol. 3, No. 1, pp. 37-53.

McHale, R. (1992), *Constructing Postmodernism*, Routledge, London.

Mclver, C. (1987), *The Marketing Mirage: How to Make it a Reality*, Heinemann, London.

Millerson, G. (1964), *The Qualifying Associations: A Study of Professionalization*, Allen and Unwin, London.

Offe, C. (1985), *Disorganised Capitalism*, Polity, Cambridge.

Pearson, G. (1993), 'Business Orientation: cliche or substance?', *Journal of Marketing*, Vol. 9, No. 3, July, pp. 167-84.

Simcock, P. (1993), 'Marketing as a Profession', Rethinking Marketing Conference, Warwick, July.

Skinner, W. (1986), 'The Productivity Paradox', in *Harvard Business Review*, July/August, p. 58.

Thomas, M. (1984), 'The education and training of marketing managers', *Marketing Digest*, Spring, pp. 28-34.

Vink, N. (1992), 'Historical Perspectives in Marketing Management: Explicating Experience', *Journal of Marketing Management*, Vol. 8, No. 3, July, pp. 180-196.

Waters, M. (1989), 'Collegiality, Bureaucratisation and Professionalization', *American Journal of Sociology*, 94(5), pp. 945-72.

Wernick, A. (1991), *Promotional Culture Advertising, Ideology and Symbolic Expression*, Sage, London.

Wong, V. (1993) 'Marketing's Ascendancy and Transcedence: Is this what it takes for business to succeed?', Rethinking Marketing Conference, Warwick, June.

10 Future imperfect? The uncertain prospects of the British accountant

Robin Roslender, Ian Glover and Michael Kelly

Introduction

Accountancy has been one of the most visible professions since the 1970s. It has consistently attracted the largest single number of British graduates as it has grown in size to approaching a quarter of a million members. It has been closely identified with the mechanisms which successive Conservative governments employed in their efforts to control public expenditure. It has also been implicated in a succession of major financial scandals including Polly Peck, BCCI and the collapse of the Maxwell empire. The academic literature on the profession is less extensive than might be expected given its public profile although in recent years this has begun to be addressed as a result of the emergence of a critical accounting project in which sociological insights have been very influential (Cooper and Hopper, 1990; Roslender, 1992; Puxty, 1993). To date, however, such attention has tended to focus on a range of institutional issues associated with the profession's many associations (Macdonald, 1984, 1985; Willmott, 1986; Robson and Cooper, 1990) and on the problematic influence which accounting controls have on British industry and commerce (Armstrong, 1987a, 1987b, 1989). Comparatively little attention has been paid to the study of accounting labour, the one notable exception being found in the work of Johnson (1972, 1977a, 1977b, 1980).

This paper seeks to catalyse more enquiry into the conditions of contemporary accounting labour. In the first section the appeal of a career in accountancy is explored. This provides a backcloth to the identification of a number of problems which those who have elected to pursue a career in this profession increasingly face, and which show few signs of disappearing. In the third section the existing literature on accounting labour is reviewed in an attempt to suggest that contemporary accountancy is an increasingly divided profession, and that the prospects for accounting careers look distinctly imperfect. Underlying the paper is the belief that for many within the lower reaches of the profession, accountancy has seen its best times and may be about to undergo a reversal in its fortunes. This is not to suggest that the use of accounting controls is about to be rejected by industry, commerce and the public sector, rather that the benefits (broadly conceived) accruing to those involved in these processes will become increasingly differentially distributed.

The appeal of accountancy

During the 1980s a widely quoted statistic was that 10 percent of new graduates were opting for a career in accountancy, resulting in it being the most favoured profession of the decade (e.g. Cooper, Lowe, Puxty & Willmott, 1985). The statistic was subsequently employed by the Institute of Chartered Accountants in England and Wales (ICAEW) who claimed that it referred to the percentage of graduates from UK universities and polytechnics choosing chartered accountancy as their first employment. Sikka, Willmott & Lowe (1989) estimated that the profession as a whole was attracting almost 20 percent of graduates by the late 1980s while Crompton (1990) noted it to be the largest single source of graduate recruitment at that time. Subsequently the numbers seeking to read for degrees in accounting in the universities have fallen slightly but given the increasing number and variety of institutions offering accountancy qualifications and the present level of interest in business studies or similar courses, the overall effect remains the same. Whatever the impression conveyed by the Monty Python team in the 1970s regarding the greyness of the accountant, the young of the later 1980s and early and mid 1990s seem to be quite happy to accept this image, or at least to take a chance with it and strive to become accountants. Why is this?

One of the major attractions of a career in accountancy is the level of financial reward generally associated with it. One legacy of the 1980s emphasis on the virtue and power of market forces has been greater or more overt acceptance of the view that people are what they earn, with status or prestige increasingly a function of earning power rather than of socially useful and/or personal achievement. High earners were widely portrayed as role models to be emulated, and amongst the professions accountants certainly appeared to fit the bill. The promise of high earnings continues today: high-profile recruitment agencies such as Michael Page report that newly qualified chartered accountants can expect to command salaries in the region of £20,000 plus benefits. Trainees are tempted with £12-£13,000, a far cry from the postwar era when many of their counterparts were experiencing for the first time the luxury of not paying for a chance to enter the profession. For experienced accountants, those with several years of post-qualifying experience (but still under 30), salaries of £30,000 plus benefits appear to be commonplace judging from the pages of the professional press. Those who elect to move into general management posts, and fully exploit the potential of an accounting qualification, can expect to eventually receive even higher levels of remuneration.

The prospect of a sustained career clearly appeals to many who choose accountancy. In a survey of new student members, the ICAEW reported that 61 percent, the highest proportion, identified the career opportunities afforded by accountancy as the reason for their choice (*Accountancy*, September 1990). In the case of the public practitioner, a three-year apprenticeship, i.e. a training contract, is followed by a period of post-qualification journeymanship, the length of which usually depends on ability and aptitude for the work at hand, which in turn leads to junior, middle and perhaps senior management posts, i.e. partnerships. The Big Six professional firms[1] have over 2,500 partners who sit at the apex of the public practice career structure. For those at the other end of the continuum opportunities still exist to set up in practice as sole practitioners or to become partners in a small sized firm.

At present half of the UK's qualified chartered accountants work outside of public practice, in industry, commerce and the public sector, having moved to such employment after qualification. Here they compete for career progression with former trainees who have normally pursued programmes of education and training in association with the Chartered Institute of Management Accountants (CIMA), the Chartered Association of Certified Accountants (CACA) or the Chartered Institute of Public Finance and Accounting (CIPFA). In contrast to many of their counterparts in public practice their early career experience is commonly one of increasingly demanding opportunities in line with examination success. Consequently they are in a position to move through the lower managerial grades more quickly than many of their chartered accountant colleagues. This has not gone unnoticed by the CA institutes who have recently provided the opportunity for some of their members to pursue their training outside of public practice, the TOPP initiative. This is bound to further intensify competition for the various managerial posts which are the principal rungs on the corporate accountancy career ladder.

A further attraction of a career in accountancy is the work that it entails. In the *Accountancy* survey mentioned earlier, half of the respondents believed that accountancy provided job satisfaction with 28 percent viewing it as a 'potentially challenging' job. Although the kinds of satisfaction traditionally associated with medicine, law, education or engineering might not be so obvious in the case of accountancy there are many potential opportunities to gain significant satisfaction from the work involved. Take, for example, the budgetary process: despite a negative image associated with the authorization function of a budget, many management accountants take great pleasure from their success in involving junior and middle management in the budgetary process. Responsibility accounting seeks to promote the empowerment of these employees rather than simply to ensure their compliance with imposed financial structures (c.f. Armstrong, 1990). Cost control need not be a euphemism for providing the basis for rationalising, i.e., reducing the size of, the workforce. Again many management accountants are intent on ensuring that increased profitability is not achieved at the expense of the workforce but reflects effective financial management throughout the organization. During the past decade the pursuit of value for money in the public sector has produced a deep-seated concern about the wholesale transfer of accounting practices to not-for-profit organizations. There can be few accountants who would disagree with the proposition that such a transfer is inherently problematic. This is the challenge which a concern with the 3Es: economy, efficiency and effectiveness, provides, one which holds out the prospect of universal benefits, government policy permitting (c.f. Greenough, 1990).

Finally it would be disingenuous to overlook the idea that some are attracted to accountancy as a consequence of power and influence which the profession has long had within British management hierarchies. This is more than simply a matter of being steeped in esoteric knowledge and able to practice using rather indeterminate skills. It is being a member of what has been described as the pre-eminent profession within British capitalist enterprises (Armstrong, 1985, 1987a). Armstrong's thesis on the power of accountants and accounting controls has been one of the most influential contributions to the literature of critical accounting which has emerged in the past decade or so. It also informs his work in the sociology of the professions published in the pages of *Work, Employment and Society* (Armstrong, 1987b, 1989, 1993). Armstrong argues that the pre-eminence of accountants is based upon their successful collective mobility project which began in the mid 1840s. At this time the solution which the early British accountancy profession offered to the allocation problems associated with bankruptcy and insolvency provided a foundation for the development of a powerful audit function. By the turn of the century the profession was in a position to sponsor its preferred methods of corporate control when conditions were favourable. Initially this was in the sphere of realization following the successful incorporation of cost accounting techniques into the mainstream of accounting. Eventually the profession was able to provide a compelling solution to the problem of controlling labour, i.e. the extraction of surplus value, particularly by means of management accounting. As Armstrong (1985) makes clear, although accountants may perform the important functions of monitoring operations and of allocating resources between them, functions distinct from the control of labour, both activities only make sense as components of an organization for doing so. Although Armstrong (1993) has begun to raise a number of points about the capacity of the CIMA to sustain its particular position of power and influence, there is little sign that the modes of control which are identifiable with the present-day accounting (and, increasingly, the finance) function will rapidly lose their appeal, a view which is effectively an axiom of the critical accounting tradition.

Storm clouds gather

The distinction between the accountancy profession and its characteristic modes of control is a significant one. While the accounting function remains pre-eminent in British enterprises there are a number of problems facing the profession which lead us to conclude that it may well have seen its better days and consequently for many accountants the future is potentially rather imperfect. In the following pages several of these problems are identified and examined.

The oversupply of professionally qualified accountants

The profession's popularity during the past decade and a half has become increasingly problematic. In the 1960s and 1970s the demand for accounting skills exceeded the available supply as British industry and commerce embraced the logic of accounting controls. This explains why presently half of the ICAEW's home membership works outside of the sphere of public practice. The figure for its Scottish equivalent, the Institute of Chartered Accountants of Scotland (ICAS), is 70 percent while the CACA reports that only a quarter of its UK members work in public practice. However, the expansion in accounting posts has inevitably begun to moderate in recent years with the result that if the supply of qualified accountants does not already exceed demand then it must soon do so. To appreciate the scale of the problem it is instructive to briefly review the patterns of membership of several of the accountancy associations. The ICAEW has experienced a doubling in its qualified membership since 1970 and presently has 16,000 students on training contracts. The growth of the CIMA during the same period has been more rapid, from 12,000 in 1971 to almost 34,000 today. In addition, it records a student membership of approximately 50,000. This in turn is rather fewer than the CACA's 80,000 plus students, although traditionally a large proportion of these are based abroad. Overall, for every two qualified accountants working in the United Kingdom and Ireland there is currently one student member in the course of training.

The growth in demand for accountancy qualifications has reinforced the important role which the examination regime plays in the profession (Power, 1991). The CACA has only recently begun to publicise its pass rate which is less than 30 percent at the final level. This is lower than the CIMA whose average rate at the final level is 38 percent. By contrast the three CA associations, ICAEW, ICAS and ICAI (the Irish institute), together with the CIPFA report finals success levels in excess of 50 percent. It has to be remembered that all of the associations have multi-level qualification programmes which means that the professional examination regime performs a vital selection and thus attrition function for the profession and its employers. It has also provided the associations with a significant source of income with which they may fund a wider range of activities, e.g. academic research, political lobbying, the exploration of international links, etc. Making the examinations more difficult in order to protect the long term interests of the qualified accountant could have the consequence of further disaffecting large numbers who believe the present arrangements to be unfair. This in turn could affect the finances of the associations. On the other hand such a move could call into question the public interest function espoused by the profession (Willmott, 1990). A restrictive practice of this sort might also attract the attention of any government committed to the ideal of promoting the operation of market forces.

The relevance of accounting qualifications

To this point in the paper reference has been made exclusively to professionally qualified accountants and those who seek to join their ranks. In the UK a relevant accounting qualification is required only by those who wish to practice auditing and insolvency. The monopoly of auditing work was established in the Companies Act 1948 and restricted to members of the ICAEW, the ICAS, the ICAI and the CACA. A member of the CIMA can also engage in auditing if s/he is in possession of a practising certificate (which effectively means a period of post-qualifying training). The Companies Act 1989 introduced a new regime intended to regulate the activities of auditing, particularly those engaged in sole practitioner or small partnership work. In the case of insolvency work there are lawyer members of the Society of Practitioners of Insolvency, the Recognized Professional Body for such work, but normally they act in an advisory capacity to qualified accountants. For any other type of accounting work, whether in the public sector, industry and commerce or practice, it is not necessary to have a professional qualification in accounting.

In principle anyone who is judged competent by their employers can carry out much accounting work, the signing-off of a set of accounts being an important exception to the rule. The availability of some extent of accounting training has matched the demand for it in the past twenty years. At one extreme of the further and higher education continuum there are business studies courses at national certificate level. At the opposite end are masters programmes in accounting and finance which may admit students with non-accounting backgrounds. The emergence of accounting degrees such as the Bachelor of Accountancy has resulted in the increased supply of academically accredited graduates who many would claim are well prepared for the roles which accountants occupy without the necessity of an extended period of professional training. Add to this the more recent emphasis upon finance and matters financial together with the development of a parallel set of financial studies programmes. And then there is the MBA option with the obligatory foundation course in accounting.

Taken together this suggests that if the professional associations were to raise the level of qualification in an attempt to balance supply and demand the effect would be negligible. More accountants would remain formally unqualified, perhaps returning us to the situation which existed before the explosion in professional association membership. If employers are satisfied with the way in which their accounting (and finance) function is performed by accountants outside of the professional bodies then the latter's activities, however well meaning, are largely irrelevant. A final observation on the relevance of professional accounting qualifications is that in the USA, Japan and Germany, three of Britain's principal competitors in the world market, there are proportionately very many fewer qualified accountants. In these economies business and business economics graduates and engineers have long been viewed as being perfectly capable of performing much of what is designated the accounting and finance function in Britain.

The emergence of the accounting technician

While the UK and Ireland have no fewer than six professional accountancy associations, the market for accounting labour is inhabited by at least as many second register (second level) associations (Renshall, 1984). Several provide impressive sounding but less substantial qualifications, e.g., the Association of International Accountants, the Society of Company and Commercial Accountants, and the Association of Cost and Executive Accountants. These should not be confused with the Institute of Company Secretaries and Administrators (ICSA) which continues to provide a joint professional legal and accounting training which is particularly valuable to those wishing to pursue a career in the small business sector. The Institute of Taxation has recently formed a technician association, the Association of Taxation Technicians which parallels the specialist technician function associated with the Institute of Internal Auditors. However, the most interesting of the three technician associations is the more generally oriented Association of Accounting Technicians (AAT).

The AAT was formed in 1981 by the ICAEW, CACA, CIMA and CIPFA in order to provide a means of qualification for accounting technicians. These were conceived of as assistants to accountants, a second tier of the profession who were to be well-versed in accounting procedures and techniques but not involved in, nor capable of, initiating financial policy. Among the job titles of accounting technicians are: accounts clerk; credit controller; payroll assistant; book-keeper; etc. The founding membership of the AAT was 6,000, together with 19,500 students. By 1992 these had grown to 16,500 and 76,000 respectively, although even before its launch the Manpower Services Commission estimated that in the UK alone there were well over a quarter of a million accounting technicians (Cropper, 1990). The AAT has worked extremely hard at raising the standard of its examination programme in an attempt to enhance both its own status and that of its members. In addition it has mirrored the first register associations in their Continuing Professional Development provisions.

What started out as the logical complement to a powerful profession could soon end up being a major competitor on the supply side for the accounting function. There are already signs of the problems to come. The AAT takes great pains to point out that many of its members now hold promoted posts and are managing technicians in the same way as senior accountants manage accountants. A feature on the AAT quoted a Big Six partner predicting that AATs would become financial controllers of medium-sized companies within a few years (*Career Accountant*, April 1990). Brandenberg (1987) outlined several elements of a hidden agenda for the promotion of AAT members in public practice: the use of AAT members would allow their employers to recruit fewer graduates; AAT members were more willing than graduates to undertake the routine work which increasingly characterises accountancy; they were cheaper to employ; and their training schedules allowed more 'chargeable time'. More recently Hanson (1992) has argued that the skills acquired by newly qualified AAT members are those of professional accounting personnel, and that with considerable post-qualifying experience, senior accounting technicians may occupy useful roles in middle management.

The Profession's outmoded structure

The continued existence of six professional associations is increasingly being recognized as a source of future difficulties for members. In 1970 the leadership of the ICAEW proposed a unified body for all accountants and although this proved acceptable to the leaders of the other associations, it was roundly rejected by its own members (Willmott, 1986). In the wake of this debâcle the profession's senior officers formed the Consultative Council of Accounting Bodies (CCAB) to provide a mechanism to co-ordinate their activities and a united voice against the profession's critics. In turn the CCAB established two key self-regulatory bodies, the Accounting Standards Committee (ASC) and the Auditing Practices Committee (APC) on which all of the associations were represented. However, at the grassroots level, a series of merger proposals between various associations has continued to be rejected, the most recent being in 1990 involving the CIPFA and the ICAEW whose members voted overwhelmingly to retain their independence and, presumably, their self-professed eminence over lesser accountants. In fact rather than support the logic of merger, sections of the ICAEW's membership have been more interested in introducing internal segmentation in the form of faculties. The first of these, the Faculty of Taxation, was formed in March 1991, followed by the Faculties of Information Technology, and Finance and Management. Members in public practice had pre-empted these developments by forming a General Practitioner Board to represent their particular views and interests on Council.

The leaderships of the six associations have become increasingly convinced of the need for what they now term a 'rationalization' of the profession's present structure. In a communication to members in February 1993, the Presidents of the six associations identified a number of arguments which they believed favour rationalization. Political influence in Britain, Europe and world-wide would be strengthened, the profession's public image would be less confused, while fewer associations would result in economic benefits to members, i.e. lower subscriptions. Two further arguments are rather more revealing. If there were fewer bodies competing for students it would be easier to raise professional standards. This suggests that the profession recognises that it is perceived in some quarters to be failing to maintain the quality of service expected of it. Secondly rationalization is viewed as providing a necessary framework for managing the relationship between the supply and demand for students. This suggests that the hitherto free market in the recruitment and qualification of new members requires some urgent regulation. Both of these observations have already been mentioned of course, together with the view that the employers of accountants might have a rather more active role to play in this market place than the profession's leadership are willing to acknowledge, at least publicly. This also points to a further argument in favour of rationalization although one not mentioned in the document: fewer accountancy bodies and less competition might result in the speedy development of a much needed protective function for their memberships. Presently their constitutions proscribe the associations acting in a unionate way, individual organizations indicating that membership of an appropriate trade union is not incompatible with professional status. Hitherto union membership has not been common among accountants, mainly because it has not been a widespread necessity. The problems which are under discussion in these pages suggest that this situation may soon change with the result that large sections of their memberships might expect associations to be in a position to act effectively on their behalf.

A loss of faith in the accountancy profession

Earlier Armstrong's thesis on the pre-eminence of accountants and accounting controls was outlined. In his initial formulations he makes much of the role which the audit function played in commending the profession to those seeking to retain their control of the organization. Subsequently he offers an alternative conceptualization of the basis for the profession's power and influence, the long-run tendency within capitalist organizations to displace trust from agents whose function it is to inspire, engineer and control the productive process to those whose task it is to monitor their activity, *inter alia*, accountants (Armstrong, 1991, p. 18). It is ironic that a further problem which increasingly confronts the accountancy profession in the UK is that it is no longer regarded with the same confidence that it once was, particularly the audit branch of the profession. Recent financial scandals such as BCCI and Polly Peck together with the affairs of the late Robert Maxwell have focused attention on the audit function's claim to act in the public interest. The high fees earned in the performance of the annual independent third party review are viewed increasingly sceptically by the business community. The resurrection of an 'audit expectations gap' defence by the profession, one which seeks to blame clients, the media and in turn the general public for misunderstanding what an audit is actually intended to achieve, has attracted the attention of a number of critical accounting researchers (Humphrey, Moizer and Turley, 1992; Sikka, Willmott, Puxty and Cooper, 1992; Hooks, 1992). One consequence of this is that talk of the need for legislation to severely curb the profession's self-regulatory powers is beginning to find support from within sections of the profession (Mitchell, Puxty, Sikka and Willmott, 1991; Mitchell and Sikka 1993; Mitchell, 1993).

Reference has also been made to the challenge which the pursuit of value for money and the 3Es in the public sector presents to the members of the profession employed there. The spread of economic calculation to every aspect of public service is how this and related initiatives have been conceptualized by Miller and Power (1992) reflecting the generally unfavourable image which accountants and their practices have established there. It is accountants rather than their political masters for the past fourteen years who are held responsible for ward closures, the withdrawal of free bus passes from the elderly, the rationalization of mountain rescue services, etc. In this respect accountants are simply continuing their work of making visible the scope for financial improvement possible in industries such as coal, heavy engineering and textiles. Their growing involvement in the financial service industries is no more likely to endear them to customers as they experience escalating bank charges and insurance premiums which have been introduced in an attempt to share the burden of losses experienced here in recent years.

Taken together it would seem that the more the accountancy profession has come into the public's consciousness, the less favourable its image has become. The growth in interest among sections of the profession in pursuing the critical accounting project has to date resulted in a literature which for the most part provides substance for heightening public misgivings about the contribution which the profession is able to make to society (Tinker, 1985; Chua, Lowe and Puxty, 1989; Cooper and Hopper, 1990). In this context even mainstream critiques of the relevance of sixty years of managerial accounting such as Johnson and Kaplan (1987) offer may serve to reduce the long term prospects for the profession further.

The conditions of accounting labour

All of the previous problems are rather general in nature and, perhaps, a little speculative. Most do have some factual basis of course, e.g., the growing number of qualified accountants or technicians, the increased scrutiny of the profession's practices, the concern with the spread of the logic of accountability, etc., all of which have been extrapolated forward in a (hopefully) reasoned way. By contrast the focus of this section is much more with the present and the (recent) past about which woefully little evidence, sociological or from critical accounting, exists. This is both surprising and disturbing since in many respects we are concerned with the most pressing problem facing many accountants - the conditions under which they perform their labour. Once reviewed it is possible to see the growth in numbers of qualified accountants, business graduates and accounting technicians in a more problematic light, further highlighting the difficulties of times to come. Accountants have never featured prominently in the literature of industrial sociology. They are normally mentioned in comparative studies of professional occupations, and usually quite favourably in terms of their place in the organizational hierarchy (Portwood and Fielding, 1981; Child, 1982; Crompton, 1990). However, there is no comparable study to Montagna's (1974) account of the American certified public accounting profession although several years previously Hastings and Hinings (1970) provided a useful foundation for the study of the UK profession when they analysed the value conflicts of chartered accountants who elected to pursue their careers in industry and commerce rather than in practice. Hopper's (1980) study of the role conflicts of management accountants in industry was equally insightful but sociology seemed content to restrict its substantive enquiries in the 1980s to a pair of historical papers on the emergence of the ICAS (Macdonald, 1984, 1985) which in turn produced a response from the accounting historians Briston and Kedslie (1986). Armstrong's work is more concerned with accountants as the practitioners of accounting controls than it is with the conditions of their labour, a subject which he has seemed content to disregard (Roslender, 1993).

The principal exception to this literature is found in the work of Johnson who in a series of explorations of the relationship between the professions and the class structure provided a preliminary set of insights on the existence of significant divisions within the UK accountancy profession (Johnson, 1972, 1977a, 1977b, 1980). Initially Johnson drew attention to the development of the modern profession being accompanied by a greater specialization of tasks, an increased routinization of function and the creation of subordinate technician grades. As a result he concluded that in contemporary accounting work the situation is increasingly one of large numbers of accountants employed in subordinate grades 'effectively excluded from entrance to the higher grade' (Johnson, 1972, p. 70). Subsequently Johnson argues that much accounting work is little more than book-keeping, being a purely technical function 'associated with the day to day implementation of systems of financial or stock control' (Johnson, 1977a, p. 107). In 1980 Johnson identified two categories of accountant: book-keepers who are 'engaged in the labour process and subject to the forms of exploitation (not appropriation) characteristic of unproductive labour under capitalism' (p. 357); and senior accountants who 'create, install and supervise control systems and regulatory procedures which operate as mechanisms of secondary control [in] the bureaucratic hierarchy' (p. 358). The full force of Johnson's view of the nature of accounting labour is summarized as follows:

> While part of the membership is incorporated into the labour process and its activities subject to routinization and fragmentation, a dominant group partakes in the functions of capital (Johnson, 1980, p. 361).

Johnson's position was informed by the work of Braverman and Carchedi. In his own 1974 text Braverman mentions accountants by name as becoming increasingly subject to the proletarian condition (p. 407; see also p. 403 for reference to finance professions). Although together with similar professionals they may continue to retain certain privileges as compared with the mass of the working class he believes that for many their subjection to a process of fragmentation and degradation will result in them experiencing their work in ways that strengthen their affinity with the mass of the working class.

Carchedi's interest in the 'middle layers of employment' or new middle class was in terms of their economic proletarianization. By this he meant the removal of particular aspects of the job contents of professional employees (such as accountants) which resulted in them performing only the function of the collective worker, i.e., a technical rather than a managerial function (Carchedi, 1975, 1977; see also Roslender, 1990). Taken together the work of Braverman and Carchedi invokes the idea of a managerial labour process in which professional employees, to the extent that they perform any managerial labour, do so within a structure which sees them as being both exploiters (of those below) and exploited (by those above). Although Johnson does not integrate this critical insight into his analysis of the accountancy profession, it is not difficult to restate his position in terms of an attenuated hierarchy of accounting positions within the organization with senior accountants at the apex and technically-oriented (qualified/unqualified) accountants at the base.

The idea of a managerial labour process is hotly contested, not least by Armstrong. Returning to Marx, Armstrong (1989) defines a labour process as the means whereby people reproduced the material means of their existence. It is possible to extend this concept to intellectual work argues Armstrong but not to managerial work, since this would permit the routine tasks involved in factory discipline to become labour processes. The crux of the problem is that the only reason why such activities as this are necessary is that in capitalist societies labour processes, whether manual or mental, exist in distorted form as a result of the existence of the on-going struggle for control between capital and labour. To talk of managerial labour processes effectively means that class has disappeared from the analytical scheme, an outcome which contradicts the Marxist foundations of Braverman's project. Two counter arguments are usefully introduced at this point. First, while it is certainly the case that the order of managerial work invoked by Armstrong contradicts the commonsense notion of a labour process, the sort of work which accountants and similar professionals engage in is not quite so crudely that of factory discipline, and in Carchedi's terms commonly involves the performance of both the global function of capital and the function of the collective worker. Secondly the concept of class structure invoked by Armstrong is wholly inadequate for understanding the nature of contemporary capitalism. Although not without their difficulties neo-Marxist class theory such as that of Carchedi, Poulantzas and Wright does at least begin to come to terms with an ever more complex economic class structure (Cottrell and Roslender, 1986). For these reasons we concur with the position embraced by Murray and Knights (1990) against Armstrong:

> ... although they may be comparatively advantaged and protected, managers do not stand above the labour process; rather they are fully implicated in it and experience parallel tensions and contradictions by virtue of their own labour and the labour of those whom they supervise.

Johnson's account, modified to take on board the idea of a managerial labour process within the profession, remains the most explicit statement on the conditions of accounting labour. It is supported by one of the very few critical accounting papers which have focused on accounting labour (Booth and Cocks, 1990). Using Australian evidence they describe much accounting work as 'specialized, organized hierarchically, subject to stringent time constraints, standardized, increasingly automated, and facing proletarianization' (pp. 400-1). They also draw attention to the increasing feminization of much lower-grade accounting work, arguing that this is a development entirely consistent with the progressive division of labour within the profession. Similar evidence has been assembled by Ciancanelli, Gallhofer, Humphrey and Kirkham (1990) in the case of UK and Lehman (1992) in the USA. Booth and Cocks conclude in terms reminiscent of Johnson that:

> A large proportion of the accountants employed by the Big Eight (sic) perform largely deskilled and fragmented tasks for small wages, while a small elite group of partners oversee the generation of surplus value which they then appropriate. (p. 403).

The relative invisibility of accounting labour may be about to end as younger researchers focus their attention on the profession. Hanlon (1992) completed a doctoral thesis on the changing experience of accounting work in the regime of flexible accumulation. Much of his empirical evidence is derived from interviews with Irish chartered accountants engaged in the auditing function. His view of the auditing labour process is that while in the early stages the work is boring, routine and highly standardized, this does not lead to the deskilling nor the proletarianization of the chartered accountant (Hanlon, 1992, p. 127; see also Puxty, 1990). It is argued that the mundane 'totting and ticking' involved is a necessary part of the training for future practice which itself has become, again of necessity, more specialized. The growing place of technology within auditing is equally beneficial as it provides a means of achieving a range of efficiency gains which translate into increased profitability. All of this is somewhat less pessimistic than the picture painted by Johnson or Booth and Cocks. It is interesting to note that in the middle of his account of the auditing labour process Hanlon observes that there is evidence of accounting technicians and non-graduates being gifted the routine work of the early training period and low grade computing roles. Again this is presented as being a beneficial development which will free up the more capable (although numerically fewer) graduate recruits, reduce their potential job dissatisfaction and accelerate their formation as the elite workers of the profession. Turning to the question of control within the auditing labour process Hanlon argues that the hierarchical structure of the work from juniors through seniors, assistant managers, managers and directors, to partners ensures a tight monitoring of performance at all levels. This is widely accepted by those subject to it because of the opportunities for mobility that are inherent within the structure itself, i.e. the promise of sustained career progression.

Career is also the focus for a second study of the accounting labour process (Grey, 1994). Drawing on insights derived from the Foucauldian literature, Grey investigates how the practices of self-management necessary for the successful pursuit of a career project commonly transforms the nature and meaning of many of the exercises of disciplinary power evident in the labour processes associated with the contemporary auditing function. The work of the young auditing trainee is variously described as the monotonous repetition of routine tasks, bean counting, ticking and bashing, a bit disillusioning, etc. But those who are committed to career projects, and who react enthusiastically to the tediousness of their chores are recognized by their superiors as the trainees who are learning the nuts and bolts of the job. They are also likely to be the employees who will respond appropriately to the many exercises of disciplinary power which they will inevitably encounter in their professional careers right up to the level of partner. Grey acknowledges that traditionally there has been a pattern of career progression in the big firms through two years of routine auditing, a third year in a more senior role which might continue for a further period on qualification and then onwards and upwards to management functions, perhaps to a partnership. However, not everyone who qualifies remains in the work. Some move elsewhere in the firm, others readily leave for jobs in industry and commerce; those less fortunate may find themselves 'counselled out' at this time or in later years, obliged to find an alternative means of realising their career aspirations. By implication very few are actually allowed to remain within the organization in a position to disrupt this highly efficient market for auditing and accounting labour.

Accountancy: a profession divided

Both Hanlon and Grey offer a more appealing image of contemporary accounting labour than either Johnson or Booth and Cocks. They do not deny that in the early stages of training much auditing labour leaves a great deal to be desired. However, they accept that the work becomes increasingly challenging in more senior posts and for the most part those who seek a career in accountancy are willing to exchange short-term boredom for long-term fulfilment. Two important issues immediately present themselves for consideration. First, in the absence of evidence why should we believe that the traditional situation of exploiting trainees has not subsequently been extended to more senior posts, those filled by qualified accountants as well as other employees deemed adequately qualified to carry out the work? Second, the promise of career progression through such 'promoted' posts, to the lower managerial grades has to be viewed in the light of greatly increased competition for such movement, again involving non-accountants. By emphasising the centrality of the career for accounting labour, Hanlon and Grey highlight its traditionally dynamic nature. While in the past the structure of the accounting function was readily capable of accommodating the aspirations and expectations, not to mention the competencies of many, many fewer accounting workers, the contemporary structure, described by Grey as a pyramid, is inevitably less effective. In this way the widespread opportunity for upward occupational mobility from some book-keeper type of role to that of a managing accountant looks more a feature of the profession's past rather than its future. An assured career for all who actively seek it is a logical impossibility. There are presently too many in the lower reaches of the profession to allow this to happen, a situation exacerbated by the fact that a large proportion of those who have experienced significant upward mobility in the recent past are comparatively young members of the profession who often have nowhere else to move to.

What is being sketched out here is the image of a significantly divided accountancy profession. The majority, which includes both trainees and professionally qualified accountants, are engaged in work which is essentially of a technical nature while the minority are employed in managerial roles, which encompass overseeing the work of other accountants in the case of junior and middle management to participating in the general management of the enterprise at the top of the hierarchy. It is the former accountants who will experience the increasingly imperfect future discussed earlier. A crucial feature of this future is already evident in the reduced opportunities which exist for the individual accountant to bridge the gap between the two groups. The term proletarianization has been used by those who have sought to conceptualise the progressive division of the profession (Johnson, 1977a; Booth and Cocks, 1990; Glover, Kelly and Roslender, 1986; Roslender, 1990, 1992). After Carchedi (1975, 1977) they recognise the significance of investing only a minority of contemporary professional-managerial work roles with a genuine work of supervision and management component. By simultaneously condemning the majority to work of a technical nature, a structural process of economic proletarianization can be seen to have affected the accountancy profession and its members. This is not to suggest that any individuals have actually experienced a changed class situation which is what the original conceptualization of proletarianization entailed (Marx and Engels, 1973). This would be an empirical question as would the extent of any upward movement across the divide, which might be taken (literally) as evidence of embourgeoisement. Economic proletarianization used in this way conceptualises the emergence of the division itself and draws attention to fundamental change that this entails in the conditions of much accounting labour.

Economic proletarianization in Carchedi's analytical scheme was not to be viewed as a precursor to political, i.e., class, action on the part of those who experience it. Influenced by the structural Marxism of Althusser and Poulantzas, Carchedi, like Wright, divorces the structure and action aspects of Marx's legacy (Crompton, 1993). The deteriorating work experiences and rapidly disappearing mobility opportunities of large sections of the accountancy profession are not likely to result in them joining, or indeed becoming the vanguard for, the working class in its struggle with capital. For one thing they are too closely associated with many of the most divisive evils of the existing order: lay-offs, redundancies and plant closures; the dismantling of the Welfare State and the underfunding of local government; abandoned development programmes; Third World poverty and its escalating debt crisis. That these might be the result of the widespread applications of accounting controls rather than the realization of the wishes of those who perform the labour of accounting is hardly a relevant consideration for those who view such individuals as well paid, securely employed and extremely powerful members of society.

There is a sense in which the accountancy profession may yet come to play a role in the new politics, i.e., the new social movements of the late twentieth century (Offe, 1985). The competition for lower level accounting posts, coupled with their limited intellectual demands must surely give way to attacks on the privileged market situation of their incumbents, attacks which are more likely to be successful given the lack of a protective function by the professional associations. As Crompton (1993) observes: what the market giveth it also taketh away. The encroachment of unemployment within the profession should not be overlooked. There can be little question that recession has played a considerable part in significantly amplifying the established 'downsizing' and rationalising practices evident in the lower reaches of public practice in recent years. However, the fact that at least one of the professional associations has started to circulate members with the particulars of colleagues seeking employment is a portent to the future. The systematic abuse of women accountants documented by Ciancanelli et al. (1990) and Lehman (1992) may serve to enlighten this growing minority within the profession that there is more to gender politics than being able to gain the opportunity to qualify as a CA. All these features of the profession's imperfect future may encourage members to reassess the integrity of the work they are engaged in and the conditions under which it is presently performed. Equally they may question their belief that accounting for externalities such as the environment, for effectiveness rather than efficiency, for the worth of employees rather than their value as (human) assets, etc., are only of theoretical interest and come to the conclusion that accounting may be reformulated as a far more socially useful activity.

Note

1. The Big Six accounting firms are, in order of UK fee income: Coopers & Lybrand; KPMG Peat Marwick; Price Waterhouse; Ernst & Young; Touche Ross & Arthur Anderson.

References

Armstrong, P. (1985), 'Competition between the organizational professions and the evolution of management control strategies', *Accounting, Organizations and Society*, Vol. 10, 1, pp. 129-48.

Armstrong, P. (1987a), 'The rise of accounting controls in British capitalist enterprises', *Accounting, Organizations and Society*, Vol. 12, 5 pp. 415-36.

Armstrong, P. (1987b), 'Engineers, management and trust', *Work, Employment & Society*, Vol. 1, 4, pp. 421-40.

Armstrong, P. (1989), 'Management, labour process and agency' in *Work, Employment & Society*, Vol. 3, 3, pp. 307-22.

Armstrong, P. (1990), 'A comment on Murray and Knights', *Critical Perspectives on Accounting*, Vol. 1, 3, pp. 275-81.

Armstrong, P. (1991b), 'Contradiction and social dynamics in the capitalist agency relationship', *Accounting, Organization & Society*, Vol. 16, 1, pp. 1-25.

Armstrong, P. (1993), 'Professional knowledge and social mobility: postwar changes in the knowledge base of management accounting', *Work, Employment & Society*, Vol. 7, 1, pp. 1-21.

Booth, P. and Cocks, N. (1990), 'Power and the study of the accounting profession' in D. Cooper and T. Hopper (eds), *Critical Accounts: Reorientating Accounting Research*, Macmillan, London, pp. 391-408.

Brandenberg, M. (1987), 'The day of the accounting technician', *Accountancy*, December, pp. 105-6.

Braverman, H. (1974), *Labour and Monopoly Capital: the Degradation of Work in the Twentieth Century*, Monthly Review Press, New York.

Briston, R. and Kedslie, M. (1986), 'Professional formation: the case of the Scottish accountants - some corrections and some further thoughts', *British Journal of Sociology*, Vol. 37, 1, pp. 122-30.

Carchedi, G. (1975), 'On the economic identification of the new middle class', Economy and Society, Vol. 4, 1, pp. 1-86.

Carchedi, G. (1977), *On the Economic Identification of Social Classes*, London, Routledge & Kegan Paul.

Child, J. (1982), 'Professionals in the corporate world: values, interests and control' in D. Dunkerley and G. Salaman (eds), *International Yearbook of Organizational Studies 1982*, Routledge & Kegan Paul, London, pp. 212-41,.

Chua, W.F., Lowe, T. and Puxty, A. (eds) (1989), *Critical Perspectives in Management Control*, Macmillan, London.

Ciancanelli, P., Gallhofer, S., Humphrey, C. and Kirkham, L. (1990), 'Gender and accountancy: some evidence from the UK', *Critical Perspectives on Accounting*, Vol. 1, 2, pp. 117-44.

Cooper, D. and Hopper, T. (eds) (1990), *Critical Accounts: Reorientating Accounting Research*, Macmillan, London.

Cooper, D., Lowe, T., Puxty, A. and Willmott, H. (1985), 'The regulation of social and economic relations in advanced capitalist societies: towards a conceptual framework for a cross-national study of the control of accounting policy and practice', First Interdisciplinary Perspectives on Accounting, Conference, Manchester.

Cottrell, A. and Roslender, R. 'Economic Class, Social Class and Political Forces', *International Journal of Sociology and Social Policy*, Vol. 6, 3, (1986), pp. 13-27.

Crompton, R. (1990), 'Professions in the current context', *Work, Employment and Society*, Vol. 4, May 1990, pp. 147-66.

Crompton, R. (1993), *Class and Stratification: an Introduction to Current Debates*, Polity Press, Cambridge.

Cropper, K. (1990), 'The first ten years of AAT', *Management Accounting*, Vol. 68, 8, p. 80.

Glover, I., Kelly, M. and Roslender, R. (1986), 'The Coming Proletarianization of the British Accountant?', *Fourth Aston/UMIST Labour Process* Conference.

Greenhough, J. (1991), 'The Audit Commission', in M. Sherer and S. Turley (eds), *Current Issues in Auditing*, 2, e, London, PCP, pp. 240-7.

Grey, C. (1994), 'Career as a project of the self and labour process discipline' *Sociology*, Vol. 28.

Hanlon, G. (1992), *Flexible accumulation and the rise of the commercialized service class: an examination of Irish accountancy*, unpublished PhD thesis, Trinity College, University of Dublin.

Hanson, J. (1992), 'The Association of Accounting Technicians' in D. Andrews (ed.), *Chartered Accountants 1993*, Charles Letts, London.

Harper, R.R. (1988), 'The fate of idealism in accountancy', Second Interdisciplinary Perspectives on Accounting Conference, Manchester.

Hastings, A. and Hinings, C.R. (1970), 'Role relations and value adaptation: a study of the professional accountant in industry', *Sociology*, Vol. 4, 3, pp. 353-66.
Hooks, K.L. (1992), 'Professionalism and self-interest: a critical view of the expectations gap', *Critical Perspectives on Accounting*, Vol. 3, 2, pp. 109-36.
Hopper, T. (1980), 'Role conflicts of management accountants and their position within organization structures', *Accounting, Organizations & Society*, Vol. 5, 4, pp. 401-11.
Humphrey, C., Moizer, P. and Turley, S. (1992), 'The audit expectations gap - plus ca change, plus c'est la meme chose?', *Critical Perspectives on Accounting*, Vol. 3, 2, pp. 137-61.
Johnson, H.T. and Kaplan, R.S. (1987), *Relevance Lost: the Rise and Fall of Management Accounting*, Harvard Business School Press, Boston.
Johnson, T.J. (1972), *Professions and Power*, Macmillan, London.
Johnson, T.J. (1977a), 'The professions in the class structure', in R. Scase (ed.), *Industrial Society, Class, Cleavage and Control*, London, Allen & Unwin.
Johnson, T.J. (1977b), 'What is to be known? the structural determination of social class', *Economy and Society*, Vol., 6/2, pp. 194-233.
Johnson, T.J. (1980), 'Work and power', in G. Esland and G. Salaman (eds), *The Politics of Work and Occupations*, Open University Press, Milton Keynes.
Lehman, C. (1992), '"Herstory" in accounting: the first eighty years', *Accounting, Organizations and Society*, Vol. 17, 3, 4, pp. 261-85.
Macdonald, K.M. (1984), 'Professional formation: the case of Scottish accountants', *British Journal of Sociology*, Vol. 35, 2, pp. 174-89.
Macdonald, K.M. (1985), 'Social closure and occupational registration', *Sociology*, Vol. 19, 4, pp. 541-56.
Marx, K. and Engels, F. (1973), 'Manifesto of the Communist Party' in D. Fernbach (ed.), *The Revolutions of 1848*, pp. 67-98, Penguin Books, Harmondsworth.
Miller, P. and Power, M. (1992), 'Accounting, law and economic calculation' in M. Bromwich and A. Hopwood (eds), *Accounting and the Law*, pp. 230-53, Prentice Hall/ICAEW, London.
Mitchell, A. (1993), 'Ending decades of opposing change', *Management Accounting (UK)*, Vol. 71, 8, p. 18.
Mitchell, A. and Sikka, P. (1993), 'Accounting for change: the institutions of accountancy', *Critical Perspectives on Accounting*, Vol. 4, 1, pp. 29-52.
Mitchell, A., Puxty, A., Sikka., P. and Willmott, H. (1991), *Accounting for Change: Proposals for Reform of Audit and Accounting*, Fabian Society, London.
Montagna, P. (1974), *Certified Public Accounting: A Sociological View of a Profession in Change*, Scholars, Houston.
Murray, F. and Knights, D. (1990), 'Intermanagerial Competition and Capital Accumulation: IT Specialists, Accountants and Executive Control', *Critical Perspectives on Accounting*, Vol. 1, 2, pp. 167-89.
Offe, C. (1985), 'New social movements: challenging the boundaries of institutional politics', *Social Research*, Vol. 52, 4, pp. 817-68.

Portwood, D. and Fielding, A. (1981), 'Privilege and the professions', *Sociological Review*, Vol. 29, 4, pp. 749-73.
Power, M.K. (1991), 'Educating accountants towards a critical ethnography', *Accounting Organizations and Society*, Vol. 16, 4, pp. 333-53.
Puxty, A.G. (1990), 'The accountancy profession in the class structure' in D. Cooper and T. Hopper (eds), *Critical Accounts: Reorientating Accounting Research*, pp. 332-65, Macmillan, London.
Puxty, A.G. (1993), *The Social and Organizational Context of Management Accounting*, Academic Press, London.
Renshall, M. (1984), 'A short summary of the accounting profession' in B. Carsberg and H. Hope (eds), *Current Issues in Accounting*, 2, e, pp. 23-38, Philip Allen, Oxford.
Robson, K. and Cooper, D. (1990), 'Understanding the development of the accountancy profession in the United Kingdom' in D. Cooper and T. Hopper (eds), *Critical Accounts: Reorientating Accounting Research*, pp. 336-90, Macmillan, London.
Roslender, R. (1990), 'The accountant in the class structure', *Advances in Public Interest Accounting*, Vol. 3, pp. 195-212.
Roslender, R. (1992), *Sociological Perspectives on Modern Accountancy*, London, Routledge.
Roslender, R. (1993), 'Armstrong on accountants: extracting straw men from historical infights', *Proceedings of the Conference on Professions and Management*, University of Stirling.
Sikka, P., Willmott, H., Puxty, A.G. and Cooper, C. (1992) '*The impossibility of eliminating the expectation gap*', Mimeo, University of East London, London.
Sikka, P., Willmott, H. and Lowe, T. (1989), 'Guardians of knowledge and public interest: evidence and issues of accountability in the UK accountancy profession', *Accounting, Auditing and Accountability Journal,* Vol. 2, 2, pp. 47-71.
Tinker, T. (1985), *Paper Prophets: A Social Critique of Accounting*, Holt, Rinehart and Winston, New York.
Willmott, H.C. (1986), 'Organizing the profession: a theoretical and historical examination of the development of the major accountancy bodies in the UK', *Accounting, Organizations and Society*, Vol. 11, 6, pp. 555-80.
Willmott, H.C. (1990), 'Serving the Public Interest?, a critical analysis of a professional claim', in D. Cooper and T. Hopper (eds), *Critical Accounts: Reorientating Accounting Research*, pp. 315-31, Macmillan, London.

11 Politics and professionalism: pursuing managerialism in personnel

Barbara Paterson

Introduction

The data presented in this paper are derived from a study which explored the two main themes of the work of personnel specialists and how they do it, and the nature of the knowledge used in personnel work. It also examined the issues of occupational choice and entry, ambiguity and role, power and influence, political behaviour and status and effectiveness (Paterson, 1991).

This paper considers some of the latter issues, and it examines personnel specialists' perceptions of managerialist aims, and how these aims are pursued both by their instrumental use of professionalism and by their involvement in political behaviour.

Study samples

Data were obtained from personnel specialists (229 respondents and 109 interviewees), and from fifteen specialist senior executive interviewees. These samples were drawn from twenty seven activity classifications, to represent a wide cross-section of personnel specialists in Scotland.

Briefly, the respondent sample was made up of 80 percent (184) males and 20 percent (45) females. The respondents' ages ranged from 23 to 64 years, with a mean age of 40.7 and a median age of 39, and eighty four percent (N=229) had 5 years' or more service in personnel work.

Under 30 percent (66) had spent the whole of their working lives in personnel, and forty percent (38) of the respondents who were aged between 40 and 59 had worked in personnel for less than half of their working lives. Overall, however, 74 percent percent (165) had spent half or more of their working lives in personnel.

Only 31 percent percent (71) of the respondents had chosen personnel as their first career, and were what Watson (1977) called 'initial choosers', while the others had arrived in the occupation by a variety of other means, and were typified only by the diversity of their occupational backgrounds.

While 45 percent percent (103) of the respondents had a first degree, 70 percent (72) of these were under the age of 40. The age group 40 and over comprised 60 percent (75) of all respondents without degrees (126). The difference between these two age groupings was strongly significant (chi-square 19.739, p= .001). Higher degrees were reported by eight percent (18) of the sample, and there were no significant differences by age.

Twenty four percent (55) of the sample had a professional qualification which was not an Institute of Personnel Management (IPM, now IPD, the Institute of Personnel and Development) one, while possession of an IPM qualification was reported by thirty five percent (81) of respondents (229). There appeared to be a clear decay of possession of the IPM qualification over the age of 40. There were two strong associations found in connection with the age of respondents and their means of obtaining an IPM qualification: securing it by a full-time course in the age group under 40 (chi-square 22.846, p = .001); and the prevalence of obtaining IPM corporate membership under the 'experience provisions' in the '40 and over' age group (chi-square 35.170, p = <.001). The 'under 40s' comprised 69 percent (27) of the initial choosers who had an IPM qualification.

While 134 survey respondents had expressed a willingness to be interviewed, 68 percent (50 percent) were selected, aiming to cover all 27 activity classifications. The remaining 41 members of the interview sample of 109 personnel specialists were non-respondents.

Managerialism in personnel

The issues of ambiguity and role must inevitably contribute to any discussion of managerialism in the personnel occupation. Several elements of ambiguity are clearly present in the idea that personnel specialists work as members of management teams. Various other facets of ambiguity have been identified in the personnel literature, and in writings on more general aspects of management.

There were legal and moral difficulties in justifying absolute managerial authority over employees (Sayles, 1964). Management was 'not a neutral function' in which managers could be impartial (Farnham, 1984). The management of resources imposed 'conflicting criteria' on managers, which created ambiguity or ambivalence which was 'fundamental to most aspects of the managerial occupation' (Watson, 1977). The conflict of interest between capital and labour contained a 'structural contradiction between the material interests of employer and employee', and managers themselves should not be 'taken in or confused by technicist ideology that disregards [this] conflict of interest' (Wilmott, 1984). While managers are agents of the employers, they are also employees.

Another kind of ambiguity was discussed by Machin and Stewart (1981). They noted how, at every level of management apart from the very lowest and the highest levels, managers were simultaneously expected to be 'leaders, colleagues, and followers'. Thus their membership of a management team could contain many elements of ambiguity. While all of the team members pursued organizational goals, specialist groups were 'likely to be mindful of the differential impacts of alternative organizational strategies upon their own sectional interests' (Wilmott, 1984). 'Something of a philosophical and psychological quagmire' could result when a member of a management team went against the team's group norms on issues of substance (Morse, 1976).

Watson (1977) argued that conflict, tension, ambiguity and ambivalence characterised personnel work, and that these problems were rarely temporary ones. Rather, they seemed to be 'intrinsic and essential' to personnel's central involvement 'with the utilization of human resources within a capitalistic industrial society'. Thus, Miner and Miner (1976) suggested that personnel managers had 'been caught at the nexus of conflict' between the orientations of traditional management, and professional personnel management. Personnel managers 'walk a tightrope' because they work 'at the nexus of competing values' (Tyson and Fell, 1986).

The aim of personnel management is the achievement of 'both efficiency and justice, neither of which can be pursued successfully without the other' (IPM, 1963). This dual aim must clearly present problems for the practitioner. Watson (1986) noted that personnel specialists had to 'look two ways at once in their work'. They were under pressure to emphasise care for employees, partly in order to make managerial authority more acceptable to the managed, and they also had to persuade other managers that personnel was an important contributor to the effective control of employees. Earlier, Watson (1977) had argued that personnel managers also experienced ambiguity between the advisory nature of their role, and being forced towards interventionist action.

Tyson (1980) suggested three ways in which ambiguity is inherent in the personnel role, 'depending on how we approach the question'. The professional role model could give rise to ambiguity, first through the expectations of other managers if they believed that personnel was an 'intercessory' role, and second because of the confusion which surrounded the question of whether or not personnel management was a profession. Ambiguity could also result from personnel's use of the control and coordination devices of policies and procedures, as these impersonal controls, impersonally administered, could result in personnel managers being the 'victim of their own impersonal rules'. A similar view was expressed by Watson (1986), who suggested that all personnel procedures 'contain the seeds of their own destruction'.

Tyson's (1980) third aspect of ambiguity concerned the role of personnel managers as negotiators of meaning. This was immediately concerned with the daily performance of personnel management. The imprecision and vagueness inherent in human relationships and in much communication could create ambiguity which personnel specialists might use to advantage. They could use interpersonal skills 'of a high order' to renegotiate and reinterpret meanings to the advantage of their organizations and of the different interest groups within them. The 'management of meaning' contributed to management as a political activity (Gowler and Legge, 1983).

Although the matter of 'role' has received a good deal of attention in the personnel literature, there are only two arguments in connection with it which are of particular relevance to the data which will shortly be discussed here. These concern the 'advisory' and the 'middleman' roles.

The notion of the advisory role in personnel work has generated a minor debate, which has suggested that the term 'advisory', with its connotations of passivity, may be at least partly inappropriate for describing the behaviour of personnel managers when they advise other managers (cf. *inter alia* Crichton, 1963; French and Henning, 1966; Ritzer and Trice, 1969). A mythical occupational image had perpetuated the view that personnel managers did not make decisions for line managers, or manipulate their decisions, when the reality was that they did (Ritzer and Trice, 1970). Watson (1977) argued that 'it seems to be something of a rhetorical device to call what are in effect executive commands 'advice''.

Both Fox (1966) and Dryburgh (1972) described the problems and dilemmas which could arise from 'man in the middle' roles. Crichton (1963) had earlier pointed to the problem that the image of personnel managers as 'liaison officers', 'go-betweens', 'buffers' or 'links', indicated 'a middle ground, communicating and interpreting role', which meant that it was 'seldom [that] their identification with the management team [was] made clear'.

The issue of whether personnel management is in between management and employees is connected both to ambiguity in the occupation, and to notions of the personnel role. The personnel specialist interviewees in the Paterson (1991) study were asked, 'Some argue that the personnel manager is 'in between' management and the employees. Do you agree with this idea of the job?'.

Fifty eight percent (63) of the 109 interviewees felt that they were on the side of management, and the majority of them expressed their views in an emphatic and spirited way:

> No! No way! A personnel manager is not functioning properly if he doesn't see himself as part of the management team (Personnel Manager, Engineering);

> Certainly not! I am part of the management team. I'm not a management shop-steward and employee conciliator (Personnel Manager, Foods);

> No - it's a fallacy. He's part of the organization. Some people like to kid themselves on (Training Officer, Furniture Manufacturer.);

> No. It's a subtle trap to take that role. You'll lose your influence on the management side. You always have to be seen as a member of management and know who your master is (Assistant IR Manager, Coal);

We are the advisers and executors of policy, and part of the management team - not conciliators. That has to be understood by all (Personnel Manager, Metal Manufacture).

Twenty eight percent (31) thought that they did have a middle-ground/buffer/mediator approach to their work. This was explained in terms of improving management-employee relationships and/or channels of communication, either as the result of a poor organizational climate historically, or because of their personal belief that personnel should be approachable by both 'sides' of the employment relationship:

... I feel that I act as a buffer. Communication here has been a problem. I act as a link (Personnel Manager, Retailing');

Yes. It is irksome and objectionable to have the conciliatory role. It's not where I want to be. Too frequently people try to put me 'in between'. Just because it happens, doesn't mean that it's right (Personnel Manager, Multiple Retailing);

I often have to represent both sides. I put the 'personnel' view to management, and then put the 'management' view to the staff (Personnel Officer, Insurance);

I think I have to agree, regrettably. I'd like to say it shouldn't be the case. I'm trying to eradicate that aspect here (Personnel Manager, Brewing/Public Houses).

Eight per cent (9) said that, on occasions, personnel was 'in the middle'. They explained that this was necessary when management had done or were about to do something which was contrary to the interests of employees, or which might cause future problems. It is worth noting however, that these interviewees saw their mediating role as a temporary and expedient measure, and not as their normal work situation:

On certain occasions, yes. Through lack of communication from management, when we are placed as the 'go-between', getting facts, and rectifying situations (Personnel Manager, Hotels, Catering & Leisure);

Sometimes it has to be. For example, I have to step in and veto management, and suggest alternatives (Personnel Officer, Furniture Manufacture);

... We have a very few managers who don't consider employees when making decisions. I have battles with those individuals more frequently than I have with the majority of our managers. It is usually seen as interfering, because it's none of my bloody business ... They're not all they might be in managing

> people and have to be straightened out (Training and Development Manager, Transport).

This manager felt that the 'problem managers' forced him into a mediating role at times. He added, however,

> I see personnel working closely with managers not 'in between' ... we've got the balance right. If managers have to come to personnel before they can breathe, it's totally unrealistic...

There were five (5 percent) 'other' responses, and these were from interviewees whose jobs were 'central staffs' or policy making ones, which did not involve (as they saw it) the management/employee interface. Only one personnel specialist felt that he favoured employees:

> ... I tend to be on the employees' side - it's 40 percent management, 60 percent employees. It's just the way I am, especially when dealing with hard line managers who want to screw blokes into the ground (Personnel Officer, Construction).

These results were almost the reverse of those reported by Watson (1977, pp. 175-7). The question was identical in both studies. Most of his sample willingly saw themselves as 'in the middle', which Watson thought was 'something of a contradiction', as 'a central aspiration' of personnel specialists was 'to achieve credibility' as members of the 'management team'.

For Watson, the apparent contradiction was explained by personnel managers preserving the appearance of neutrality, which served as a means of contributing to organizational goals. In this, they presented objectivity or neutrality to employees, and acted as a channel of communication for managers. In comparison, while 28 percent (31) of the interviewees in the our study said they were 'in the middle', as their interview extracts show, some were strongly opposed to the idea, and wished to change their position, while others felt that they had little alternative because of the historical background of management/employee relations in their organizations.

Six percent (6) of Watson's interviewees were 'equivocal' in their replies, a trait not found in our interviewees, who forthrightly stated their position, whatever it was.

Watson reported that twenty seven percent of his respondents 'were concerned to reject the 'in between' notion ... sometimes quite strongly'. In this study, fifty eight percent (63) felt that they were unequivocally members of management.

As the composition of the interview sample for this study was broadly similar to that of Watson's in terms of gender and backgrounds, we must look elsewhere for some explanation of the dissimilar results.

First, the data which were obtained about our respondents showed that industrial relations was an important element in most of their jobs. Watson (1977) related some of his own experience in industrial relations, where 'one always stressed that in the long run one was bound by management's decisions'. It is possible therefore that incumbents of jobs with a substantial industrial relations content will see themselves more clearly as 'management' than those whose jobs contain a greater emphasis on other personnel activities. It should be said here, however, that strong 'managerial' responses were received also from people whose involvement in industrial relations was negligible/nil.

Second, it could be that the timing of this study's interviews (spring/summer 1985) may have had some bearing on the responses. It is very possible that during the period of recession, personnel work was more 'managerial' in its relationships with the workforce in private companies.

This point will be pursued further shortly, when we consider personnel specialists' views about the compatibility of justice and efficiency in their work. Mackay (1986) noted that in 1984, the majority of her interviewees showed tendencies towards being more aggressive and 'bullish', with a 'harder and more confident' management approach, which led to the finding that 'the macho manager is alive and kicking in a surprisingly large number of organizations'.

The third possibility relates to the information our interviewees gave us about their relationships with other management. It is possible that the position of 'man in the middle' might detract from their credibility with line/other management (cf. Crichton 1963; Fox 1966).

The fourth possibility is that, in the period between Watson's (1977) study and our one, the number of personnel specialists who were members of management teams had increased, and that the 'central aspiration' described by Watson in the mid-1970s had become more of a reality for many personnel practitioners in the course of the next decade.

We shall now consider the justice/fairness source of ambiguity which was outlined earlier. It is to do with the notion that there is a conflict of interests between labour and capital (cf. Watson, 1977; Wilmott, 1984) and it also considers the view that the aim of personnel management is to achieve both efficiency and justice (IPM, 1963).

The interviewees were asked a question which was similar to one which Watson (1977) asked his sample; 'Some people argue that there is an inevitable conflict between an organization being efficient on the one hand and being just and fair to its employees on the other. How do you feel about this?'.

The majority of the 29 percent (32) who said that justice and efficiency go together, emphasised efficiency. For some, the central argument was organizational survival, and that efficiency kept people in work, and facilitated the payment of benefits. Others saw that efficiency coupled with injustice was not good business sense, while yet another group thought that their organizations were normally both fair and efficient:

> ... the reality is that what is good for the company is good ultimately for the workforce. If you are profitable, you are able to return to those who are generating the profits: good salaries; good conditions; job opportunities; and

guaranteed employment. If you are inefficient, and more than fair to your workforce, you may in fact disadvantage them. It is not fair to cosset people. Companies which do that go to the wall (Personnel and Senior IR Officer, Brewing);

It is an expensive view that organizations should buffer individuals from economic sanctions like redundancy (Employee Relations Manager, Metal Manufacturing.);

... personnel management is part of management, which should be just and fair - not meaning 'kind' (Personnel Manager, Electro-optical Equipment);

... there's nothing that gives personnel a bad name quicker than someone dithering on the side of the employee, because it's the kinder thing to do, rather than actually being the correct thing to do (Personnel Officer, Oil exploration).

Twenty-two percent (24) felt that justice/fairness bred efficiency:

you've got to be fair, honest, consistent and reasonable ... It is less efficient to have a disgruntled workforce. However, to run the business efficiently, you don't take the soft options (Personnel Officer, Synthetic Pigments);

... you've got to be fair and reasonable, otherwise people won't work for you. I don't mean give everything they ask (Personnel Officer, Electronics).

Eighteen percent (20) saw some potential for conflict, but felt that it could be contained by striking a balance between fairness and efficiency; the conflict could be mitigated by compromise:

it's a question of compromise. The pendulum swings one way, and then another (Assistant Area Personnel Officer, Health Board).

Other interviewees in this group felt that the justice/fairness element of the 'balance' took place in the context of ensuring an efficient, viable organization:

I agree, but you have to minimise the conflict. I am of the view that the company is efficient first. It is better to be lean, fit, and efficient - keeping 100 people in jobs, rather than have 200 in work for three months, and we are all out of a job ... It is really a matter of balance (Personnel Manager, Construction).

One hundred and forty five (15) of the interviewees did not see that there was any conflict involved in the employment relationship. Many of these views were strongly expressed, and they centred on organizational survival through efficiency, and effective management:

> Rubbish! If a company is not profitable, then there are no jobs. If management can't manage, then people are made redundant. Redundancy and unemployment is hardly fair or just (Personnel Manager, Multiple Retailing);

> Absolute nonsense! This company is a fair employer, profitable and efficient (Personnel Officer, Defence Electronics);

> ... I don't see any conflict between justice or fairness, and being efficient. We are all employees including the directors. If the company is in trouble, we are all in trouble (Personnel Officer, Electro-optical Goods).

Twelve percent (13) saw different degrees of conflict, variously resulting from specific matters, such as working practices, the availability of resources, the actions of line managers, or the unwillingness of employees to accept/understand managerial decisions or actions:

> Yes, I agree. We have to take the two sides into consideration - especially in engineering, which is often subject to demarcation (Personnel and Training Manager, Machine Tools);

> There's got to be a conflict - especially where cash is a problem ...' (Personnel Officer, Education);

> There's always conflict ... I've seen unfairness in this industry and spoken out against it (Personnel Officer, Road Haulage).

Some of these interviewees however, added a sour note in their analysis of the justice/efficiency argument:

> ... Most organizations like to think that they are tolerant of social justice. The extent to which they are prepared to put their money where their mouth is, when there is economic crisis? - I think social justice would come low in their order of priorities (Senior Industrial Relations Officer, Local Government).

Five percent (5) said that it was not always possible to reconcile fairness and efficiency:

> ... There are always conflict situations where the two are not always reconcilable ... however, we shouldn't shrink from the occasions when the view has to be one-way (Personnel Officer, Oil Production).

Only one person said that employee interests should sometimes be put before cost-effectiveness. This was the personnel officer who felt that he was 'on the employees' side' because of line managers' attitudes towards staff:

> ... employees are assets as much as machinery ... to treat loyal servants unfairly sticks in my throat. I don't know how other personnel people feel about that (Personnel Officer, Construction).

Overall, 65 percent (71) of the interviewees in our study did not see conflict between justice/fairness and efficiency, or felt that if it was possible in theory, it was not inevitable in practice.

Forty five percent of Watson's (1977) sample felt that conflict was inevitable, of whom 18 said that they had to 'keep a balance'. Eighteen percent (20) of our study's interviewees thought that a balance had to be achieved, while 17 percent (18) felt that there was a conflict between justice/fairness and efficiency. The majority of those, however, saw conflict not as a permanent state of affairs; rather, it arose from specific circumstances or managerial/employee attitudes and/or actions.

We saw earlier that our interviewees were more 'managerialist' than Watson's (1977) sample in connection with the possibility of being 'in between'. Once again, in the findings just reported, there is a strong managerialist emphasis in our study, almost always related to the issue of efficiency for economic survival.

Throughout, there has been evidence of a 'hard-nosed' approach where the organization has to come first, even though this might result in unfairness or injustice for some parts of the labour force. We have seen a strong awareness of what is necessary to make organizations 'healthy', cost-effective, profitable, lean and fit. For many, this meant redundancy programmes, unjust to those whose employment was terminated, but justifiable on the grounds of 'good for the greatest number'.

Many accounts indicated that personnel should not 'cosset' or 'buffer' employees from economic reality, that it should not take the 'soft option', 'dither on the side of the employee', 'give everything they ask', or be 'kind'. There was evidence also that being just and fair was seen as instrumental for the achievement of efficiency, because dissatisfied employees 'won't work for you'. There is therefore, some support for Watson's (1977) view that personnel specialists were 'forced to be concerned' with employee welfare or social justice, and employed a 'lesser of two evils' strategy to prevent the disruption of progress towards organizational objectives.

A few interviewees were openly welfare-oriented in their views, but their responses related to challenging instances of injustice, rather than their active promotion of justice/fairness as an ongoing feature of their work. The views of the majority of the sample, however, are best summarised in the words of one that 'we are not here to be just and fair alone'.

Indeed, if we look at the practical world of management which our personnel specialists were reporting, one of private sector recession and reduced budgets in the public sector, we might possibly ask whether a more welfare oriented approach would have been at all realistic. Many of the interview extracts have shown that the participants saw their priorities in terms of saving jobs, including their own in some cases.

Tyson and Fell (1986) wrote that personnel specialists walked a 'tightrope' in view of the competing values in their jobs. It would appear from this sample's responses for both the 'in between' and the 'justice versus efficiency' questions, that the majority of our practitioners had both feet firmly on management ground, or otherwise perceived the 'tightrope' to be so low that they were able to step on and off it at will, to suit the circumstances.

Politics, persuasion and professionalism

For the purposes of the analysis which follows, being 'professional' has the layman's meaning of being good at one's job; of being skilled, knowledgeable, expert and competent. This is primarily because the study sample expressed their 'professionalism' thus, and because even those who were IPM members did not describe what they did in their jobs in terms of any broader occupational reference. In this there are parallels with Guest and Horwood's (1981) study where the personnel managers felt that while education and experience were 'desirable', the essential minimum characteristics needed for effective performance were appropriate social skills and personality; 'it is who you are and where you have been rather than 'academic' knowledge and skills'.

Lawrence (1986) argued that personnel managers saw the techniques and procedures which they used in their work 'not only as tools for doing the job but the accoutrements of professional status *per se*'. A further sort of instrumentalism was noted by Watson (1986), in that personnel managers 'are professionals when it suits them, and part of the organization when it does not'.

Our study was interested in the ways in which the sample interacted with other management in their organizations in the everyday course of their jobs. Two of the interview questions were of particular relevance to this investigation, and these concerned the means our personnel specialists used to influence other management, and whether they were conscious of using knowledge/information for political purposes.

Our specialists were asked how they 'got their way' in their relationships with other departments, either in policy matters, or in day-to-day managing. This question looks, for the most part, at lateral power which is exhibited across an organization in the relationships between departments (cf. Hickson et al., 1971, 1986).

The method most preferred, by 45 percent (49) of the sample (108) was the use of a logical argument, which presented information in a reasoned and credible way:

> People in other management disciplines tend to expect Personnel to come along and waffle, and not have a concrete input. Most take account of what the personnel person says if he comes along with a reasoned, prepared case (Personnel Officer, Petrochemicals).

Eighteen percent (20) used persuasion, and for some of these interviewees, their own personality was seen as an aid to effective persuasion:

> I persuade - by personality, common-sense, and logic. There are precedents which show the inherent risks of not taking our advice (Personnel Officer, Vehicle Manufacture).

Eighteen percent (19) emphasised their credibility, achieved through previous good contact and/or advice and a track record of effectiveness:

> ... it's more than persuasion. It's about track record, and the capability of our suggestions (Personnel Manager, Metal Manufacture);

> ... previous effective contact helps (Personnel Manager, Telecommunications).

Yukl (1989) felt that it was essential for managers to build a reputation for expertise, which was established by a mixture of showing expertise and impression management. Others' perceptions of expertise had, however, to be reinforced by logical argument and the presentation of credible evidence before expert power could be exerted. Bucher (1970) saw the ability to be articulate as '*a sine qua non* of effectiveness in interdepartmental arenas' which could enhance perceived stature beyond that prescribed in the formal organization structure. In order to argue forcefully for an argument, however, the proposer had first to have a firm belief in it (Bem, 1972).

Eight percent (9) of our interviewees used their knowledge of personalities and/or the political situation in connection with personnel activities to ensure a successful outcome of their initiatives with other management:

> ... by using my knowledge of management relationships by knowing which people to approach, when, and how and by putting the case to them in a way geared to their expected response. I tailor the strategy for best effect (Personnel & Administration Manager, Oil Drilling Machinery);

> You look at the politics - the whole situation, and what you want to achieve. You gear your approach to the particular managers. Some, you approach directly, and openly persuade. Others, you take the back-door approach with. You assess each situation as it arises (Personnel Manager, Construction).

Only five percent (5) mentioned 'pulling rank', either their own or that of their superior. Two interviewees felt that their view must succeed always in the face of line management opposition, and that they would use any means necessary to secure this, while another two took the approach of 'being helpful' as a way to both maximise the image of the personnel function, and minimise aggressive tendencies on the part of line management. Two interviewees gave 'other' responses, one of which concerned the practitioner's unwillingness to try to get his own way: '... my job is to interpret what management really wants ...'.

Overall, however, the interviewees saw their dealings with other management as a test of their interpersonal skills, in which their ability to assess and/or respond to situations relied on their knowledge of their subject and the other manager(s) involved. Many emphasised their communication skills, and their ability to use their personality to advantage in relationships with other managers. While most of the interviewees seemed to take a fairly open approach in the process of influencing others, there were some who admitted to 'tailoring' their strategy for best effect. An even more covert approach was reported by one manager:

> I sow a seed and nurture it. I let them think that they have thought it (Assistant Personnel Manager, Electrical Contracting).

Watson (1977) asked his interviewees a similar question about 'getting their way', and although the results for our study were analysed in a different way to Watson's, some areas of comparison are possible. Watson's interviewees placed more emphasis on formal authority, planting ideas, threatening/bullying than our interviewees, who more often mentioned their effective past performance, expertise and credibility. The interviewees in our study also placed a greater emphasis on the combined activities of logic and persuasion, which together included working on relationships, than Watson's sample did.

As we have already seen, some of the interviewees in our study identified the behavioural adjustments they made when in contact with other management as 'political' in nature. As one personnel manager put it,

> Personnel is a minefield, because nobody asks a question to get a straight answer. You have to find out what they really mean. And *your* answer is remembered.

Mintzberg (1985, p. 134) felt that political behaviour was 'typically divisive and conflictive'. According to Kakabadse (1983) however, it was 'impossible to escape the power/political interactions that take place between people at work'. In most organizations, 'dynamic political processes' occurred, mostly with the intention of influencing decisions (Bacharach and Lawler, 1980).

While organizations were run by a 'series of games', there was no implication that there was any consensus as to the rules of play (Crozier and Friedberg, 1980). Managers had to anticipate that 'more than one team will be playing in the organization and not find this immoral or upsetting' (Sayles, 1964). Thus, personnel specialists had 'to understand the power politics in their organizations if they [were] going to influence events' (Johnston, 1978).

Our interviewees were asked if they were conscious of themselves or others using information and knowledge for 'political' means (N = 96). Fifty eight percent (56) gave 'yes' responses, although the amount of their involvement in political behaviour varied: 27 percent (26) engaged in it to secure a good outcome; 15 percent (14) were actively involved all of the time, because of the attitudes of their line management towards personnel; and 16 percent (16) felt that political behaviour was a fact of life, and that all managers engaged in it.

Wilmott (1984) wrote that managerial work research had tended not to depict the political reality of managerial work. In view of the responses we have seen above, it seems sensible to suggest that if researchers ask specific questions about political behaviour, the deficiency noted by Wilmott may be remedied. Indeed, Stewart (1983) has argued along broadly similar lines.

Our interviewees who said that they engaged in organizational politics, and used knowledge/information to do so, knew precisely what the nature of their involvement was, to the extent that they manipulated people and events to qet what they wanted:

> Of course! Anyone who denies it - well! People who succeed are politically successful *and* competent at their job. To be merely competent will not lead to success (Personnel Officer, Electronics);

> Every organization is a jungle. No-one has not got information they can use in a political sense (Personnel Manager, Food, Drink and Tobacco);

> Always - you manipulate people to get what you want (Employee Relations Officer, Vehicle Manufacture).

Some interviewees mentioned areas of their jobs where they were more likely to engage in political behaviour:

> Yes. I use it in recruitment, in proposing people for posts. I use my knowledge of the people and the departments to get suitable placements(Personnel Officer, Gas);

> ... Information can be used in ways it wasn't designed for. Take manpower statistics for example - politics show in their interpretation (Employee Relations Manager, Steel);

> Oh yes - everyone must do to an extent. How honest they'd be in admitting it, I don't know. It's using knowledge and information responsibly, to build up your credibility in the eyes of other management (Training Officer, Energy).

Fifteen percent (14) of the interviewees felt that political behaviour was rarely overt in their organizations, and they attributed this to 'open' styles of management, or alternatively, the small size of the organization which meant that there was not much scope (or necessity) for internal politics. 'No' responses were received from 25 percent (24) of the interviewees, and their lack of participation was expressed in terms of feeling that political behaviour was inappropriate for personnel, or indeed against their principles.

A noticeable feature of the interviews however, was the level of awareness of political behaviour which was shown by the sample, regardless of whether or not they classed themselves as participants. Those who admitted to engaging in political behaviour said that they did so to secure the success of their departments' policies, ideas and strategies. Both credibility and being useful could be used as political tools. Small organization size, and/or the strength of top management had some bearing on whether political behaviour was evident, or even possible. There seemed to be a greater emphasis on teamwork and cooperation in smaller concerns.

Conclusions

Perhaps it was not surprising that our interviewees took a strong line about their role as 'management'. Other data obtained about them showed that most were involved in personnel work at the 'sharp end', with industrial relations generally a major feature of work. While their work could be challenging, it was also stressful. Personnel was described as 'a lonely occupation', and doing the work or certain aspects of it created various degrees of stress for 84 percent (91) of the interview sample. While the interviewees held predominantly managerialist views, another theme emerged which might at face value present a kind of contradiction to managerialism. This was the interviewees' emphasis on professionalism. For this sample, and as noted, 'professional' meant doing their jobs well, and being seen to do so. There was a strong element of instrumentalism in this which hinged on credibility. The interviewees exhibited the task-centred approach which Tyson and Fell (1986) felt embodied the 'professional ethic'. Credibility enhanced their ability to influence others, and to participate in decision-making proactively. For many, their competence and expertise were sources of political 'clout' which they used to advantage, especially when other managers made mistakes. Personnel's use of knowledge and expertise was seen as a major source of power and/or influence by the senior executive interview sample. For this interview group, organizational/sector-specific knowledge was as important as any 'professional' personnel knowledge. Thurley (1981) wrote that personnel managers used professionalism instrumentally because they were 'caught in a mismatch between a pretentious abstract model of human resource management and the reality of a fragmented set of activities carried out with little recognition of their value by other managers'. While the results of this study show that personnel specialists do use their 'professional' credibility in their relationships with other managers, it is questionable whether they do so to mitigate the 'mismatch' noted by him.

Rather, it appears that their professionalism furthered entirely practical situation-specific ends. This involved them helping other managers to consider the personnel implications of their decisions, often to prevent 'bad' decisions which could have a detrimental effect on labour relations, or which could leave their employers open to legal action. In this, the protection of employer interests, rather than the promotion of personnel policies or procedures and/or theory for their own sake, came through strongly in the interviews.

The specialists in our study have shown us that they have shaken off the idea that they should be fairer and more caring than other managers. Instead, they have presented evidence that other managers require education in personnel matters, and need to recognise that personnel management is part of all managerial jobs. Indeed, the resistance of other managers to this idea was a feature of the interview data, and it is apparent that other managers' refusal to recognise that personnel work is an integral part of management gives personnel specialists a high first hurdle to jump before they can proceed with whatever task they have in hand.

References

Bacharach, S.B., and Lawler, E. (1980), *Power and Politics in Organizations*, Jossey-Bass, London.

Bem, D. J. (1972), 'Self-Perception Theory', in L. Berkowitz (ed.), *Advances in Experimental Social Psychology*, pp. 1-62, Academic Press, New York.

Bucher, R. (1970), 'Social Process and Power in a Medical School', in M.N. Zald (ed.), *Power and Organizations*, pp. 3-48, Vanderbilt University Press, Nashville.

Crichton, A. (1963), 'A persistent stereotype? The personnel manager: the outsider', *Personnel Management*, December, pp. 160-67.

Crozier, M. and Friedberg, E. (1980), *Actors and Systems: the Politics of Collective Action*, Chicago University Press, Chicago.

Dryburgh, G. D. M. (1972), 'The man in the middle', *Personnel Management*, May, p. 3.

Farnham, D. (1984), *Personnel in Context*, IPM, London.

Fox, A. (1966), 'From welfare to organization', *New Society*, Vol. 17, pp. 14-16.

French, W. and Henning, D. (1966), 'The authority-influence role of the functional specialist in management', *Academy of Management Journal*, Vol. 9, September, pp. 187-203.

Gowler, D. and Legge, K. (1983), 'The Meaning of Management and the Management of Meaning: a view from social anthropology', in M.J. Earl (ed.), *Perspectives on Management*, pp. 197-233, Oxford University Press, Oxford.

Guest, D. and Horwood, R. (1981), 'Characteristics of the Successful Personnel Manager', *Personnel Management*, May, pp. 18-23.

Hickson, D.J., Hinings, C.R., Lee, C.E., Schneck, R.E. and Pennings, J.M. (1971), 'A Strategic Contingencies Theory of Intraorganizational Power', *Administrative Science Quarterley*, Vol. 16, pp. 216-29.

Hickson, D.J., Butler, R.J., Cray, D., Mallory, G.R. and Wilson, D.C. (1986), *Top Decisions: Strategic Decision Making in Organizations*, Blackwell, Oxford.

IPM (1963), 'Statement on personnel management and personnel policies', *Personnel Management*, March, 11-15.

Johnston, N.M. (1978), 'Planners come of age', *Personnel Management*, November, p. 5.

Kakabadse, A. (1983), *The Politics of Management*, Gower, Aldershot.

Lawrence, P. A., (1986), *Invitation to Management*, Basil Blackwell, Oxford.

Machin, J. and Stewart, R. (1981), 'Directions for future research into managerial effectiveness', in J. Machin, R. Stewart and C. Hales (eds), *Towards Managerial Effectiveness*, Gower, Aldershot.

Mackay, L. (1986), 'The Macho Manager: it's no myth', *Personnel Management*, January, pp. 25-27.

Miner, J.B. and Miner, M.G. (1976), 'Managerial characteristics of personnel managers', *Industrial Relations*, Vol. 15, No. 2, May, pp. 225-34.

Mintzberg, H. (1985), 'The Organization as a Political Arena', *Journal of Management Studies*, Vol. 22, No. 2, March, pp. 133-54.

Morse, N. (1976), 'Management by Norms', *Management Today*, February, pp. 66-69.

Paterson, B.E. (1991), 'Personnel Specialists in Scotland: a Study of Managerial Work and Knowledge Use', Unpublished PhD thesis: University of Abertay, Dundee.

Ritzer, G. and Trice, H.M. (1969), *An Occupation in Conflict*, Cornell University Press, Ithaca.

Ritzer, G. and Trice, H.M. (1970) 'A Mythical Occupational Image', *Human Mosaic*, Vol. 4, Spring Part 2, pp. 69-78.

Sayles, L.R. (1964), *Managerial Behaviour*, McGraw-Hill, New York.

Stewart, R. (1981), 'The relevance for managerial effectiveness of my studies of managerial work and behaviour', in J. Machin, R. Stewart and C. Hales (eds), *Toward Managerial Effectiveness*, pp. 7-31, Gower, Aldershot.

Stewart, R. (1983), 'Managerial Behaviour: how research has changed the traditional picture', in M. Earl (ed.), *Perspectives on Management: a Multi-disciplinary Analysis*, pp. 82-98, Oxford University Press, Oxford.

Thurley, K. (1981), 'Personnel Management in the UK - a case for urgent treatment?', *Personnel Management*, August, pp. 24 -29.

Tyson, S. (1980), 'Taking Advantage of Ambiguity', *Personnel Management*, February, pp. 45-8.

Tyson, S. (1986), 'The Management of the Personnel Function', Journal of Management Studies Conference on Industrial Relations Strategy and Management, Manchester Business School, September, 1986.

Tyson, S. and Fell, A. (1986), *Evaluating the Personnel Function*, Hutchinson, London.

Watson, T.J. (1977), *The Personnel Managers: A Study in the Sociology of Work and Employment*, Routledge & Kegan Paul, London.

Watson, T.J. (1986), *Management, Organization and Employment Strategy*, Routledge & Kegan Paul, London.

Wilmott, H.C. (1984), 'Images and Ideals of Managerial Work: A Critical Examination of Conceptual and Empirical Accounts', *Journal of Management Studies*, Vol. 21, No. 3, pp. 349-68.

Yukl, G.A. (1989), *Leadership in Organizations* (2nd edition), Prentice Hall, Englewood Cliffs, N.J.

12 The undisclosed bankers

Mark Hughes

Introduction

Bankers perceive themselves as professional, regarding recent changes within banking as a challenge to their professional status (Morison, 1989, p. 99; Richardson, 1992, p. 4; Lloyd, 1992, p.20). The Chartered Institute of Bankers (CIB) with over 100,000 members is a major professional association (Morse, 1993, p. 62). Despite bankers perceiving themselves as professionals, their reputation appears to have been tarnished over the past decade.

> The evidence, such as it is, therefore, is that the exchange of old professional ethos for the new commercial one has reaped considerable reputational liabilities. There is good cause to suspect, if not reliable means to demonstrate, that the change has produced more losses than gains. (Lloyd, 1992, p. 20).

This chapter, through reviewing research into banking and relating these findings to the sociology of professions, seeks to further our understanding of bankers' claims to professional status. Before reviewing the research it is necessary to introduce key terms within the chapter and the historical background.

Managers and other senior officials in the joint stock banks began using the title 'banker' in the second half of the nineteenth century (Green, 1979, p.xix). In this chapter, it is used in a similar fashion to denote those bank employees in managerial positions. Whilst, the majority will be employed in the branches, the title also includes managers at regional and head offices.

In discussing banks the chapter is concerned with retail banking (Howcroft and Levis, 1986) as opposed to wholesale banking. In particular, although not exclusively this encompasses the high street operations of the 'big four' clearing banks.

Banking was not widely regarded as a profession before the third quarter of the nineteenth century, with commentators describing the business as a trade rather than as a specialist profession (Green, 1979, p. xviii). Prior to the third quarter of the nineteenth century banking had not been dominated by the current large joint stock banks, but instead by many private partnerships working in a small scale. The formation of the joint stock banks led to the displacement and absorption of many of the old private bankers. There was now a need for managers who could manage branch networks and supervise head office departments ... 'many of those working in the banks realized that the growing awareness of technical skills could be harnessed to a system of banking qualifications' (Green, 1979, p. xx).

Green (1979, p. xx) suggests that the support and initiative for professional qualifications came from junior managers and clerks. At this stage, the notion of the 'general's baton', implying that every entrant to banking displaying sufficient ability, had the opportunity to rise through the ranks to the position of general manager was evident. This was reflected within a desire not to make the new professional body restrictive.

> The founders of the Institute, including senior bankers and the clerks who had advocated the introduction of a banking qualification in the 1870s, made certain that its role as a professional body was not in any way restrictive. In contrast to professional associations which used their membership and qualifications as a licence to practice, the Institute was launched on the understanding that its qualifications would be accessible to many thousands of employees (Green, 1979, p. xx).

The Institute of Bankers was incorporated by Royal Charter in 1987. Glover (1985) suggests that the objectives of the Institute of Bankers remained the same since it was founded in 1879, although the means of fulfilling them have changed frequently and considerably. The three main objectives are:

> to facilitate the consideration and discussion of matters of interest to bankers;
>
> to afford opportunities to its members for the acquisition of a knowledge of the theory of banking;
>
> to take any measures which may be desirable to further the interests of banking.

The Institute has suffered in recent times from recessional problems affecting the whole of banking.

> In 1992-93 as the UK recession continued and banks went on reducing staff numbers, things became more difficult for the Institute and many of its members. Membership of the Institute, which had declined by more than 10,000 during the previous year, fell again by a similar amount to approximately 100,000, thus coming back to levels last seen in the 1970s (Morse, 1993, p. 62).

In July 1993, the Chartered Building Society Institute and the CIB merged, adding 6,500 members to the CIB. This may be viewed as a response to falling numbers and convergence in the business of banks and building societies (Morse, 1993, p. 62).

A review of banking research

The review is based upon research published between 1983 and the early to mid 1990s, which discusses the UK banks in general and the work of bankers in particular.

Smith and Wield (1983) identified the ethos within the clearing banks as 'autocratic paternalism' which they view as encouraging conformity amongst bankers. Child et al (1983) considered how jobs of service providers are changing with the introduction of new technologies. In discussing the semi-professional status of senior bank staff, it is suggested that technology could be used to support a policy of degradation, through the introduction of 'idiot-proof systems' (1983, p. 176). However, uncertainty and the resulting indetermination within service task dimensions make it more difficult to transfer the provision of a service to a technological system (Child et al, 1983, p. 183). Child et al (1983) offer the example of bankers sanctioning loans and overdrafts where there has traditionally been an element of uncertainty.

> Compared with doctors, bank officers have a weaker public identity as professional experts whose judgement must be consulted. Loans, for example, are being offered by many sources today and it is relatively easy for the customer to weigh up alternatives and decide on the best methods of financing (Child et al, 1983, p. 186).

In the case of doctors, qualifications allow a degree of market power. Bankers are felt to lack such market power for the following reasons:

> In banking, the structure of qualifications offered by the Institute of Bankers has never provided a basis for this degree of market power, because the banks have always controlled the volume of new entrants into training and have maintained the dependence of staff on the employer for career progression by refusing to recruit from each other (Child et al, 1983, p. 187).

Crompton and Jones (1984) in a similar fashion encourage the consideration of professionalism within its own organizational context.

> Banking is widely regarded as a profession; and is explicitly presented as such in the recruitment literature; professional examinations denote full entry to professional status. However, banks train their own personnel for their own specific purposes, and, as we have seen the no-poaching agreement with regard to career staff ensures that such employees are confined to organizational submarkets (Crompton and Jones, 1984, p. 233).

Child and Tarbuck (1985) examined the positions adopted by managements and trade unions over the introduction of new technologies in the retail sector of banking. They suggested that the historical development of banks influences their culture.

> Banks are founded on an appearance of soundness, conservative respectability and orderly administration (Child and Tarbuck, 1985, p. 31).

Whilst research into the work of bankers was not evident within sociological journals, there was one exception. Crompton (1986) considered the implications of the increase in professional qualifications amongst women. Focusing upon a range of professions including banking, reference was made to three ideal typical strategies (Brown, 1982) underlying individual choices and actions in relation to work and employment.

> Entrepreneurial - where resources are such that self-employment is possible.
>
> Organizational - where advancement is sought within an employing organization.
>
> Occupational - where skills and qualifications are used to move from employer to employer.

Although distinctions are difficult as classifications will depend upon specific employment contexts, the Institute of Bankers was regarded as fitting the organizational strategy (Crompton, 1986, p. 30).

Collinson (1987) revealed a lack of equal opportunities in banking with regards to recruitment, training and promotion. In explaining the lack of success of the Banking, Insurance and Finance Union to challenge the prerogative of management over recruitment and promotion Collinson suggests the following:

> Indeed, it is precisely this question of managerial power and prerogative, as it is presently mediated through unaccountable and secretive practices and a highly paternalistic banking culture, which lies at the heart of the continuing barriers to equal opportunities (Collinson, 1987, p. 12).

One of the few observational studies of the work of bankers was undertaken by Lawrence (1987). The research conducted in National Westminster Bank involved observing 12 managers drawn from branch managers, area directors and senior managers from the Bank's five divisions. One of the interesting elements in this work, is the attempt to offer an interested outsider's view of bank culture:

> Highly structured
> Vertically Differentiated
> Career-For-Life
> Careerist

Homogeneous
Classless
Co-operative
Service Sector Personnel
Conformist or Unconventional?
Status-conscious
Generalist
Polite
Literate
Deliberate
Orderliness
Rationality
Control-oriented
Paternalist

Although some of these labels now appear dated (career-for-life, polite) and others questionable (generalist, paternalist), they do provide a unique perspective about the work of bankers and their claims to professional status.

Howcroft (1988) has addressed changes in management resulting from the transition from traditional retail banks to emerging retail banks. The following are identified:

i) *Traditional Retail Bank* Conservative prudent risk averse, emphasis on lending skills, administration general, management divisional, not profit conscious and not cost conscious.

ii) *Emerging Retail Bank* Dynamic creative risk aware, specialized flexible matrix style, market-oriented, selling-oriented, profit-conscious and cost-control conscious.

Lee and Piper (1988) studied promotion processes within a single region of Midland Bank, identifying what they called a 'promotion culture'. The following major themes of the promotion culture were identified. The bank was perceived by its employees to be an autocratic organization, which was hierarchical, status conscious and demanding loyalty. Also, there was a belief in onward and forever upward career movements.

In 1989, Lee and Piper published a further paper focused upon recruitment and promotion of graduates in Midland Bank, providing insights into the 'subjective', 'informal' and 'political' aspects of the promotion process (Lee and Piper, 1989, p. 46).

Research commissioned by banks rarely appears in the refereed journals. However, an article in *Personnel Management* provides an insight into work being undertaken. The research identified 11 high performance managerial competencies within National Westminster Bank relevant to rapidly changing environments and flexible forms of organization (Cockerill, 1989, p. 54). The competencies identified included conceptual flexibility, a developmental approach and a proactive orientation (Cockerill, 1989, p. 55).

Cressey and Scott (1991, p. 84) have identified cultural changes resulting from banks moving from mechanistic forms to more organic forms of organization.

i) *Old Model* Paternalistic, cautious, hierarchical, trustee role, staff are a cost item, attention to detail, specific specialist roles, loyalty, bureaucratic and command oriented.

ii) *New Model* Technocratic, performance-oriented, flexible, commercially driven, staff are a resource, sales oriented, outgoing and adaptable, educated, competitive and commitment oriented.

McGoldrick and Greenland's (1992) discussion of competitive forces highlights the environment in which bankers operate. Banks along with other financial institutions are increasingly being viewed as retail institutions that have a direct interface with the consumer market (McGoldrick and Greenland, 1992, p. 170).

In recent years, the term financial services has been adopted to help classify the variety of money-based services on offer to consumers at a time when the traditional barriers between different suppliers looked like breaking down (Fifield, 1989, p. 33). As traditional barriers between banks and other suppliers break down in the future, it may be possible to generalize research findings across organizations: examples of financial service research include Storey (1987), Hope et al (1988), Kerfoot and Knights (1992) and Knights and Willmott (1992).

The professional banker?

In the following section, the professional status of bankers is discussed in terms of perspectives on professionalisation, occupational control and banking as an organizational profession.

Perspectives on professionalization

Johnson (1972, p. 21), whilst being critical of such an approach identifies four ways in which the term professionalization has been used. These perspectives provide an introduction to the professionalization of bankers.

The first approach refers to broad changes in occupational structure whereby professional or even white-collar jobs increase in number relative to other occupations. Cotterrell and Patrick suggest that whilst there had been increases in the number of bankers, employment levels had recently fallen:

> The number of full-time bankers (employees in banking) grew by more than 100,000 between 1979 and 1989 - an increase of 31 per cent ... Full-time employment then fell dramatically between 1989 and 1993, by more than 80,000 (Cotterrell and Patrick, 1994).

The second approach to professionalization refers to an increase in the number of occupational associations. In the case of bankers the main association remains the CIB. The exception to this has been specialists working within the banks, in areas such as computing, law and accountancy.

The third approach refers to an occupation exhibiting a number of attributes which are essentially professional. Greenwood (1957) identifies the following attributes:

Basis in Systematic Theory
Licence to Practice
Code of Ethics
Community Sanction
Professional Culture

There is a systematic theory of banking embodied within the objectives of the CIB and the courses leading to the CIB qualifications. The associateship qualification is still regarded as a prerequisite for career bankers, although whether this can be regarded as a licence to practice is doubtful. The CIB does not have a code of ethics, although the Banking Ombudsman has recommended that banking ethics should be included as part of their syllabus in future (*Banking World*, 1994). Research undertaken by the University of Westminster (commissioned by the Co-operative Bank) suggests that bank managers are perceived as ethical (Thomas, 1993, p. 20). In terms of community sanction the public image of the banks appears to have been tarnished (Lloyd, 1992, p. 20). The final attribute is the presence of a professional culture. The tradition of paternalism (Collinson, 1987 and Lawrence, 1987) within banking is likely to have led bankers to relate primarily to their respective banks, rather than their professional body.

The final approach identified by Johnson refers to professionalization passing through predictable stages of organizational change, the end state being professionalism. In the case of banking, there was a considerable effort to establish professional qualifications in the 1870s (Green, 1979, p. xx), but since then bankers to not appear to have moved towards professionalism. As Glover (1985) noted their objectives have remained unchanged. Also, they have remained a broad based association, lacking a code of ethics. In the next section, an explanation for the difficulties in developing as a profession is offered.

Occupational control within banking

Johnson (1972, pp. 37-38), in criticizing professionalization theories, suggests that more fruitful results can be obtained through considering occupational control. The following discussion is based upon a framework developed by Child and Fulk to analyse occupational control which they suggested might be applicable to other occupations (1982, p. 184). They offer the following definition of occupational control.

> The concept of occupational control refers to the collective capability of members of an occupation to preserve unique authority in the definition, conduct, and evaluation of their work and also to determine the conditions of entry to an exit from practice within occupational parameters (Child and Fulk, 1982, p. 155).

There are four areas in which conditions affecting occupational control in professions might usefully be examined (Child and Fulk, 1982, p. 159).

Restriction of access to the occupation's knowledge base

Context of professional employment

Power and authority in the relationship of client and professional

Relationships between the profession and agencies of the state.

Firstly, access to the occupation's knowledge base has involved studying for the CIB professional qualifications. However, parallel to this easily codified knowledge, bankers have suggested that there is an element of tacit knowledge within their work. This is effectively captured by Hanson.

> The art of lending, if art it be, may often lie in the judgement or, indeed, sixth sense of a bank manager - by sheer experience he will acquire a nose for the good or not so good proposition (Hanson, 1982, p. 63).

The uncertainty element in the work of bankers is being eroded through technological changes (Child et al, 1983). A consequence of this is that whereas in the past bankers could have maintained occupational control through drawing upon their experience based tacit knowledge this appears to be diminishing.

Secondly, the employment context has a number of implications for the occupational control of bankers. Child and Fulk (1982, p. 165) suggest that in heteronomous organizations the definition of work objectives and evaluation criteria may no longer be in the sole control of occupational members. Banks have traditionally emphasised unitary objectives (Lawrence, 1987).

Also Child and Fulk suggest that employees will be dependent upon the internal labour market and large organizations will generate substantial vertical differentiation among occupational members. The dependence upon internal labour markets within banks has been demonstrated (Child et al, 1983; Crompton and Jones, 1984). Vertical differentiation has always been a by-product of the traditionally hierarchical structures within the banks (Lawrence, 1987). The emerging retail banking form identified by Howcroft (1988) suggests a flexible matrix structure, with implications for the traditional vertical differentiation. Whilst the employment context is changing, it is difficult to view changes as aiding bankers in maintaining occupational control.

Thirdly, there appears to have been a considerable shift in power and authority from banker to client, captured in the following quote.

> It is not easy being a banker these days. From being a figure of power the bankers has become a figure of fun, even pity (Bose, 1992, p. 21).

As consumers of banking services have become better informed, they have become more sophisticated in the demands they place upon the banks and consumerism has led to a higher profile for pressure groups, particularly those reflecting the interests of small business owners.

The power and authority of the banker in relations with clients has been further eroded through the presence of alternative service providers. Banks are beginning to use technology to by-pass their branches.

> A gradual detachment of historic branch functions and their fragmentation in the wider external economy is evident in developments such as EFTPOS, home banking, and the Midland Bank's recently launched First Direct branchless telephone banking service, for example (Cressey and Scott, 1992).

The emergence of alternative service providers, such as the building societies, insurance companies and chain stores (such as Marks and Spencer) has been particularly significant for bankers who were used to operating under virtual monopoly conditions.

A consequence in the shift of power and authority from banker to client, has been the inability of bankers to maintain occupational control through claiming to protect clients' interests. This can be contrasted with National Health Service doctors who in defending their status have 'focused directly upon the protection of the interests of the patient' (Crompton, 1990, p. 163).

The fourth area affecting occupational control in professions is the relationship between professions and agencies of the state. Whilst financial services legislation in the 1980s was intended to deregulate the UK financial system, the fear is that it transformed the system into one of the most regulated in Europe (Gardener and Molyneux, 1989). Criticisms of the activities of the banks from the National

Consumer Council and the Director General of Fair Trading are being backed up with the threat of the imposition of statutory codes (Hughes, 1993, p. 3).

This section has revealed little support for bankers' claims to professionalization or the maintenance of occupational control. There are even indications that their professional status is declining (declining numbers, less power and authority in relations with clients, threat of state regulation). Crompton (1990, p. 163), one of the few sociologists to have researched the area, suggests that:

> It is not a matter of coincidence that expert occupations operating in the market, for example in accountancy, banking and management have taken on the mantle of professionalism, through such formal bodies such as the Institute of Bankers, the Institute of Chartered Accountants of England and Wales, and so on, and would relinquish it with extreme reluctance.

Whilst it is difficult to reconcile this desire with the preceding discussion, it is possible that bankers as managers belong to an organizational profession.

Banking as an organizational profession

A theme of this chapter has been that bankers are more closely attached to their respective banks, rather than the occupational category 'banker'. This may be a by-product of the traditionally paternalistic employment methods evident within the banks (Collinson, 1987 and Lawrence, 1987) This reasoning suggests that we need to consider bankers in terms of organizational control, rather than occupational control.

In the earlier discussion of the historical evolution of banking qualifications, the motivation appeared to be the need to identify managers in the newly formed joint stock banks (Green, 1979, p. xx). Since the formation of the joint stock banks there has been a demand for managers, as a consequence of their size and geographical spread.

Drawing upon the work of Larson (1977) Reed and Anthony (1992, p. 600) suggest that management displays the characteristics of the prototype of an 'organizational profession'.

The following characteristics which apply to bankers may be identified, although research evidence is limited:

> There is a high degree of organizational dependence (Crompton, 1986, p. 39 and Cressey and Scott, 1991, p. 84).
>
> There is a high degree of work-related and occupationally-related heterogeneity (Lawrence, 1987, p. 15).

The knowledge base is organizationally diverse and difficult to codify. This was the case, although the ability of bankers to resist codification of knowledge has been questioned (Child et al, 1983).

Bankers possess a limited degree of monopoly control over the knowledge base (Crompton and Jones, 1984). This is related to professional qualifications being accessible to all employees in principle (Green, 1979, p. xx).

There are significant constraints on the exercise of discretion and autonomy. Lawrence (1987, p. 11) highlights the significance of controls in banking.

Internal functional differentiation and hierarchical stratification is present with banking, largely as a consequence of the size of these organizations. However, there are indications that this is changing (Howcroft, 1988 and Cressey and Scott, 1991).

In terms of the characteristics of organizational professions suggested by Reed and Anthony (1992) there are indications that bankers as managers may belong to such an organizational profession.

Discussion

Despite the size of the banks and the fact that the Institute of Bankers was founded in 1879, the only research studies to consider the professional status of bankers occurred in the mid 1980s (Child et al, 1983; Crompton and Jones, 1984; Crompton, 1986). The problem has been further compounded by the fact that research studies rather than focusing upon the work of bankers, appear to reflect the discipline interests of researchers: technology, industrial relations, marketing and so on.

Before concluding this chapter, reasons for the paucity of empirical work informing our understanding of the professional status of bankers are discussed.

Bankers may remain undisclosed due to problems of gaining research access to information in the banks, e.g. 'unaccountable and secret practices' (Collinson, 1987). One of the cornerstones of banks is their assurance that information about customers will always remain confidential. Such a cultural barrier is likely to make negotiating research access problematic. Also, the fact that banks remain large and hierarchical means that requests to do research often are referred to head offices, possibly resulting in research that challenges the status quo being filtered out. For researchers to fully understand working methods within the banks they need to understand the multiple perspectives that exist within different departments and at different levels within banks. However interdepartmental politics may complicate matters further.

A final explanation why the work of bankers remains undisclosed is sociological antipathy towards researching bankers. Collins (1979) in reviewing *The Bankers* by Martin Mayer highlights a problem with sociological research in the USA which may be generalizable to the UK.

> Money is doubtless the single most important neglected topic in sociology. For that matter, it is probably the most important neglected topic in all the social sciences. Sociologists ignore it as if it were not sociological enough (Collins, 1979, p. 190).

There appears to be a need to exercise the 'sociological imagination' (Mills, 1953) with reference to bankers.

Conclusions

In the introduction it was suggested that bankers perceived themselves as professionals and perceive change as a challenge to their professional status. However, their claim has been questioned in terms of the lack of evidence needed to substantiate such a claim. It was demonstrated that bankers display few of the characteristics of professionals and lack the means of occupational control exhibited by other professionals. However, bankers as managers display many of the characteristics of an organizational profession.

In conclusion, claims of bankers to be professionals are questionable. If professionalism is viewed as a continuum, bankers appear to be far removed from professions such as law and medicine. Their reluctance to relinquish the professional label (Crompton, 1990) is an understandable counter position to the growing consumerism and subsequent calls for greater state regulation of the banks.

Whilst it is possible to offer explanations for why the work of bankers remaining undisclosed, difficulties are compounded by the rapidly changing environment in which bankers operate (Howcroft, 1988 and Cressey and Scott, 1991). This was effectively captured in the rationale for the research of Lawrence '...our understanding of the world will never quite catch up with our experience of it' (Lawrence, 1987, p. 2). The prospects for an incremental development of a theoretical approach to the professional status of bankers based upon earlier work is problematic within a rapidly changing environment.

However, whilst specific research into bankers as professionals and more generally the work of bankers remains limited, it is difficult to conclusively challenge the bankers claims to professional status. In this instance, the truism about the area meriting further research does appear relevant. As long as bankers remain undisclosed they may maintain the mystique of the professional.

Note

I wish to thank Professor Aidan Berry for providing constructive critiques of draft versions of this chapter. Responsibility for the views expressed rests with the author.

References

Banking World (1994), 'Putting ethics on syllabus', Vol. 12, No. 1, p. 7.

Bose, M. (1992), 'The ghosts of Captain Mannering', *The Director*, Vol. 45 (12).

Brown, R. (1982), 'Work histories, career strategies and class structure', in A. Giddens and G. Mackenzie (eds), *Social Class and the Division of Labour*, Cambridge University Press, Cambridge.

Child, J. and Fulk, J. (1982) 'Maintenance of occupational control - the case of professions', *Work and Occupations*, Vol. 9, No. 2, pp. 155-92.

Child, J. Loveridge, R., Harvey, J. and Spencer, A. (1983), 'Microelectronics and the quality of employment in services', in P. Marstrand (ed.), *New Technology and the Future of Work and Skills*, Frances Pinter, London.

Child, J. and Tarbuck, M. (1985), 'The introduction of new technologies: managerial initiative and union response in British banks', *Industrial Relations Journal*, Vol. 16, No. 3, pp. 19-33.

Cockerill, T. (1989), 'The kind of competence for rapid change', *Personnel Management*, pp. 52-56.

Collins, R. (1979), Review of 'The Bankers' by Martin Mayer, *American Journal of Sociology*, Vol. 85, pp. 190-94.

Collinson, D. (1987), 'Banking on women: selection practices in the finance sector', *Personnel Review*, Vol. 16, No. 5, pp. 12-20.

Cotterrell, A. and Patrick, K. (1994), 'A job for life?', *Banking World*, Vol. 12, No. 6, pp. 43-44.

Cressey, P. and Scott, P. (1991), 'Industrial relations and innovation in services: the British banking sector', mimeo, University of Bath.

Cressey, P. and Scott, P. (1992), 'Employment, technology and industrial relations in the UK clearing banks: is the honeymoon over?', *New Technology, Work and Employment*, Vol. 7, No. 2.

Crompton, R. (1990), 'Professions in the current context', *Work, Employment and Society*, Special Issue, May, pp. 147-66.

Crompton, R. and Jones, G. (1984), *White Collar Proletariat: Deskilling and Gender in Clerical Work*, Macmillan, London.

Crompton, R. with Sanderson, K. (1986), 'Credentials and careers: some implications of the increase in professional qualifications amongst women', *Sociology*, Vol. 20, No. 1, pp. 25-42.

Fifield, P. (1989) 'Consumer financial services', in P. Jones (ed.), *Management in Service Industries*, Pitman, London.

Gardener, T. and Molyneux, P. (1989), 'Banking regulation in the UK - converging towards complexity', *Banking World*, Vol. 7, No. 2, pp. 35-37.

Glover, E. (1985), 'Professional education for bankers', in B. Livy (ed.), *Management and People in Banking*, Institute of Bankers, London.

Green, E. (1979), *Debtors to their Profession: a History of the Institute of Bankers 1879-1979*, Methuen, London.

Greenwood, E. (1957), 'Attributes of a profession', *Social Work*, Vol. 2, No. 3, pp. 44-55.

Hanson, D.G. (1982), *Service Banking*, The Institute of Bankers, London.

Hope, V., Knights, D. And Willmott, H. (1988), 'The ambivalence of personnel in life assurance: the challenge of change', *Personnel Review*, Vol. 17, No. 1, pp. 32-37.

Howcroft, J.B. (1988), 'The evolution of retail branch banking in the UK', *Loughborough University Banking Centre Research Paper Series*, No. 55.

Howcroft, J.B. and Levis, J. (1986), *Retail Banking*, Basil Blackwell, Oxford.

Hughes, M. (1993), 'Code of conduct attack on banks', *The Guardian*, July 23, p. 3.

Johnson, T.J. (1972), *Professions and Power*, Macmillan, London.

Kerfoot, D. and Knights, D. (1992), 'Planning for personnel? Human resource management reconsidered', *Journal of Management Studies*, Vol. 29, No. 5, pp. 651-68.

Knights, D. and Willmott, H. (1992), 'Conceptualizing leadership processes: a study of senior managers in a financial services company', *Journal of Management Studies*, Vol. 29, No. 6, pp. 761-82.

Larson, M.S. (1977), *The Rise of Professionalism: a Sociological Analysis*, University of Californian Press, Berkeley.

Lawrence, P. (1987), 'Work and its context: senior managers in a clearing bank', Loughborough University Banking Centre Research Paper Series, No. 39.

Lee, R.A. and Piper, J. (1988), 'Dimensions of promotion culture in Midland Bank, *Personnel Review*, Vol. 17, No. 6, pp. 15-44.

Lloyd, T. (1992), 'How courteous reliable banks became uncaring and selfish', *Banking World*, Vol. 10, No. 6, pp. 20-25.

McGoldrick, P.J. and Greenland, S.J. (1992), 'Competition between banks and building societies in the retailing of financial services, *British Journal of Management*, Vol. 13, No. 3, pp. 169-79.

Mills, C.W. (1953), *The Sociological Imagination*, Oxford University Press, New York.

Morison, I. (1989) 'The cultural revolution in banking: a 20 year perspective', in Institute of Bankers (ed.), *Jack of All Trades ... Master of None*, Institute of Bankers, London.

Morse, J. (1993), 'President's Statement', *Banking World*, Vol. 11, No. 7, pp. 62.

Reed, M. and Anthony, P. (1992), 'Professionalizing management and managing professionalization: British management in the 1980s', *Journal of Management Studies*, Vol. 29, No. 5, pp. 591-613.

Richardson, L. (1992), *Bankers in the Selling Role*, Wiley, New York.

Smith, S. and Wield, D. (1983), 'Features of technical and organizational change in the clearing banks; an outline discussion with reference to Greater London', *LETR Working Paper No. 1*, The Open University, Milton Keynes.

Storey, J. (1987) 'The management of new office technology choice, control and social structure in the insurance industry', *Journal of Management Studies*, Vol. 24, No. 1, pp. 43-62.

Thomas, T. (1993), 'The banker as ethical businessman', *Banking World*, Vol. 11, No. 3, p. 20.

Yukl, G.A. (1989), *Leadership in Organizations* (2nd edition.) Prentice Hall, Englewood Cliffs, N. J

13 Managing IT professionals: a crisis in management control?

Wendy Currie and Colin Bryson

Introduction

Throughout the 1980s a wealth of literature emerged which linked competitive advantage with IT strategy (Kantrow, 1980; McFarlan, 1984; Porter and Millar, 1985; Porter, 1985; Clark, 1989; Feeny, 1988). The normative approach was founded largely on the precept that carefully crafted IT strategies led to competitive advantage, measured by increased market share and higher profits. Yet the 1990s saw a spate of IT failures such as the ambulance computer fiasco (Currie, 1995a), the Wessex Health Authority computer failure, and the highly publicised TAURUS disaster (Cohen, 1993; Currie,1995a; Tilley, 1990; Financial Times, 1993; Waters, 1993; Waters and Cane, 1993). In the case of TAURUS, it emerged that project management oversights of the legal, financial, political and logistical issues played a significant part in the demise of the £400 million computer project (Currie, 1994). In fact, a recent survey found that some twenty-five per cent of companies believed that most of their IT projects were unsuccessful either because they were delivered too late and over budget, or because they had failed to meet user-needs (Financial Times, 1994).

However, the assumption that the above IT failures are labelled computer disasters, tends to deflect attention away from management and to absolve project managers of the responsibility for failures (Willcocks and Griffiths, 1994). But against a backcloth of large scale IT failures which have come to light in recent years, more attention is now being focused upon the human dimension of managing change. Indeed, simple interpretations which look only at the number of technical malfunctions are misguided, as the majority of IT failures stem from a complex web of economic, political and technical factors (Sauer, 1993; Currie, 1995b; Financial Times, 1994). Perhaps a more appropriate focus is to discern the skills and experience essential for managing large scale IT projects in contemporary private and public sector organisations.

In this context, different interpretations emerge regarding the types of skill required for managing people and technology (Thamhain, 1992). In recent years, many writers have postulated that generalist skills are most appropriate for managing IT, since these individuals are perceived to combine technical awareness with business acumen (Adler et al, 1992; Boynton et al, 1992; Morone, 1993; Rockart, 1988; Rockness and Zmud, 1989). In this article, we consider the literature on the generalist versus specialist debate vis a vis managing technology. In addition, we reflect on some empirical work conducted by the authors on the management of large scale IT projects in the private and public sectors. Here we contend that the management of large scale IT projects and people is highly complex and fraught with difficulties. As a result, human resources management concerns regarding whether to use generalist or technical managers, or even hybrid managers is immaterial in isolation of other important political, market, sectoral and economic considerations.

However, our research into private and public sector organisations suggests that one of the key problems associated with managing large scale, high risk IT projects is indeed a lack of skills, both at management and technical levels. Whilst the technical skills shortages are well documented and seemingly ongoing, less attention is given to management skills shortages. Our research suggests that in a climate of rapid technological change, with many new languages and packages entering the commercial marketplace, project managers are faced with an ongoing requirement to learn new skills. In addition, the current emphasis upon business process reengineering (BPR) and process innovation (Davenport, 1994) also poses new challenges to project managers to seek a competitive advantage through IT.

Many large organisations attempt to impose a formal-rational structure upon managers and technologists by designing complex IT architectures and strategies led by steering committees and project boards. These organisations are also likely to adopt menu driven methodologies for managing large scale IT projects. Yet our case study research shows that such approaches often impose an overly formal and rigid framework upon managers and technologists, and are by no means a guarantee of IT project success. Moreover, the imposition of formal-rational IT architectures tend to serve as a direct financial control strategy of senior executives. In doing so, they invariably exert undue pressure upon project managers and IT staff to meet rigid project deadlines, often ignoring other performance indicators such as quality and business effectiveness. The research was funded by the Scottish Higher Education Funding Council (SHEFC) and was part of an interdisciplinary project on managing IT.

Methodology

Questionnaire survey

The selected methodology comprised a questionnaire survey to over 900 private and public sector organisations throughout the UK. A response rate of about twenty per cent was achieved. The sample for the mail questionnaire was selected from a large commercial database which contained over 8000 UK and Eire organisations who subscribed to the Computer User's Handbook (CUH, 1994). The CUH was up to date and represented a significant number of organisations with a large annual IT spend.

The survey questionnaire was sent to a sample of UK organisations within particular sectors and who made significant use of IT. They were categorised as follows: Public (UK SICC codes 91-95), Financial/Services (UK SICC codes 81-83, 96), Manufacturing (UK SICC codes 21-26, 30-49).

The addressee for the questionnaire was the contact name given in the commercial database. This was predominantly the most senior manager responsible for IT in the organisation. In about 20 percent of responses, the questionnaire was completed by a manager other than the addressee. This person was usually the addressee's deputy, or an IT manager in cases where the addressee was a non-IT manager (e.g. Managing Director). The researchers recognised the inherent difficulties of using a questionnaire survey, such as the possibility of inappropriate or misinterpreted questions leading to inadequate or incomplete answers, etc (Galliers, 1993). For example, some questions were essentially sector specific (e.g. more appropriate to either the private or public sector). To avoid some of the more notable methodological problems, a case study approach was used where on site interviews were carried out with selected organisations from the questionnaire survey.

On site interviews (case studies)

The questionnaire survey was also followed up by an inductive case study approach. Interviews were conducted with general and technical managers and technical personnel in the IT department. Here a semi structured questionnaire was used which focused on some of the themes from the questionnaire survey. The case study exercise was particularly useful for exploring these themes in greater depth. For example, many IT managers in the public sector were interested to discuss government policy on market testing and compulsory competitive tendering (CCT). In this context, public sector IT managers faced new challenges as many were unsure if their department would still exist after 1996 or be disbanded or even outsourced to an IT company. Other respondents were also keen to discuss the skills demarcation between general and IT managers, and even the wide skills gap between managers and IT staff. In addition, the case study research enabled more focused questions to be raised about the success rate of IT projects and the use of project management methodologies as a control strategy of senior executives.

The generalist IT manager

The growth in annual IT budgets throughout the last two decades, coupled with the popular precept that IT is a 'strategic device' serves to reinforce the view that IT should be managed by senior level personnel (Boynton, et al, 1992; Earl, 1988; Rowe and Herbert, 1990). Such a view implicitly supports the intervention of the generalist manager in technical decisions, since technical skills are rarely seen as a prerequisite or requirement for senior level managerial positions (Adler et al, 1992). Indeed, the generalist manager usually possesses a wide array of non-technical skills which include: a working knowledge of the functional areas of finance and accounting, personnel, marketing and sales, etc. In this context, the technologist as manager is not seen as an appropriate model (Currie, 1995a). Yet the political and skills boundaries which exist between managers and technologists are likely to impose severe difficulties for those who manage IT projects, and also for the technical staff being managed. In this section, we consider some of the literature which addresses the issue of managerial responsibility for IT.

One of the key themes arising from this literature is who should take control of IT? Here, the choice is often between general (non-technical) managers or managers with a technical (IT) background.

Boynton et al (1992, p. 32) claim that 'over the last decade, general managers who report to functional areas other than information systems 'line managers' have increasingly gained information technology (IT) management responsibilities'. The authors stress that the most important factor which underlies this phenomenon is the growing requirement for line managers to 'manage interdependencies within and external to the firm in the light of pressures to globalise operations and competitive requirements (increasing product quality and decreasingly time to market'.

Whilst recognising the importance of IT as a means of solving 'business and strategic challenges', the authors argue that, 'Although IT managers possess important technical and systems know-how, IT applications are best led by line managers who thoroughly understand the business situation' (Boynton et al, 1992, p. 32). They further point out that, in the past decade, organisations are encountering greater technological and strategic complexities which, in turn demands a re-evaluation of the 'IT management architecture'. This is the 'locus of decision making for IT-related processes within a firm' Similarly, Rockart (1988, pp. 57-64) claims that:

> In the 1980s, especially in the last five years, it seems that a quantum change has taken place. This change can be summed up easily. Information technology has become inextricably intertwined with the business. It has, therefore, become the province not only of information systems professionals, but of every manager in the business no matter what his or her level.

The issue of whether IT should be managed by general or technical managers is a critical one in the literature (Rockart, 1988; Zmud et al, 1987; Rockness and Zmud, 1989; Rowe and Herbert, 1990; Adler et al, 1992. Smits et al, 1993; Morone, 1993). The issue has become more important as the *strategy-technology connection* (Kantrow, 1980) urges senior executives to align business strategy with IT strategy. Indeed, other writers caution against a lack of senior management involvement in the strategic management of technical functions, as this is seen to result in the fragmented and piecemeal implementation of technology. Here, functional managers may take technical decisions without adhering to the overall corporate strategy (Currie, 1994b). Adler et al (1992, p. 1 9) claim that, 'Too many businesses leave the technical functions - research and development (R&D), management information systems (MIS), manufacturing engineering, and so on - out of the business strategy process and exempt them from senior management's expectation that all the functions manage their internal operations strategically'.

A central theme relating to this debate is whether IT should be managed centrally by a single IS department, unit or function, or decentralised to the business units. Boynton et al (1992, p.33), claim that:

> the best way to link IT consistently to a firm's day to day, core business processes is to centrally distribute IT management responsibilities to line managers. If the central IS function dominates IT management, this alignment will not occur for two reasons. First, in firms with dominant central IS functions, line managers have to place the fate of their operations and their careers in the hands of others. Thus they resist relying on IT resources that they neither control nor, most likely, fully understand. As the importance of IT resources increases, we believe that line managers will increasingly resist extreme dependence on a central IS function, even if the IS staff has been responsive to their needs in the past. With dispersed responsibility, line managers will use IT resources more effectively, learning to apply IT to business tasks just as they apply human, financial, and other key resources to business opportunities, problems, and threats.

Complications arise, however, where IT is embedded into core business processes, and is therefore operationally cross-functional. Here it is likely that companies will retain a centralised IS function, although this scenario poses problems in terms of management responsibility and control. For example, a UK bank has addressed the issue of how best to manage IT by developing a strategic framework designed to fuse business understanding with IT knowledge. Whilst this organisation continues to operate a centralised IS division, it is forced to address the 'knowledge gap' which exists between business managers and technologists. The solution is seemingly to create a 'hybrid' manager - someone who possesses both managerial and technical skills (Earl and Skyrme, 1992; Meiklejohn, 1990; Palmer and Ottley, 1990). At the bank in question, relationship managers are senior managers with an understanding of the business, who liaise with line managers (from the business units) and project managers (technical specialists). This organisational framework is designed to ensure that managers from the business units will request the most appropriate technical solution from the IS division, since the relationship manager (theoretically) understands the business problem as well as the most appropriate technical solution. Hybrid managers theoretically represent the most practical solution to the knowledge gap which exists between managerial and technical functions. Indeed, the subject of hybrid managers is an important one in the literature.

Hybrid managers. myth or reality?

A significant theme emerging from the recent literature on managing IT supports the view that problems of evaluation and implementation are the result of mismanagement and not technical mishap (Earl and Skyrme, 1992; Keen, 1988; Sparrow et al, 1989). Yet the notion of a technical or computer failure often disguises poor project management methods and practices which seemingly contribute to such disasters (Currie, 1994a).

The problems of managing IT become ever more complex and difficult to resolve in a climate of almost constant organisational and technical change. New languages and packages are introduced into organisations at an alarming rate. At the leading edge of IT systems development, the rapid technological changes guarantee an acute and continuing skills shortage. Those organisations with a large annual IT spend often resort to using external technical contractors and management consultants to offset the skills shortage problem.

At the user end, staff often complain of requirements to learn new packages such as word processing or spreadsheets. This often produces the inverse of what the packages are intended to achieve. Productivity levels fall as new skills are learned.

This scenario is a constant challenge to managers and staff. Coupled with the human problems of introducing technical change, the growing financial costs impose greater burdens on managers to ensure a successful outcome from IT. Success from IT is usually measured in the form of performance improvements. Here the accent is on developing information systems in line with business process re-engineering (BPR) strategies, cost cutting through headcount reduction and the generation of new IT-led businesses.

However, skills shortages (managers and IT staff) create an ongoing managerial dilemma. This is because managers and technical specialists are trying to make sense of the technical changes, often from a skills base that is outdated and redundant. At senior levels, project managers are assigned to large scale IT projects even in circumstances where they do not understand the technology. Similarly, the in-house IT department may comprise people with predominantly mainframe skills, even though many of the latest technical developments are PC related, e.g. client server and networks (Currie, 1995a).

The problem is compounded by management's reluctance to train and retrain existing staff. At the user level, staff may find that technology is simply imposed upon them. Or, perhaps worse, individuals personally decide which system they wish to use, leading to the ubiquitous problem of systems not being able to interface with one another. Such a situation is often the result of an ad hoc approach to IT implementation where sub-strategies are adopted sometimes in conjunction with a single IT strategy.

The lack of skills for managing IT, in turn, creates further confusion as traditional career paths tend to favour those with general management skills (budgeting, planning, coordinating, controlling, etc). This is in spite of the seemingly greater demands for managers to understand how the latest technology will effect business process reengineering changes.

A likely solution to the problem is therefore presented in the literature in the form of the hybrid manager (Earl and Skyrme, 1992; Kerr, 1989; Meiklejohn, 1990; Mercer, 1990; Palmer and Ottley, 1990). Whilst these individuals are likely to exist more as a figment of our imagination as opposed to a reality, the theory surrounding the hybrid manager at least addresses the problem of fusing business skills with technical knowhow. According to Earl and Skyrme (1992, p. 172) the hybrid manager is a concept, 'a capacity for a role'. Indeed, it is a formidable management development challenge and is not found in conventional organisational charts in most British companies.

In a report published by the British Computer Society, a recommendation was made for UK companies to train some 10,000 people to become hybrid managers by 1995 (Palmer and Ottley, 1990). The report recommended that UK companies should develop people to 'conceive and implement' information systems in line organisations which would attract global customers and help the organisation to compete in the global marketplace. Key performance indicators were to improve time to market, cost, quality, service or any other factor relating to competitiveness.

Earl (1989) defines hybrid managers as 'people with strong technical skills and adequate business knowledge, or vice versa ... hybrids are people with technical skills able to work in user areas doing a line functional job, but adept at developing and implementing IT application ideas'.

Whilst there is not a wealth of literature on the hybrid manager phenomenon, Earl and Skyrme (1992) inform us that the topic is discussed in other disciplinary territories to include: information systems management (particularly project management); management of analogue functions (e.g. finance and R&D); studies of general management (e.g. the issue of generalists v specialists). They say that *hybrids* are commonly business managers with IT experience rather than the opposite scenario. This scenario is likely to mean that a generalist manager is given the responsibility of the IT department, or that a technical specialist has moved into general management. What is significant here is that technical skills seem to take second priority to the skills commonly associated with general managers. This is important in the light of research into managing IT projects in the private and public sectors (Currie and Bryson, 1995).

The role of the project manager

Prescriptive contributions on project management recommend the development of general management skills for the planning and control of large scale IT projects. Indeed, an inability to develop these skills is often cited as a key reason for the high failure rate of IT projects (Financial Times, 1994).

Writing on the topic of project management for information systems, Yeates (1991, p. 11) identifies eight skill prerequisites for planning and controlling IT projects. They include:

1 Communication skills
2 Effective planning
3 Organisationally powerful
4 Good controller
5 Sensitive to problems of change
6 An effective manager of teams
7 A good trainer
8 Technical competence

Yeates (1991, p. 11) argues that the project manager's success 'will be measured by how clearly the agreed project or service is delivered within budget, time-scale and to quality'. He concedes that it is important for the project manager to be technically competent so as to choose the technical computing strategies most appropriate for the application development. But the remaining seven skill areas are also crucial if the IT project is going to succeed.

The linear approach to IT project development is also commonplace in the literature. Yeates (1991, p. 22) asserts that, irrespective of whether an IT project is large or small or is intended for a commercial or non-commercial environment 'the development process can be broken down into its constituent parts. The basic building blocks are the same in all cases, and are in turn, feasibility, analysis, design, programming, implementation and support.

This six stage model is designed to ensure that IT projects are carefully planned and controlled. The first stage refers to the extent to which the envisaged project is worth developing. This is essentially a management question, since it is unlikely that resources will be allocated to a proposed IT project unless it is perceived to enhance efficiency, productivity and reduce costs. The analysis stage is concerned with two distinct activities. One is the collection of information about the operation of the existing systems and, two, the identification of difficulties, problems and bottlenecks with those systems. This stage will specify how the proposed IT project will provide an appropriate business solution to the problem. Structured methodologies are seen as useful for this stage so as to ensure that a 'deliverable product' is the end result. The design stage is to specify the new computer-based system in terms of its technical content: the output of which is a design specification. According to Yeates (1991, p. 30). 'First the logical design is developed which defines the user's outputs, inputs and processes. This is then mapped on to the computer system in terms of data files, program modules and supporting software to define the physical design. This physical design specification will also include the operational requirements, security levels and authorised user list'. This stage is followed by the programming and testing processes, which are concerned to produce the actual computer programs to handle the system data. It is usual for senior analyst/programmers to undertake the more complex modules, with the less experienced programmers carrying out the coding of simpler routines. Once the modules are complete, they will undergo testing, with any errors in the programs corrected. Stages five and six are concerned with the implementation of the information system and the post-implementation stages.

A standard project management methodology using the PRINCE system is also advocated for the development of IT projects in private and public sector organisations. PRINCE is essentially a methodology for project management, rather than IT project development. Although it is intended to provide a framework for the latter. Like other methodologies recommended to guide IT projects, PRINCE also advocates a sequential or linear approach to the completion of clearly defined stages. The PRINCE project management organisation is outlined in Figure 13.1.

Here it can be seen that at the apex of the organisation, an information systems steering committee (ISSC) oversees the work of the entire project management team. The ISSC is primarily responsible for developing an alignment between the corporate strategy and IT. In this context, the ISSC formulates the IT strategy and allocates resources to large scale IT projects. The information technology executive committee (ITEC) also has an important role in that it prioritises proposed IT projects and also widely influences financial and staff resources. The project board is also perceived as an important part of the PRINCE project management model. It is allocated three essential roles: executive, senior user and senior technical.

The project board is largely concerned with the operational management of the IT project. It is responsible for appointing a project manager and authorises resources to initiate the project. Once the IT project is under way, the project board reviews and approves further plans and conducts formal end-of-stage assessments. It then signs off each completed stage before commencing a new stage. The project board also pays particular attention to deviations from the original project plan. By and large, the project board attempts to keep the project within budget and to timescale. Once the IT project is complete, the project board ensures that implementation

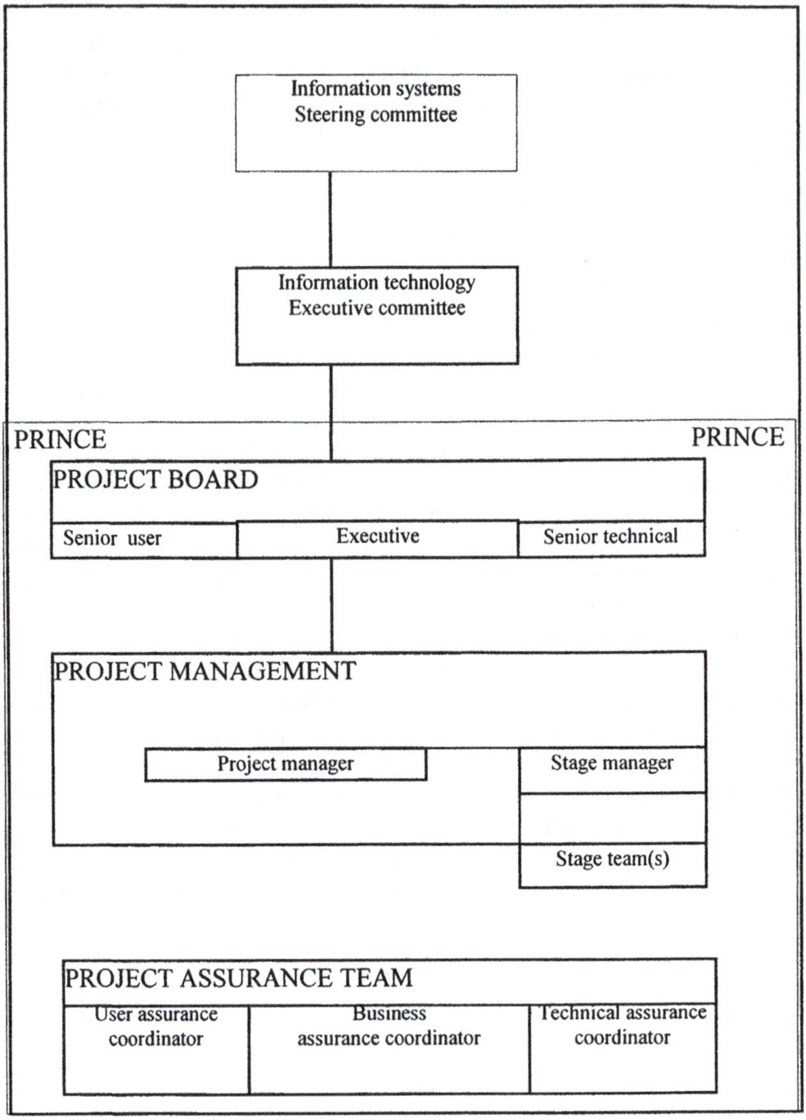

Figure 13.1 The PRINCE project management system

Source: Yeates, 1991, p.41

plans are under way and initiates a project evaluation. Formal-rational project management methodologies of this nature are usually adopted in private and public sector organisations with large annual IT spends. Their role is predominantly to impose a formal framework for managing large scale IT projects.

Managing large scale IT projects in the private and public sectors: a crisis in management control?

A survey was conducted into some 900 private and public sector organisations in the UK, with a response rate of about 20 percent. The survey was multidisciplinary and focused upon key areas of IT strategy, evaluation, implementation and human resources. The questionnaire was mailed to IT managers in the financial services, manufacturing industry and public sector. Clearly, there are methodological problems in conducting comparative surveys of this nature, given that some of the questions were not relevant to all sectors. However, the questionnaire design was intended to encapsulate a broad picture of some of the key interdisciplinary themes and issues of managing IT, rather than detailed knowledge pertaining to each area.

One of the key areas relevant to our discussion concerned the structuring of IT activities within the three focus sectors. Of the 174 organisations who responded to this question, it was interesting to find that as many as 118 organisations, most notably in financial services, retained a centralised IT division or department. This compared with only 30 of organisations claiming that IT was a sub-section of a larger department (usually finance, administrative services, communications or operations).

Whereas this finding might suggest that IT was deemed important enough to warrant being a separate division or department in the majority of organisations, a closer examination of the status of IT found that senior IT managers were unlikely to occupy a board level position, or even be able to represent IT at board level meetings. Even where organisations employed an IT director, the role and responsibility of this individual was not always in line with the status one usually ascribes to director level. Indeed, in one public sector organisation, the IT director with overall responsibility for 280 personnel was not even a member of the Management Group. Consequently, he was unable to represent his vision for IT at the meeting held by the Management Group. Instead, he was forced to convey his views vis a vis IT strategy to a board member who would, in turn, convey them to the meeting. According to one IT manager who worked under this regime, 'The possibilities for distortion of information about IT are endless. Usually, the main decision of the Management Group is simply to cost-cut. They simply don't understand the fundamentals of IT'.

Nevertheless, some eighty per cent of organisations (from a total of 184) claimed to have an IT strategy which was developed at senior level management. Interestingly, the questionnaire survey found that although the IT strategy was developed by senior level managers, many of these people did not possess a technical background. Figure 13.2 gives a breakdown of who was responsible for developing IT strategy. It is important to differentiate between the processes of strategy formation (development) and strategy implementation. It shows that, over fifty-six per cent of those responsible for developing the IT strategy were senior level managers, compared with only four per cent of middle managers. However, inductive case study investigations into the IT strategy formation process found that different interpretations were given for the concept of *strategy*. For example, a number of senior managers talked about strategy essentially as a planning process in line with a formal project management methodology such as PRINCE. In this context, strategy appeared to be a formal statement about organisational objectives for IT. It was also a formal statement about resource allocation for those projects which were deemed *strategic* by management.

Interviews with senior managers also confirmed a division of labour between those who develop the IT strategy (senior managers) and those who implement it (usually middle or junior level IT managers). The level of responsibility for IT strategy formation was further linked with resource allocation. This was reflected in a document acquired from a leading UK bank outlining a 'partnership structure for information technology projects' which stressed that, 'The structure described in this document is intended to provide a formal framework within which information technology (IT) can work in partnership with the business divisions of the bank to initiate and deliver systems projects when they are needed and at an appropriate cost'. It further stressed that:

> The structure described here covers all projects initiated on behalf of business divisions and also projects initiated by technology in order to improve service levels or quality of the IT service. It does not cover the day to day management of the IT delivery function nor does it cover the mechanism and standards for project development which are covered in the bank's X methodology.

Documentation from many of the case study organisations confirmed that IT strategy formation was often concerned with defining the organisational structure in which IT would fit, as well as resource allocation procedures. Indeed, the Group Technology Steering Committee's remit was 'to approve initiation of all projects above £1 million budgeted expenditure and above £0.2m unbudgeted expenditure (all projects above £5m required board approval from the bank)'.

In spite of the majority of organisations claiming to have a formal IT strategy in place, its implementation was usually the responsibility of middle level project managers within the IT department. Interviews with project managers and IT professionals about the processual nature of strategy formation and implementation raised some interesting questions about this relationship. One such question concerned the skills demarcation between project managers and IT professionals. For example, a number of project managers held the view that 'successful project management' involved the acquisition of business skills in the form of planning, coordination, budgeting, communication and control. A sizeable number of project managers did not have technical backgrounds, although they were managing high expenditure and high risk IT projects. One project manager with a degree in archaeology said that

> In my opinion, it is not important that project managers understand the technology. They just need to know what is the most appropriate technical solution for the business problem. Besides, techno-speak is gobbledegook.

Comments of this nature were often treated by the IT professionals with contempt.

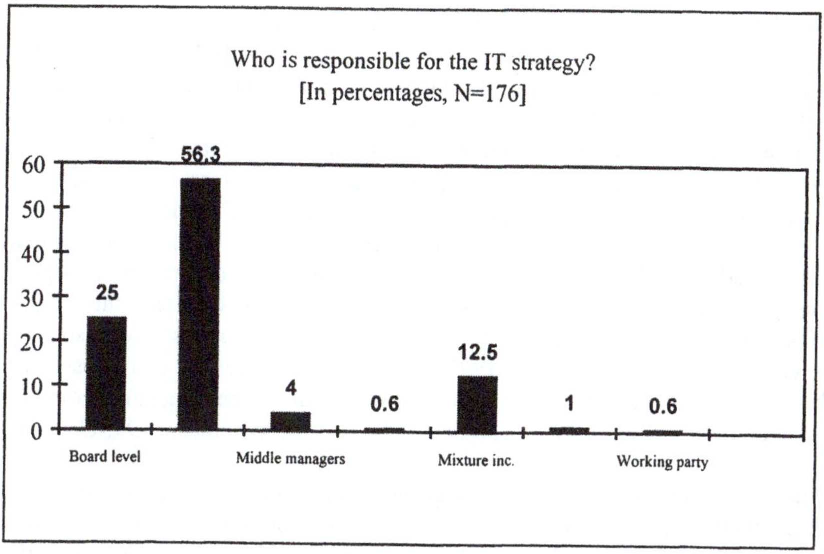

Figure 13.2 Management responsibility for IT strategy formation

Interviews conducted with both permanent and contract IT staff (usually analyst/programmers) suggested that, whereas the quest to promote non-technical personnel to IT project management positions was the norm in many organisations, their lack of technical skills was perceived by those whom they manage (analyst/programmers) as a serious impediment to the success of IT projects. This issue arose time and time again when interviewing IT professionals as opposed to (generalist) project managers.

Comments from one analyst/programmer at a UK bank were particularly pertinent to this issue. Thus 'The traditional methodology driven approach to project management adopts a linear approach where specific modules are completed before going on to the next stage. The trouble is, the customer (business department requesting the information system) is often confused about what they want. We (the analyst/programmers) are therefore sent off in a number of different directions. The project manager then becomes worried about the budget going out of control and the failure to meet deadlines. To counteract this, we are then given strict deadlines even though the customer is likely to change the scope of the project time and time again. Project managers rarely understand today's technology and, because of this, they resort to draconian performance measurement controls'.

A salient observation from the case study research into managing IT in private and public sector organisations suggested that a crisis in management control was emerging from the transition from mainframe technology to new PC based technologies in the form of client server and networks. Project managers were reluctant to confirm this crisis, although a closer examination of the interview data showed that two competing perceptions of management control were held by managers and technical personnel. The former were usually keen to advocate the effectiveness of formal project management methodologies for managing IT projects and personnel. In addition, project managers often implied that a thorough understanding of these methodologies was an adequate prerequisite for managing large scale IT projects. Rarely did project managers stress the importance of technical skills as a necessary requirement for controlling IT work.

Conversely, IT professionals at the sharp end of systems development contradicted this view. Many believed that the inability of project managers to understand the practical aspects of systems development work (i.e. the languages and packages) was directly linked to IT project failures. Recent studies also support this view (Currie, 1995a; Sauer, 1993). Indeed, the failure rate of IT systems is a subject which is now receiving more attention from the academic community (Willcocks and Griffiths, 1994) and the media (Financial Times, 1994; *Computing*, 1994a).

The extent to which a crisis in management control of IT existed in organisations was difficult to quantify. Managers were keen to avoid questions about IT project failures, although many admitted that 'IT was a problem area'. Organisational policies and practices it seemed fuelled the IT problem, particularly insofar as managers and IT staff were encouraged to pursue different career trajectories. For example, project managers were keen to stress that technical skills were not a component of managerial work. They said that generalist skills such as an understanding of the business, the ability to communicate and manage budgets, etc, were in greater demand.

IT professionals, on the other hand, were often critical of this approach, as many saw themselves as 'more highly qualified' than their project managers. Politically, the issue was explosive. Yet pay and reward scales were sometimes at odds with individual perceptions of status and ability in regard to project managers and IT professionals. For example, a number of star rated contract IT analyst/programmers earned more than the project managers to whom they reported. At one leading UK bank, a cluster of contract IT staff with scarce skills were able to command high freelance salaries on the grounds that permanent IT staff with complementary skills were non-existent. This situation was all the more contentious as many of these individuals were offered repeat contracts of six months, though their initial status was described as a stop-gap.

Case study research further confirmed that the euphemistic notion of the hybrid manager was not fully integrated into organisational life in both private and public sector settings. As one project manager observed 'If you want to get on in this organisation (local authority), you need to abandon your technical skills to become a manager. Very rarely do managers retain or even acquire technical skills'.Similarly, in manufacturing, technical staff also abandoned their IT background to join the managerial career ladder. In some manufacturing firms, a separate career structure existed for managers and technical personnel, with the former career spine overtaking the latter in terms of pay, conditions and rewards.

Discussion and conclusion

The article has considered a number of themes relating to the management of IT projects and staff in contemporary private and public sector organisations. We contend that a simple choice between general or technical managers in the management of large scale, high risk IT projects is too simple. Indeed, very few technical managers charged with managing IT projects actually retain their detailed IT knowledge. This is because formal human resource policies encourage those seeking managerial positions to abandon their technical skills in favour of adopting general skills (budgeting and planning, etc). In addition, project managers are also encouraged to adopt formal-rational methodologies for controlling IT projects. However, many organisations are concerned about the high failure rate of IT projects. As a result, they are encouraged by the rhetoric surrounding the development of hybrid managers. However, empirical research in private and public sector settings suggests that few organisations possess hybrid managers. Moreover, few organisations are making any headway in this direction, since the majority of them continue to adopt a centralised IT division, often with a separate IT career management structure. This forces IT staff to seek a management career outside their IT division (e.g. in one of the business units) or, alternatively, remain within the centralised IT department. Consequently, the skills gap between managerial and professional staff remains, with many IT personnel commenting upon the lack of technical awareness among project managers. In this context, we contend that this situation gives rise to a crisis in management control, where project managers attempt to overcome their lack of technical knowledge by imposing rigid and inflexible performance targets upon the technical team. However, this is not an effective solution since IT staff merely resort to workarounds. In this scenario, IT projects become date driven where insufficient attention is given to issues of quality and skills development.

Whilst is it outside the scope of this article to offer solutions to the problem, we nevertheless contend that IT departments are often seen as adjuncts to the core business divisions. In turn, they are given the status of service providers and are, in turn, treated as cost centres. Consequently, the IT department is more likely to be outsourced to a third party than other departments or activities. Such a situation does not bode well for those who work in IT, in either a management or technical capacity. We therefore contend that, in the present climate, managerial and technical divisions are likely to remain, in spite of the popular rhetorical justifications, separate and with senior managers unable to integrate IT fully within their organisations and, more specifically, their business divisions.

References

Adler, P.S., McDonald, D.W., and MacDonald, F. (1992), 'Strategic management of technical functions', *Sloan Management Review*, Winter.

Boynton, A.C., Jacobs, G.C. and Zmud, R.W. (1992), 'Whose responsibility is IT management?', *Sloan Management Review,* Summer, pp. 32-38.

Clark, K.B. (1989), 'What strategy can do for technology', *Harvard Business Review*, November/December, pp. 94-98.

Cohen, N. (1993), 'Settlement time to decrease'. *Financial Times,* 2 July, p. 10.

Computer Users' Handbook (1994) VNU Publications, London.

Currie, W. (1994a), *The strategic management of advanced manufacturing technology,* CIMA, London.

Currie, W. (1994b), 'Outsourcing - the new IT strategy?', published by Cost A3 Conference Organisers, Glasgow Business School/Commission of European.

Currie, W. (1995a), *Management strategy for information technology: an international perspective*, Pitman, London.

Currie, W. (1995b), 'The IT strategy audit: formulation and performance measurement at a UK bank', *Managerial Auditing Journal, Vol.* 10, No. 1.

Currie, W. and Bryson C. (1995), 'Generalist managers, IT specialists and IT project development: a crisis in management control', paper presented at the Technological Innovation and Global Challenges conference, Aston Business School, July 5-7.

Davenport, T.H. (1994), 'Saving IT's soul: human-centred information management', *Harvard Business Review,* March/April, pp. 119-31.

Dixon, P.J. and John, D.A. (1989), 'Technology issues facing corporate management in the 1990s', *MIS Quarterly,* September, pp. 247-55 .

Earl, M.J. (1988), *Information Management,* Prentice Hall, New York.

Earl, M.J. and Skyrme, D.J. (1992), 'Hybrid managers - what do we know about them?', *Journal of Information Systems,* Vol. 2 , pp. 169-87.

Edwards, B., Earl, M. and Feeny, D. (1989), 'Any way out of the labyrinth for managing IS?', Research & Discussion papers, RDP 89/3, Oxford Institute of Information Management, Templeton College, Oxford.

Feeny, D (1988), 'Creating and sustaining competitive advantage with IT', in M. Earl (ed.) *Information Management,* Prentice Hall.

Financial Times (1993), 'Taurus the octopus', 22 January.

Financial Times (1994), 'Computers in Finance', 15 November.

Galliers, R. (ed.). (1993), *Information systems research: issues, methods and practical guidelines,* Alfred Waller, Henley on Thames.

Kantrow, A.M. (1980), 'The strategy-technology connection', *Harvard Business Review,* July-August.

Keen, P. (1988), 'Rebuilding the human resources of information systems' in M. Earl (ed.), *Information management: the strategic dimension*, pp. 254-71, Oxford University Press. Oxford.

Kerr, S. (1989), 'The new IS force', *Datamation,* 35, pp. 18-22.

Kumar, K. (1990), 'Post-implementation evaluation of computer-based IS: current practices', *Communications of the ACM,* Vol. 33, No. 2. 203-12.

McFarlan, F.W. (1984), 'Information technology changes the way you compete', *Harvard Business Review,* May-June.

Meiklejohn, I. (1990), 'Whole role for hybrid', *Management Today,* March, pp. 113-16.

Mercer, C. (1990), 'Hybrid managers: a role analysis', MSc thesis, Social & Applied Psychology Unit, Sheffield University.

Morone, J.G. (1993), 'Technology and competitive advantage - the role of general management', *Research-Technology Management,* pp. 6-25.

Palmer, C. and Ottley, S. (1990), 'From potential to reality: hybrids - critical force in the application of information technology in the 1990s', a Report by the BCS Task Group in Hybrids, British Computer Society, London.

Porter, M.E. (1985), *Competitive advantage: creating and sustaining superior performance,* Free Press, London.

Porter, M.E. and Miller, V.E. (1985), 'How information gives you competitive advantage', *Harvard Business Review,* July-August.

Rockart, J.F. (1988), 'The line takes the leadership - IS management in a wired society', *Sloan Management Review,* Summer 1988, pp. 57-64.

Rockness, H. and Zmud, R.W. (1989), *Information Technology Management: Evolving Managerial Roles*, Financial Executives Research Foundation, Morristown, New Jersey.

Rowe, C. and Herbert, B. (1990), 'IT in the boardroom: the growth of computer awareness among chief executives', *Journal of General Management,* Vol. 15, No. 4, pp. 32-44.

Sauer, C. (1993), *Why information systems fail,* Alfred Waller, Henley.

Smits, S.J., McLean, E.R. and Tanner, J.R. (1993), 'Managing high-achieving information systems professionals', *Journal of Management Information Systems,* Vol. 9, No. 4, pp. 103-20, Spring.

Sparrow, P., Gratton, L. and McMullan, J. (1989), *Human resource issues in information technology,* P.A. Consulting Group, London.

Thaimhain, H.J. (1992), 'Developing the skills you need', *Research Technology Management,* March/April, pp. 42-47.

Tilley, L. (1990), 'A revolution in share registration', *Banking Technology,* November.

Waters, R. (1993), 'The plan that fell to earth', *Financial Times,* 12 March, p. 19.

Waters, R. and Cane, A. (1993), 'Sudden death of a runaway bull', *Financial Times*, 19 March, p. 11.

Willcocks, L. and Griffiths, C. (1994), 'Predicting risk of failure in large-scale information technology projects', *Technological Forecasting and Social Change,* 47, pp. 205-228.

Willcocks, L.P. and Mark, A.L. (1989), 'IT systems implementation: Research findings from the public sector', *Journal of Information Technology,* Vol. 2, part. 2, pp. 92-103.

Yeates, D. (ed) (1991) *Project management for information systems,* Pitman, London .

Zmud, R.W., Boynton, A.C. and Jacobs, G.C. (1987), 'An examination of managerial strategies for increasing information technology', proceedings of the Eighth International Conference on Information Systems .

14 The triumph of hierarchies over markets: information systems specialists in the current context

Stephen Ackroyd, Ian Glover, Wendy Currie and Stephen Bull

Introduction

In this chapter we will be considering the work, employment and modes of organization of information systems specialists. In the following pages we will consider the ways in which this increasingly important occupation is being organised in the contemporary world. However, while commenting on the behaviour, work and organization of information systems analysts and programmers, we also have our eye on a broader area of debate. The background question of importance to us concerns the way the organization and use of information and knowledge is developing in the contemporary world. Information system specialists are the architects of the new technology, and their activity is intimately connected with key changes taking place in economy and society. Analysing what they do, their organization and the effects of these features of this emerging occupation is likely to be a valuable source of insight into the character of contemporary change. As is set out in the next section, our presentation regarding information systems analysts will take the form of a systematic critique of what is called the 'knowledge worker thesis'.

It is commonly argued that we are living through a period in which the dominant forms of organising human affairs are changing dramatically: we are supposedly moving away from formal organization in general, and its classical form, that of the bureaucracy, in particular, towards what are called 'loosely-coupled systems' and 'networks'. Although analysts differ in the way to characterise the dominant features of contemporary change, it is common enough to see new forms of organization as involving the attenuation if not the replacement of hierarchy. Many analysts of contemporary society assume that the huge development of information technology is one of the main sources of what they see as the erosion of the old forms of hierarchy which have for so long been a feature of social organization. The argument has two sides and runs as follows: first, because information technology is now widely used in firms and organizations, relationships need no longer be coordinated by authority. Rapid and effective information exchange at a distance allows the old hierarchical structures to be replaced by more decentralised and mutually co-operative relationships involving the extension of autonomy to individuals and groups. Secondly, at the same time and for the same reason, more effective communications allow one of the key conditions for effective market exchanges - complete information - to be much more closely approximated. Hence, market relations are also becoming more effective and will penetrate more areas of formal organization. New organizational forms and new market relations have a similar structure. They both may be described as networks. In the new circumstances then, there is a problem about the boundaries between hierarchies and markets. For some analysts, both hierarchies and markets are being replaced by networks. On the other hand, since what appears to be happening is the dissolution of hierarchies and the extension of markets, for economists, and some others, what we are witnessing is the triumph of markets over hierarchies.

We shall argue against such accounts of contemporary change, suggesting instead that patterns of change are not adequately understood in terms of the emergence of extensive and increasingly homogeneous networks. The extent to which there is any abandonment of hierarchy in favour of market is much more apparent than real. Instead, we propose that what is happening is a set of related changes in which patterns of formal organization are being extensively recast. Hierarchies in the new forms and combinations are not familiar to us; that is all. We will argue that this sort of effect can be seen with clarity from the consideration of what is happening to occupation bringing about the implementation and development of information technology.

We begin by discussing the work of various writers who have commented on changes in knowledge and understanding in the contemporary world and who have linked their understanding of these things to more general patterns of socio-economic re-organization. We will then counterpose these arguments with what we suggest is a more firmly grounded argument of our own, in which we suggest that it is not the removal but the transformation of hierarchy that is the principal direction of organizational change that can be identified in the contemporary world.

The knowledge worker thesis

Numerous social theorists and commentators in the post war period have pointed to the increased importance of knowledge in contemporary society. Raymond Aron, Ralph Dahrendorf, J. K. Galbraith, Clark Kerr, Daniel Bell and Anthony Giddens, have all emphasized the increasing prevalence of codified and theoretical knowledge to work organization and social development, and the growing power of those who possess such knowledge. In spite of many criticisms of the utopianism and political naivete of Daniel Bell (1973) and other supporters of the notion of a post-industrial society (in effect, a society allegedly run by a new elite of knowledge workers), such ideas in one form and another have continued to be influential.

These days, however, it is conventional to begin an account of the idea of the "knowledge worker" with a discussion of the work of Peter Drucker (1969, 1993). Although he is clearly not a social or economic theorist of any great analytical power, Drucker has the happy knack of spotting subjects that will become important. As early as the mid-nineteen sixties, he was suggesting the importance of the 'knowledge industries' to the 'knowledge economy'. According to Drucker, in the US economy of 1965, the 'knowledge sector' was allegedly producing a third of the country's Gross National Product. Farm workers and machine operators were allegedly being replaced by teachers, office workers, scientists, engineers, accountants, marketing men, health care professionals, computer specialists, and skilled industrial workers whose expertise would consist much more of knowledge than of skill. While specific skills would always be the most vital component of work, skills were increasingly being acquired 'on a knowledge foundation', enabling people to learn how to learn, and bringing the worlds of work and knowledge together on a large and unprecedented scale.

Extended education in particular meant higher expectations of employment, with salaries, careers and mental work replacing wages, jobs and manual effort. Indeed, Peter Drucker is amongst the first to enunciate what has become a recurrent theme in the writing about knowledge workers, to the effect that it is the supply of labour - rather than the demand for it - that is creating the knowledge society and economy. Several reasons for this are put forward. Primarily Drucker invoked 'discontinuities which were calling into being the new groupings of knowledge workers'. He sees discontinuities between different areas of institutional life as arising in four areas: the growth of new science-based technologies and industries, incipient economic globalisation, societies dominated by big organizations run by managers, seemingly often for managers, and above all the emergence of knowledge as 'the central capital, the cost centre and the crucial resource of the economy' (1969, p.ix). Spontaneous developments of knowledge seemingly just occur. As in much of his work, here Drucker is not so much wrong as inexplicit and tendentious.

There are many similarities between the propositions of Drucker and the more recent, influential and subtle writings of Robert Reich (1991). Reich refers to the 'symbolic analyst' rather than the knowledge worker; but it is clear that, in many ways, what he has to say about the emerging cadres of new workers and the consequences of their actions, is very much the same as earlier ideas. According to Reich, symbolic analysts are different from other groups of service workers - called by Reich 'in person servers' - such as taxi drivers, waitresses, cashiers and janitors. All service workers are becoming more numerous, but, by contrast with the in-person servers, the symbolic analysts are highly creative with their activity focused on problem identification and solution. They are children of the age of information technology and they 'manipulate symbols, juxtapose patterns, collate information from diverse sources, [and] transform reality into abstract images which are intelligible to fellow analysts' (Balasubramanyam, 1994, p. 441). They 'push the production frontier outwards' as well as generating increased efficiency. They included 'research scientists, design engineers, software engineers, civil engineers, investment bankers and, as Reich puts it, even a few creative accountants' (p. 441) For Reich, symbolic analysts are very much the new elite in the USA much as the 'new class' portrayed by Galbraith (1958) were argued to be in *The Affluent Society* (Balasubramanyam, 1994).

However they are not merely highly qualified people like the new class; they are highly creative, and their activity is a source of innovation and adds value to economic processes. According to Reich, analysts are products of the new US originated and dominated world order in which 'global webs' (networks of global enterprises) roam the world in search of suitable labour and materials and customer needs to satisfy. Thus the analysts are not necessarily traditional professionals - that is, people who have mastered a pre-existing and systematised body of knowledge - nor do they follow standard career paths of seniority and hierarchy. Nevertheless, Reich estimated the new 'knowledge workers' accounted for about 20 percent of the US workforce in 1990, with in person servers accounting for a further 30 percent and routine production workers a declining 25 percent. Moreover, in a clear echo of the views of Drucker, the fortunes of the symbolic analysts are secured by their own actions, in that the supply of the analysts work stimulates and creates demand. Thus analysts make their own work, among other things, telling their employers and clients what to want before delivering it to them. Hence, analysts have skills which are greatly sought after, and the growth in their numbers is linked to the spread of large companies and increasingly large and diverse markets in which they operate. Reich, rather optimistically, advocates the upgrading of most US workers to symbolic analyst level so as to eradicate growing income disparities between them.

More recently, a group of influential writers has emerged in Britain, whose work, which although conceptually more sophisticated in many ways than either Drucker's or Reich's, shows continuities and similarities with the pioneers (cf. Prichard, 1996). This is the Lancaster Group - principally Frank Blackler (1988, 1995) and Michael Reed (1991, 1996a). (See also: Blackler, Reed and Whitaker, 1993a, 1993b). These writers have discussed the production of new forms of knowledge and new groups of knowledge worker. Blackler, Reed and Whitaker espouse the notion of 'knowledge workers' as absorbers, creators and resolvers of uncertainty and as 'new generation' workers employed to 'deal with options that their employing organizations are unable to address through their established routines'. For these writers, cadres of 'esoteric knowledge workers', employed in new kinds of flexible organizations such as knowledge intensive firms (KIFs), are contributing to the emergence of the knowledge society. Hence, their research interests may be economically described as attempting to cast light on the 'organizational symptoms of the knowledge society'. In a later paper, Blackler (1995) produces 'an overview and interpretation' of the roles of knowledge, knowledge workers, knowledge intensive firms (KIFs), such as consultancies, in the management and organization of work in the contemporary world.

Following a review of relevant writings on the nature and use of knowledge in organizations Blackler goes on to argue that it is better to think in terms of 'knowing as something that people do, rather than in terms of knowledge as something that they have'. Again there is an emphasis on the relevance of 'esoteric experts' (like management consultants) who are seen as being different from and much more important than exponents of formalised knowledge (such as traditional professionals). But it is in considering the connection of change at the level of knowledge with social organization, that the work of the Lancaster Goup is an improvement on earlier work. For example, Blackler (1995) makes a more concerted attempt to show why we might confidently accept that the work of the new knowledge worker adds value. For Reich (1991), such knowledge workers command high rewards because their skills are hard to duplicate. But while he is, fairly obviously, strongly influenced by Reich, Blackler is more careful to specify the contribution of the knowledge workers to economic processes. Thus, the skills of the knowledge worker include 'problem solving (research, product design, fabrication), problem identification (marketing, advertising, customer consulting), and brokerage (financing, searching, contracting)' (1995, p. 1027). Blackler asserts that such combinations of skills can and do link complex production and marketing processes together in new ways: technical insights are linked with product design expertise and to marketing know-how; or financial acumen is connected with strategic planning to produce goods and services in attractive and timely packages. Each step in the value chain depends for its effective realisation upon the esoteric 'embrained knowledge' of particular individuals. Thus it is relationships between people who have this kind of knowledge, Blackler holds, which underpins new forms of organization which are constructed around 'networks, partnerships or contractual arrangements'. The requirement for these new forms of knowledge is explained by the widespread reorganization of capitalism at the present time.

Reed has also made some contributions to understanding the (presumed) linkages between new forms of knowledge and organizational and societal arrangements. One of the early concerns for Reed has been the tendency for IT to be used to manipulate, control and monitor economic and societal development (1991). The main beneficiaries of this shift towards 'programmed societies' would be the 'service class' of managers and other experts who, it is felt, would alone have the specialised knowledge needed to manipulate the increasingly fragmented and disorganised society that they had brought into being. However, according to Reed, there is consensus amongst several major researchers to the effect that the members of the service class lacked both the material power and political will, not to mention the organization to do this. Indeed most of them were ideologically conservative and often reliant on traditional bureaucratic structures to function at all, let alone effectively. In other work, however, Reed has gone much further. In his discussion of 'expert power' in 'late modernity', Reed (1996a, p. 573) suggests that increasingly 'reflexive and flexible terms of capital accumulation' will strongly affect the main forms of 'expertise, organizational design and class power'. Divisions of labour 'within and between the professional and managerial middle classes' would become more intensely contested and fragmented, with certain expert groups having a strategic role to play in restructuring professional work organization and control.

Reed also considers related changes in class formation. Here he compares and contrasts three perspectives. On the one hand, the 'new service class thesis' suggested that a new, cohesive, powerful and mature professional/managerial class was emerging in the post-industrial, information society of the late twentieth century. By contrast, the 'new technocracy thesis' was far more pessimistic: the latter envisaged socio-economic polarization within the middle class between an emerging global technocratic elite and more localised and 'deskilled, delayered and dispossessed ranks of managers, technicians and bureaucrats'. To these two however, there is a third alternative: a 'class fragmentation' thesis which sees the middle class becoming highly 'fragmented and diffused' due to the ferocity of expert power struggle, so much so that it was too weak to mobilise itself into any form of collective action either on its own behalf or in alliance with 'other groups in superordinate or subordinate positions in the class structure'. Liberal, organizational and entrepreneurial (knowledge worker) professions were all divided against each other instead of forming a dynamic service class or a reactionary technocratic elite. Reed tends to favour this third view.

Although there are clear differences of outlook and tone between Blackler and Reed (while the former looks optimistically at the emergence of the knowledge worker and sees much that is positive in their supposedly growing spheres of activity, the latter, by contrast, has much more perception about the likelihood of conflict), they do share a common view about likely origins and likely patterns of associated social and economic development following the emergence of the knowledge worker. Both these writers, like Drucker and Reich before them, believe there will be more and more knowledge workers in the near future. Indeed there is a belief that the growth of these groups, once set in motion, will be self-reinforcing and the epicentre for a widening cycle of social and economic change. The key is that knowledge work is a new way of adding value. Indeed, knowledge workers, whose skills are an effective compound of ingredients: esoteric and local knowledge, social skills and connections and entrepreneurship, scarcely need formal organizations. The emergence of networks of knowledge workers will, in fact, be synonymous with the development of new kinds of organization. Organizations that are based on informal relationships, and that are indistinguishable from networks, will be more and more prevalent. The networks of knowledge workers are themselves proto-organizations, and scarcely need institutional support. Hence, the emergence of the knowledge worker and network organization imply the simultaneous redundancy and deconstruction of traditional forms of organization as an associated development.

This is a beguiling story. But it is a thesis which we believe will not stand careful appraisal, let alone sustained interrogation. Hence, we now propose to offer a critique and assessment of these ideas. We agree with (and applaud) some aspects of the overall explanatory strategy: it is necessary to connect what is happening to ideas and practice with organizational changes at other levels. Ultimately, social science must undertake the explanation of social change. Hence, our discussion will be equally if not more wide-ranging than the knowledge worker thesis itself: we are working with and connecting the organization of occupations, organizational changes and connections of these with general patterns of socio-economic change. Needless to say perhaps, we think that, in its present form, the knowledge worker thesis is both lacking in conceptual rigour and empirical reference. With regard to the first point, there is a lack of agreement over the way to define key terms and the concepts needed to delineate central processes. But, in our view, it is the empirical weakness of the argument which is more of a problem. It is not clear what occupational groups - or even what kinds of expertise - are the centre of the argument being mounted about knowledge workers. The knowledge worker thesis looks, at first sight, to be an argument which is grounded, and which refers to empirical events occurring round us. But the terms in use are woefully imprecise, and it is by no means clear to what extent propositions in the argument have empirical reference.

It is for this reason that we have grounded our critique in the consideration of a particular - if highly important - occupation. In the following pages we shall be testing the knowledge worker thesis against what research tells us of the situation of the information systems analyst. If there is a central, key, occupation in the information revolution it is this one. Information technology is a key part of the contemporary infrastructure of business and this group is central to the deployment and use of this technology. Hence, at the end of the day our critique is mainly an empirical one: we argue that because the knowledge worker thesis does not make much sense of the experience of this key occupation, it is of questionable value.

An alternative view: I. not knowledge but information

We begin by suggesting that the idea of the knowledge worker, and that of its *doppelganger*, the symbolic analyst, is obfuscatory. We suggest instead that the nature of changes in the division of labour of skilled people needs to be more adequately understood.

A basic problem for the idea of the knowledge worker is that the growth occupations of the contemporary world, and information systems analysts are a good example here, do not produce or handle knowledge. If academic knowledge is taken as the model - a not unreasonable procedure since this is a widely recognised ideal of what knowledge is - it does not describe new occupations such as information systems analysts very well. Academic knowledge is usually both articulated and formalised, being produced in this form so that it can be taught and so that competency in handling it certificated. Academics also still operate with an idea of knowledge as being, in principle at least, a 'free good' which should be available for anyone and everyone to use. But such conceptions are actually alien to ideas increasingly current in the contemporary world.

It is perhaps surprising to find that practitioners in new occupations such as information systems analysis are quite content to assert that they do not deal in knowledge, as opposed to the much more prosaic 'information'. As has frequently been asserted, we live in an age of burgeoning information, and it is actually difficult to equate this with the idea that we are in an era of increasing knowledge as it has been traditionally understood. The new occupations in the forefront of innovation, do not typically aspire to produce or to use knowledge. Such groups are, however, very clear that the commodity they handle is anything but free. It is not free in multiple senses, not least of which being that not everyone can gain access to it or make use of it. Certainly, if we mean by knowledge articulated, formalised and synthetic understanding - as distinct from intuitive or implicit skill - very few occupations have ever had or aspired to have knowledge. A strong definition of knowledge - which features developed understanding - simply cannot be applied to the majority of occupations in the contemporary - and still less the historical - world of work. Understood in this sense, and in general, only academics, scientists and traditional and senior professionals are or have been concerned with knowledge.

Faced with this sort of embarrassing fact, contemporary students of the new occupations wishing to use the idea of knowledge workers, have either to exclude large numbers of new workers from consideration (because they do not develop or use knowledge) or they have had to redefine the meaning of knowledge. Some of the knowledge worker writers - Frank Blackler in particular - have put a great deal of effort into undermining and displacing traditional definitions of what counts as knowledge, and have attempted instead to develop ideas about 'new' forms in which knowledge can be held and made available for use. In Blackler's writing, for example, we have a series of suggestions to the effect that there are new kinds of knowledge being actively created at the present time. A key procedure here is to make the suggestion that forms of unarticulated and tacit 'knowledge' are found which are increasingly effective in practical applications. It is argued that these are now much more effective than the traditional form of knowledge, because they are, supposedly, a key source of value added. But it is, in fact, difficult to specify forms of knowledge that have not existed before, or new forms which have not been implicated in economic processes hitherto.

Many, if not most, traditional kinds of work have embodied skills - many of them largely implicit and not formalised - which is one source of their value. Business leaders, craftspeople, farm workers, skilled factory workers, most clerical and almost all professional people have always been 'knowledge workers' in this sense. Virtually all jobs have long relied on their incumbents having a great deal of personal, social, practical and tacit knowledge to accompany their professional expertise and formal training and or articulated 'knowledge'. What seems different today - although we suspect that the phenomenon has always seemed and been portrayed by interested parties as different - is not that there are new forms of knowledge, but that there are new occupations in which implicit skills are key components of their owners' capacities to contribute to economic processes. These skills do not need to be a source of value in themselves, so long as they allow processes to take place in which value is created. Hence, we would argue that there is no need to depart far from conventional modes of explanation when trying to account for the emergence of new occupations. The key to understanding this sort of thing derives, as in the past, from understanding the forces which are shaping a division of labour in which some occupations are advantageously placed. In brief, we argue that information systems analysts and other new occupational groups have found a lucrative position within emerging economic processes. In this, knowledge in its traditional forms is often redundant and groups with little formal knowledge (and, often, we think, little special competence) are sometimes able to charge premium rates for their work.

The development of the occupational group of information systems analysts, programmers and managers - has been rapid. But there is little sign of a weakening of their position in the labour market. On the contrary, there is a lot of evidence accumulating that employees and managers in these occupations are often very well rewarded. In a recent study of small information technology firms Ackroyd (1995) found that many highly dynamic firms were efficient and profitable and, indeed, brought high rewards to their staff. A recent survey found that freelance IS specialists have 'broken through the six figure salary barrier' (*Computing*, 5 February, 1998). For example, the average IT manager now earns £1,936 per week, which is slightly more than £100k per annum. The figures for project managers, business analysts and analyst programmers are £1,884, £1,624 and £1,343 per week respectively.

Why certain new occupational groups, of which informational system analysts are a good example, are in a strong position in labour markets can, fairly obviously, be explained by changes in the organization of the economy. It is this that is dictating the reorganization of productive activities and, inter alia, creating an abnormal demand for certain skills. What is of interest is that these groups are choosing to exercise the power that their market scarcity bestows through certain patterns of re-organization and not others. As we shall suggest, based on a consideration of the available stock of contemporary research, these occupations are choosing to reorganise themselves in particular ways and not others. The reasons for this are not accidental. As we will show, information system analysts are tending to organise themselves in entrepreneurial rather than traditional professional forms. Against expectation, perhaps, they tend to eschew professionalisation as a way of improving their collective status and react to their increasingly powerful position within corporations, not by taking more control within them, but by organising themselves independently and creating new forms of organization to market their skills.

II. Not de-professionalisation but entrepreneurship

In the early 1970s data processing staff tended to be unqualified or to have secondary education qualifications like GCE O and A levels rather than degrees. Their successors have increasingly tended to be graduates, but able recruits to the occupation are sought from any background, and a lack of formal qualification is not an impediment to practice or advancement. If the majority of practitioners are graduates today, they are people who hold all kinds of degree, rather than qualifications in computing or information systems analysis. If employers expect IS specialists to have some sort of degree or professional qualifications, recruits who do not have these may undertake part-time or distance learning qualifications. But it would be wrong to see any strong trend towards professionalisation. Opportunities for professionalisation are conspicuously neglected. For example, the British Computer Society (BCS) offers professional qualifications and is a member institution of the UK's Engineering Council, but the number taking advantage of the facility is low. Similarly, there are emerging professional associations for business consultants and business consultancy firms, but the membership of relevant professional bodies is an unexpectedly low proportion of the rapidly growing numbers in the occupation. We have been told, informally, that only about one in twenty of those eligible to join the BCS actually belong it. However other professional groupings are often similarly under-organised in the UK although not usually anything like as dramatically as IS specialists.

A number of writers have envisaged that rising groups with scarce expertise will undertake professionalisation as a means to collective mobility. Peter Armstrong, for example, has put forward an influential account of the collective mobility 'project' of management accountants in the UK since 1945 (Armstrong, 1993). In order for the members of the Chartered Institute of Management Accountants (CIMA) to experience upward mobility they needed to expand their expertise into areas that would be obviously relevant to the concerns of senior management. At the same time they had to de-emphasize their function-specific knowledge, useful for management control, because of its subordinate status. This meant that 'the managerial credibility of professional knowledge is in tension with its secure possession' (p. 1). More recently, and while CIMA had grown into a large body with numerous members in senior management positions, it felt increasingly under threat from growing use of operational, rather than financial information, for management control, and from the widespread and growing teaching of management accounting to business and cognate, for example, engineering, medical, students at both undergraduate and masters' levels (cf. Roslender et al, chapter 10 in this book). As we will discuss more fully in the next section of this chapter, there is little reason to think that information systems analysts are generally making or seeking to make these sorts of compromises with senior managements in corporations.

Amongst many sources, contributors to Orlikowski et al (1996) offer ample evidence of the growing complexity and variety of information technologies, of the artificiality of distinctions between social and technical influences which becomes apparent from studying the development of IT in different contexts, and of the confusing and illusory actions of many claims about knowledge work in this area. But the balance of evidence is that information systems specialists are not taking advantage of the scarcity of their expertise by making claims about the indispensability of understanding information systems to effective strategic management. As we have seen the available empirical evidence shows that professionalisation is not being given a high priority. But clearly, the lack of evidence for professionalisation, including the lack of interest in developing claims to be the guardians of a definite area of knowledge is evidence that should not be interpreted as the weakness of these groups. Nor is it to be understood as evidence for the decline of professionalism as such.

There is implicit in the work of both Blackler and Reed, an evolutionary hypothesis concerning the trend of development in the organization of groups that hold authoritative knowledge. For both of these authors, we have supposedly passed through an era dominated by the independent or liberal professionals, to the new period in which knowledge workers (in command of new forms of knowledge) are dominant. However, against this, history shows that the path of the development of professional groups has seldom been linear. Periods of consolidation in which groups mount professionalisation projects and use such expedients as formalisation of knowledge and the licensing of practitioners, follow periods of remission in the growth of professions when new occupations following much more entrepreneurial policies are the leading points of occupational development. It would be a mistake to designate these periods of innovation as involving de-professionalisation, since the decline in the numbers of professionals is seldom experienced. What we see are periods of remission in which tendencies for growth in professionalisation are limited, whilst new skills are delivered by entrepreneurial forms of organization. In a recent study of management consultants, for example, it has been shown that the numbers of solicitors has been relatively static in the last ten years, whilst the number of business consultants has nearly doubled (Wilbey, 1998).

More generally, as Johnson suggested some time ago (1972) professionalism is a mode of organising an occupation as well as a set of attributes of one, and for this reason, professions are as capable of adapting to new environmental exigencies as organizations are. Indeed professions have found ways of making large organizations an aspect of their environment (Ackroyd, 1996). Reed seems to be developing a similar line of argument when he contrasts the independent/liberal professions with less well-organised 'entrepreneurial professionals', but this promising line is left under-developed in his writing (Reed, 1996). But if this line of argument is correct, the adoption of a professional mode of organising could well be developed by information systems analysts, when, at some later point, they find themselves in a different position in the market from their present situation of extreme scarcity. But, for the moment, it seems that there is relatively little to be gained from adopting professionalism as a mode of organising, as the costs of making credible claims of this sort would be large in terms of the time and resources required. Professionalisation, after all, involves the formalisation of knowledge into teachable curricula, the development of the means for delivering teaching, not to mention the testing and certification of recruits. At the moment, because of the extreme scarcity of competent practitioners in the information systems field, quite different forms of entrepreneurial organization recommend themselves.

III. Not disorganization but re-organization I: Changes in the corporation

We now turn to the question of what is happening to information systems analysts within organizations. The crucial area of intra-organizational change is one considerably neglected by many analysts of contemporary change, including the knowledge worker writers. However, a good deal of empirical research now bears on this question and this may be systematically appraised. For example, there is widespread evidence suggesting that there is a recurrent problem of the integration of information systems specialists into existing managerial hierarchies. In recent years, much academic and practitioner attention has focused upon what are perceived problems of managing information systems specialists (Forester, 1980; 1985). Against a background of organizational restructuring and downsizing, many researchers have considered the integration of IT as simply one aspect of the broader question of how the 'new' corporation will be structured, managed and controlled (Allen and Scott-Morton, 1994). But what is there to be observed is not accurately seen simply as a problem of this kind.

The factors influencing the strategic integration of information services into core business activities and change processes of the organizations that employ them are usually held to be dependent upon the ways in which information systems specialists and their colleagues are educated, trained, deployed and managed (cf. Child, 1987; Knights and Murray, 1994; Sorge and Hartmann, 1980). Education and training tend to be perceived to be among the main building blocks for success in information systems and other forms of technical development. The conventional wisdom is that if information systems specialists (and their colleagues in other business areas) are educated to understand and to satisfy each other's needs, and if significant proportions of all specialist groups have the breadth of outlook and knowledge to be good candidates for top management, then the capacity to develop and to use information systems strategically will be optimal. But this assumes much too readily that what will happen regarding the corporation's internal structure will be decided simply by reference to the question of the functional requirement for different kinds of expertise.

As an alternative, we suggest that at least three influential forces must be considered to understand the organization of information technology functions with the corporation. These are: firstly, strategic considerations about corporate development. Here it matters greatly whether the firm in question is large or small, and the extent to which it is undertaking reorganization to meet the challenge of increasing competition and particularly the effects of globalisation. Secondly, and related to this strategy/structure area of consideration, there is the related question of the internal politics of the organization. Meeting the challenge of development in a situation where key skills are extremely scarce has led to some typical and largely new forms of intra-organizational politics. In fact information systems specialists find themselves in a strong position within corporations but they are generally not exploiting their situation to achieve more influence within organizations. Finally, then, we are led on to consider the area we have been exploring in previous sections: this concerns the views of IS personnel about their own advantage and their chosen projects in pursuit of them. The combination of these factors seems, quite frequently, to be pushing towards the outsourcing information systems, rather than its secure integration as a corporate function.

Researchers have already pieced together some of these connections. An association between decisions about information systems and the ways in which information systems can best contribute to competitive advantage have often been proposed (Porter and Millar, 1985). More specifically, competitive advantage has been linked with the issue of whether or not to outsource information systems work (Currie and Willcocks, 1998a, 1998b). Decisions about how information systems work should articulate with the design of organization structures focus on the relationship between organization structure and information systems. In particular, they are often concerned with the issue of whether information systems departments should be centralised or decentralised, and whether they should be cost or profit centres (Shank and Govindarajan, 1992).

Budgets for information systems and the notion of information as a strategic resource have grown since the 1970s, suggesting that information systems should be managed from the highest organizational levels. However, despite this it has also been found that information system skills are still widely seen as not relevant to 'managerial' work (Boynton, Jacobs and Zmud, 1992). While in many areas senior line managers have increasingly been vested with responsibility for managing IT, they are increasingly expected to manage interdependencies within and outside their companies as businesses become more subject to competitive pressures. The potential for information systems to enhance competitive performance has become a key consideration for line managers. Indeed, the growing emphasis on the links between effective strategy and new technology in the management literature has pressurised senior executives into trying to align information systems and general business strategies. As a result managers have also debated whether information systems should be managed centrally or devolved to business units. Centralisation, it is felt, makes line managers reluctant to depend on information systems departments for resources that they nominally control but do not understand (Adler, McDonald and McDonald, 1992). However, it is often the case that information systems are already deeply embedded into core business processes and both cross-functional and hierarchical companies tend to keep information systems centralised. By so doing, they experience problems of management responsibility and control.

It is clear from the above discussion that the issue of strategy as mediated by technology is a key issue in determining the politics between occupational groups in organizations today. An issue of control has emerged. This is not infrequently conceptualised as the question of whether technical or general managers should be in charge of information systems (Adler, McDonald and McDonald, 1992); the importance of senior management commitment to information systems; the perceived need to develop 'hybrid managers' (Currie and Glover, 1999); the character of relationships between senior managers and information systems managers and management control; the political aspects of information systems management; the ongoing development of information systems management; and the varied and evolving methods for interpreting the performance of information systems (Farbey, Land and Targett, 1993). Such considerations are relevant to the degree of integration information systems specialists are likely to experience.

But, despite their obvious importance to contemporary organizations, there is evidence which points towards information systems specialists having been pushed from core into peripheral and external labour markets. The tendency for information systems departments to be defined and treated as cost centres, the historic split in the UK between technical specialists and generalist managers and the solitary nature of a good deal of information systems work have all been associated with such tendencies by researchers (Currie, 1995; cf. also Glover and Kelly, 1987; Glover, 1999). Some recent evidence suggests that integration of technical management at the highest levels of higher-performing UK manufacturing and construction companies has been improving, however (Glover, Tracey and Currie, 1998). Yet, this is more likely to involve engineers than systems analysts and other information systems people, because engineering production and design, in manufacturing and construction, are understood to be very obviously central, strategic, profit-generating, and so on, at least following two decades of massive public criticism by social scientists, politicians and journalists of companies which were failing to recognise the fact. However, information systems are more easily identifiable as a support or service function, rather like personnel or human resource management, only more of a nuisance because its level of technical expertise is higher and developing faster, making it harder to manage and control. The influence of information systems is pervasive but rarely uniformly so, and only effective at the strategic and operational core of some companies and organizations, such as those in financial services, or public sector organizations which depend completely on large scale information processing. This means that, in general, in most organizations, information systems functions are rarely permanently central and powerful (Huber, 1993).

Currie (1995), who surveyed 174 UK organizations, found that separate career structures and salary scales for IS professionals and managers were common, and that managers and technical staff tended to be referred to, respectively, as generalists and specialists. However interviews with both groups found consensus on the idea that their education and qualifications could be similar. Generalist middle managers earned significantly more than senior analysts and programmers of the same age, justifying this by their 'greater responsibility'. However both groups consisted of graduates and information systems specialists who very often had far more real responsibility than the middle managers who were crucially dependent on their highly complex technical judgements, ones which often had major commercial and financial implications. On the other hand, the usual complaints about technical staff not communicating well with users and generalist managers were justified in some cases. But, at the same time, senior information systems staff also complained that 'communication' was actually the responsibility of generalist managers. One said that the 'cliché that technical people can't communicate is false', and he and others argued that generalist managers did not listen to descriptions of information systems couched in everyday language and did not want to learn about information systems even though their employees were spending very large amounts of money on it, and on the provision of information systems training. Generalist information systems managers tended to define their responsibilities, and to be judged by their superiors themselves, in non-technical terms such as those of planning and budgeting control. The imposition of deadlines and performance targets on technical staff following a linear process was common. Yet technical staff argued that their work was often too unpredictable and dynamic to satisfy performance targets in this way, and that it had an iterative rather than a linear quality. Management, according to technical staff, had little understanding of the risky nature of their work, and too often used administrative and budgetary controls as inadequate substitutes for genuine project management skills. To technical staff, the imposition of arbitrary and often premature deadlines by general managers had harmful effects on quality. Generalist project managers had a Pontius Pilate approach to the notion of success. They defined successful information systems project work as that which was finished on time and within budget, and which they could sign over to the client, with any future technical problems being the responsibility of technical staff.

Yet it is also clear that there are factors leading competent information systems specialists to seek employment outside the established corporate sector. As we shall consider more fully in the next section, there is a burgeoning market for the services of independent information systems analysts. Pay is often very much higher for those selling services as independent contractors than for those in traditional employment. For one thing, individual specialists gain in employability as they accrue varied and usually cutting-edge experience. Thus, information systems contract work is not poorly paid and degrading in the same way as many other forms of contract work. Those with scarce high level premium skills are very highly paid and greatly in demand. They earn high-level managerial salaries while working as highly valued information systems professionals. As has been suggested earlier, a recent survey found that freelance information systems specialists have 'broken through the six figure salary barrier'. The reasons for the skill shortages are historical and are therefore not only a phenomenon created by the speed at which new technologies are introduced into the marketplace.

Thus, ongoing skill shortages at all levels of employment lead managers to use costly external information systems contractors and management consultancies. In some contexts it may be true that the successful management of information systems can offer considerable efficiency gains, cost savings and the prospect of yet further development and/or outsourcing specialists are called in to take over the running of IS work. Freelance IS specialists offer a range of packaged solutions and back-up services to their clients. Smaller IS consultancies offering specialist services are usually much cheaper but less resourceful and flexible (Ackroyd, 1995). However, the danger of the upward trend towards outsourcing information systems work to third-party firms is that it will strip companies of their information systems resources (hardware, software, people and processes). Once a large information systems consultancy purchases a client's IS assets in an outsourcing arrangement (for example when the former takes over more than 70 percent of the latter's information systems facility) it is unlikely that the client organization will retain any significant information systems knowledge. Information systems skills development and training will therefore become the responsibility of the IS consultancy. It was recently pointed out that:

> Today, only half of the jobs in the information technology industry are in the MIS departments. Now a third of the information technology jobs are filled through outsourcing or consulting profession versus in-house MIS departments. A limited number of jobs that design, develop, manufacture and sell hardware and software products are still in-house at companies. Systems development has been moved to the user departments in many organizations, leaving the MIS department to maintain the tools and the databases (Juliussen and Juliussen, 1996, p. 447).

The tendency for IS work to be outsourced by companies has resulted from heightened competition and a search for cost savings (Lacity, Willcocks and Feeny, 1995). The rhetoric about constant self-appraisal surrounding such contemporary management fads and practices as business process re-engineering and process innovation and so on has also fuelled the IS outsourcing marketplace (Currie and Willcocks, 1998a). Outsourcing activities are very numerous, and range from small scale IS trouble-shooting and systems development to large-scale systems building and integration, through software engineering, maintenance, network services and education and training and so on (Currie and Willcocks, 1998b).

IV. Not disorganization but re-organization II: New structures

In North America and the UK the information systems specialist is often perceived, and accurately so, as existing outside the mainstream organizational hierarchy. Many now contribute their skills to teams providing information systems and support as independent contractors (Ackroyd, 1995). They have become people who sell their experience of many different work environments and their fruits of accumulated technical expertise to client companies, often, as we have seen, for premium rewards. The current skill shortages have enabled many competent information systems specialists to command high salaries in markets which are otherwise dynamic and unpredictable.

Whilst this may offer employers cost savings in that information systems specialists are hired for separate contracts and therefore become a variable rather than fixed cost, this strategy has many disadvantages. Serious skill shortages continue to prevent companies achieving their information systems goals and objectives. That contemporary firms will achieve competitive advantage by using high levels of information technology and highly skilled knowledge workers utilising bespoke information systems sits uncomfortably alongside the upwards trend towards outsourcing. In fact, information skills and capabilities are now routinely being stripped out of companies. Companies which rely solely on external sources for the provision and maintenance of their information systems become vulnerable to unforeseen problems. Clearly, one of the perils of large-scale outsourcing is that companies become completely dependent upon their suppliers. This can create power asymmetries which take the form of suppliers dictating future IS strategies, frameworks and possibilities (not to mention prices) to clients (Currie and Willcocks, 1998b).

However, from the point of view of the information system professionals themselves the trend has some obvious advantages. The trend towards outsourcing can only have been damaging for those who have weak or inadequate skills and who have found themselves (with little choice) working in low discretion capacities, either as subordinate employees within corporations or, less likely, as low level associates in information systems consultancies. For many the loss of the traditional career path - which would involve progressing through a specialist hierarchy thence into general management - is now impossible for many information systems specialists - many of whom work without security of employment fulfilling fixed term contracts. But research as well as popular perception shows that many information systems consultants are very highly paid in compensation for their loss of contractual security and the possibility of career progression. The average information systems consultant is at least as highly paid as the senior professional such as the doctor, lawyer and accountant. Moreover, many are able to choose projects that are of interest, rather than being forced to work on routine tasks (Ackroyd, 1995).

But it would be wrong to suggest that the situation of the information systems professional is best understood in terms of the further development of market relations. The alternative to existing in a special enclave within a large corporate hierarchy is not the market: it is to occupy a place in a new form of organization. The uncertain and tenuous position of information systems specialists in many large and medium sized companies and their undoubted market strength means that they are, in many cases, able to organise themselves as groups of consultants and contractors. The dominant form of such new organizations has already been identified in the literature: it is the so called knowledge intensive firm or KIF. The rise of a new and highly distinctive type of organization in the KIF has been widely noted. These are small and highly adaptable firms which supply specialised and usually also business-related services. Although there are manufacturing firms that have been identified as KIFs, such organizations are usually identified as management consultancies and contractors of various kinds such as systems designers, computer programmers, financial marketing and advertising agencies. The KIF is, undoubtedly a compelling organizational phenomenon of the late twentieth century.

And yet commentators of the KIF have run into trouble trying to specify their character. Various, often contradictory, definitions of KIFs exist. At first there was a tendency to argue that KIFs are distinguished by the fact that they employ large numbers of professional or other highly trained people. However this would mean that traditional professional practices - which are often anything but dynamic and innovative - would have to be included as well as new service firms such as management consultancies and software houses. Mats Alvesson, one of the few perceptive commentators on the KIF (1995), specifically distinguished professional organizations from KIFs because he had felt that the majority of the work of such organizations was highly standardized, which the work of KIFs seldom was. The KIFs which Alvesson discusses did employ numbers of conventional professionals as well as significant numbers of new and emerging occupations including systems analysts and programmers. Thus he lists 'accountants, advertising workers, architects, computer experts, engineers, management consultants and psychologists' in his organizations. While he found it increasingly difficult to draw a clear line between professions and non-professions, leaving 'space for a concept or category that can illuminate occupations characterized by long formal education and the traits that normally accompany this - prestige, work tasks broadly perceived as complicated and high salaries' (cf. Fores, Glover and Lawrence, 1991) he clearly suggests that the character of KIFs was dictated by the new kinds of expertise they purvey. Alvesson (1995, p. 6) calls KIFs 'human-capital intensive structures' (p. 158) and asserts that the their typical form is the management consultancy. Actually, it is their distinctive relationship with their clients, that makes them notable.

For writers who see in the KIFs exemplary new kinds of organization, they are important because of the contributions that the knowledge workers in them make to value added. This, it has to be admitted, can be both large and an indispensable element in business processes as they are currently organised. However, for their exponents, the value added which KIFs produce is achieved mainly as a result of their extensive use of team working. Considered organizationally, KIFs are usually de-centred and highly developed matrix structures. These features also mean that KIFs embodied new forms of management and new devices to incorporate and control staff: friendly and informal relations, distinctive cultural values, employee-centred personnel policies and so on. Hence, for many commentators, KIFs were highly significant developments in the modern world, for here was the re-emergence of the open and participative organization that also makes a major contribution to increasing wealth. Thus a KIF was a very labour-intensive kind of firm, with a high density of people with complementary skills needed to make it work (p. 159).

But whether this new type of structure is particularly efficient or likely to be of much enduring significance is highly questionable. A case can clearly be made that the significance of KIFs has been exaggerated because of their ideological appeal and because of considerable misunderstanding about their nature and role. While the KIF is, in some respects, the opposite to Taylorist/Fordist organizations because of its emphasis on professional as opposed to managerial(ist) co-ordination of work, it is very unlikely that this is an emerging new pattern of organization which will be adopted widely. Ackroyd, (1995, 1999) and Ackroyd, Louche and Letiche (1997), have argued from the findings of their research that the organizational forms found in KIFs are not found in all high-technology or even all information technology firms. Clearly, there is evidence which suggests that KIFs are much less common and much less significant for understanding contemporary economic change than some writers on them have suggested. Arguably, KIFs fill specific market niches servicing large dominant corporations. In this role, KIFs are the necessary antithesis of large Fordist and other large and powerful organizations. They are the marginal products of market imperfections and hardly likely to displace, still less overpower, their client organizations, however (temporarily) advanced, scarce and expensive their knowledge and skills. Their long-term future is very uncertain.

According to Alvesson, even the idea that KIFs possessed exceptionally high amounts and levels of expertise is difficult to defend. Even if KIFs were outstanding contributors to wealth creation, in the real world, however, all KIFs operated in environments of considerable ambiguity, and the apparently widespread acceptance of the myth that they were unusually rational and efficient actors was simply part of the mystique that had long been built up around modern management and organization. Indeed much of their activity was far from esoteric or innovative, being designed to help client companies through periods when established staff were overloaded. In these circumstances it is normally very hard to judge the value of their outputs, to demonstrate their technical competence, whatever the nature of their contribution. The validity of these kinds of suspicion could be reinforced by the finding by Alvesson that the 'best' or 'right' KIFs and the 'right' or 'best' client companies appeared to seek each other out and to work on enhancing each others' reputations. In Alvesson's view socialization and leadership within KIFs were often 'social, non-formal and anti-technocratic', designed to reinforce specific approaches to work and working philosophies. The particular companies studied in some detail by Alvesson are perhaps unusual in their emphasis on social and project management skills as opposed to technical knowledge. He argues that this could have been a function of the characteristic of their clients' employees' not inconsiderable technical knowledge. To differentiate themselves from these, Alvesson's companies appeared to be emphasising their distinctiveness in terms of non-bureaucratic working patterns and specially subjective orientations to workplace cultures.

Other KIFs known by Alvesson were more technocratic in their approaches. Even so, KIFs are, in general, held to be 'systems of persuasion'. They exploited the contemporary over-dependency on information. People gathered much more information than they could use and they often spoke about it in ways designed to make themselves appear 'careful, rational, reliable, even intelligent' (p. 1011). Alvesson noted how paradoxical this was. KIFs and all those in larger client companies which exaggerated the value, and virtue, of information and of knowledge appeared to do so in order to appear, to others as well as to themselves, as 'advanced, progressive, responsive, intelligent, etc.' (p. 1011). They deny the ambiguities inherent in all practical use of knowledge and information, and they acted and thought as if they could always fall back on a bedrock of 'hard' data, (i.e. formal, codified knowledge), while also calling from time to time on such 'other cultural values ... as creativity, originality and interactive capacities' (p. 1011). Alvesson is keen not to deny the strictly practical value of knowledge for work. However he also noted how its presence is used for creating community and social identity, for providing a shared language, for boosting self-esteem, for persuasion in dealing with customers and others, for image-building, for promoting legitimacy and good faith, and for obscuring uncertainty and counteracting reflection.

Alvesson clearly thinks that the most interesting features of KIFs were their 'claims of knowledge (or other rare skills)' (p. 1012), rather than whatever actual knowledge they possessed. This is partly because expert power was being boosted, and its importance emphasised, by proselytisers for and sellers of 'knowledge' and 'knowledge work'. It certainly is important not to lose sight of the dependence of KIFs on rhetoric. The traditional rhetoric of professions concerned science and knowledge. That of employees of KIFs is focused more on the ability to handle uncertainty in contexts of change which tended to present themselves as local and unique but demanding energetic use of 'intuition, flexibility, creativity and social skills' (p. 1013). Therefore a 'crucial dimension of KIFs is ... as systems of persuasion or local sites for rhetoric' (p. 1013). These special cultural features of KIFs clearly have consequences for the mode of engagement of associates and employees. Clearly, managements sought employee compliance on a broader scale than that of developing and using knowledge to effect, but they could exploit the ambiguities which inevitably and usefully surround knowledge use to their own advantage. It is tempting, in fact, to suggest that this ability to exploit the ambiguity of knowledge use is the key ability of both 'modern' and 'post-modern' management (cf. Legge, 1995).

None of this is to deny that many KIFs are genuinely 'knowledge-intensive', even if 'ambiguity-suppressive' might be a more accurate description of their function. While KIFs were often internally open and participative, and their employees self-directed, they also are often engaged in constructing technical and managerial systems of control for client organizations. Where they are not directly engaged in augmenting the wealth creating capacities of the major companies that are their clientele, KIFs clearly draw their earnings from augmenting and contributing to the functioning of larger business units. Blackler (1995) and Reed (1992) had both written about KIFs as firms dominated by symbolic analysts or other knowledge workers whose flexible, organic, human-centred, decentralised, autonomous, expert-dependent, anti-bureaucratic ways of working were increasingly diffusing themselves across and transforming all kinds of contemporary organization. However advocates of KIFs as exemplary organizational forms are rarely if ever specific about the sources of and the reasons for the emergence of new knowledge and of the contribution to value added of the supposedly growing cadres of knowledge workers. Commentators too often rely on the implication that KIFs do create value independently of their clients, and that once a new method of creating value has been found it will be spontaneously adopted and copied. Alternatively, it is clear that KIFs develop and succeed, not because of their human co-ordination and supposedly specially intensive use of human talents, but because of some extremely fortuitous market conditions in which they find themselves. Typically the market niches in which KIFs operate exist in interstices between the operations of large corporations, 'where it is possible for small companies to sell their products on advantageous terms' (Ackroyd and Lawrenson, 1996b, p. 164).

Clearly then, there are good reasons for thinking that the sudden emergence of new kinds of knowledge postulated by Blackler begins to appear less plausible. When the way the organizations employing large numbers of knowledge workers actually function is appreciated, the likelihood of the forms of organization adopted by KIFs being widely copied seems very unlikely. For Ackroyd and Lawrenson, KIFs are relatively few in number, and conspicuous only because they are so differently organized from most of the firms, 'high-tech' and otherwise, that surround them, which tend to be organized in quite orthodox ways (1996b). There is no noticeable general process of organizational diffusion: both orthodox and innovative structures co-operated and coexist (Ackroyd, 1995; Ackroyd, Louche and Letiche, 1997). Also, the new organizations, as Alvesson (1995) has suggested, tended to be in the periphery rather than at the centre of their national economies. They are also at least as often associated with commerce and services as with manufacturing. If all this is true, the faith of some writers in the future of the symbolic analyst and the knowledge worker is very hard to justify.

Ackroyd and Lawrenson (1996b) are almost alone in paying considerable attention to the organizational conjunctures in which KIFs operate. These authors regard economic globalisation, which has especially important commercial and financial, communications/media/entertainment, and educational and political features, not only industrial ones, as the most promising basis for explaining contemporary changes. They are interested in occupations, organizations, and global economic development. They contrast three theoretical positions relevant for understanding the role of KIFs and more generally, recent changes in the use of knowledge and expertise. These are the power-dependency and the neo-liberal approaches, and their own view, which focuses on the new, more complex and diffuse, power relations associated with the extensive development of trans-national companies and growing importance of global economic relations. Ackroyd and Lawrenson favour the last of these approaches because they see a world economy emerging, one in which occupations, professions and organizations increasingly develop in supranational contexts. (They do not apprehend the role of economic globalisation unreservedly; they are aware of its media and financially amplified aspects, cf. Hirst, 1996, and Hirst and Thompson, 1995, 1996). However the first of the two approaches that they discuss tend to focus on occupations and organizations within nations. The power-dependency perspective emphasises the continuity of existing forms and practices by arguing, for example, that there is nothing new about the flexible firm in particular and flexible employment practices in general. Historical patterns of economic competition and domination have not altered very much and are unlikely to alter in any fundamental sense and those who argued otherwise tended to be apologists and propagandists for the powerful. Neo-liberal theory, on the other hand, did argue that new organizational forms were emerging. It conceptualized inter-organizational relations more in terms of contributions to added value, rather than, as in the previous case, purely in terms of competition, power, domination and dependency. Rising incomes, new technology and fragmenting market demand meant that genuinely new profitable relationships between firms were emerging, with very large firms much less dominant than hitherto. Economic integration is increasingly a product of flexible specialization across interfirm networks and of help from non-market support agencies. Ackroyd and Lawrenson criticize this view heavily for being an idealized one with little evidence available to give it empirical support.

Clearly, there is, as these writers suggest, scope for an improved approach, superior for being based on the sounder elements of each of the two former ones as well as on a perception of the real changes taking place in the world economy. Markets based on increased international trading have continued to develop even when national economies have been in recession. International, even global, markets for many goods and for products of the mass media had developed enough to 'reduce the capacity of even the very largest manufacturers to sustain monopoly power' (p. 152). Increasing levels of global trading have only been possible by dint of a huge growth of commercial organizations. The global production arrangements of large trans-national corporations increasingly consists of small units, dispersed across the world, with operational power increasingly decentralized to them (Bartlett and Ghoshal, 1989). Globally extensive manufacturing and trading corporations, Japanese-style, were being copied by many non-Japanese multinationals. Their physical dispersal and the apparent fragmentation of their power often masked growth of the latter across localities and regions. Similarly, there is too little perception of the many commensurate changes in the relationships between larger and small businesses which have followed, especially the development of management consultancies and business services companies catering to the needs of global corporations. Many of the small businesses that have been emerging are flexible and 'human-centred' - along the lines that neo-liberal arguments prescribe - and the KIF is a new organizational form that has been called into being and functions 'well in the interstices between the large corporations' (p. 153). But the need for them exists only so long as the large organizations themselves are at their present stage of development.

In the UK in the 1980s, policy-oriented research had been designed to show how new configurations of technology could be used by innovative small and medium sized companies to generate new and highly successful forms of manufacturing. New and flexible working practices plus higher levels of skill would be underpinned by developments in information and production technology. All such thinking was based on faith in capital intensiveness, in achieving greater productivity with less labour than is used within traditional institutions. While some more sophisticated versions of it used such terminology as the 'social shaping of technology', technological determinism and over-optimism underpinned it all. This was partly because the influence of information technology on work and work organization had often been misunderstood and exaggerated. Information technology was a part-facilitator of new corporate configurations of capital. The latter had been massively neglected in the 1980s UK literature on technology policy and in most thinking about recent economic and organizational trends. IT was merely a necessary but not a sufficient condition for the further dramatic development of the global economy now in process.

This sort of development, by organizations which managed increasing proportions of world-wide production and trading of goods and services, was connecting many previously unconnected parts of the world. It involved the creation of new forms of organization on the part of unprecedentedly large and wealthy multinationals, such as capital extensive firms, or CEFs. They tended to be concentrated densely in a number of related industrial sectors, and increasingly powerful in spite of their dispersal, which often served to conceal their power in national or regional contexts. It was very misleading to think of the current stage of capitalism as 'disorganized' (cf. Lash and Urry, 1987), simply because the dominant level of organization had been moving up from that of the national economy to that of the global one. For Ackroyd and Lawrenson, the emerging global economy was 'increasingly orchestrated by the activities of major corporations' (1996b, p. 155).

Although the most obvious examples of CEFs are global manufacturing and trading conglomerates (M-TCEFs) pioneered by the Japanese but now quite widely copied, there are more significant examples in commerce and commerce-related companies. These sectors are becoming dominated by what can be called I-BCEFs, or information-based capital extensive firms, such as those which offered banking, insurance and financial services. These have grown from their connections with nationally based trade to facilitating trade and commerce across the world. Japanese firms also tended, although to a smaller extent, to dominate this sector. However, there is another type of I-BCEF, distinct from those which use information for commerce, and which make commerce out of information, in media, communications, entertainment and advertising combines whose organizational forms tended to be the same as other I-BCEFs. Like M-TCEFs, I-BCEFs are built around capital-extensive technologies, and characterised by huge capital investments. All kinds of commercial and information-providing service companies, apart from I-BCEFs, had been growing up all over the world, generally underwritten by developments in manufacturing and, in particular, the high density commerce promoted by highly productive and profitable manufacturing for world trade.

As in the past with the employment of commission agents, factors and book-keepers, however, CEFs, I-BCEFs and M-TCEFs with far-flung activities do not need to employ large numbers of highly skilled people to manage them or to conduct their operations. What they did now have, as in the past and by most past standards, were state of the art information transfer technologies, designed and operated at the centre by very small numbers of elite system designers and strategic managers, serviced by workers at globally dispersed plants and offices with far less training and knowledge. Thus in M-TCEFs and their important variants, I-BCEFs, very large scale and dispersed activities were co-ordinated using IT in ways which meant that organizations could be both capital and labour intensive in many respects, although they were predominantly extensive in both.

One of the main effects of the spatial extent of the present development of these new global organizations is that they have fostered the development of KIFs. By this argument, far from KIFs being a growth point from which there will be the proliferation of new organizations of a similar type, they are transient and depend for their continued existence on unstable relationships of mutual dependency with large corporations. They are likely to be limited in both number and importance considered in the longer term and using an appropriate frame of reference.

Conclusion

This paper is partly a critique and partly a clarification and synthesis and of existing evidence. We regard IT, and, more particularly, the utilisation made of IT by specific groups, as extremely influential in influencing change. In this sense, IT, as with all new forms of technology that are widely adopted, is clearly something that releases potent forces. However, our view of IT is far from being a technologically determinist position: we do not assert that there is anything inevitable about the effects of the adoption of a new technology. This is because what happens depends on the way that this technology is appropriated and used: it matters a great deal which groups have control of the technology and how they are disposed to utilise it. Hence we also do not see the new technology as having important properties in its own right; as being, somehow, an additional actor (or "actant") in an already complex situation, as in actor network theory (Callon, 1987; Latour, 1987, 1991). In contrast to both these views, we think of IT as just another resource (like money, raw material, other technology or labour) to which groups of actors have differential access and in which they have particular interests. As with other resources, IT will continue to be a subject over which contending groups will negotiate and develop interests.

The fact that this sort of technology has all sorts of possibilities, which are presently being realised and developed in different ways in different parts of the world should not mislead us into thinking that our existing ways of analysing social development no longer apply. It is true that, among other things, information technology has the capacity to revolutionise the way business is conducted, and give a powerful boost to the development of effective global organizations. But in order for such possibilities to be realised, particular groups of people must take up and utilise the new technology. In so doing they will have to enter alliances and arrange particular divisions of labour in order to realise plans and bring new forms of production and distribution into being. Our analysis in this chapter has taken precisely this form: we have identified the groups which have an interest in the technology and how they are disposed to act in order to develop their organization and spheres of influence.

At the most basic level, the new technology has prompted the formation of series of new occupations, the most distinctive of which, it is now becoming apparent, is the one we have been considering at length in this chapter - the information systems specialists. We have also argued that features of the situation of this group - which has made a successful claim to the day to day responsibility for the new technology in businesses, is not acting in the way that commonsense, experience and a good deal of social science might lead us to expect. The balance of the evidence seems to be that these influential new specialists are not trying to take over more powerful positions within management by mounting professionalisation projects. The most conspicuous trend is for this occupation to organise themselves as specialist business service providers outside corporations. We may confidently expect further developments of this kind. Already there are emerging very large international business consultancy groups providing comprehensive information and management services. For one reason or another the days of the small flexible business consultancy company may be numbered.

The recognition of a new fluidity in business relations is the starting point of the approach to social change which has been our critical foil in this chapter. In this, the knowledge worker writers share with us at least two important perceptions about change. Firstly, it is true that there are significant developments in the numbers and internal organisation of small companies. The KIF with its large numbers of employees whose work is new - being outside any of the established areas of professional competence - is a reality. Such firms are so different from traditional structures that they have to be recognised. Secondly, it is also true that large organisations are tending to reduce the scale and inclusiveness of their operations in any one site. As they move much more into multi-national operations, they are more and more entering into co-operative relations with other firms and outsourcing many of the things they need from firm and contractors. We would argue, of course, that these two processes are intimately related. As major corporations gear themselves up for global operations, they are forced to spread themselves more thinly as they disperse their capital in more sites; this, in turn, makes them draw much more heavily on local suppliers and external service providers to supply their needs. For the reasons we have examined in this chapter this reliance extends to such important requirements as information systems design. The huge growth of management consultancy suggests that even local management is sometimes being drawn from contractors.

But whereas we have seen in such developments the need to understand the particular objectives and interests of specific groups - the way that the emerging occupation of systems analysts is responding to its situation, for example, and the designs and intentions of the strategists in major corporations - others, such as the exponents of the knowledge worker thesis, have been disposed to think that we are facing a new and unprecedented situation. The knowledge worker writers want to suggest that there are new forms of knowledge which are, to considerable extent, producing current change. They suggest that because of the availability of new ways of thinking, people are actually able to transform their situations. We suggest, by contrast, that knowledge - and more importantly conceptions of knowledge - are intimately related to particular interests and relations of power. If there are new forms of knowledge, it will be because there are groups disposed to define what they know as new in order to attempt to persuade others of its relevance. But groups will be able to develop their interests only insofar as they are allowed to do by the constraints exerted by other groups with different powers and interests.

At the most general level, there is a theoretical question concerning the patterns of development of contemporary capitalism. In our view, emergent patterns are the result of the interactions of the groups, but the expectation is that there will be decided advantages for those groups already controlling the use of resources. In the medium term the controllers of the large organisations we have discussed in the previous section of this chapter will have more influence than any new occupation, whatever its temporary market advantages. Here again there is a contrast with the ideas of knowledge worker writers and others who assume that the changes in business that are being analysed are absolutely unprecedented and of entirely unpredictable outcome. Given that they assume change proceeds mainly from the creative activities of individual and groups, it could hardly be otherwise. In his two-page response to Prichard's (1996) critique of his thinking, Blackler (1996) refers to the 'The partial replacement, in the processes of wealth creation, of concentrations of capital or labour by the use and development of specialist knowledge and experience'. As if to clinch the argument, he lists a number of far-reaching changes ... 'taking place in the processes by which wealth is created in contemporary capitalism'. He then lists six, which are together meant to distinguish the late twentieth century and to be the context of the supposedly rapidly growing significance of knowledge work and workers (see Figure 14.1 below).

However, from our point of view, we suggest that there are clearly cycles and phases of activity in the development of capitalism. What is happening today is part of a process of development which, according to the definitions one chooses, began between 200 and 500 years ago. What we are talking about in our discussion of the changes taking place today has to do with the emerging shape of the next stage of the developments of economy and society set in motion by industrialization. This process will, eventually, come to be seen as having major phases, of which we would distinguish three: mechanization, electrification, and info-technologization. Just as clearly there are massive continuities in these stages of technological development, with each of the latter borrowing extensively from the former. Electrification is the development and extension of particular aspects of mechanisation, just as information technology is the development and extension of electrification. We suggest that a fourth phase, bio-technologization, will in due course be clearly perceivable, although we ourselves are unable to see clearly as yet how it might borrow extensively from the former three or the extent to which it will come to be seen as more independent from their development than they have been from each other. However, to give a more empirical point to this very general argument, we have listed in Figure 14.1 at the end of the text of this chapter the technical and other developments which Blackler claims make the end of the twentieth century unique. (He ignores biotechnology but this is reasonable given his priorities). Next to each point, we have listed examples about the prevalence of similar developments in the half-century or so around the turn of the last century in 1900 - beginning in 1875 or so and continuing until the middle of the 1920s. Against these changes, those of the second half of the twentieth century do appear quite as unique and as dramatic as some would have had us believe. Radio, flight, the telephone, motor transport, mass production, universal pensions, television and the development of the modern corporation, modern systems of government and of social welfare and of health care are hard acts to follow, but it seems that we might well be experiencing some approximation to technological renaissance at the present time

Blackler's changes of the second half of the twentieth century	'Equivalent' changes circa 1875 - 1925
Proliferation of centres of capital	New York, Paris, Berlin and others as well as London.
Interpenetration of regional economies	Europe and South and North America, Europe and Africa and the Middle and Far East, North America and numerous others.
Emergence of a global division of labour	European empires and their colonies, dominions, dependencies and other trading partners and many other examples of trading of primary, secondary and tertiary products.
Changing government policies towards the redistribution of wealth	Developments in taxation and in the provision of pensions and social insurance payments in several industrial countries.
New information and communication technologies	Calculating machines, electric light, submarine and other telegraphy, typewriters, telephones, television, radio, flight, motor cars, buses, lorries, motorcycles.
New approaches to organization	Very large and relatively numerous civil service departments; major developments in local government, health care, retailing, chemicals, electricity generation and supply, financial services and construction project organization; most of the major organizational and public sector professions; mass production, large scale vertical integration in mass production, Alfred Sloan and the M-form; multinationals; unprecedentedly large scale military organization and production; the Dupont Formula for management accounting.

Figure 14.1 **Blackler's (1996) far-reaching changes of the second half of the twentieth century**

References

Ackroyd, S. (1995) 'On the Structure and Dynamics of Some Small, UK-Based Information Technology Firms', *Journal of Management Studies*, Vol. 32, No. 2, pp. 141-61.

Ackroyd, S. (1996) 'Organization Contra Organizations: Professions and Organizational Change in the United Kingdom', *Organization Studies*, Vol. 17, No.4, pp, 599-621.

Ackroyd, S. (1999) 'In Search of the European Knowledge Intensive Firm' in F. Blackler, D. Courpasson and B. Elkejar (eds) *Knowledge-Work and European Competitiveness,* Sage, London.

Ackroyd, S. and Lawrenson, D. (1996b), 'Knowledge-Work and Organizational Transformation: Analysing Contemporary Change in the Social Use of Expertise', in R. Fincham (ed.), *New Relationships in the Organizational Professions*, Avebury, Aldershot, pp. 149-70.

Ackroyd, S., Louche, C. and Letiche, H. (1997), 'The Managerial Regimes of European High Technology Firms: Some Findings from Comparative Research', in R. Oakey and S.-M. Mukhtar (eds) *New Technology-Based Firms in the 1990's* (volume III), Paul Chapman, London, pp. 197 -210.

Adler, P.S., McDonald, D.W. and MacDonald, F. (1992), 'Strategic Management of Technical Functions', *Sloan Management Review*, Winter, pp. 19-37.

Allen, T.J. and Scott-Morton, M. (1994) *Information Technology and the Corporation of the 1990s*, Oxford University Press, Oxford.

Alvesson, M. (1995), *Management of Knowledge-Intensive Companies*, Walter de Gruyter, Berlin.

Armstrong, P. (1993), 'Professional Knowledge and Social Mobility: Postwar Changes in the Knowledge-Base of Management Accounting', *Work, Employment and Society*, Vol. 7, No. 1, pp. 1-21.

Balasubramanyam, V.N. (1994), 'The New Knowledge Workers?', *Organization*, Vol. 1, 2, pp. 439-56.

Bartlett, C.A. and Ghoshal, S. (1989), *Managing Across Borders*, Harvard Business School Press, Boston, Mass.

Bell, D. (1973) *The Coming of Post-Industrial Society*, Basic Books, New York.

Blackler, F. (1988), 'Information technologies and organizations: Lessons from the 1980s and issues for the 1990s', *Journal of Occupational Psychology*, Vol. 61, pp. 113-27.

Blackler, F. (1995), 'Knowledge Work and Organization: An Overview and Interpretation', *Organization Studies*, Vol. 16, No. 6, pp. 1021-46.

Blackler, F. (1996), 'Response', *Organization Studies*, Vol. 17, No. 5, pp. 858-60.

Blackler, F., Reed, M. and Whitaker, A. (1993a), 'Editorial Introduction: Knowledge Workers and Contemporary Organizations', *Journal of Management Studies*, Vol. 30, No. 6, pp. 851-62.

Blackler, F., Reed, M. and Whitaker, A. (1993b), 'Epilogue - An Agenda for Research', *Journal of Management Studies*, Vol. 30, No. 6, pp. 1017-20.

Boynton, A.C., Jacobs, G.C., Zmud, R.W. (1992), 'Whose responsibility is IT management?', *Sloan Management Review*, Summer, pp. 32-38.

Callon, M. (1987), 'Society in the Making: Technology as a Tool for Sociological Analysis', in A. Bijker et al (eds) *The Social Construction of Technical Systems: New Directions in the Sociology of History and Technology,* MIT Press, London and Cambridge, Mass.

Child, J. (1987), 'Managerial Strategies, New Technology and the Labour Process', in D. Knights, H. Willmott and D. Collinson (eds), *Job Redesign, Managerial Strategy, New Technology and the Labour Process,* Gower, Aldershot, pp. 107-41.

Currie, W. (1995), *Management Strategy for IT: An International Perspective,* Pitman, London.

Currie, W. L. and Glover, I.A. (1998), 'Hybrid Managers: An Example of Tunnel Vision and Regression in Management Research', to appear in W.L. Currie and R. Galliers (eds), *Reinventing Information Systems*, OUP, Oxford.

Currie, W. and Willcocks, L. (1998a) *New Strategies in IT Outsourcing*, Business Intelligence, London.

Currie, W. and Willcocks, L. (1998b) 'Analysing Four Types Of IT Sourcing Decisions In The Context Of Scale, Client/Supplier Interdependency And Risk Mitigation', *Information Systems Journal,* Vol. 8, No. 2, pp. 119-43.

Drucker, P.F. (1969), *The Age of Discontinuity*, Heinemann, London.

Drucker, P.F. (1993), *Post-Capitalist Society*, Butterworth-Heinemann, Oxford.

Farbey, B., Land, F., and Targett, D. (1993), *IT Investment: a Study of Methods and Practice,* Butterworth-Heinemann, London.

Fores, M., Glover, I. and Lawrence, P. (1991), 'Professionalism and Rationality: A Study in Misapprehension', *Sociology*, Vol. 25, No.1, pp. 79-100.

Forester, T. (1980), *The Microelectronics Revolution*, Blackwell, Oxford.

Forester, T. (1985), *The Information Technology Revolution*, OUP, Oxford.

Glover, I.A. (1999), 'British Management and British History: Assessing the Responsibility of Individuals for Economic Difficulties', *Contemporary British History*, forthcoming.

Glover, I.A. and Kelly, M.P. (1987), *Engineers in Britain: A Sociological Study of the Engineering Profession,* Allen and Unwin, London.

Glover, I.A., Tracey, P.J., and Currie, W.L. (1998), 'Engineering Our Future Again: Towards a Long Term Strategy for Manufacturing and Management in the United Kingdom', in R. Delbridge and J. Lowe (eds) *Manufacturing in Transition*, Routledge, London, pp. 199-223.

Hirst, P. (1996), 'Globaloney', *Prospect*, February, pp. 29-33.

Hirst, P. and Thompson, G. (1995), 'Globalization and the future of the nation state', *Economy and Sociology*, Vol. 24, No. 3, pp. 408-42.

Hirst, P. and Thompson, G. (1996), *Globalization in Question: The International Economy and the Possibilities of Governance*, Polity Press, Cambridge.

Huber, R.L. (1993) 'How Continental Bank outsourced its crown jewels', *Harvard Business Review*, January/February, pp. 121-29.

Johnson, T.J. (1972), *Professions and Power*, Macmillan, London.
Juliussen, K.P. and Juliussen, E. (1996), *The Eighth Annual Computer Industry Almanac*, The Reference Press, Austin, Texas, USA.
Knights, D. and Murray, F. (1994), *Managers Divided: Organization Politics and Information Technology Management*, Wiley, Chichester.
Lacity, M.C., Willcocks, L.P. and Feeny, D.F. (1995), 'IT Outsourcing: Maximise Flexibility and Control', *Harvard Business Review*, May-June, pp. 84-93.
Lash, S. and Urry, J. (1987), *The End of Organized Capitalism*, Polity, Oxford.
Latour, B. (1987), *Science in Action*, Open University Press, Milton Keynes.
Latour, B. (1991), 'Technology as a society made durable' in J. Law (ed.) *A Sociology of Monsters? Essays on Power, Technology and Domination*, Routledge, London.
Legge, K. (1995), *Human Resource Management: Rhetorics and Realities*, Macmillan, Basingstoke.
Orlikowski, W.J., Walsham, G., Jones, M.R. and Degross, J.I. (1996), *Information Technology and Change in Organizational Work*, Chapman and Hall, London.
Porter, M.E. and Millar, V. (1985), 'How information gives you competitive advantage', *Harvard Business Review*, July/August, pp. 149-60.
Prichard, C. (1996), 'A Commentary and Response on Blackler's "Knowledge Work and Organization: An Overview and Interpretation"', *Organization Studies*, Vol. 17, No. 5, pp. 857, 58.
Reed, M.I. (1991), 'The End of Organised Society: A Theme in Search of a Theory?', in P. Blyton and J. Morris (eds) *A Flexible Future? Prospects for Employment and Organisation*, Walter de Gruyter, Berlin.
Reed, M.I. (1996a), 'Expert Power and Control in Late Modernity: An Empirical Review and Theoretical Synthesis', *Organization Studies*, Vol. 17, No. 4, pp. 573-97.
Reed, M.I. (1996b), 'Rediscovering Hegel: The New "Historicism" in Organisation and Management Studies', *Journal of Management Studies*, Vol. 33, No. 2, pp. 139-47.
Reich, R.B. (1991), *The Work of Nations: Preparing Ourselves for the 21st Century*, Simon and Schuster, London.
Roslender, R., Glover, I. and Kelly, M. (1999), 'Future Imperfect: The Uncertain Prospects of the British Accountant', chapter 10 in this book.
Shank, J.K. and Govindarajan, V. (1992), 'Strategic cost analysis of technological investments', *Sloan Management Review*, Fall, pp. 39-51.
Sorge, A. and Hartmann, G. (1980), 'Technology and Labour Markets', Discussion Paper 80-39, International Institute of Management, Berlin.
Wilbey, A. (1998), 'A New Profession? Understanding Management Consultancy', unpublished MA thesis, Department of Behaviour in Organisations, University of Lancaster.

Further reading

Ackroyd, S. and Procter, S. (1998) 'British Manufacturing Organisation and Workplace Relations' *British Journal of Industrial Relations*, Vol. 36, No, 2, pp. 136-83.

Ackroyd, S. and Lawrenson, D. (1996a), 'Manufacturing Decline and the Division of Labour in Britain: the Case of Vehicles', in I. Glover and M. Hughes (eds), *The Professional-Managerial Class: Contemporary British Management in the Pursuer Mode*, Avebury, Aldershot, pp. 171-94.

Alvesson, M. (1990a), 'Organization: from Substance to Image?', *Organization Studies*, Vol. 11, No. 3, pp. 373-94.

Alvesson, M. (1990b), 'On the Popularity of Organizational Culture', *Acta Sociologica*, Vol. 33, No. 1, pp. 31-49.

Alvesson, M. and Willmott, H. (eds.), (1992), *Critical Management Studies*, Sage, London.

Alvesson, M. (1993), 'Organizations as Rhetoric: Knowledge-Intensive Firms and the Struggle with Ambiguity', *Journal of Management Studies*, Vol. 30, No. 6, pp. 997-1015.

Anthony, P.D. (1994), *Managing Culture*, Open University Press, Celtic Court.

Armstrong, P. (1987), 'Engineers, Management and Trust', *Work, Employment and Society*, Vol. 1, No. 4, pp. 421-40.

Astley, G. (1984), 'Subjectivity, Sophistry and Symbolism in Management Science', *Journal of Management Studies*, Vol. 21, No. 3, pp. 259-72.

Baber, Z. (1996), *The Science of Empire: Scientific Knowledge, Civilization and Colonial Rule in India*, Albany, State University of New York Press.

Barnes, B., Bloor, D. and Henry, J. (1996), *Scientific Knowledge: A Sociological Analysis*, Athlone, London.

Bendix, R. (1975), 'Science and the Purposes of Knowledge', *Social Research*, Vol. 42, No. 2, pp. 331-59.

Berggren, C. and Nomora, M. (1997), *The Resilience of Corporate Japan*, Paul Chapman, London.

Bird, J. (1996), 'Disinformation Technology', *Management Today*, June 1996, pp. 78-80.

Bloor, G. and Dawson, P. (1994), 'Understanding Professional Culture in Organizational Context', *Organization Studies*, Vol. 15, No. 2, pp. 275-95.

Blyton, P., Hassard, J., Hill, S. and Starkey, K. (1989), *Time, Work and Organization*, Routledge, London.

Bohn, R.E. (1994), 'Measuring and Managing Technological Knowledge', *Sloan Management Review*, Fall, pp. 61-73.

Boisot, M.H. (1986), 'Markets and Hierarchies in a Cultural Perspective', *Organization Studies*, Vol. 7, No. 2, pp. 135-58.

Boisot, M.H. (1995), *Information Space: A Framework for Learning in Organizations, Institutions, and Cultures*, Routledge, London.

Borgmann, A. (1984), *Technology and the Character of Contemporary Life: A Philosophy Inquiry*, University of Chicago Press, Chicago.

Bourdieu, P., Passeron, J-C. and de Saint-Martin, M. (1996), *Academic Discourse: Linguistic Misunderstanding and Professorial Power*, Polity Press, Oxford.

Brooke, C. (1995), 'Analyst and Programmer Stereotypes: a Self-fulfilling Prophecy?', *Journal of Information Technology*, Vol. 10, pp. 15-25.

Brown, A.D. and Starkey, K. (1994), 'The Effect of Organizational Culture on Communication and Information', *Journal of Management Studies*, Vol. 31, No. 6, pp. 807-28.

Burke, G. and Peppard, J. (eds.) (1995), *Examining Business Process Reengineering-Current Perspectives and Research Directions*, Kogan Page, London.

Carchedi, G. (1977), *On The Economic Identification of Social Classes*, Routledge, and Kegan Paul, London.

Causer, G. and Jones, C. (1996), 'Management and the Control of Technical Labour', *Work, Employment and Society*, Vol. 10, No. 1, pp. 105-23.

Chaudhury, A., Nam, K. and Rao, H.R. (1995), 'Management of Information Systems Outsourcing: A Bidding Perspective', *Journal of Management Information Systems*, Vol. 12, No. 2, pp. 131-59.

Child, J., Fores, M., Glover. I, and Lawrence, P. (1983), 'A Price to Pay? Professionalism and Work Organizations in Britain and West Germany', *Sociology*, Vol. 17, No. 1, pp. 63-78.

Cohen, B. (1985), 'Skills, Professional Education and the Disabling University', *Studies in Higher Education*, Vol. 10, No. 2, pp. 175-86.

Cooper, R. and Burrell, G. (1988), 'Modernism, Postmodernism and Organizational Analysis: An Introduction', *Organization Studies*, Vol. 9, No.1, pp. 91-112.

Corfield, P.J. (1995), *Power and the Professions in Britain 1700-1850*, Routledge, London.

Cross, J. (1995), 'Outsourcing at British Petroleum', *Harvard Business Review*, May-June, pp. 94-102.

Cross, J., Earl, M.J. and Sampler, J.L. (1997), 'Transformation of the IT Function and British Petroleum', *MIS Quarterly*, December, pp. 401-23.

Davenport, T.H., Jaarvenpaa, S.L. and Beers, M.C. (1996), 'Improving Knowledge Work Process', *Sloan Management Review*, Summer, pp. 53-63.

Delbridge, R. and Lowe, J. (1997), 'Managing Human Resources for Business Success: A Review of the Issues', *The International Journal of Human Resource Management*, Vol. 8, No. 6, pp. 857-73.

Demirag, I.S. (1996), 'The Impact of Managers' Short-Term Perceptions on Technology Management and R and D in UK Companies', *Technology Analysis and Strategic Management*, Vol. 8, No. 1, pp. 21-32.

Dingley, J. (1996), 'Durkheim, Professions and Moral Integration', in I. Glover and M. Hughes (eds), *The Professional-Managerial Class: Contemporary British Management in the Pursuer Mode*, Avebury, Aldershot, pp. 155-69.

Dingwall, R. and Lewis, P. (eds) (1983), *The Society of the Professions: Lawyers, Doctors and Others*, Macmillan, Basingstoke.
Dopson, S. and Stewart, R. (1993), 'Information Technology, Organizational Restructuring and the Future of Middle Management', *New Technology, Work and Employment*, Vol. 8, No. 1, pp. 10-20.
Du Gay, P. (1968), *Consumption and Identity at Work*, Sage, London.
Earl, M. (1989), *Managerial Strategies for Information Technology*, Prentice Hall, London.
Earl, M.J. (ed.) (1996a), *Information Management: The Organizational Dimension*, Oxford University Press, Oxford.
Earl, M.J. (1996b), 'The Risks of Outsourcing IT', *Sloan Management Review*, Spring, pp. 11-20.
Earl, M. and Skyrme, E. (1992), 'Hybrid Managers - What Do We Know About Them?', *Journal of Information Systems*, Vol. 2, pp.169-87.
Elias, N. (1997), 'Towards a Theory of Social Processes: a Translation', *British Journal of Sociology*, Vol. 48, No. 3, pp. 355-83.
Enteman, W. (1993), *Managerialism: the Emergence of a New Ideology*, University of Wisconsin Press, Madison, Wisconsin.
Etzioni, A. (ed.) (1969), *The Semi-Professions and their Organization*, Free Press, New York.
Evans, P. (1995), *Embedded Authority: States and Industrial Transformation*, Princeton University Press, Princeton, 1995.
Feenberg, A. (ed.) (1995), *Alternative Modernity: The Technical Turn in Philosophy and Social Theory*, University of California Press, Berkeley and Los Angeles.
Firstenberg, R.P. and Makiel, B.G. (1994), 'The Twenty-First Century Boardroom: Who Will Be in Charge?', *Sloan Management Review*, Fall, pp. 27-35.
Fleck, J. (1992), 'Expertise: Knowledge, Tradeability and Power', paper presented to Workshop on Exploring Expertise, Edinburgh, November.
Floyd, S.W. and Wooldridge, B. (1997), 'Middle Management's Strategic Influence and Organizational Performance', *Journal of Management Studies*, Vol. 34, No. 3, pp. 465-85.
Fores, M. (1996), 'The Professional as a Machine: Death of Each Day's Life', in I. Glover and M. Hughes (eds), *The Professional-Managerial Class: Contemporary British Management in the Pursuer Mode*, Avebury, Aldershot, pp. 109-26.
Fores, M. (1985), 'Newton on a Horse', *History of Science*, Vol. 23, No. 4, pp. 351-378.
Fores, M. and Pratt, J. (1987), 'Engineering: Our Last Chance', *Higher Education Review*, Vol. 19, No. 3, pp. 5-26.
Forester, T. (1987), *High-Tech Society: The Story of the Information Technology Revolution*, Basil Blackwell, Oxford.
Francis, A., Turk, J. and Willman, P. (1983), *Power, Efficiency and Institutions: A Critical Appraisal of the 'Markets and Hierarchies' Paradigm*, Heinemann, London.

Freidson, E. (1994), *Professionalism Reborn: Theory, Prophecy and Policy*, Polity Press, Cambridge.

Frenkel, S., Korczynski, M., Donoghue, L. and Shire, K. (1995), 'Re-constituting Work: Trends Towards Knowledge, Work and Info-normative Control', *Work, Employment and Society*, Vol. 9, No. 4, pp. 773-96.

Fulcher, J. (1997), 'Did British society change character in the 1920s or the 1980s?', *British Journal of Sociology*, Vol. 48, No. 3, pp. 514-21.

Galbraith, J.K.(1958), *The Affluent Society*, Hamish Hamilton, London.

Gardner, H. (1984), *Frames of Mind: the Theory of Multiple Intelligences*, Heinemann, London.

Glover, I.A. (1992), 'Wheels within Wheels: Predicting and Accounting for Fashionable Alternatives to Engineering', in G. Lee and C. Smith (eds), *Engineers in Management: International Comparisons*, Routledge, London, pp 20-40.

Glover, I. and Hughes, M. (eds) (1996), *The Professional-Managerial Class: Contemporary British Management in the Pursuer Mode*, Avebury, Aldershot.

Glover, I. and Tracey, P. (1997), 'In Search of *Technik*: Will Engineering Outgrow Management?', *Work, Employment and Society*, Vol. 11, No. 4, pp. 759-76.

Grandori, A. (1997), 'Agency, Markets and Hierarchies', in *The International Encyclopaedia of Business and Management Handbook of Organizational Behaviour*, A. Sorge and M. Warner (eds), International Thomson, London, pp. 64-78.

Hales, C. (1993), *Managing Through Organization: The Management Process, Forms of Organization and the Work of Managers*, Routledge, London.

Hassard, J. and Parker, M. (eds) (1994), *Towards a New Theory of Organization*, Routledge, London.

Herrigel, G. (1996), *Industrial Constructions: The Sources of German Industrial Power*, Cambridge University Press, New York.

Hickson, D.J. (ed.) (1997), *Exploring Management Across the World*, Penguin, Harmondsworth.

Higgins, W. and Clegg, S.R. (1988), 'Enterprise Calculation and Manufacturing Decline', *Organization Studies*, Vol. 9, No. 1, pp. 69-89.

Irwin, A. (1995), *Citizen Science: A Study of People, Expertise and Sustainable Development*, Routledge, London.

Jenkins, D. (1996), *Managing Empowerment*, Random House, London.

Jewkes, J., Sawers, D. and Stillerman, R. (1958), *The Sources of Invention*, Macmillan, London.

Jones, T.C., Currie, W.L. and Dugdale, D. (1993), 'Accounting and Technology in Britain and Japan: learning from field research', *Management Accounting Research*, Vol. 4, pp. 109-37.

Kochen, M. (1984), 'A New Concept of Information Society', in B. El-Hadidy and E.E. Horne (eds), *The Infrastructure of an Information Society*, Elsevier, Amsterdam, pp. 25-38.

Kotter, J. R. (1982), *The General Managers*, Free Press, New York.

Kumar, K. (1995), *From Post-Industrial to Post-Modern Society: New Theories of the Contemporary World*, Blackwell, Oxford.

Lane, C. (1989), 'From 'Welfare Capitalism' to 'Market Capitalism': A Comparative Review of Trends Towards Employment Flexibility in the Labour Markets of Three Major European Countries', *Sociology*, Vol. 23, No. 4, pp. 583-610.

Langrish, J., Gibbons, M., Evans, W.G. and Jevons, F.R. (1972), *Wealth from Knowledge: A Study of Innovations in Industry*, Macmillan, London.

Locke, R.R. (1984), *The End of the Practical Man: Entrepreneurship and Higher Education in Germany, France and Great Britain, 1880-1940*, Jai Press, Greenwich, Connecticut.

Lorenz, A. (1990), 'Out of the Race', *The Sunday Times*, 22 July, 4.9.

Loveridge, R. and Pitt, M. (1992), *The Strategic Management of Technological Innovation*, Wiley, Chichester.

Lyles, M.A. and Schwenk, C.R. (1992), 'Top Management, Strategy and Organizational Knowledge-Structures', *Journal of Management Studies*, Vol. 29, No. 2, pp. 154-74.

Lyon, D. (1988), *The Information Society: Issues and Illusions*, Polity, Cambridge.

Macdonald, K.M. (1995), *The Sociology of Professions*, Sage, London.

Machlup, F. (1980), *Knowledge: Its Creation, Distribution and Economic Significance: Volume 1*, Princeton University Press, Princeton.

Maffin, D., Thwaites, A., Alderman, N., Braiden, P. and Hills, B. (1997), 'Managing the Product Development Process: Combining Best Practice with Company and Project Contexts', *Technology Analysis and Strategic Management*, Vol. 9, No. 1, pp. 53-74.

McKinlay, A. and Starkey, K. (1988), *Competitive Strategies and Organizational Change*, Vol. 9, No. 4, pp. 555-71.

McRae, H. (1992), *The World in 2020: Power, Culture and Prosperity*, Harvard Business School Press, Boston, Mass.

Meiksins, P. and Smith, C. (1996), *Engineering Labour: Technical Workers in Comparative Perspective*, Verson, London.

Meyer, J.W., Boli, J., Thoman, G.M. and Ramirez, F.O. (1997), 'World Society and the Nation-State', *American Journal of Sociology*, Vol. 103, No. 1, pp. 144-81.

Mills, C. W. (1956), *The Power Elite*, OUP, New York.

Molloy, S. and Schwenk, C.R. (1995), 'The Effects of Information Technology on Strategic Decision-Making', *Journal of Management Studies*, Vol. 32, No. 3, pp. 283-307.

Nichols, W.A.T. (1969), *Ownership, Control and Ideology*, Allen and Unwin, London.

Pavalko, R.M. (1971), *Sociology of Occupations and Professions*, Peacock, Ithaca, Illinois.

Pavitt, K. (1990), 'What We Know About the Strategic Management of Technology', *California Management Review*, Spring, pp. 17-26.

Pitt, M. and Clarke, K. (1997), 'Frames of Significance: Technological Agenda-forming for Strategic Advantage', *Technology Analysis and Strategic Management*, Vol. 9, No. 3, pp. 251-69.

Poster, M. (1990), *The Mode of Information: Poststructuralism and Social Context*, Polity Press, Oxford.

Powell, W.W. and DiMaggio, P. (1991), *The New Institutionalism in Organizational Analysis*, University of Chicago Press, Chicago and London.

Prichard, C. and Willmott, H. (1997), 'Just How Managed is the McUniversity?', *Organization Studies*, Vol. 18, No. 2, pp. 287-316.

Raelin, J.A. (1992), 'Cross-cultural Implications of Professional/Managerial Conflict', *Journal of General Management*, Vol. 17, No. 3, pp. 16-30.

Reed, M.I. (1988), 'The Problem of Human Agency in Organizational Analysis', *Organization Studies*, Vol. 9, No. 1, pp. 33-46.

Reed, M.I. (1989), *The Sociology of Management*, Prentice-Hall, London.

Reed, M.I. (1997), 'In Praise of Dualism: Rethinking Agency and Structure in Organizational Analysis', *Organization Studies*, Vol. 18, No. 1, pp. 21-42.

Reid, S. and Garnsey, E. (1997), 'The Growth of small high-tech firms: destinies and destinations of Innovation Centre 'graduates'', *New Technology, Work and Employment*, Vol. 11, No. 2, pp. 84-91.

Rowlinson, M. (1997), *Organizations and Institutions: Perspectives in Economics and Sociology*, Macmillan, London.

Rubery, J. (1994), 'The British production regime: a societial-specific system', *Economy and Society*, Vol. 23, No. 3, pp. 335-54.

Saul, J.R. (1992), *Voltaire's Bastards: The Dictatorship of Reason in the West*, Free Press, New York.

Scarbrough, H. (1993), 'Problem - Solutions in the Management of Information Systems Expertise', *Journal of Management Studies*, Vol. 30, No. 6, pp. 939-55.

Scott, W.R. (1995), *Institutions and Organizations: Theory and Research*, Sage, Thousand Oaks, California.

Sorge, A. (1989), 'An Essay on Technical Change: Its Dimensions and Social and Strategic Context', *Organization Studies*, Vol. 10, No. 1, pp. 23-44.

Sorge, A. (1991), 'Strategic Fit and the Societal Effect: Interpreting Cross-National Comparisons of Technology, Organization and Human Resources', *Organization Studies*, Vol. 12, No. 2, pp. 161-90.

Sorge, A. and Warner, M. (1986), *Comparative Factory Management*, Gower, Aldershot.

Star, S.L. (1995), *Ecologies of Knowledge: Work and Politics in Science and Technology*, SUNY, New York.

Starbuck, W. (1992), 'Learning by knowledge intensive firms', *Journal of Management Studies*, Vol. 29, No. 6, pp. 713-740.

Stehr, N. (1991), 'The Power of Scientific Knowledge - and its limits', *Canadian Review of Sociology and Anthropology*, Vol. 28, pp. 461-80.

Sviolka, J.J. (1996), 'Knowledge Workers and Radically New Technology', *Sloan Management Review*, Summer, pp. 25-40.

Thompson, G., Frances, J., Levacic, R. and Mitchell, J. (eds.) (1991), *Markets, Hierarchy and Networks: The Coordination of Social Life*, Sage, London.

Tordenstahl, R. and Burrage, M. (1990), *The Formation of the Professions: Knowledge, State and Strategy*, Sage, London.

Webb, J. (1996), 'Vocabularies of Motive and the 'New' Management', *Work, Employment and Society*, Vol. 10, No. 2, pp. 251-71.

Webster, J. (1995), 'The Difficult Relationship between Technology and Society', *Work, Employment and Society*, Vol. 9, No. 4, pp. 797-810.

Wentworth, D.S. and Glover, I.A. (1998), 'Small Business Success: the Sectoral and the Dialectical', in M.G. Scott, P. Rosa and H. Klandt, *Educating Entrepreneurs for Wealth Creation*, Ashgate, Aldershot.

Whitley, R. (1988), 'The Management Sciences and Management Skills', *Organization Studies*, Vol. 9, No. 1, pp. 47-68.

Whitley, R. (1987), 'Taking Firms Seriously as Economic Actors: Towards a Sociology of Firm Behaviour', *Organization Studies*, Vol. 8, No. 2, pp. 125-47.

Whitley, R. (1974), *Social Processes of Scientific Development*, Routledge and Kegan Paul, London.

Williamson, O.E. (1975), *Markets and Hierarchies: Analysis and Antitrust Implications*, The Free Press, New York.

Willmott, H. (1997), ''Outing' Organizational Analysts: Some Reflections Upon Parker's Tantrum', *Organization*, Vol. 4, No. 2, pp. 255-68.

Willmott, H. (1993), 'Paradigms and Organizational Analysis', *Organization Studies*, Vol. 14, No. 5, pp. 681-719.

Wood, R.C. (1994), 'Postmodernism', *Work, Employment and Society*, Vol. 8, No. 3, pp. 459-63.

Wood, S.J. (1989), 'New Wave Management?', *Work, Employment and Society*, Vol. 3, No. 3, pp. 379-402.

Woodiwiss, A. (1996), 'Searching for Signs of Globalisation', *Sociology*, Vol. 30, pp. 799-810.

Part V

Discussion

15 Fragmentation, cooperation and continuity: towards a flexible technocratic synthesis?

Ian Glover and Michael Hughes

Introduction

What relevance do the contents of this book have for the future of management in the UK? We have chosen to define the term profession quite widely for our purposes: a knowledge base of some kind, and a fiduciary element in the relationship between the expert labour in question and either its clients or employers or both or all that we have required. This means that we are concerned with most of the UK's qualified and expert 'managers' and specialist members of management teams, and thus directly with the majority of all of the UK's managers, and indirectly with virtually all of them.

In this final chapter we review arguments and evidence contained in its predecessors and go on to suggest that 'business and professional technocracy' is the best term available for describing and explaining the kind of regime that is evolving to manage employment, work and work organizations in the UK. To do this, we first briefly discuss and consider the general direction of the UK's economy and of the character of its management. Second, we briefly consider the general prospects for the UK's professions and for each of the three kinds of them, independent, public and organizational.

Thirdly, we take specific examples from each of the three kinds, namely doctors as our example of independent and public sector professionals, the police as a specific example of the latter, and engineers, bankers and IT specialists as examples of organizational professionals. We have chosen these particular examples because of their divergent character: they span the independent, public and organizational sectors; they include very long-established, firmly if relatively recently established, and new professional occupations, and all have experienced considerable change in recent years.

We then briefly discuss all of the professions and sectors of professional employment which the chapters in the book have dealt with, and in doing so we refer when necessary to other professions like those of architects, social workers, academics and scientists, whose members work alongside 'our' professionals. Our intention here is to explore the general character and flow of contemporary changes, and to pave the way for the fifth and final main section of the chapter before its concluding one. In this fifth section we describe and discuss the probable evolution of management in the UK from the 1950s to the early twenty-first century as one from 'gentlemen and players' to a 'business and professional technocracy'. In our discussion of the relevant changes we consider some of their implications for education and training for most kinds and sectors of employment and for patterns of employment including those related to age, the life cycle and aspects of social welfare. Finally, in the concluding section of the chapter we briefly summarise the main arguments of the book, and make a few suggestions for policy and research.

The general direction of change

Our perception of the UK's recent and current economic performance is guardedly optimistic. We see the UK as having experienced various and varied kinds of economic difficulty since the time, in the middle decades of the nineteenth century, when in spite of the varied difficulties of *that* period, the UK was the world's leading economy. The era from the reign of England's first Queen Elizabeth to that of its second (and the UK's first) was one of 'unprecedented and almost unbelievable success' by virtually any standard (Glover, Tracey and Currie, 1998). In overseas exploration and trade, in engineering and industrialization, in exploration, colonisation and settlement, in political life, in war, in intellectual and leisure pursuits, and in influence, the achievements were *normally* path-breaking and dramatic. However differences in resource endowments and in aspirations made *relative* economic and, to a lesser extent, political, decline inevitable. Thus and as was also argued elsewhere, the 'notion that the UK underwent some kind of collective identity crisis and failure of will, as if a declaration had been made that [a degree of] (self-imposed) failure ought to be experienced after centuries of continuous development or success, [was] very compatible with the conclusions about educational and occupational choices (Coleman, 1973) and social movements and ideological and organizational choices (Glover, 1985, 1991) long apparent in writings on the UK's relative decline' (Glover, Tracey and Currie, op cit).

What we are discussing here is a matter of national confusion and uncertainty, of 'problems of success' writ very large and manifested in such things as institutions and invented traditions with partly celebratory assumptions built into them; in half-hearted, arms'-length approaches to core activities like factory production in particular and to wealth creation in general; and in a belief in the value of generalism rather than in that of the sector-specific or preferably both, influencing vocational higher education; and in the notion of engineering as the 'mere' application of new scientific knowledge, drawing on the partly Victorian assumption that hard work was unfit for a gentleman. Displacement activities have been conspicuous parts of the syndrome: examples from recent years include human resource management, business process re-engineering and total quality management. Each of these can add unnecessary complexity to management and organization without getting to the bottom of the problems that they are ostensibly remedies for. There has also been much interesting confusion about the supposed problem of short-termism in financing private and public sector activities, including the development of human capital. What is long-term on one side of the Pyrenees (or the North Sea) is short-term on the other and at different times as well as in different places, and apparently short-termist structures can be operated in long-term ways, and vice-versa.

Since the rather worrying 1970s a great deal of powerfully argued but often contradictory ideas have been deployed in attempts to explain the UK's perceived economic and other difficulties (e.g., Wiener, 1981; Barnett, 1972, 1986, 1995; Sorge and Warner, 1986; Locke, 1989; Edgerton, 1991; Rubinstein, 1993; Coates and Hillard, 1995). Yet whatever the true character of the UK's economic performance in the last 150 or so years, which have produced and witnessed almost earth-shattering economic, social, technical, political, military, scientific and other developments, the impression persists of 'a deeply conservative yet very resilient and sophisticated society which is capable of making itself dramatically open to experience' (Glover, Tracey and Currie, 1998). A very powerful tradition of creativity and innovativeness at all levels of society is part of this, along with such ongoing problems as a tendency 'to overvalue inspiration and to undervalue perspiration, to defer too much to commanding social presence ..., and celebrity and heroism, and even heroic failure ... [and belief] in biologically fixed levels of ability ... out of tune with Japanese and much Western European management practice ... and ... archaic, undemocratic sentimentality about the past and its living embodiments like the monarchy' (Glover, Tracey and Currie, 1988).

The UK's economic performance compared with its competitors has suggested, at times in the 1980s, but especially in the mid-1990s, that a century and half or so of relative decline is drawing to a close. Other mature economies have been experiencing their problems of success and UK management is increasingly highly and more or less relevantly educated, and also more confident, pragmatic and determined than it has been for decades (on economic performance, see O'Mahony and Wagner, 1995, and O'Mahony and Wagner with Paulson, 1995, and on UK management quality, see Lawrence, 1990, Barry, Bosworth and Wilson, 1997; and Glover, Tracey and Currie, 1998). Manufacturing performance appears to have been improving significantly in ways which suggest that many of the failures and excesses of the 1950s, 1960s and 1970s were too bad to be true. Many old problems, of short-termist and arms'-length management, persist in many manufacturing sectors, but the average and general trends appear to be positive. This suggests that Wiener's (1981) slightly romantic perception of the UK as 'an industrial society with an anti-industrial culture', always exaggerated (Edgerton, 1991), is increasingly out of date: there was a disease, but it never infected the whole body economic and politic, and it is on the run.

Our perception of the general future of the UK's economy and society also tends towards guarded optimism. The UK has long traditions of innovation and pragmatism, very considerable strengths in education and research of virtually all kinds, rediscovered concern for detail and hard work, renewed humility and openness to foreign experience following an era of perceived failure, very efficient farming, long and successful experience of international finance, of overseas trade and of overseas contact in general, considerable political and diplomatic experience, experience of complex project management and of managing multinationals and a willingness to make fundamental changes once they are felt to be really needed. On the other hand weaknesses in qualifications and skills persist, especially at the lower levels of employment, and also take the form of social, economic and educational polarisation, the uncertain and varied status and power of experts of different kinds, over-complicated divisions of labour, cynicism and sentimentality about past glories and present realities alike, ongoing tendencies in parts of the education system and the civil service to encourage arms'-length attitudes towards detail, and confusion about moral and other values in a society under strain from rapid economic and sociopolitical change which is associated with shallow forms of elitism and stereotyping.

There is much uncertainty in the UK, as is the case with many other countries, about how its overseas trading and other economic activities will develop. However the growing variety and complexity of the qualifications and expertise of UK management do not augur badly in a world offering many opportunities. The UK generally has closer relationships with the Far East and North America than its Continental partners have, and this is also clearly positive.

In chapter one we noted how Crompton (1990) and Ackroyd (1994) had suggested that the UK's professions tended to prosper in softer times and to have their growth stifled in harder ones. Both had tended to be more focused on the public sector caring or welfare professions than on others when they made these suggestions, and they had also noted how some of the organizational and private sector professional activities like IT work and commercial law prosper considerably during periods of tough and aggressively entrepreneurial wealth creation and rapid technical change.

Also in chapter one, we discussed ways in which, in the last two decades or so, professions and their members might be being outflanked by the production of vocationally educated but not professionally qualified graduates so that 'when everybody is somebody, nobody is anybody'. We felt that they might be undermined by commercialism and subordinated by managerialism as their management became more unified, simplified, customer-responsive and controlling. We suggested, as many of the authors of chapters two to fourteen do, that all of these threats have often been real and effective. However we cannot see how most of the more established or the currently newer or expanding professions, in the context of the ideas about their current and future situation that we have just described, can fail to prosper. The future looks as if it will combine a mixture of tough and thrusting times, and softer, and in the fully negative sense, harder ones. Tougher times should favour the more hard-nosed professions and softer times the more caring ones, as before. Professional and other senior occupations which have less overtly sophisticated and complex knowledge and skill bases, and ones which are more understandable by and accessible to lay people, such as those of the police, school teachers, social workers and librarians, are likely either to remain or to become almost entirely graduate occupations with professional aspirations and with some professional attributes, and more often professions *de facto* than *sui generis*.

The general prospects for professions

These may be summarised as follows, partly on the basis of the arguments of the last few paragraphs. The power bases of the emerging so-called 'knowledge' professions like those of IT specialists, management consultants, public relations experts and counsellors and therapists of various kinds tend, except in the first of these cases, to be much less tangible and public than those of the more traditional independent and organizational ones. Together competition between the latter and the growth of the former create a picture of fragmenting power structures. However most professional groups or groupings have strengths which derive largely from a combination of their expertise and the asymmetrical power relations characteristic of virtually all advanced (and other) societies. Thus much continuity is apparent, although professions are increasingly subject to strong external forces and increasingly equipped to cooperate creatively with each other. Management teams and organizations are likely to become more efficient, but not much more democratic, as a result.

IT specialists are really engineers. Their main professional association is the British Computer Society which is a constituent member of the Engineering Council, which, in name and intention at least, represents all of the UK's engineers. They design or engineer hardware and software and they programme computers and analyse and develop the systems whereby computers are put to use in the real world. Their power bases are relatively intangible and private more because of their novel character than because of their specificity to user attributes and needs. In this way they tend to differ from the other three types of so-called knowledge professionals mentioned along with them above: management consultants, public relations experts, and counsellors and therapists. The knowledge bases of some of these three types of professional vary considerably in terms of substance. In general, such 'knowledge workers', as was argued in chapter fourteen, are unlikely ever to be as powerfully established as professionals as accountants, doctors, engineers and lawyers, whose knowledge bases and skills are much more tangible and substantial as well as much more established.

As was also noted in chapter fourteen, many jobs are nowadays performed by people who are over-qualified for them. Such people, whose qualifications are often at least nominally on an intellectual par with those of professionally qualified graduates, are naturally tempted to try to dignify their work and their employment with professional status and the other trappings of professionalism.

The independent professions, law, medicine, accountancy, architecture, civil and other consulting engineering, management consultancy, surveying and so on, generally enjoy broadly good long-term prospects. In some cases, as with doctors and public health care, and architects and big building and other construction companies and direct labour organizations, hierarchical coordination may continue to remove large numbers of professional clients from their markets. However this is not a generally new phenomenon, and on the whole the services of independent professionals are likely to be increasingly affordable and attractive as incomes, personal and corporate, continue to rise.

The public sector professions have been vulnerable to commercialisation and privatisation and to stronger managerial control. The main responses available to public sector professional occupations are 'self-imposed' efficiency savings and the development of such 'management' abilities as marketing, public relations and financial control, making self-management an obviously efficient option and making individual practitioners look like excellent candidates for strategic management teams. In local government, public utilities, the police service, health care and education, professionals generally *are* the line managers, with considerable and crucial hands-on expertise as well as the potential to manage it strategically. A major argument deployed against private sector professionals in the past was that they pursued their own interests and developed their own practices at the expense, as in engineering, of normally far more important core line functions like production (Child et al, 1983). This argument has been used, inappropriately in some key respects, against public sector professionals (see Chaston and Badger, 1993, for example). The onus is on such professionals to stand up for themselves by pointing this out. Doctors, for example, should reclaim lost territory in the NHS, by equipping themselves with relevant accounting, financial, marketing and personnel management knowledge. Academics should do the same in universities, too. In all such cases management expertise should be the servant and not the master of professional practices and sector-specific concerns.

Similar points apply to organizational professionals although with even more force in most cases: self-management and managerial resources should be used to create climates of constructive cooperation and organizational learning. Some of the research reported by Glover, Tracey and Currie (1998) and by Glover and Tracey (1997) suggests that in many of the more competent UK manufacturing and construction companies, this is what has been happening. Criticisms of professional groupings working against each other have apparently been heard and acted upon.

In all sectors the dangers and issues are broadly the same although their specific nature and relevance varies. Professions are, at best, bulwarks against the overweening and irresponsible exercise of state and market power. In the public sector responsible professional self-management should mean responsible use of public resources on the behalf of and for taxpaying citizens. In the private sector, the organizational professionals employed there should be examples of ethical and responsible accounting, employment, production, design, marketing and so one. Independent professionals should exemplify, not least and not only because it is very much in their own interests to do so, the highest ethical and technical standards. There points are both elementary and old but they are nonetheless often forgotten or ignored, especially in particularly soft or particularly hard times, or in ones immaturely misperceived as such.

Some specific examples

Professions at bay generally need to be professions adapting themselves to changing circumstances. Here we use five examples of this: bankers, engineers and IT specialists as organizational professionals, the police and doctors as public sector ones and, again, doctors as independent ones. In the case of IT specialists and doctors our points are relatively brief, because most of what needs to be said here is in chapters thirteen and fourteen regarding the former, and in chapter four regarding the latter.

In chapter twelve, Mark Hughes discussed bankers as members of an organizational profession whose terms and conditions and kinds of employment were largely employer-determined. Since he wrote and developed his paper further, further changes have been taking place in banking, ones which were spelt out at length to us in an extended interview with a senior executive of a high street clearing bank in the summer of 1998. Mark Hughes had located bankers quite firmly among organizational professionals. They were qualified and trained like professionals but they were first and foremost employees of the banks, and in these ways they resembled accountants, engineers and sales and marketing experts employed in industrial and commercial companies and in the public sector.

Our interviewee agreed with this perception. Bank managers and other expert specialists in high street banking in the UK were professional insofar as most sat the professional examinations of the Chartered Institute of Banking, and insofar as they provided services to lay people and businesses. The Chartered Institute of Banking's examinations were of degree standard and bankers had to pass them in order to gain promotion in almost all cases. However the Institute had nothing to do with banking business and management. It existed for study and educational purposes and it neither advised nor became otherwise directly involved with the tasks of those who managed banks.

His own bank recruited graduates from all disciplines. Newly recruited graduates had to pass the Chartered Institute of Banking's examinations within two years of joining the bank, or leave, or at least be taken off its 'fast track' route to promotion. Banking careers were less secure in general than they had been twenty or forty years earlier. The 'ban' on inter-bank recruitment had more or less gone, too, although in practice only a small percentage of a given bank's staff had worked for other banks. Banks were less paternal as employers than in the past, with even the cheap mortgages given to staff no longer as cheap relative to others as they once were.

The banks' emphasis on marketing had increased with better targeting of customers and with more integration of market positioning and overall strategy. The new culture was one of banks as shops selling money in the form of mortgages, overdrafts, loans and so on. Older members of staff had sometimes found the new culture a bit hard to adopt. Banking seemed to be more and more about closing deals. The old-fashioned 'Captain Mannering' culture of providing a service to local businesses and individuals had been replaced by one emphasizing efficiency and the bottom line, and quite hostile to costly 'fat' of any kind. There had been quite a dramatic change of image since the 1980s: an avuncular sort of organization had transformed itself into a group of thrusting retail outlets. Some of this had been mainly presentational, and to varying degrees the banks were still good employers. However expectations of staff had increasingly taken the form of quantified targets and the work was now 'far from cushy', with the experience of stress quite common.

Management fads of recent years, like total quality management, had not been used for very long or very widely by the banks. However control by costs had been developed and the banks were continually and increasingly judged by the stock market by their ratios. The key ratios included cost to income, with much emphasis on non-interest income such as arrangement fees and commission, and on employment costs. Traditionally staff had represented about 70 percent of a bank's costs. This percentage was now much lower than in the past. All of the clearing banks judged each other by their staff costs, with the ratio of overall costs to income being seen as the major guide to efficiency by all parties.

Some of the high street banks had had large scale early retirement and redundancy programmes and others had relied more on natural wastage to reduce staff costs. Some had put much more effort into training and retraining than others. The shape of banking employment had altered massively. For example older secretaries had either become expert with information technology, or mainstream bank staff such as tellers. Promotion, in the past, had tended to be more of a matter of seniority, of dead men's shoes, of gentlemanly behaviour and length of service. Nowadays, however, the ability to process work and to produce solutions was emphasized much more. People were wanted who could sell, who could recognise sales potential and who could reel people in, who had a pleasant manner and a hard nose. It was important neither to undersell nor to oversell the banks' products. Overselling was likely to displease the regulatory authorities. There was significantly greater use of credit scoring than in the past. It was used for all sorts of products and although it was by no means an infallible guide to lending its use did seem to reduce losses significantly.

There had been no shift of power from head offices to branches. The balance of power in banks had always been towards the centre and this would almost certainly never change. Branch managers had less power to lend money than in the past, and were more than ever subject to the application of systematic rules and sanctions. The most able staff tended to be sucked into the centre earlier in their careers than in the past. Branch management was only middle management. The role of branch manager had shrunk considerably. Nevertheless the staff of branch banks had to sell, to be more proactive sales people than in the past. Such people were 'customer service officers' and on the whole the term 'bank clerk' no longer meant much. Staff were almost all front office people now. There were virtually no back office staff. All of the work that such people had done in the past, processing cheques and so on, was now picked up by vans and done elsewhere.

Loyalty had traditionally been a major force in banking employment. To some extent it still was. Historically banks had been paternalist employers, who helped employees in financial trouble for example. This had changed somewhat. Nowadays really poor performers got into trouble, in a generally tougher climate. The banks still had a lot to learn about using information technology. IT was still not 'core banking' and the banks tended to oscillate between employing IT staff and outsourcing their work. However there was considerable investment in staff IT training and many older, as well as younger, employees were now reasonably and often very expert users of computers.

Deregulation of financial services and growing competition between growing numbers and kinds of provider had been changing the balance of power between the stakeholders and pressure groups associated with banking. Regulatory bodies like the various Ombudsman schemes and investment, banking, insurance and pensions authorities had been developed and revamped in various ways and this had direct effects on how the banks worked. The banks feared bad publicity and were keen to be or to continue to be regarded as helpful yet discriminating lenders. The Bank of England continued to monitor the banks to make sure that they did not lend too much money. The issues of whether state deregulation had led to more public and industry regulation was an academic one, but the banks did seem increasingly subject to pressures from several directions. The national financial market was more complex than in the past. Now that banks gave mortgages they were subject to building society regulations, for example. One set of controls and rules often seemed to be replacing another. The banks had always operated in sector-specific ways to some extent, with managers in rural communities being knowledgeable about farming, and so on. One of the high street banks had made itself expert in recent times in the organization and financing of management buy-outs.

This example of bankers as organizational professionals is one of members of commercial organizations providing services to the public in ways which are profitable but also largely self-regulating in the cause of economic and social responsibility. There is little evidence of very fundamental changes in what banks and bankers do, although plenty of evidence about important ones in how they do it.

In chapter one, in discussing Jane Goodsir's chapter, we described police officers as not untypical of other professions which provide services under state mediation and control. Jane Goodsir's chapter was written in 1993 at a time when police professional autonomy faced a major challenge. The points which follow come from recent discussions with Jane Goodsir and with contacts in the police and our own reading. The more radical reforms proposed by Sheehy were shelved, as the police became involved in internal debates about reconfiguring the service. Some important reforms have been carried through, affecting the accountability of more senior officers. At lower levels, police discipline and control remain influenced by the 'double jeopardy' principle. Internal disciplinary proceedings relating to serious offences, such as deaths in custody, are still conducted to the high legal standard of proof required in a criminal trial. The Police Complaints Authority and the Association of Chief Police Officers have however successfully argued for a reduction in the burden of proof, and change will take effect in 1999. However the number of complaints against the Police from the public has risen. Within the police service there have been a number of high profile sex discrimination cases brought by serving women officers, indicating that there may be difficulties in changing the culture of the service. By proceeding slowly with a series of low profile internal reforms the police have successfully resisted external bids to impose root and branch change, despite internal pressure. In this respect, they have retained a good deal of autonomy in relation to the conduct of police business in comparison with other public sector 'quasi-professions'.

There has been a somewhat cyclical aspect to the ways in which the Police have effectively fended off external pressures for reform to the system in the 1990s. All external proposals regarding pensions, performance related pay and performance evaluation have been defeated by promising internal reforms, which it was claimed would exceed public expectations. Cases of particularly bad management, or the sexual abuse and harassment of women officers, have effectively served to divert attention from underlying problems and the managerialist attempts on behalf of governments to attack them. Through discussion of underlying problems, to the proposal of managerialist remedies, to promising, and to a small degree delivering, internal reforms as an alternative, while using specific instances of bad practice as smokescreens, to general but inevitably poorly informed debates about bribery and corruption, the police have in effect seen everyone off. In doing so they have been aided considerably by their highly competent legalistic approach to problems, which acts as a quiet but powerful weapon against often confused and diffuse managerialist efforts at reform.

The increasing employment of graduates in the police service has been associated with changes to police education and training. However such changes have not done much to address the tasks of police officers on the ground. To develop a stratum of 'police managers' would be unlikely to make a difference to the ability of streetwise police officer to cheat and lie. The service contains two cultures: top managers, traditionally looking outwards, at the top, and/or versus operational managers who always protect their 'men' against criticisms from the former and from external sources. It appears to be very difficult for the police to strike an appropriate balance, especially in the big hard cities.

There is an officer class in the police, consisting primarily of fast track graduate recruits, often recruited in mid-career, aged thirty-plus. However the service remains a closed community impenetrable by the notion of Police Management and able to fend off, not only attempts to use bureaucratic management controls, but also attempts to use new technology in ways which would make them more accountable and efficient. One obvious asset possessed by the Police in the defence of its territory is, of course, the uniquely vulnerable character of its clientele.

Another is the high level of public relations competence, underpinned in many respects by genuinely good intentions, of top police officers.

Police officers, with their near-monopoly of state-sanctioned violence, enjoy *de facto* self-regulation. They have always enjoyed considerable autonomy in going about their work. They have learnt, for over a century and a half, how to guard this autonomy jealously, and with the support of various state sanctions and privileges. Yet their knowledge base is diffuse, to say the least, both even if and partly because its foundations include jurisprudence and moral philosophy. Moreover their average level of qualification is not high: 'neither thick nor genius' was one way in which the preferred standard of candidate has been described. The internal police examinations are essential for promotion and are in three parts: basic police duties, criminal, and road traffic. They are normally taken in the early years of a career and are based on a mixture of legal and other practical knowledge. It is not necessary to be a graduate in order to be promoted, and graduates are not favoured explicitly when applying for promotion although a degree can be seen as another string to an applicant's bow. However Graduate Entrants are eligible for and expected to seek to secure places in the accelerated promotion scheme. Most of them succeed in doing this, but in order to do so they have to have undergone a two-year probationary period and to have passed all of the police examinations at their first sitting.

Once on the fast track an officer can achieve promotion to sergeant in three years and to chief inspector in seven. This is relatively new and somewhat different to the traditional culture of everyone starting as a probationary constable, as everyone still does, but with there being a more or less completely level playing field for promotion irrespective of education or social background. Policing is changing in some respects but the strong traditional culture of pragmatism sensibly persists, underpinned by state and public support. Managerial fads and fashions appear to have had little long term effect. For example the title of Chief Superintendent (Personnel) has sometimes been altered to Director of Human Resources, and then back to the original, without the tasks being performed changing much at all. More civilian support staff are employed than in the past, and they often enter the service at senior levels. However their roles are advisory and supportive rather than executive or operational. Amalgamations of forces are currently being considered and are thought to be likely to happen in some quarters. The changes of title from 'force' to 'service' and the slowly growing recruitment of women and members of ethnic minority groups and the relaxation of height restrictions signify, like the use of IT, genetic fingerprinting and the psychological profiling of offenders, a public sector organizational profession adapting to changes in society without changing in any fundamental sense. The police service is probably less vulnerable to commercialisation, privatisation and managerialism than most if not all other public sector professions because of the unique, uniquely entrenched, and powerful, nature of its role. It is difficult for other kinds of expert labour to encroach on or outflank the police and their work because it is so, perhaps exceptionally, practical, and with so diffuse a knowledge base.

Similar points apply to doctors, insofar as they also perform a unique, virtually indispensable role in society. However, unlike the police service, the NHS is relatively vulnerable to use as a political football in the name, although not necessarily the cause, of greater efficiency (Kelly and Glover, 1996). The knowledge base of doctors has much more of a monolithic quality than that of the police and it also tends to be much more prestigious. State sanction and support of the activities of doctors is, like that of the police, very strong and entrenched, if not perhaps quite so unquestioning.

Goodwin (1998, p. 27) attributed the continuing power of doctors in the NHS to the long-established state-sanctioned influence and power of their professional associations and to their individual power in hospitals, health authorities and general practices. Doctors were ' "production managers" ... [who] determine[d] the outputs by the admission, diagnosis, treatment and discharge of patients'. Their 'organisation power ... and the often enormous resource implications of their decisions' meant that the NHS had put great efforts into involving them in management, 'rather than them being managed at arm's length as a discrete professional group'. Such involvement is likely to strengthen the already (and still) dominant hand of doctors within the NHS. Medical education is gradually being broadened to include more 'management' components and practising doctors are increasingly taking postgraduate taught masters' degrees such as MBAs in Health Care Management. Like engineers of our acquaintance, doctors taking such courses tend *not* to find such courses exceptionally intellectually demanding as opposed to stimulating, useful and interesting.

As for engineers themselves, these largely organizational professionals - though significant numbers of them are employed in the public sector in education, central and local government, the armed forces and so on, and as both independent professionals and employees in consultancies - are unlikely to face the kinds of difficulty that they have experienced when industry in the UK was either in the doldrums or in serious decline. The tide appears to have turned, or at least to be turning: the problems understood, a range of solutions known, the context more international, go-ahead and outward-looking than in the past. Engineers are no longer less well paid than accountants or university professors and civil servants. They are overwhelmingly graduates, they generally dominate senior executive posts in industry and they are increasingly conversant with financial data and marketing and strategic management expertise (Barry, Bosworth and Wilson, 1997; Tracey and Glover, 1997; Glover, Tracey and Currie, 1998; Tracey, 1998). Their professional collective organization is still rather fragmented but the umbrella body for the specialist engineering institutions has a reasonable to good record, since its establishment in the early 1980s, of improving public perceptions of engineers and engineering, of encouraging the broadening and other development of qualifications, and of working towards greater intra-professional unity.

Public perceptions of engineers, especially those of mechanical ones, still sometimes tend, in our experience at least, to associate them with a grimy past, whereas 'technology', especially that of the microelectronic variety, has newer and cleaner connotations. This is a positive factor for the future of the engineering profession because IT professionals, most of whom are in reality engineers of various kinds, are largely unorganized, but heavily in demand and very well paid and likely to remain so for a considerable time. There is much evidence to suggest (cf. Currie, 1995) that many of them are dissatisfied with poor management of themselves and their talents, and their main professional association, the British Computer Society (BCS), as noted earlier a member institution of the Engineering Council, stands to benefit greatly from the present situation. The BCS currently (mid-1998) has about 35,000 members. Of these about 8,000 are students and about 7,000 overseas members, leaving a core membership of about 20,000 people. BCS staff have estimated that its potential membership is 500,000. Even if the BCS was to recruit 25 percent of these the result would be a considerable boost to the income and to the power, image and status of the engineering profession.

There can be little doubt that - far from constituting a chimerical and soft-edged 'knowledge worker' professional grouping - members of IT occupations have substantial, albeit usually latent, power available to them. The scale and severity of the problems associated with their employment, as discussed by Wendy Currie and Colin Bryson in chapter thirteen, is evidence of this. The point is reinforced further when the breadth of the considerations raised or linked to their work and employment, discussed by Stephen Ackroyd, Ian Glover, Wendy Currie and Stephen Bull and in chapter fourteen is appreciated. While quasi-populist notions of knowledge work and of information societies may be exaggerated, the importance of efficient production and use of information for managing all kinds of organization in increasingly complex and international contexts cannot be ignored.

The three types of profession

There can be little doubt that the main perceived threats to professional control over employment and work in the UK are external. Faster rates of technical change and more intense competition may mean that increasingly global markets subject occupational and organizational hierarchies to pressures that they can find very hard indeed to withstand. Outflanking of professional authority is more credible when professionals increasingly work alongside graduates rather than people significantly less highly qualified than themselves, as was the case before foreign competition helped to generate pressures for higher education to expand and become more vocational. When senior executives are subject to strong external pressures to perform it is tempting for them to co-opt, informally as well as formally, non-professional line managers and/or auxiliary and support staff in order to control (to undermine and to subordinate) professionals whom they perceive as being too individualistic.

The main pressures to which the independent professions have been subjected have been those associated with deregulation. Interestingly, the case of banking, with banking members of an organizational profession, suggests that deregulation actually takes the form of the replacement of state regulation by self-regulation, by private but also public bodies financed, organized and run by professionals and sectors themselves. This 're-regulation' often appears to be more effective and indeed forceful than the sometimes quite weak and often unenforced and occasionally almost completely moribund forms of state regulation which preceded them.

The two chapters on law and management consultancy as independent professions offer considerable evidence of commercialisation of professional activities. Commercial and other forms of civil law are now, quite overtly, big business, and criminal law is hardly a poor man's profession conducted solely with the welfare of the general public, including its more vulnerable members, in mind. Management consultancy is arguably only a pseudo-profession, a source of employment for charlatans and failures. However this cynical and extreme view should be balanced by one which recognises that much consultancy work is mere outsourcing, by managements which find the consultancy market a more cost-effective source of expertise than their own staff. Also many consultants are in possession of serious and weighty knowledge and expertise. Further, while it may take many years before management consultants are organized and respected enough to have a royal charter, if indeed they ever are, many of them are chartered members of established professions and employed by clients in ways similar to those associated with traditional independent fee-taking professionals.

Regarding doctors, members of a profession which is partly independent as such, and which still enjoys considerable independence and power within and around the public sector, the arguments of chapter four by Kelly and Glover emphasize the ongoing relevance of medical authority in conditions of populist and sometimes childishly frivolous mass affluence. They also suggest, if largely in implicit ways, that medical dominance in the UK's NHS is being upgraded or modernized, rather than destroyed, by attempts at top-down managerial and commercial 'reform'. Doctors appear likely to be medical technocrats in the future, equipped with serious and effective commercial, financial and political understanding, rather than the often intellectually impressive but sometimes narrow professional expertise of the present and past.

Doctors form a particularly powerful public sector profession as well as a traditionally and partly independent one. Our sort of tentative optimism about their future in the public sector is not much apparent in the view expressed by Charles Booth in his chapter on UK local government bodies' codes of professional ethics. He finds these rather weak, hypocritical and ineffectual, and evidence of lack of competence and commitment on the part of the relevant professions. However the professions that he deals with are weaker, newer ones, leisure professions whose members are almost entirely local government employees of sometimes uncertain status. It is possible to reconcile the (apparent) disparity between our views and those of Booth by suggesting that public sector professionals of all kinds are being better integrated into and involved in the management of their employing organizations than in the past.

This interpretation is fully in accord with the conclusions of Stuart Davies in his chapter on the museums profession, which has become more efficient and productive without losing its integrity and purpose. It is not completely at odds with Jane Goodsir's views about the police, spelt out earlier in this chapter as well as in her own, although the management into which that profession has long been integrated is principally and ultimately that of the state.

Both doctors and the police form powerful organizational professions in the public sector. The chapters on the organizational professions as such cover professions whose members are generally employed in private industry, commerce and finance. We have discussed engineers and IT specialists earlier in this chapter: suffice it to say here that their prospects both as employees and as members of professions look generally good. However one slightly worrying possibility would be for IT people, probably as members of the British Computer Society, to break away from the Engineering Council and most other engineers to form their own 'high-tech' professional grouping. For various reasons we consider this possible rather than probable, and think that even if it were to happen the long term effects would probably not be damaging, either to the relevant professionals, or to the economy and to society.

In chapter one we suggested that marketing might sensibly be described as an anti-profession, insofar as its most obvious goals are commercial. However the influence and membership of the Chartered Institute of Marketing continue to grow (Tracey, 1998) and as Don Bathie's chapter and the work of some marketing educators suggests (McDonagh and Prothero, 1996), the concerns of marketing professionals may becoming broader and more socially responsive than in the past. Marketing specialists are increasingly graduates in marketing or in similar business subjects with significant marketing content and are thus less often educated in non-relevant ways, or with little knowledge of operational, financial and human resource issues. Marketing and sales specialists probably form the largest occupational/functional/professional grouping in private sector management in the UK and have always been well represented at board and other senior levels. We do not think that this situation is likely to change greatly in the future, although all things remain possible, of course.

Similar kinds of argument apply to accountants, in spite of the pessimistic elements of the arguments of Robin Roslender et al, in chapter ten. These arguments do not deny the indispensability, perceived as well as real, of accounting and financial work in and for management. While they suggest that the golden years for careers in accountancy may be over they do nonetheless assume that accountants will be influential although not necessarily dominant members of top management teams for the foreseeable future. However we feel far more uncertain about the long-term future of personnel and human resource specialists. In chapter eleven Barbara Paterson shows how keen they have been to present themselves as useful to employers in different ways at different stages of business cycles. However they form the least numerous functional specialism in UK management and most of their specialist contributions are capable of being made by line managers and others, as when the former manage recruitment, staffing, deployment, training and appraisal, and when accountants manage reward systems and lawyers handle employment disputes. There is a sense in which the twentieth century history of welfare, personnel and human resource management in the UK is inseparable from that of post-imperial *angst* with undertones of the provision of hopefully simultaneously useful and caring employment for non-relevant graduates (Glover, 1992). Attempts to interpret the sociopolitical and economic role of personnel and human resource management in the UK in terms of its unusual and unusually strong historical roots seem to us more likely to be fruitful than ones which recruit explanations from recent and contemporary and often foreign philosophical developments, like postmodern thinking, most of which cannot have influenced many of the events to which they have been related, because they took place after the latter happened (cf. Legge, 1995). We do not think that practitioners of and proselytisers for personnel and human resource management will be any less resourceful in the future than they have been so far in justifying their existence. However we are less certain about the receptions that they will receive from colleagues in more credible and substantial specialisms.

We have already discussed bankers and IT specialists at some length in this chapter. Both groups had, and have, most attributes of organizational professionals: knowledge bases, qualifications, professional association, mainly salaried employment and some element of social responsibility. Both performed important economic roles and both were subject to managerial controls. The major difference between them was that whereas bankers were a well established group subject to significant externally imposed change, IT specialists formed a rapidly expanding new one which tended to impose change on others. The historical elements in the relevant chapters, by Hughes, Currie and Bryson, and Ackroyd et al, suggest, along with points included in this chapter, that all triumphs of markets over hierarchies, and all those of the latter over the former, are provisional in whatever people describe as developed and developing societies.

There are limits to the pressures that have been affecting all of the three kinds of profession that we have been discussing. Commercialism in the form of deregulation of independent professions and the imposition of internal markets and labour market flexibility in public and private sector organizations and the removal of restrictive practices, and commodification more generally, have tended to engender efficiency and entrepreneurial and other innovative activity. Managerial controls imposed on all sorts of profession have almost certainly, however, inhibited innovation and crushed ambition, albeit not universally. More, and more vocational, but non-professional, educational provision have clearly meant that professionals are no longer as dominant, unique or otherwise special within managerial teams as they were in the 1970s and earlier.

Reed (1996) quoted a wide range of well-known commentators (for example, Zuboff, Reich, Giddens and Foucault) to argue that the institutional forms characteristic of modernity were being undermined and disembedded by economic globalization in the late twentieth century. To facilitate this process expert systems and knowledge were being applied using advanced forms of information storage and retrieval over vast distances. Occupational boundaries and divisions were being splintered and blurred within it. The power bases of the independent or liberal professions were being attacked to effect by various competing and 'corporate agencies'. The organizational professions were both beneficiaries and victims of contemporary rationalization processes. However the new kind of expert professional, 'knowledge workers' or Reich's (1991) 'symbolic analysts' had benefited greatly from recent changes. Their knowledge was very esoteric and intangible and directed at complex problems, using 'symbolic systems and information techniques focused on the "management of uncertainty"'. Their 'highly refined and portable expertise' was virtually impossible for competing groups to penetrate or take over or for bureaucratic managers to rationalize.

The natural habitats of such people were such major 'knowledge-intensive ... industries' as education, research and development, artistic creation and communication, communication media, information services, and information machines' (cf. Machlup, 1980). In these industries there was a premium on unique, innovatory and exceptional forms of expertise which were used to pursue 'future value' rather than immediate returns. Such kinds of expertise were almost impossible to codify and control. Knowledge workers tended to fit well into deregulated, flexible, organizational and political-economic settings. It was relatively easy for them to be independent from independent and organizational professions and to fend off attempts at control by corporate managements and government regulators.

We find these arguments somewhat uncertain. As Flood's chapter in this book suggests, lawyers, as traditional independent professionals, often conform to the stereotype of knowledge worker, with very unique and portable and esoteric forms of knowledge. So too, perhaps, do organizational professionals as the 'technicians', who Reed uses an example. Technicians are not really professionals, and exist on the bottom edges of managerial strata, rather than clearly within them. They are superior kinds of skilled worker. However engineers, accountants and marketing and sales specialists who are presumably among the 'managers' and 'administrators' who are Reed's other example of organizational professionals have long - in an important sense since time almost immemorial - very often worked as knowledge workers or symbolic analysts in the ways described by Reed and Reich. Many have been self-employed, often as consultants, and many still are. Most of the UK's major management consultancy firms have been formed by or from accountancy practices, also. Even when employed as organizational professionals their expertise and work here have been very hard for managements or rival professionals to penetrate and control. In other words they have always been knowledge workers of a kind - which is why it is not surprising that Reed uses such people - 'financial/business consultants; project/R and D engineers; computer/IT analysts' - as his major examples of them.

We find the category 'knowledge worker' too general and at times too value-laden to be seriously helpful for understanding recent and contemporary developments. Its use generally ignores the kinds of major international differences in the production or formation of expert and managerial labour that we discussed and described in chapter one. Its use exaggerates, we feel, the complexity of contemporary problems facing managements compared with those facing them in the past. Such decisions as the ones to reorganize (or to organize effectively for the first time) General Motors by Alfred Sloan in the 1920s, or of the decisions by European monarchs and governments to support various attempts at geographical exploration and colonial expansion between the fifteenth and twentieth centuries, hardly appear to have been even simple or routine ones by the standards of the writers or readers of this chapter. Also the sectors or industries or activities identified as somehow special or new by Machlup, above, are not so on the whole. It is true that entertainment, the mass media and information technology are either much expanded or genuinely new elements, as for example with the development of video, microprocessors, electronic mail and so on, in some key respects. But education, artistic activities, 'research and development' (however portrayed or prosecuted) and communication are all both ancient and modern phenomena. Mass affluence and the very large scale internationalization of some business activities, and of a very great deal of communication and finance, *are* genuinely new. Whether they have an inherent tendency, in conjunction, to help engender a convergence and expansion of 'hype' about knowledge work and workers and about the novelty of 'symbolic analysis' is an open question.

There is a general and recurring tendency to re-invent the wheel in many discussions of expert labour (see for example Currie and Glover, 1998 - on the currently fashionable notion of the 'hybrid manager'). Hanlon (1998), for example, writes to very good effect of 'divisions within the service class ... [not being] new' (p. 45) but without explaining just how old they are. After noting how Bourdieu (1984) and Savage et al (1992), had distinguished between economic and cultural capital in Bourdieu's case and economic, cultural and organizational assets in that of Savage et al, as power bases of different and often competing branches of the service class or types of professionalism, Hanlon goes on to discuss the fairly recent growth of competition, in the UK especially, between what he calls social service professionalism and commercial professionalism. The former had emerged in the 1930s and 1940s under a broadly Fordist era of social consensus. Under it, rights to health care, social welfare, education and so on were guaranteed to all on the basis of citizenship, and delivered by professionals. The latter version of professionalism had emphasized, much more strongly, and mainly since the 1970s, the value of entrepreneurial and managerial skills and it had 'emerged most strongly in areas of the private sector such as accountancy ... law ... and engineering' (p. 50). Such professionals needed more than the technical ability required to deliver a service: they needed to be able to manage money, employees and relationships with clients, and the ability to bring in and expand business. In this latter case there was less emphasis on serving clients in need (the deserving poor) and more on involving large corporations and/or clients in the determination of their own needs, and more emphasis, too, on managerial and entrepreneurial skills, as opposed to technical ones, in the assessment of success and in decisions about career advancement.

Commercial professionalism tended to define social service professionalism as 'a luxury which the state can no longer afford as it shifts its priorities from a Keynesian welfare state to one where the state's primary function is to ensure international competitiveness rather than welfare based on citizenship' (p. 52). State deregulation of some professional services and the imposition of managerial controls and internal markets in the public sector had had mixed effects on different professions. Stronger state control of public legal aid funding and the encouragement of non-legal counsellors for divorce and of licensed conveyancers for house purchases had made life harder for many small law firms, although sales of public housing and privatisation programmes had tended to counterbalance such developments in the short term, with the newly-permitted expansion in the size of law practices (as discussed by Flood in chapter two of this book) facilitating expansion of commercial law. In business generally there had been many winners and many losers. Many large private sector companies now controlled their in-house professionals more tightly than hitherto, or they had outsourced their work. Internationalisation of business, corporate restructuring and developments in markets, IT and taxation had also, however, stimulated or facilitated growth in accountancy and management consultancy, banking, marketing, and (as noted above) commercial law.

However professionals in all sectors were increasingly expected to follow the norms of commercial (and managerial) professionalism, to work in ways driven by 'a commercial rather than a technical logic'. Thus NHS doctors were increasingly expected to be competent managers and expected less often to share information with health professionals in competing NHS units. Engineers and scientists in manufacturing were expected to conform to financial pressures even more than in the past. In big accountancy and law firms guaranteed professional career paths were being replaced by insecure employment and continual appraisal based on financial performance standards. Senior staff in local authorities, as in the NHS and elsewhere, were increasingly employed on short-term contracts, and professionals and other non-supervisory staff in both local and central government were increasingly subject to overt managerial control and to expectations and perceptions about their 'personal' qualities. Professionals increasingly needed to prove their trustworthiness regularly and according to commercial and managerial rather than the technical and fiduciary criteria more often associated with social service professionalism. The most rewarding careers were increasingly those linked to large scale commercial professional environments, where prestige, financial resources, major clients and superior professional and other contacts tended to be more plentiful.

Hanlon goes on to discuss the varied and shifting political allegiances of social service and commercialised professionals of several kinds and to discuss various examples of resistance to commercialism and managerialism as well as a number of different and related political and professional scenarios. Both the social service and commercial camps were still struggling to 'impose their vision on society and hence to legitimise their cultural capital' (p. 55). The public-private sector split had been blurred and the service class, at the upper end of the labour market, was in no sense conservative or homogeneous. Hanlon warns against critics who might regard the changes he considers as 'superficial and ... ephemeral'. They were real, in the form of changing kinds of work and conflicts that would 'spill over into the political arena' over many years (p. 59).

We find almost all of Hanlon's arguments well-founded but we also concur with his manifest and other less explicitly stated doubts about how new the relevant cleavages around, between and within different professional groupings are. We are also uncertain about what he seems to regard as the new and relatively monolithic status of the external economic and political influences that he discusses. He, like us, is concerned with professions coping, recently as they have in the past, with economic recession and political change. There is much evidence in his arguments, and in the work of those whom he cites in his references, of considerable resistance and resilience on the part of professions, and of the incorporation, temporary and permanent, of commercial and managerial norms and procedures. There are few if any references in Hanlon's account to past and ongoing divisions within the UK's middle classes in general and its professionals in particular, between carnivores and herbivores, the 'hard' and the 'soft', and between 'players' and 'gentlemen'. These distinctions and divisions have been discussed for over a century with the writings of Matthew Arnold on barbarians and philistines and so on, and of Rudyard Kipling on hooligans and gentlemen, being amongst the earlier examples. Elements of such themes were picked up nearly forty years ago by the American economist David Granick in *The European Executive* (1962), and it has long (certainly since the 1950s) permeated writings on 'hard and soft' in personnel and human resource management in the UK (Legge, 1995). Elements of the distinction can also be found in popular comparisons of *Guardian* and *Telegraph* readers, and in historians' ones of Whigs and Tories, and even, perhaps, of Cavaliers and Roundheads.

From gentlemen and players to business and professional technocracy

In the 1950s, as Granick (1962) and others noted, qualified managers in the UK fell into two main categories: graduates and professionals. At that time these terms corresponded broadly to those of generalist and specialist, and gentlemen and player. Graduates were few in number, largely from the oldest universities, and tended to gravitate to the top jobs in larger organizations. Their degrees tended to be in academic subjects, in the humanities or the so-called pure sciences. They were more likely to be humanities or arts graduates than science ones and the terms amateur and philosopher king have also been applied to them. The authors of the most comprehensive and by far the most influential study of the backgrounds of UK managers ever conducted found that in the early to mid 1950s the most advantageous qualification to possess in management, industry and commerce in the

UK was an arts degree from Oxford or Cambridge university (Acton Society Trust, 1955). Holders of such degrees tended to occupy the top jobs. Beneath them were the specialists, usually with functional responsibilities. Such people tended to have degrees in scientific and engineering subjects, or professional qualifications in accountancy and engineering. These people tended to be 'on tap but not on top' although boards of directors usually contained small numbers of them, usually as directors of finance, production and engineering. Top jobs in sales and marketing tended to be filled by arts graduates. At all levels it was more helpful to have attended a public school than a grammar school and much more helpful to have attended either of these than a technical or elementary or secondary modern one. The distinction between gentlemanly amateur generalist graduates and specialist professional players had grown up from later Victorian times following Gladstone's decision in 1870, effectively to staff the highest levels of the civil service, its Administrative Class, with holders of degrees in arts subjects from Oxford or Cambridge. Such people were valued for their detachment, integrity and trained minds, and were felt able to adopt a broader and more effective approach to management than those whose minds had been focused on the study of professional specialist and/or vocational subjects either at university or for professional qualifications. (The three original professions of the clergy, the law, and medicine were excluded from this). The latter also tended to have attended local grammar schools, whereas the former tended to have been boarders at public schools. The former group tended to see themselves and to be seen as members of the 'first eleven' in their employing organizations, and the latter tended to dominate management in the civil service, to armed forces and in most large commercial, financial and industrial private sector organizations for the first two thirds or four fifths of the twentieth century. In many sectors and in most respects it still does. However in sectors in which managers have tended to have grammar school, provincial and local backgrounds, rather than metropolitan (public school and London, Oxford, Cambridge, the Home Counties and so on in England and to some extent Edinburgh, Glasgow, Aberdeen, St Andrews and so on in Scotland) ones, and which tended to have developed slightly later than ones dominated by management with metropolitan backgrounds, a different and in many respects opposite pattern was apparent. This was 'provincial' and professional rather than metropolitan, and under it professionally qualified specialists tended to dominate management hierarchies (Glover and Kelly, 1987). This pattern has tended to be found in local government and the National Health Service, elsewhere in the public sector apart from the civil service and the British Broadcasting Corporation, and in small and medium sized enterprises.

Compared with managers and specialist management-level expert labour in other industrial countries, UK managers have generally been less highly and relevantly qualified. However professional education and training, combined with rigorous primary, secondary and university education with high academic standards and effective systems of apprenticeship and pragmatic attitudes to skill, knowledge, tasks, work and employment probably meant that until the 1970s, that widely publicized shortfall between the qualifications of UK and foreign management and labour were more apparent than real as far as their effects were concerned. In the 1960s and 1970s apprenticeship went into serious decline and at the same time higher education began a long period of massive expansion and vocationalisation. Since then concern about declining academic standards in schools and universities has been aired regularly. In our experience and opinion there is probably a good deal of justification for this concern. However loss of precision in the use of language, loss of arithmetical skills and reduced concern for learning and truth as ends in themselves amongst the average products of the system is probably outweighed very considerably by the massive increases in the numbers of qualifications gained both in and after secondary education.

Public concern with different aspects of education for the world of work has been manifested periodically in the thinking of such committees as the Bolton one on small business which was partly concerned with the management of SMEs and which reported in 1971, the Finniston Committee of Inquiry into the Engineering Profession which reported in 1980, and the various public inquiries concerned with management qualifications and development which reported between 1985 and 1987 and which helped to lead to the Management Charter Initiative. Since the 1950s the qualifications of UK managers have become much more numerous, varied and vocational. At the time of writing the proportion of each age cohort of school leavers attending university is approaching two fifths, and the numbers and types of vocational masters and doctoral degrees and student are also expanding along with the numbers of professionally qualified people and mature students. More and more graduates have postgraduate and professional qualifications and the expansion of degree level work in polytechnics under the Council for National Academic Awards from the 1960s to the early 1990s and the conversion of polytechnics into new universities in 1992 has been an important feature of the creative growth of a system of mass higher education with a diverse elite core of institutions, university departments and so on. The present system manifests many strains including overly managerialist employment policies, especially in the former polytechnics or 'new universities', and a kind of emphasis on research across the whole system which can valorize the activity of academics writing for each other and for the benefit of their own careers more than for the public enlightenment and good.

Some of the last few paragraphs above briefly summarize some of the arguments of the first few pages of chapter one of this book. There, we wrote that management-level people in the UK are becoming 'a mixture of products of all three ways of producing people [professional-managerial, university-formed technocratic and company-centred technocratic] - they are becoming more technocratic - with elements of the custodian [the gentleman, above] still around' (Glover and Tracey, 1997, p. 774). Thus Glover, Tracey and Currie (1998) argued that 'Because vocational (and academic) higher education in the UK has been expanded and developed since the 1960s to meet, anticipate or even create a wide range of market and other needs, often very imaginatively, because the traditionally open-ended approach to learning of the system has generally been maintained, and because the age participation rate is increasingly close to the average of other industrial countries, the prospect of the UK's approach to higher education leapfrogging those of its competitors has become genuinely possible', and these 'changes are not merely products of UK responses to foreign competition and practice: many are largely or entirely domestic in origin'.

In our title of this section we use the term business and professional technocracy to describe the emerging character of UK management. This is because the backgrounds and expertise of UK managers are increasingly diverse and vocational and with strong and continuing emphases on wealth-creation and money-making on the one hand (business) and on responsible autonomy, and specialist and sustained professional practice on the other. There is thus substantial improvement in UK management quality since the 1970s, when it was possible to write realistically of there being 'a non-system of matching education and work as far as the requirements of a modern industrial economy are concerned' (Glover, 1978). This is clearly positive and a big step in the right direction. The professional mode of occupation formation and government is likely to remain significant and influential because of its value to practitioners in the shorter term and to employers and society in the longer one for coordinating the production, organization and control of complex expertise and for protecting it against the ravages of both unfettered state dominance and chaotic market forces. For an account of how this mode of occupation formation is at least potentially, with occasionally and judiciously applied state intervention, the least worst of the available alternatives, see Dingley (1996) on how professions have helped to constitute the social and moral order since medieval times.

So that readers will not accuse us of ending on too positive a note, we will make a final point before our conclusion. This is that the demise of apprenticeship appears to have been the price paid for the expansion of graduate status and its promise of upward social mobility in the UK since the 1950s. Education for management-level work (not management education - a different and less important phenomenon and issue) has been developed greatly in the UK since the 1950s. While such a task can never be complete, perhaps the time has now come for those seeking to influence relevant policies to focus far more on the needs of the economy for less privileged forms of labour and on the needs of those who are to perform it.

Conclusion

The main arguments of this book have been summarised in the previous section of this chapter. The professional mode of occupation formation has a useful and flexible quality that makes it resilient in the face of attacks from big business and the state. It and its products will be more useful to society if they are understood properly. To be understood properly they need to be apprehended in their full historic and comparative context, and considered critically, dispassionately, respectfully and sympathetically, simultaneously(!).

The main policy implications of this book, and of its two 1996 companion volumes *The Professional-Managerial Class* and to a smaller extent *Beyond Reason,* are obvious and simple and they concern babies and bathwater. Further, we feel that professions and managers in the UK should not only not be studied and developed in isolation from their historical and internationally comparative contexts: they should also be studied and developed in conjunction with the study and development of what we have just referred to as less privileged forms of labour. We are unconvinced, after some decades of experience of teaching and various forms of employment, that the innate intellectual potentials of people vary as greatly as some educators and psychologists conventionally assume. We know that machinery is now able to perform a huge amount of what used to be called physical and mental donkey work. We also know that the life span is increasing and that many of the less well qualified young people in our very affluent society suffer considerably from lack of purpose, with many older employees also falling victims to ageism and social snobbery. In this situation the way forward - or out - seems obvious: an assumed 75 to 90 year plus life span divided roughly equally between learning and self-discovery, doing challenging work, and a mixture of relaxation, civic and social activities and teaching the younger generation (Branine and Glover, 1997). Remaining physically and psychologically threatening and damaging or socially demeaning jobs like refuse disposal or bar work should perhaps be reserved mainly for younger adults from *all* social backgrounds, to be done while they are also studying. Most of the jobs performed by people between their late twenties and late fifties should be complex and challenging enough for them to have at least some profession-like characteristics. Retirement should be flexible and genuinely earned; and equitably financed, with those who lack occupational pensions not allowed to live in poverty but given state pensions significantly larger than current ones. None of these suggestions are radical: they reflect existing trends and the facts of the situation.

Regarding future research, if we are to understand management in the UK, we need to know properly what the characteristics of those responsible for it consist of. Since the broadly excellent Acton Society Trust (1955) study of the early to mid 1950s, referred to above, surveys of UK managers' backgrounds have been regionally based (and biased), of top managers only, or otherwise unrepresentative. All that is known for sure is that UK managers' educational and occupational backgrounds are much more varied, with the average level of qualification much higher, than in the past. There is a similar paucity of accurate evidence on the backgrounds, qualifications and skills of other employees. Thus it would be helpful for data on the social, educational, occupational, professional and sectoral backgrounds of all kinds of employee, professional and manager, and on their skills, training, careers and so on, to be much more readily available than it is at present. In particular very little indeed is known about the marketing and sales specialists and managers who form the most numerous and arguably the most powerful occupational specialist group in the UK. Unlike accountants, engineers, HRM specialists and others, marketing and sales specialists have not attracted much of the attention of management researchers, yet in many respects they constitute the glue which holds management together in many, probably most, sectors of employment.

Finally, we wish to reassert our faith in the better characteristics of the professional ideal, such as the long term and lifetime reflective development of personal skills, understanding and wisdom, the sense of responsibility to others, and the healthy scepticism towards both Mammon and the state. As we suggested in chapter four of this book and earlier in this one, we find both the left wing position on professions, associated with Terry Johnson, and the right wing one, associated with Talcott Parsons, too extreme. Yet professions and their members are often quite rightly accused of mystification and exploitation of lay people, and of acting monopolistically in their own interest in ways which retard economic and social advance. Nonetheless they do very often supply lay people and businesses and government with invaluable and sophisticated expertise and, at times, highly altruistic endeavour. They also provide their members with challenging and exciting work, opportunities to develop considerable expertise and wisdom, and justified feelings of achievement and personal satisfaction. In an era of potentially sustainable high affluence it should not be beyond human wit to work effectively towards a situation in which many elements of such rewards are available to most people at most levels of employment.

References

Ackroyd, S.J. (1994), 'Professions, their Organisations and Change in Britain: Some Private and Public Sector Similarities and their Consequences' paper to ESRC Seminar Series on Professions in Late Modernity, University of Lancaster, 30 June 1994.

Acton Society Trust (1955), *Management Succession*, Acton Society Trust, London.

Barry, R., Bosworth, D. and Wilson, R. (1997), *Engineers in Top Management*, Institute for Employment Research. Warwick.

Barnett, C. (1972), *The Collapse of British Power*, Eyre Methuen, London.

Barnett, C. (1986), *The Audit of War: the Illusion and Reality of Britain as a Great Nation*, Macmillan, London.

Barnett, C. (1995), *The Lost Victory: British Dreams, British Realities, 1945-1950*, Macmillan, London.

Bourdieu, P. (1984), *Distinction: A Social Critique of the Judgement of Taste*, Routledge and Kegan Paul, London.

Chaston, I. and Badger, B. (1993) 'The Professional - an Obstacle to Creating Customer-Oriented Public Sector Organizations', paper presented at conference on Professions and Management in Britain, Stirling, 1993.

Child, J., Fores, M., Glover, I. and Lawrence, P. (1983), 'A price to pay? Professionalism and work organisation in Britain and West Germany', *Sociology*, Vol. 17, No. 1, pp. 63-78.

Coates, D. and Hillard, J. (eds) (1995), *UK Economic Decline: Key Texts*, Prentice Hall and Harvester Wheatsheaf, London.

Coleman, D.C. (1973), 'Gentlemen and Players', *Economic History Review*, Vol. 26, No. 1, pp. 92-116.

Crompton, R. (1990), 'Professions in the Current Context', *Work, Employment and Society*, Vol. 4, No. 2, pp. 147-66.

Currie, W.L. (1995), *Management Strategy for IT: An International Perspective*, Pitman, London.

Currie, W.L. and Glover, I.A. (1998), 'Hybrid Managers: An Example of Tunnel Vision and Regression in Management Research', forthcoming in W.L. Currie and R. Galliers (eds), *Reinventing Information Systems*, OUP, Oxford.

Dingley, J. (1996), 'Durkheim, Professions and Moral Integration', in I. Glover and M. Hughes (eds), *The Professional-Managerial Class: Contemporary British Management in the Pursuer Mode*, Avebury, Aldershot, pp. 155-70.

Edgerton, D. (1991), *England and the Aeroplane*, Macmillan, London.

Glover, I.A. (1978), 'Executive Career Patterns: Britain, France, Germany and Sweden', in M. Fores and I. Glover (eds), *Manufacturing and Management*, HMSO, London.

Glover, I.A. (1985), 'How the West was lost? decline in engineering and manufacturing in Britain and the United States', *Higher Education Review*, Vol. 17, No. 3, pp. 3-34.

Glover, I.A. (1991), 'The Hobsbawm-Wiener Conundrum: Economics History and Sociology in the Study of British Decline', *International Journal of Sociology and Social Policy*, Vol. 11, No. 3, pp. 1-17.

Glover, I. (1992), '*Technik*, Uncertainty and the Ethical Significance of Human Resource Management', conference on Business Ethics, Sheffield Hallam University, Sheffield.

Glover, I. and Hughes, M. (1996), 'British management in the pursuer mode', in I. Glover and M. Hughes (eds) *The Professional-Managerial Class: Contemporary British Management in the Pursuer Mode*, Avebury, Aldershot.

Glover, I.A. and Kelly, M.P. (1987), *Engineers in Britain: A Sociological Study of the Engineering Dimension*, Allen and Unwin, London.

Glover, I. and Tracey, P. (1997) 'In Search of *Technik*: Can Engineering Outgrow Management?', *Work, Employment and Society*, Vol. 11, No. 4, pp. 759-76.

Glover, I. Tracey, P. and Currie, W. (1998), 'Engineering our Future Again: Towards a Long-term Strategy for Manufacturing and Management in the United Kingdom', forthcoming in R. Delbridge and J. Lowe (eds) *Manufacturing in Transition*, London, London.

Goodwin, N. (1998), 'Leadership in the UK NHS: where are we now?', *Journal of Management in Medicine*, Vol. 12, No. 1, pp. 21-32.

Granick, D. (1962), *The European Executive*, Wiedenfeld and Nicholson, London.

Hanlon, G. (1998), 'Professionalism as Enterprise: Service Class Politics and the Redefinition of Professionalism', *Sociology*, Vol. 32, No. 1, pp. 43-63.
Hirst, P. and Thompson, G. (1995), 'Globalization and the future of the nation state', *Economy and Society*, Vol. 24, No. 3, pp. 408-42.
Kelly, M.P. and Glover, I.A., (1996), 'In Search of Health and Efficiency: the NHS 1948-1994', in J. Leopold, I. Glover and M. Hughes (eds), *Beyond Reason: The NHS and The Limits of Management,* Avebury, Aldershot.
Lawrence, P.A. and Barsoux, J-L. (1990), *The Challenge of British Management*, Macmillan, Basingstoke.
Legge, K. (1995), *Human Resource Management: Rhetorics and Realities*, Macmillan, Basingstoke.
Locke, R.R. (1989), *Management and Higher Education since 1940: The Influence of America and Japan on West Germany, Great Britain and France*, Cambridge University Press, Cambridge.
Machlup, F. (1980), *Knowledge: Its Creation, Distinction and Economic Significance*, Princeton University Press, Princeton.
McDonagh, P. and Prothero, A. (1996) (eds) *Green Marketing: A Reader*, Dryden, London.
McRae, H. (1994), *The World in 2020: Power, Culture and Prosperity*, Boston, Mass., Harvard Business School Press.
Meiksins, P. and Smith, C. (eds) (1997), *Engineering Labour: Technical Workers in Comparative Perspective*, Verso, London.
Nairn, T. (1977), *The Break-Up of Britain: Crisis and Neo-Nationalism*, New Left Books, London.
Nichols, W.A.T. (1986), *The British Worker Question*, Allen and Unwin, London.
O'Mahony, M. and Wagner, K. (1995), 'Relative Productivity Levels: UK and German Manufacturing Industry, 1979 and 1989', *International Journal of Manpower*, Vol. 16, No. 1, pp. 5-21.
O'Mahony, M. and Wagner, K. with M. Paulson (1995), *Changing Fortunes: an Industry Study of British and German Productivity Growth over Three Decades*, Report Series Number 7, National Institute of Economic and Social Research, London.
Reed, M.I. (1996), 'Experts, Professionals and Organizations in Late Modernity: the Dynamics of Institutional, Occupational and Organizational Changes in Advanced Industrial Societies', *Organization Studies*, Vol. 16, No. 2, pp. 401-28.
Reich, R. (1991), *The Work of Nations*, Simon and Schuster, London.
Rubinstein, W.D. (1993), *Capitalism, Culture and Decline in Britain, 1750-1990*, Routledge, London.
Savage, M., Barlow, J.,Dickens, P. and Fielding, T. (1992), *Property, Bureaucracy and Culture,* Routledge, London.
Scott, J. (1996), *Stratification and Power*, Polity, Cambridge.
Sorge, A. (1979), 'Engineers in management: a study of the British, German and French traditions', *Journal of General Management*, 5, pp. 46-67.

Sorge, A. and Warner, M. (1986), *Comparative Factory Organization: An Anglo-German Comparison of Management and Manpower in Manufacturing*, Gower, Aldershot.

Tracey, P.J. (1998), Drafts of unpublished PhD thesis on Engineers and Management in Manufacturing and Construction, University of Stirling, Stirling.

Wiener, M. (1981), *English Culture and the Decline of the Industrial Spirit 1850-1980*, Cambridge University Press, Cambridge.

Zuboff, S. (1988), *In the Age of the Smart Machine*, Heinemann, Oxford.

Index

For Product Safety Concerns and Information please contact our EU representative GPSR@taylorandfrancis.com Taylor & Francis Verlag GmbH, Kaufingerstraße 24, 80331 München, Germany

Printed and bound by CPI Group (UK) Ltd, Croydon, CR0 4YY
08/06/2025
01897001-0011